Human-AI Dynamics in Higher Education

Muhammad Mooneeb Ali
https://orcid.org/0000-0002-0356-320X
Saudi Aramco, Saudi Arabia

Mujtaba Asad
Sukkur IBA University, Pakistan

IGI Global
Scientific Publishing
Publishing Tomorrow's Research Today

Vice President of Editorial	Melissa Wagner
Director of Acquisitions	Mikaela Felty
Director of Book Development	Jocelynn Hessler
Production Manager	Mike Brehm
Cover Design	Jose Rosado

Published in the United States of America by
IGI Global Scientific Publishing
701 East Chocolate Avenue
Hershey, PA, 17033, USA
Tel: 717-533-8845 | Fax: 717-533-7115
Website: https://www.igi-global.com E-mail: cust@igi-global.com

Library of Congress Cataloging-in-Publication Data

(CIP Data Pending)
ISBN13: 979-8-2600-1458-5
Isbn13Softcover: 979-8-2600-1459-2
EISBN13: 979-8-2600-1460-8
British Cataloguing in Publication Data
A Cataloguing in Publication record for this book is available from the British Library.

Table of Contents

Detailed Table of Contents

Private HEIs in Malaysia are critical in creating digitally competent graduates as the country works toward fulfilling the Malaysia Education Blueprint and to support the UN's Sustainable Development Goals. Nevertheless, these aspirations have created an inconsistent ability to obtain 21st century competencies in critical thinking, digital balance, and self-regulation. Based on the Social Cognitive Theory, this research examined the relationship of digital homo-ignorance, digital self-control, digital well-being, satisfaction with life, and social anxiety towards universities' student academic performance. The analysis of the variables showed that none of the predictors were significantly correlated with student academic performance. The research provides one contribution by challenging systemic assumptions to better understand a possible theoretical contribution based on the quantitative evidence provided, and beyond the policy implications to better frame curriculum design, digital hygiene, and student support interventions while creating opportunities for broader impact.

This chapter analyzes the divergent potentials of artificial intelligence (AI) in higher education across the Global North and Global South, emphasizing the intersection of innovation and digital inequalities. It underscores that while AI facilitates specific types of education, efficient management, and sophisticated research in technologically advanced environments, its unequal global distribution exacerbates underlying inequities. Authors utilize a bibliometric analysis and institutional case study method to illustrate differences in digital infrastructure, research capability, policy frameworks, and pedagogical preparedness. The chapter presents an integrative framework for equitable AI adoption, using ideas of the digital divide, diffusion of innovation, and the political economics of knowledge. Ultimately, it contends that inclusive and contextually aware deployment is crucial for AI to act as a catalyst for educational reform rather than a tool that exacerbates current imbalances.

In the context of AI-driven education, the chapter examines the interaction between posthuman texts and the human imagination, presenting a significant avenue for understanding modern literary learning. It traces how human imagination coexists with intelligent machines, exploring the readers' and students' engagement with literary texts as consumers and co-creators, and reshapes ethics and academic integrity in pedagogy. The analysis adopts a poststructuralist posthuman perspective, utilizing the poststructuralist literary critic Roland Barthes' (1967) declaration of 'the death of the author'. The chapter validates that AI technologically reinforces this claim, as digital texts destabilize human intentionality, positioning authorship distributed across human and algorithmic agencies. By integrating the posthuman, poststructural, and literary pedagogical concerns, the chapter proposes a practical approach for educators to engage with AI critically and ethically within literary education.

This chapter explores the integration of Artificial Intelligence (AI) into literature review within research. Traditional literature review methods, while foundational to scholarly inquiry, often face challenges of scale, efficiency, and comprehensiveness due to the rapid expansion of academic publications. AI technologies provide innovative solutions to these challenges by automating the identification, categorization, and synthesis of relevant research. The chapter examines how AI can enhance systematic literature reviews, uncover emerging trends, and facilitate deeper insights into scholarly discourse. It also addresses methodological and ethical considerations, such as the reliability of AI-assisted analysis, potential biases in algorithms, and the importance of maintaining critical human oversight. Drawing on recent studies and practical examples, the chapter demonstrates the opportunities and limitations of AI in literature review processes.

The chapter analyses cyber consciousness in the context of post-humanism and the role of artificial intelligence in developing a post-human digital consciousness. It focuses on the popular Amazon Prime series Upload (2020-2025). The paper argues that, even though technology, particularly biotechnology, offers new human experiences, including “biotechnological fantasies” of a mind existing outside the body. However, such existence may prove damaging to human nature itself. It draws on the theoretical underpinnings of William Haney's book Cyberculture, Cyborgs, and Science Fiction: Consciousness and the Posthuman (2006). This chapter challenges the traditional Cartesian view of consciousness, “I think, therefore I am.” It also examines the cybercultural and cyber-social implications of digitising the mind and the act of creation. The conclusion aligns with Haney’s belief that it is better to develop a natural consciousness rather than to pursue a purely digital existence void of soul.

Integrating artificial intelligence (AI) into educational ecosystems to cultivate civic skills among students is the central emphasis of this study. Based on cybersociology as a theoretical framework, this study reframes learning as a social negotiation between humans and AI, with the latter influencing the former in terms of civic identity, media literacy, inclusion, ethical reasoning, and data literacy. One hundred and ten first-year students participated. Students' attitudes and competencies were measured before and after the use of the CALLEBAI teaching model using a 20-item Likert-scale questionnaire. Students' civic communication, data analysis, tolerance for variety, ethical awareness in political decision-making, and capacity to recognise misinformation all showed significant gains. The study found that human-AI partnerships (via debate simulations, NLP, adaptive platforms, and AI-based data visualisation) address modern political issues like corruption, polarisation, and disinformation in Indonesia.

The rapid proliferation of generative artificial intelligence challenges the model of mass universities, as analytical and synthetic activities traditionally regarded as core academic competencies become increasingly automated. This chapter examines how universities can respond by transforming from reproduction-oriented institutions into curated knowledge economies centered on the cultivation of judgment. Methodologically, the analysis combines a structural comparison of historical university models with a systematic review of recent research on AI in teaching, assessment, and governance. The main result is a dual-path institutional model of the AI university that distinguishes practice-oriented implementation tracks from research-oriented innovation tracks, while normatively linking both through judgment as a guiding principle. The chapter further shows that AI necessitates a realignment of assessment, teaching roles, and governance. The university thus emerges not as replaceable by AI, but as a key institution for social judgment in a technologically saturated knowledge order.

University programs often struggle to integrate project-based learning, essential for developing professional competencies. The 2018 reforms in France, aligned with the European competence-based framework, highlight interdisciplinary projects to bridge academic training and professional demands. At the same time, generative AI is reshaping skills across sectors, requiring critical, ethical, and adaptive use. This study examines AI use in a project-based Instructional Design course, exploring tools, collaboration, and student perceptions across project phases. Findings aim to inform teaching strategies, curriculum design, and AI literacy integration in higher education.

Preface

The rapid evolution of artificial intelligence (AI) is redefining the landscape of higher education in profound and often unpredictable ways. Once confined to experimental laboratories and niche applications, AI has now become an integral component of teaching, learning, research, and institutional governance. From intelligent tutoring systems to generative models capable of producing human-like text, the boundaries between human cognition and machine assistance are increasingly blurred. This transformation calls for a critical and multidimensional examination of how human–AI dynamics are reshaping academic ecosystems across the globe.

This edited volume, *Human–AI Dynamics in Higher Education*, brings together a diverse group of scholars to explore the opportunities, challenges, and ethical considerations emerging at the intersection of humans and intelligent systems. The contributions span geographical, disciplinary, and methodological boundaries, offering both empirical insights and theoretical reflections. Importantly, the book does not treat AI merely as a technological tool, but as a socio-cultural force that influences cognition, creativity, equity, and institutional structures.

A central theme running through the volume is the tension between enhancement and disruption. While AI promises efficiency, personalization, and innovation, it also raises pressing concerns about equity, academic integrity, human agency, and the future purpose of universities. The chapters collectively interrogate these tensions, emphasizing the need for responsible, inclusive, and human-centered approaches to AI integration.

Another key contribution of this volume lies in its global perspective. By including voices from both the Global North and Global South, the book highlights uneven access to AI technologies and the risk of deepening existing educational inequalities. At the same time, it showcases context-sensitive strategies that can enable more equitable adoption and meaningful impact.

Ultimately, this book aims to serve as a resource for researchers, educators, policymakers, and students who seek to understand not only how AI is transforming higher education, but also how human values, judgment, and creativity can continue to shape its future. Rather than positioning AI as a replacement for human intellect, the chapters advocate for a collaborative paradigm, one in which human and artificial intelligence co-evolve to enrich learning and knowledge production.

CHAPTER OVERVIEW

Chapter 1. Clicks, Stress, and Success

This chapter investigates whether digital behaviors and psychosocial factors meaningfully influence students' academic performance in private higher education institutions in Malaysia. Drawing on Social Cognitive Theory, it examines constructs such as digital self-control, digital well-being, and social anxiety. Interestingly, the findings challenge prevailing assumptions by revealing no significant relationship between these variables and academic performance, prompting a reconsideration of how digital competencies and student success are conceptualized.

Chapter 2. Global North-South's Diverging Potentials of AI in Higher Education

Focusing on global disparities, this chapter explores how AI adoption differs between technologically advanced regions and developing contexts. Through bibliometric and case study approaches, it highlights how infrastructural gaps, policy environments, and institutional readiness shape AI's impact. The authors propose a framework for equitable AI integration that addresses the digital divide while promoting inclusive innovation.

Chapter 3. Posthuman Textualities and Imagination

Adopting a poststructuralist and posthuman lens, this chapter examines how AI reshapes literary learning and authorship. It engages with the concept of distributed authorship and the evolving role of imagination in AI-mediated textual production. The discussion highlights ethical considerations and offers pedagogical strategies for integrating AI into literary education without undermining critical engagement.

Chapter 4. Integrating AI into Literature Review Practices

This chapter explores how AI can enhance the efficiency and depth of literature reviews by automating processes such as data extraction, categorization, and synthesis. While demonstrating clear benefits, it also raises concerns about algorithmic bias, reliability, and the necessity of human oversight. Practical insights are provided for researchers seeking to responsibly incorporate AI into scholarly workflows.

Chapter 5. Textualizing Cyber-Consciousness and AI Integration in Sci-Fi Fiction

Through the analysis of the Amazon Prime series *Upload*, this chapter investigates the concept of digital consciousness and its philosophical implications. Drawing on posthuman theory, it critiques the notion of disembodied existence and questions the desirability of purely digital forms of consciousness, ultimately advocating for the preservation of human essence.

Chapter 6. The Cybersociology of Learning as Human-AI Partnerships

This empirical study examines how AI-enhanced teaching models can foster civic competencies in political education. Using a cybersociological framework, the chapter demonstrates how human–AI collaboration improves skills such as ethical reasoning, media literacy, and data analysis. The findings highlight AI's potential to address contemporary political challenges through interactive and adaptive learning environments.

Chapter 7. The Future of the AI University

This chapter envisions a transformation of universities from mass education systems to curated knowledge economies centered on judgment and critical thinking. It proposes a dual-path institutional model that integrates practical implementation with research innovation, arguing that universities will remain essential as spaces for cultivating human judgment in an AI-driven world.

Chapter 8. Using Generative AI in Project-Based Learning

Focusing on a case study from a French university, this chapter explores how generative AI can be integrated into project-based learning environments. It examines student experiences, collaboration patterns, and the role of AI across different stages of project development, offering insights into curriculum design and AI literacy.

Chapter 9. Applications of AI in Educational Research

This chapter provides a comprehensive overview of AI applications in educational research, including data analysis, adaptive learning, and predictive modeling. It also addresses critical ethical issues such as bias, transparency, and data privacy, emphasizing the importance of responsible AI use in advancing educational outcomes.

Chapter 10. Accurate or Artificial? Comparing AI and Human Peer Review Feedback

The final chapter evaluates the effectiveness of AI-generated peer review compared to human reviewers. The findings suggest that AI tools can produce high-quality and consistent feedback, though often differing from human judgments. This raises important questions about the future of academic evaluation and the role of AI in scholarly communication.

Chapter 1
Clicks, Stress, and Success:
Do Digital Habits and Social Factors Really Shape Students' Academic Performance?

Sharfika Raime
http://orcid.org/0000-0003-2649-0610
City University Malaysia, Malaysia

Aervina Misron
http://orcid.org/0009-0006-5104-2800
Quest International University, Malaysia

Norsafriman Abd Rahman
UNITAR College, Malaysia

ABSTRACT

Private HEIs in Malaysia are critical in creating digitally competent graduates as the country works toward fulfilling the Malaysia Education Blueprint and to support the UN's Sustainable Development Goals. Nevertheless, these aspirations have created an inconsistent ability to obtain 21st century competencies in critical thinking, digital balance, and self-regulation. Based on the Social Cognitive Theory, this research examined the relationship of digital homo-ignorance, digital self-control, digital well-being, satisfaction with life, and social anxiety towards universities' student academic performance. The analysis of the variables showed that none of the predictors were significantly correlated with student academic performance. The research provides one contribution by challenging systemic assumptions to better understand a possible theoretical contribution based on the quantitative evidence

DOI: 10.4018/979-8-2600-1458-5.ch001

provided, and beyond the policy implications to better frame curriculum design, digital hygiene, and student support interventions while creating opportunities for broader impact.

1. INTRODUCTION

Malaysia's higher education sector is a strategic engine for national development, talent creation, and economic competitiveness (Ooi, 2025). Alongside public universities, private higher education institutions (HEIs) play a pivotal role in expanding access, attracting international students, and supplying industry with digitally capable graduates (Mohamad Fadzil et al., 2022). National policy agendas, such as the Malaysia Education Blueprint (Higher Education) 2015–2025, the Malaysian Qualifications Framework (MQF), Industry4WRD, and the Malaysia Digital Economy Blueprint (MyDIGITAL), consistently emphasise graduate outcomes, lifelong learning, and digital readiness as foundations for Malaysia's transition to a high-value, innovation-led economy (Osman et al., 2025). These priorities align with the Sustainable Development Goals (SDGs), particularly SDG 4 (Quality Education), SDG 3 (Good Health and Well-Being), and SDG 8 (Decent Work and Economic Growth).

At the same time, university learning has been rapidly reshaped by smartphones, social media, AI tools, and always-on connectivity (Shahzad et al., 2024). While these technologies create opportunities for flexible and personalised learning, they also introduce risks like digital distraction, reduced self-regulation, information overload, avoidance of difficult decisions online, and heightened anxiety in social or evaluative settings (Li et al., 2024; Marsh et al, 2022; Shahzad et al., 2024). These dynamics are especially salient in Malaysia's private HEIs, where competitive positioning, student satisfaction, and graduate employability are closely watched by students, parents, and employers (Moo & Wan, 2023).

This research addresses these realities by focusing on academic performance conceptualised as the acquisition of skills and competencies (Pascarella et al., 2011). Rather than relying solely on grades, performance is operationalised through students' attainment of 21st-century skills; learning, literacy, and life skills valued by employers across industries (Stauffer, 2022). The research examines four technology and well-being–related antecedents namely, digital well-being (the conscious, positive use of technology that maximises benefits and mitigates harms), digital self-control (the capacity to inhibit impulses and prioritise long-term goals), satisfaction with life (a cognitive appraisal of life quality), digital homo-ignorance (tendencies to avoid available information, disregard incongruent facts, or abstain from decisions), and social anxiety (lasting fear or nervousness in social situations). Together, these factors capture how students engage with digital environments and how such engagement may translate into or undermine the skills that employers and the nation require.

2. PROBLEM STATEMENT AND LITERATURE REVIEW

2.1 Problem Statement

Private HEIs in Malaysia face a managerial challenge that sits at the heart of their mission and market viability, ensuring robust academic performance measured by demonstrable skills and competencies. Despite strong policy support for outcome-based education (Moo & Wan, 2023) and graduate employability (Tee at al., 2024), many programmes report uneven attainment of 21st-century skills (Razak et al, 2025). Employers continue to signal gaps in critical thinking, information literacy, collaboration, self-management, and responsible technology use, capabilities that the MQF, the Education Blueprint, and MyDIGITAL all prioritise (Osman et al., 2025). When performance is understood as skills acquisition rather than grades alone, the researchers deemed these shortfalls become more visible and more urgent.

The contemporary digital learning environment intensifies this problem. Low digital self-control can fuel procrastination, multitasking, and off-task behaviour (Deng et al., 2024). Meanwhile, suboptimal digital well-being can lead to fatigue, reduced focus, and emotional strain (Neagu & Vieriu, 2025). Digital homo-ignorance on the other hand is reported can manifest as avoidance of credible information or indecision in the face of conflicting sources (Mayiwar et al., 2025); and lower satisfaction with life can sap motivation and persistence (Aydin et al., 2024). Collectively, these factors can depress the very skills, learning agility, literacies (information, media, and technology), and life skills (flexibility, initiative, social awareness) that define academic performance in this research. For private HEIs, where student experience and graduate outcomes strongly influence enrolment and reputation, unmanaged digital and psychosocial risks translate into weaker programme outcomes and reduced competitive advantage (Carvalho, 2024).

If this performance gap persists, several implications are likely to happen. First, graduate employability may stagnate (Malay Mail, 2024), undermining national goals under SDG 4 and SDG 8 and challenging the ambitions of MyDIGITAL to expand a high-skill digital workforce. Second, student satisfaction and retention may decline (Ong & Ramasamy, 2024), threatening tuition-dependent business models typical of private HEIs. Third, institutional standing in local and international markets may be eroded (Ong & Ramasamy, 2024), compromising Malaysia's aspiration to be a premier regional education hub. Finally, misalignment with the MQF's learning-outcome orientation and the Education Blueprint's holistic, entrepreneurial, and balanced graduate agenda could expose institutions to quality-assurance risks and missed accreditation opportunities (Carvalho, 2024; Osman et al., 2025).

Addressing this managerial issue requires an evidence-based model that links students' digital behaviours and well-being to skill-based academic performance outcomes. By empirically testing the effects of digital well-being, digital self-control, satisfaction with life, digital homo-ignorance, and social anxiety on the acquisition of 21st-century skills, the study will identify which levers most strongly predict performance in Malaysia's private HEIs. The findings can inform targeted interventions like curriculum design, digital hygiene initiatives, self-regulation supports, information-literacy training, and student well-being services, thereby advancing institutional performance, meeting policy expectations, and contributing to Malaysia's human-capital and SDG commitments.

2.2 Literature Review and Hypotheses Development

2.2.1 Digital Well-being and Academic Performance (H1)

Digital well-being refers to conscious, balanced use of digital technologies that maximises benefits while minimising harms (e.g., screen fatigue, information overload) (Arslankara et al., 2022). Research indicates that unhealthy digital habits such as excessive screen time, incontrollable social media use, and unregulated use of productivity-displacing apps, are associated with reduced attention, lower cognitive functioning during study, and increased burnout (Leonhardt et al., 2025; Sidiq et al., 2025). Conversely, interventions that foster digital mindfulness, digital hygiene rules, or intentional scheduling of online/offline time have been found to restore focus and improve subjective learning experiences (Osborne et al, 2023), suggesting a plausible pathway from healthier digital engagement to improved learning outcomes.

Viewed through Social Cognitive Theory (SCT) coined by Bandura (1986), digital well-being arises from reciprocal interactions between the learner and the digital environment, learners can learn adaptive patterns through mastery and modelling. For instance, when students develop confidence (self-efficacy) in managing their digital environment, they convert potentially disruptive tools into scaffolds for learning (e.g., using apps for deliberate practice, collaborative platforms for meaningful interaction, and AI tools for guided skill development). Thus, SCT explains how changes in digital behaviour and beliefs about control produce different learning trajectories and competency accumulation. Thus, H1 is proposed as, there is a significant association between digital well-being and academic performance among the students from private higher education institutions in Malaysia.

Notwithstanding these insights, research gaps persist. Many studies treat "screen time" as a crude metric, ignoring qualitative differences between passive scrolling and active, goal-directed use of digital tools (Bahar et al., 2024). There is also limited empirical work linking digital well-being directly to 21st-century skill acquisition rather than to broad measures of academic satisfaction or mental health (Maskun et al., 2025). Crucially, evidence from Malaysian private HEIs is sparse: institutional digital policies, pedagogy, and student digital cultures in Malaysia may moderate how digital well-being translates into competency gains. Research that operationalises digital well-being with vivid definition and tests its effect on skill-based performance in local private HEIs is therefore needed (Bahar et al., 2024; Devisakti et al, 2024).

2.2.2 Digital Self-Control and Academic Performance (H2)

Research on self-regulation (e.g., (Biedermann et al., 2024); (Deng et al., 2024)) consistently shows that students' ability to manage impulses, regulate attention, and structure study behaviour is strongly associated with improved academic outcomes. Empirical work in higher education has linked various self-control behaviours like time management, focused study sessions, or resisting distractions to better learning engagement and higher attainment of skills and competencies (Biedermann et al., 2024; Park et al., 2025). These studies typically demonstrate that students who deliberately limit multitasking, organise study schedules, and use attention-management strategies report greater depth of learning and better transfer of knowledge into applied tasks, simultaneously to the "acquisition of skills and competencies" conceptualised as academic performance in this research.

SCT explains this relationship by positioning self-efficacy and behavioural capability at the centre of successful self-regulation. Students who believe they can control digital temptations (high self-efficacy for digital self-management) are more likely to implement strategies that reduce interruptions and sustain deliberate practice (Omar et al., 2023). From the SCT perspective, these mastery experiences (e.g., successfully concentrating despite distractions) strengthen efficacy beliefs, which in turn reinforce future self-regulatory behaviour and cumulative skill acquisition (Senin et al., 2023). Observational learning also supports the adoption of effective strategies when students model peers or mentors managing digital use well (Senin et al., 2023). Hence, H2 is proposed as, there is a significant association between digital self-control and academic performance among the students from private higher education institutions in Malaysia.

Despite this evidence, several gaps remain. First, much prior research measures self-regulation in general terms (e.g., time management) without isolating digital self-control as a distinct construct that captures behaviours specific to phones, social media, and AI tools (Biedermann et al., 2024). Second, most studies focus on grades or test scores rather than skill acquisition framed as 21st-century competencies (critical thinking, digital literacies, collaboration) (Csernoch et al., 2024). Third, very few studies have tested these dynamics within private HEIs in Malaysia, which have unique student profiles, programme designs, and market pressures that may shape both digital habits and the demands for demonstrable competencies (Halim et al., 2024). These gaps justify examining digital self-control as a predictor of skill-based academic performance in Malaysian private universities.

2.2.3 Satisfaction with Life and Academic Performance (H3)

Satisfaction with life is an overall cognitive appraisal of one's life circumstances which has been linked in the literature to improved motivation, persistence, and cognitive resources available for learning (Mohamed et al., 2024). Studies in educational psychology show that students with higher life satisfaction often exhibit greater intrinsic motivation, better emotional regulation, and a more optimistic orientation toward academic challenges (Mohamed et al., 2024). These psychological benefits foster sustained engagement with learning tasks, willingness to take on challenging assignments, and resilience in the face of setbacks, all behaviours that support the gradual development of complex skills and competencies (Wang et al., 2025).

Under SCT, life satisfaction functions as a personal factor that shapes outcome expectations and self-efficacy (Kadum & Karpudewan, 2025). Students who evaluate their lives positively are more likely to expect favourable outcomes from effortful study and to believe in their capability to meet academic demands. These beliefs are purported to increase goal persistence, proactive help-seeking, and strategic learning behaviours too (Kadum & Karpudewan, 2025). Moreover, satisfaction with life may buffer against the demotivating effects of digital distraction and social stress, thus preserving capacity for deep learning and experiential practice, the mechanisms that are crucial for skill acquisition (Chong & Guan, 2022). Therefore, H3 is proposed as, there is a significant association between satisfaction with life and academic performance among the students from private higher education institutions in Malaysia.

However, gaps remain in how satisfaction with life has been linked to competency-oriented academic performance in higher education. This is because, much of the prior work (e.g., (Chong & Guan, 2022); (Shahzad et al., 2024); (Wang et al., 2025)) focuses on grades, dropout risk, or mental health outcomes rather than on concrete skill development (e.g., critical thinking, collaboration, digital literacy). Additionally, many studies are from Western contexts or public institutions (Abd Malek & Ahmad, 2023; Cynthia & Chong, 2023) and few examine these dynamics within Malaysia's private HEIs, where students' life circumstances (financial pressures, work-study balance, international enrolments) may distinctively shape life satisfaction and its consequences. This underlines the need to test satisfaction with life as a predictor of skill acquisition in Malaysian private HEIs and to explore potential mediating roles (e.g., self-efficacy) in this pathway.

2.2.4 Digital Homo-Ignorance and Academic Performance (H4)

Digital homo-ignorance is operationalised as tendencies to avoid available information, disregard conflicting facts, or abstain from decision-making (O'Brien et al., 2024). Literature on information avoidance and motivated reasoning suggests that avoidance reduces exposure to corrective feedback, narrows perspective taking, and limits critical engagement, all of which are essential for building higher-order cognitive skills (Cavlovic et al., 2024). For students, habitual avoidance of complex or challenging digital information can thus lead to gaps in knowledge, underdeveloped critical evaluation skills, and weaker problem-solving competencies (Cavlovic et al., 2024).

SCT frames digital homo-ignorance as a maladaptive interaction among personal beliefs, environment, and behaviour. Low information-processing self-efficacy and negative outcome expectations make students more likely to avoid confronting conflicting evidence or seeking clarifying information online (Mayiwar et al., 2025). This avoidance deprives them of observational learning opportunities (for example, modelling critical appraisal skills), reduces behavioural capability, and prevents mastery experiences that build confidence (Mayiwar et al., 2025), thereby undermining competency development and academic performance in skills-oriented tasks. Consequently, H4 is proposed as, there is a significant negative association between digital homo-ignorance and academic performance among the students from private higher education institutions in Malaysia.

Despite the theoretical plausibility, empirical research linking information-avoidance behaviours in digital contexts to competency-based academic outcomes is limited. Much work on information avoidance focuses on specific domains like health (Jia & Li, 2024) or politics (Bilandzic & Gall, 2024) rather than study behaviours and rarely measures downstream effects on 21st-century skill acquisition. Furthermore, there is little evidence from Malaysian private HEIs regarding how cultural, curricular, or pedagogical factors may either impair or mitigate digital homo-ignorance (Devisakti et al., 2024). Addressing this gap requires focused investigation into how avoidance of digital information impairs students' critical literacies and practical competencies in the local higher education setting.

2.2.5 Social Anxiety and Academic Performance (H5)

Social anxiety in academic contexts is defined as fear of negative evaluation, reluctance to speak up, and avoidance of group tasks (Ifenthaler et al., 2023). There is a robust literature tying it to reduced class participation, lower help-seeking, and diminished collaborative learning (Mou et al., 2024). Empirical studies indicate that socially anxious students are less likely to volunteer answers, engage in group work, or present ideas, depriving them of practice in communication, teamwork, and leadership, skills central to the competency-based conception of academic performance. The lack of exposure to social learning contexts also reduces opportunities for feedback and corrective experience that refine these competencies (Mou et al., 2024).

SCT explains the social anxiety–performance link through self-efficacy and vicarious learning mechanisms (Ponton & Rhea, 2006). Social anxiety undermines mastery experiences in social tasks and reduces attention to models of effective social/academic behaviour, thereby lowering self-efficacy for communication and collaboration (Mou et al., 2024). Without experiential reinforcement, students' behavioural parameter remains limited as they avoid interactive contexts where many 21st-century skills are practised and assessed (Xethakis et al., 2024). The SCT perspective also predicts reciprocal effects (Szczuka et al., 2023). For example, poor performance in social academic tasks feedback into greater anxiety and further avoidance, creating a detrimental cycle limiting competency growth. Hence, H5 is proposed as, there is a significant negative association between social anxiety and academic performance among the students from private higher education institutions in Malaysia.

Research gaps justify deeper research of social anxiety in the Malaysian private HEI context. Many studies on social anxiety and academic outcomes are general or concentrated in secondary schools (Mohamed et al., 2024), fewer investigate how social anxiety specifically impairs acquisition of employer-valued competencies in HEI settings. Cultural considerations (e.g., norms about deference, classroom participation styles) and institutional factors (class size, pedagogical approaches, use of online or blended formats) may moderate these effects in Malaysia, yet empirical evidence is scarce (Le, 2024; Zheng & Lee, 2023). Investigating social anxiety's impact on skill-based performance within private HEIs will therefore inform targeted pedagogical and support interventions to improve competency outcomes.

Across all five relationships there are common limitations in the existent literature namely, constructs are often studied in isolation rather than together. Besides, outcomes are frequently limited to GPA or pass rates rather than skill-based competency measures. Third, empirical evidence from Malaysian private higher education institutions is limited. Moreover, the changing digital landscape (AI tools, hybrid learning, algorithmic recommendation systems) demands updated empirical models that capture technology-specific behaviours (digital self-control, digital well-being, and digital homo-ignorance) and their interactions with socio-psychological factors (life satisfaction and social anxiety). By testing these variables concurrently and anchoring academic performance in the acquisition of 21st-century skills, this research addresses a clear empirical need and generates actionable insights for curriculum designers, student support services, and institutional policymakers in Malaysia's private HEIs.

2.3 Research Framework and The Underpinning Theory

Figure 1. Proposed Research Framework

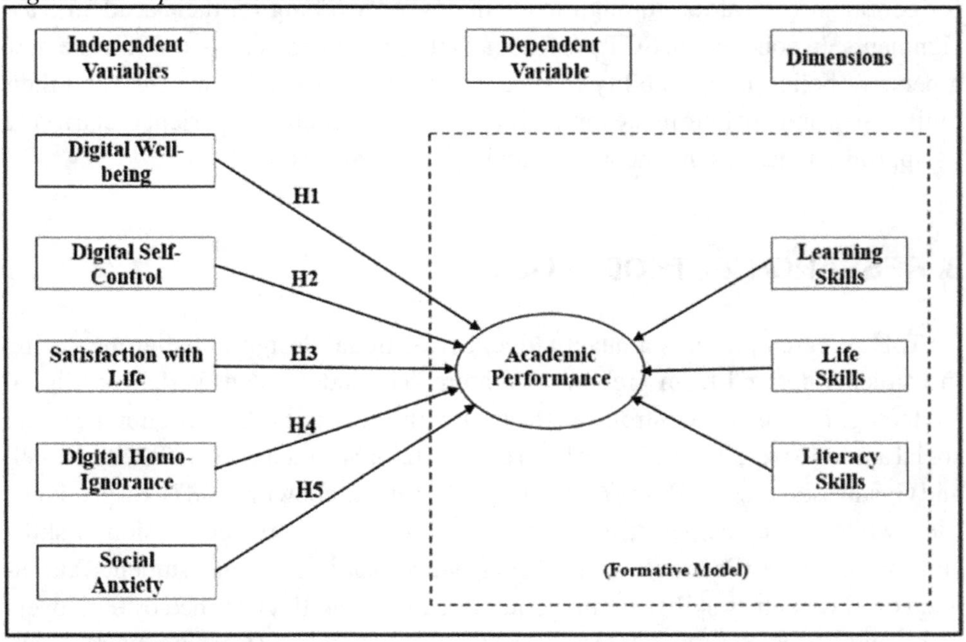

Source: Authors' owns work

Social Cognitive Theory (SCT), introduced by Albert Bandura in 1986, provides a strong theoretical foundation for the proposed framework. The theory posits that human behaviour results from the dynamic interaction between personal factors, environmental influences, and behavioural choices, a process referred to as reciprocal determinism. Central to SCT is self-efficacy, defined as an individual's belief in their capability to perform tasks successfully, which directly influences motivation, persistence, and performance. This perspective is particularly relevant for explaining how digital self-regulation, digital well-being, life satisfaction, and socio-psychological factors influence students' academic performance, as these constructs reflect the interplay between personal beliefs, digital environments, and behavioural responses.

SCT provides an analysis of the student's digital behaviour control and management, a function of their level of perceived self-efficacy, where higher levels of self-efficacy led to effective digital behaviour management. This also means that students will be able to maintain or enhance motivation toward overcoming obstacles to learning or thrive academic performance. On the other hand, students who have a low level of perceived self-efficacy may respond to their digital environments with a tendency toward avoidance or anxiety, thereby limiting engagement in learning, limiting the development of skills, and reducing their opportunity for growth. Life satisfaction and positive expectations for outcomes provide an additional challenge for continual motivation through resiliency when working on their academic assignments. In conclusion, SCT provides an integrative perspective to illustrate how a person's belief in their ability to succeed, their actions and responses, and their digital environment interrelates and influences their academic experience, clarifying its appropriateness as the theoretical underpinning of this research.

3. RESEARCH METHODOLOGY

This research presents a quantitative, correlational design utilising measuring instruments derived from previous literature. The independent variables (digital wellbeing, digital self-control, satisfaction with life, digital homo-ignorance, and social anxiety) were adapted from Lind et al. (2020); Stromback et al. (2020); Hultell and Gustavsson (2008); Barrafrem et al. (2024); and Liebowitz (1987), respectively. Meanwhile, academic performance was conceptualised as the possession of skills and competencies (Pascarella et al., 2011), operationalised through students' attainment of 21st-century skills; learning, literacy, and life skills cherished by employers across industries (Stauffer, 2022). Therefore, the dimensions (learning, literacy, and life skills) that operationalise academic performance in this research were measured using the scale adapted from Ahmad et al. (2019); Dogru et al. (2022); Hixson et al. (2012); Kalaycı and Esgi (2024); Sahin et al. (2019); and Upadhyaya and Vrinda (2021). The researchers confirmed the operational concepts initially proposed and adapted the measuring instruments, accordingly, ensuring their appropriateness for the research context.

The research involved students from private universities in Selangor only. Convenient sampling technique was employed. The use of a convenience sampling technique in this research, despite its acknowledged limitations, was considered appropriate given the practical and contextual constraints faced by the researchers. The research focused on students from private universities in Selangor, and access to respondents across all such institutions was limited due to the absence of a comprehensive sampling frame and restricted institutional contacts. Under these circumstances, convenience sampling offered a feasible and efficient means of data collection. Moreover, recent methodological literature recognises that convenience sampling is commonly adopted in educational research when the target population is difficult to access and when institutional or administrative barriers constrain probability-based sampling approaches (Etikan & Bala, 2017).

After approximately 2 months, a total of 408 completed questionnaires were received, thus the researchers have decided to proceed with the data analysis. Data screening was conducted using SPSS version 29, while both the measurement and structural model analyses were performed using SMART PLS 4.0.

4. DATA ANALYSIS AND DISCUSSION

4.1 Data Screening

For this research, the data screening phase involved three important procedures namely, identification of missing data and outliers, common method variance (CMV), and normality analysis.

4.1.1 Missing Data and Outliers

This research possesses no missing data issue since data were collected using Google Form. The platform enables the researchers to apply the "must answered question" with the asterisk symbol, abstaining the respondents from submitting their incomplete form. Meanwhile, for data screening, the researchers employed both the boxplot method and the Mahanalobis Distance (as shown in Figure 2 and Figure 3) to identify potential outliers that could bias the results.

Figure 2. Boxplot

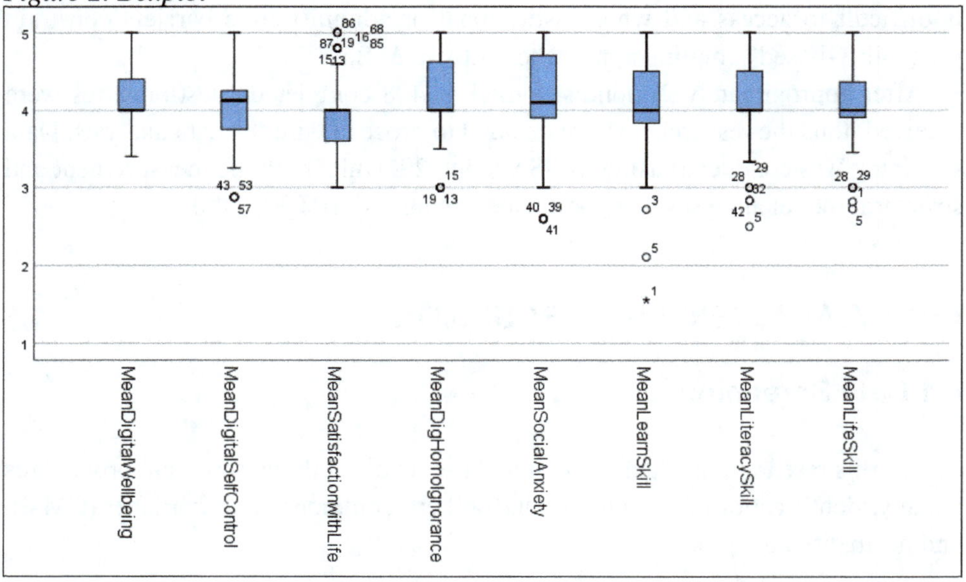

Figure 3. Mahanalobis Distance (P-value)

	Case	MAH_1	PValue
1	14	57.663	.000
2	18	19.142	.008
3	116	19.127	.008
4	126	17.167	.016
5	15	16.808	.019
6	26	16.446	.021
7	176	16.375	.022
8	207	16.245	.023

The decision of adopting both methods is because, the P-value generated from the Mahalanobis Distance procedure could help the researchers to clearly determine the most influential outliers, simultaneously protect the researchers from omitting unnecessary case with insignificant influence. Figure 3 reveals only one (1) case with P-value lower than 0.001, which could potentially distort the results (Barnett & Lewis, 1994), hence deleted. Subsequently, this leaves a total of 407 cases for the next stage of analysis.

4.1.2 Common Method Variance

Common Method Variance can either inflate or deflate the observed correlations between constructs, resulting in inaccurate parameter estimates and potentially misleading conclusions (Tehseen et al., 2017). Table 1 presents the results of the Total Variance Explained, summarising that the first component has an eigenvalue of 18.111 and explains 25.51% of the total variance, followed by the second component with an eigenvalue of 9.406, accounting for 13.25% of the variance. Cumulatively, the first two components account for 38.77% of the total variance. Importantly, the first factor explains less than 50% of the total variance, which is a commonly cited threshold in the literature for assessing the potential impact of CMV (Podsakoff et al., 2003). The results suggest that common method bias is unlikely to be a significant issue in this research.

Table 1. Total Variance Explained

Component	Initial Eigenvalues			Extraction Sums of Squared Loadings			Rotation Sums of Squared Loadings		
	Total	% of Variance	Cumulative %	Total	% of Variance	Cumulative %	Total	% of Variance	Cumulative %
1	18.111	25.508	25.508	18.111	25.508	25.508	16.812	23.678	23.678
2	9.406	13.247	38.756	9.406	13.247	38.756	8.433	11.878	35.556
3	6.702	9.440	48.196	6.702	9.440	48.196	5.499	7.745	43.301
4	4.202	5.919	54.115	4.202	5.919	54.115	3.761	5.298	48.599
5	3.047	4.291	58.406	3.047	4.291	58.406	3.266	4.599	53.198
6	2.200	3.098	61.505	2.200	3.098	61.505	2.813	3.962	57.161
7	1.832	2.580	64.085	1.832	2.580	64.085	2.421	3.409	60.570
8	1.762	2.481	66.566	1.762	2.481	66.566	2.150	3.028	63.597
9	1.671	2.353	68.919	1.671	2.353	68.919	2.107	2.968	66.566
10	1.652	2.327	71.246	1.652	2.327	71.246	1.958	2.757	69.323
11	1.361	1.917	73.162	1.361	1.917	73.162	1.871	2.636	71.958
12	1.305	1.839	75.001	1.305	1.839	75.001	1.446	2.037	73.996
13	1.200	1.690	76.691	1.200	1.690	76.691	1.372	1.933	75.929
14	1.067	1.502	78.193	1.067	1.502	78.193	1.350	1.901	77.829
15	1.037	1.460	79.654	1.037	1.460	79.654	1.295	1.824	79.654

Extraction Method: Principal Component Analysis

4.1.3 Normality Analysis

In addition to conducting the boxplot and Mahalanobis Distance procedures, the researchers carried out a normality test to assess the data's skewness and kurtosis. Establishing normality is essential, as many statistical analyses assume that the data follows a normal distribution. This analysis also aids in preventing misleading conclusions (Kline, 2011). A skewness value between -2 and 2 (Kline, 2011) indicates that the data is symmetrically distributed, without significant left or right bias. A kurtosis value between -3 and 3 (Kline, 2011) suggests that the data follows a distribution that is neither excessively flat nor overly peaked. As presented in Table 2, the skewness and kurtosis values are within these acceptable ranges, confirming that the data's normality is not problematic.

Table 2. Skewness and Kurtosis

	Mean	Skewness	Kurtosis
	Statistic	**Statistic**	**Statistic**
Digital Homo Ignorance	4.1957	0.004	0.104
Literacy Skill	4.1771	-0.188	0.686
Digital Wellbeing	4.1681	0.438	-0.410
Life Skill	4.1471	0.151	0.239
Learn Skill	4.1374	-0.347	0.782
Social Anxiety	4.1058	-0.438	-0.392
Digital Self-Control	4.0483	-0.203	0.294
Satisfaction with Life	3.8715	0.129	-0.235

4.2 Measurement Model Analysis

4.2.1 First Order Analysis / Lower Order Analysis for the Dependent Variable

4.2.1.1 Reliability Analysis

The assessment of internal consistency reliability, composite reliability, and convergent validity constitutes a critical step in evaluating the robustness of the measurement model (Dijkstra & Henseler, 2015; Hair et al., 2019).

Table 3. Internal Consistency, Composite Reliability and Convergent Validity

	Cronbach's alpha	Composite reliability (rho_a)	Composite reliability (rho_c)	Average variance extracted (AVE)
Learning Skill	0.951	0.954	0.956	0.550
Life Skill	0.918	0.921	0.931	0.553
Literacy Skill	0.896	0.896	0.920	0.658

Figure 4. PLS SEM Algorithm for Lower Order Constructs Analysis

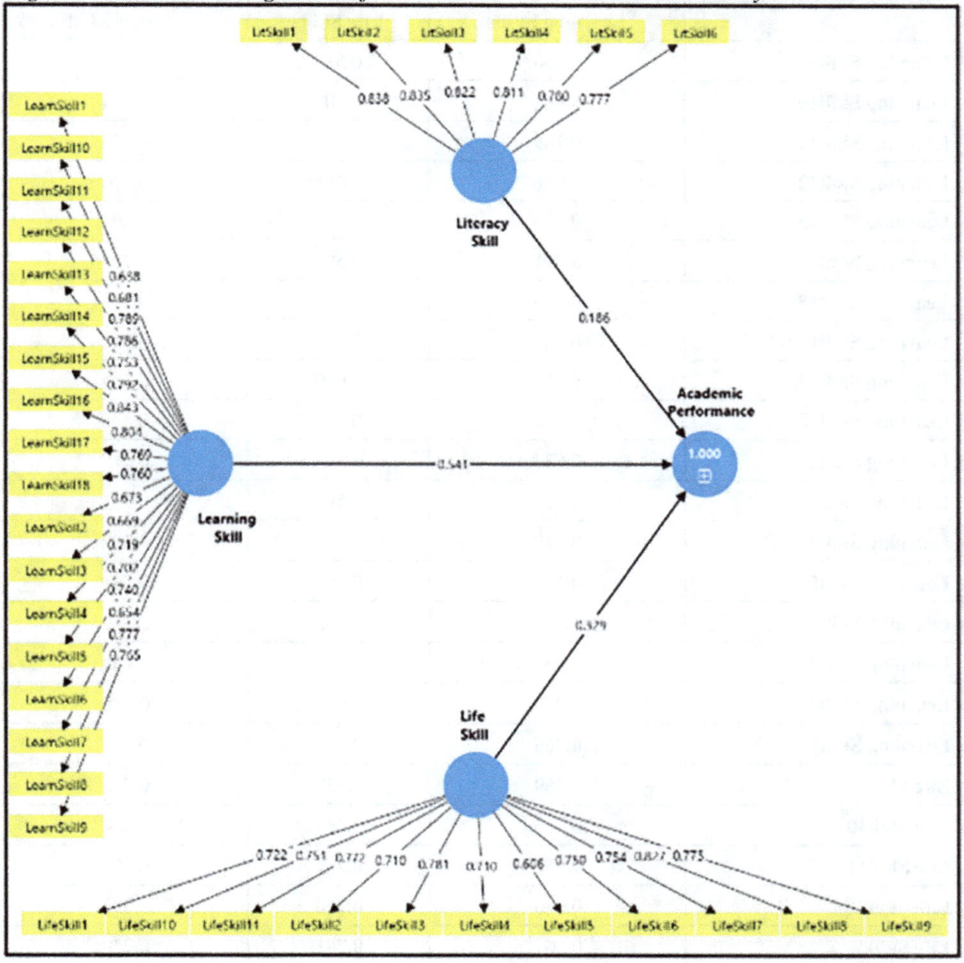

4.2.1.2 Discriminant Validity

Discriminant validity was done to ensure that each construct within the measurement model is conceptually and empirically distinct, confirming that each dimension represent unique components forming the latent variable (academic performance). This step ensures that every indicator not only aligns with its theoretical construct but also demonstrates a stronger empirical association with its intended construct than with any other (Hair et al., 2019). Table 4 presents the cross-loading results for all indicators that measure Learning Skills, Life Skills, and Literacy Skills.

Table 4. Cross-Loading

	Learning Skills	**Life Skills**	**Literacy Skills**
Learning Skill1	**0.638**	0.510	0.495
Learning Skill10	**0.681**	0.500	0.544
Learning Skill11	**0.789**	0.656	0.573
Learning Skill12	**0.786**	0.665	0.670
Learning Skill13	**0.753**	0.662	0.697
Learning Skill14	**0.792**	0.698	0.727
Learning Skill15	**0.843**	0.749	0.784
Learning Skill16	**0.804**	0.700	0.741
Learning Skill17	**0.769**	0.640	0.684
Learning Skill18	**0.760**	0.673	0.686
Learning Skill2	**0.673**	0.574	0.517
Learning Skill3	**0.669**	0.594	0.531
Learning Skill4	**0.719**	0.610	0.592
Learning Skill5	**0.702**	0.585	0.531
Learning Skill6	**0.740**	0.563	0.492
Learning Skill7	**0.654**	0.492	0.444
Learning Skill8	**0.777**	0.614	0.588
Learning Skill9	**0.765**	0.562	0.637
Life Skill1	0.559	**0.722**	0.575
Life Skill10	0.576	**0.751**	0.604
Life Skill11	0.655	**0.772**	0.623
Life Skill2	0.640	**0.710**	0.695
Life Skill3	0.661	**0.781**	0.729
Life Skill4	0.590	**0.710**	0.593
Life Skill5	0.502	**0.606**	0.577

continued on following page

Table 4. Continued

	Learning Skills	Life Skills	Literacy Skills
Life Skill6	0.608	**0.750**	0.624
Life Skill7	0.677	**0.754**	0.540
Life Skill8	0.712	**0.827**	0.723
Life Skill9	0.601	**0.775**	0.578
Literacy Skill1	0.692	0.703	**0.838**
Literacy Skill2	0.679	0.661	**0.835**
Literacy Skill3	0.676	0.678	**0.822**
Literacy Skill4	0.658	0.665	**0.811**
Literacy Skill5	0.696	0.650	**0.780**
Literacy Skill6	0.620	0.735	**0.777**

Since the dependent variable for this research (academic performance) consists of or formed by three (3) dimensions (e.g., learning skills, life skills, and literacy skills), the researchers are compelled to conducting the measurement model analysis, entailing reliability analysis and discriminant validity, for the latent variable of academic performance first (lower order construct). The rationale is to confirm that the academic performance that is operationalised and measured by the 21st century skills attainment is formed by the three (3) dimensions, specifically in the context of private higher education in Malaysia. Results presented in Table 3 confirm all three dimensions did not possess internal consistencies, composite reliability and convergent validity issues with Cronbach Alpha, rho_a and rho_c are all above 0.70 (Dijkstra & Henseler, 2015; Hair et al., 2029; Nunnally, 1978).

Besides, the convergent validity for all dimensions that is measured through the Average variance extracted (AVE) showing results above the minimum threshold 0.50 (Fornell & Larcker, 1981). This is further strengthened based on the cross-loading results presented in Table 4. The results indicate that all items achieved their highest loading on the constructs to which they were assigned, confirming construct specificity and empirical distinctiveness (Hair et al., 2019). Figure 4 is illustrating the PLS SEM diagram for the lower order constructs analysis (learning skills, life skills, and literacy skills).

4.2.2 Second Order Analysis / Higher Order Analysis (IVs to DV)

Upon the confirmation of the lower order construct, the researchers then proceeded to the measurement model analysis for the higher order constructs that involve the independent variables and the dependent variable.

4.2.2.1 Reliability Analysis

The initial PLS-SEM algorithm run to the model produced results with composite reliability and convergent validity issues as presented in Table 5a. Abiding to the principle coined by Hair et al. (2022), in order to rectify the issues, the researchers are advised to scrutinised the outer loading results for each indicator and to delete indicators with lowest loading and that did not meet the minimum requirement value of 0.70. For this research, seven (7) indicators (2 from digital wellbeing, 1 from satisfaction with life, and 3 from digital self-control) were deleted.

Table 5a. Internal Consistency, Composite Reliability and Convergent Validity

	Cronbach's alpha	Composite reliability (rho_a)	Composite reliability (rho_c)	Average variance extracted (AVE)
Digital Homo-Ignorance	0.892	0.995	0.902	0.553
Digital Wellbeing	0.791	0.548	0.658	0.334
Digital Self-Control	0.827	0.840	0.853	0.426
Satisfaction With Life	0.833	0.662	0.815	0.491
Social Anxiety	0.961	1.080	0.964	0.730

After the deletion of the seven (7) indicators, results presented in Table 5b confirm all variables did not possess convergent validity problem as all variables showing AVE reading that is higher than 0.50. Besides, all variables are showing no internal consistency or composite reliability problem with Cronbach's Alpha, rho_a and rho_c are all above the acceptable value 0.70 (Nunnally, 1978).

Table 5b. Internal Consistency, Composite Reliability and Convergent Validity

	Cronbach's alpha	Composite reliability (rho_a)	Composite reliability (rho_c)	Average variance extracted (AVE)
Digital Homo-Ignorance	0.898	0.902	0.917	0.620
Digital Self-Control	0.772	0.790	0.836	0.506
Digital Wellbeing	0.736	0.752	0.767	0.543
Satisfaction With Life	0.813	0.821	0.847	0.594
Social Anxiety	0.941	0.960	0.964	0.730

4.2.2.2 Discriminant Validity

As for the discriminant validity for the measurement model analysis that involved the independent variables and the dependent variable, the researchers have decided to undergo comprehensive procedure that includes Heterotrait-Monotrait Ratio (HTMT0.85), Fornell-Larcker Criterion, and cross-loading. The aim is to ensure that each construct within the measurement model is conceptually and empirically distinct.

Table 6. Heterotrait-Monotrait Ratio (HTMT)

	Academic Performance	Digital Homo-Ignorance	Digital Self-Control	Digital Wellbeing	Satisfaction With Life	Social Anxiety
Digital Homo-Ignorance	0.125					
Digital Self-Control	0.124	0.477				
Digital Wellbeing	0.095	0.265	0.485			
Satisfaction With Life	0.055	0.346	0.420	0.286		
Social Anxiety	0.052	0.308	0.289	0.455	0.412	

Table 7. Fornell-Larcker Criterion

	Digital Homo-Ignorance	Digital Self-Control	Digital Wellbeing	Satisfaction With Life	Social Anxiety
Digital Homo-Ignorance	**0.788**				
Digital Self-Control	0.411	**0.711**			
Digital Wellbeing	-0.003	0.261	**0.737**		
Satisfaction With Life	0.063	0.171	-0.159	**0.770**	
Social Anxiety	0.198	0.245	-0.312	-0.292	**0.854**

Table 8. Cross-Loading

	Digital Homo-Ignorance	Digital Self-Control	Digital Wellbeing	Social Anxiety	Satisfaction With Life
Digital Homo-Ignorance 1	**0.445**	0.207	0.141	-0.374	0.532
Digital Homo-Ignorance 2	**0.729**	0.127	-0.042	-0.022	0.165
Digital Homo-Ignorance 3	**0.869**	0.376	-0.062	0.197	0.062
Digital Homo-Ignorance 5	**0.807**	0.223	0.075	0.094	-0.028
Digital Homo-Ignorance 6	**0.831**	0.324	0.096	0.352	-0.285
Digital Homo-Ignorance 7	**0.931**	0.376	0.011	0.177	0.119
Digital Homo-Ignorance 8	**0.806**	0.532	-0.068	0.183	0.211
Digital Self-Control 1	0.329	**0.785**	0.294	-0.016	0.260
Digital Self-Control 2	0.126	**0.597**	-0.128	0.218	0.231
Digital Self-Control 4	0.150	**0.715**	-0.044	0.234	0.133
Digital Self-Control 6	0.408	**0.718**	0.384	0.318	-0.168
Digital Self-Control 7	0.457	**0.728**	0.301	0.248	0.211
Digital Wellbeing 3	0.194	0.138	**0.451**	-0.270	0.038
Digital Wellbeing 4	-0.047	0.296	**0.723**	-0.343	-0.041
Digital Wellbeing 5	-0.004	0.199	**0.950**	-0.230	-0.196
Social Anxiety 1	0.290	-0.002	-0.314	**0.779**	-0.422
Social Anxiety 10	0.290	0.178	-0.278	**0.827**	-0.272
Social Anxiety 2	0.087	0.084	-0.423	**0.849**	-0.318
Social Anxiety 3	0.016	0.164	-0.353	**0.892**	-0.173
Social Anxiety 4	0.095	0.198	-0.400	**0.883**	-0.145
Social Anxiety 5	0.140	0.402	-0.257	**0.853**	-0.246
Social Anxiety 6	0.122	0.088	-0.287	**0.923**	-0.285
Social Anxiety 7	0.221	0.208	-0.108	**0.845**	-0.117
Social Anxiety 8	0.300	0.214	-0.145	**0.880**	-0.278

continued on following page

Table 8. Continued

	Digital Homo-Ignorance	Digital Self-Control	Digital Wellbeing	Social Anxiety	Satisfaction With Life
Social Anxiety 9	0.083	-0.041	-0.091	**0.802**	-0.585
Satisfaction With Life 1	0.067	0.146	-0.240	-0.252	**0.952**
Satisfaction With Life 2	-0.035	0.177	-0.020	-0.423	**0.882**
Satisfaction With Life 3	0.221	0.291	0.205	-0.269	**0.507**
Satisfaction With Life 5	0.081	0.066	-0.053	-0.013	**0.658**

Figure 5 – PLS SEM Algorithm for Higher Order Constructs Analysis (after indicator deletion)

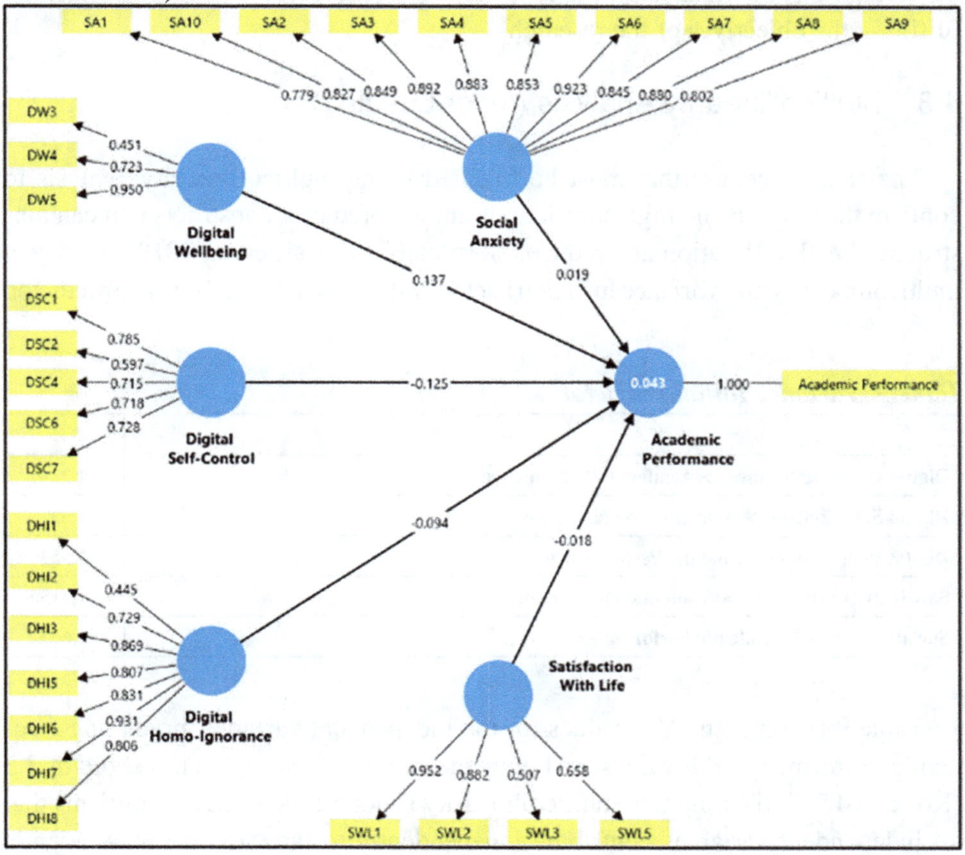

Based on the results displayed in Table 6 to Table 8, it can be concluded discriminant issue does not exist in this research. This is because, the HTMT results for all variables are showing less than 0.85 (Henseler et al., 2015). Besides, for Fornell-Larcker criterion, all diagonal values (square roots of AVE) exceed their corresponding inter-construct correlations (Fornell & Larcker, 1981). The cross-loading too showing that all items accomplished their highest loading on the constructs to which they were assigned to. This indirectly means that all indicators are measuring what it supposed to measure concurrently confirming each construct distinctiveness and uniqueness with no overlapping problem (Hair et al., 2019). Figure 5 representing the PLS-SEM for the higher order construct analysis.

4.3 Structural Model Analysis

Since the research did not encounter any issue during the measurement model analysis phase, it is deemed safe for the researcher to proceed with the structural model analysis. This analysis is implemented to test the research hypotheses, thereby fulfilling the objectives of the research.

4.3.1 Multicollinearity Analysis (Inner Loading)

The first procedure that must be fulfilled is the multicollinearity analysis to confirm there will be no high correlations among predictor constructs that can bias structural path estimation and reduce interpretability (Hair et al., 2019). To detect multicollinearity, the Variance Inflation Factor (VIF) was calculated for each predictor.

Table 9. Variance Inflation Factor

	VIF
Digital Homo-Ignorance -> Academic Performance	1.228
Digital Self-Control -> Academic Performance	1.687
Digital Wellbeing -> Academic Performance	1.553
Satisfaction With Life -> Academic Performance	1.415
Social Anxiety -> Academic Performance	1.667

Table 9 presents the VIF values for the independent variables predicting Academic Performance. All values are below the commonly accepted threshold of 3.3 (Kock, 2015), indicating that multicollinearity is not a concern. This confirms that all independent variables contribute independently to the variance in Academic

Performance, without problematic overlap, providing confidence in the structural estimates and supporting the validity of subsequent path coefficient analyses.

4.3.2 Path Coefficient

Table 10. Path Coefficient and Hypotheses Summary

	Original sample (O)	Standard deviation (STDEV)	T statistics (|O/ STDEV|)	P values	Hypothesis Summary
Digital Homo-Ignorance -> Academic Performance	-0.094	0.073	1.284	0.199	Unsupported
Digital Self-Control -> Academic Performance	-0.125	0.099	1.259	0.208	Unsupported
Digital Wellbeing -> Academic Performance	0.137	0.095	1.447	0.148	Unsupported
Satisfaction With Life -> Academic Performance	-0.018	0.093	0.188	0.851	Unsupported
Social Anxiety -> Academic Performance	0.019	0.094	0.204	0.838	Unsupported

Figure 6. PLS SEM Bootstrapping Diagram

Figure 6 displayed the bootstrapping diagram to obtain the path coefficient results, simultaneously to test the research hypotheses. The structural model results as presented in Table 10 indicate that none of the proposed relationships between the independent variables and academic performance are statistically significant. Digital homo-ignorance shows a negative but weak effect on academic performance ($\beta = -0.094$, $t = 1.284$, $p = 0.199$), while digital self-control also exhibits a negative and non-significant relationship ($\beta = -0.125$, $t = 1.259$, $p = 0.208$). Digital wellbeing demonstrates a small positive effect; however, this relationship is not statistically significant ($\beta = 0.137$, $t = 1.447$, $p = 0.148$). Satisfaction with life ($\beta = -0.018$, $t = 0.188$, $p = 0.851$) and social anxiety ($\beta = 0.019$, $t = 0.204$, $p = 0.838$) likewise show negligible and non-significant effects on academic performance. Overall, as all path coefficients fail to reach statistical significance at conventional thresholds, none of the hypotheses are supported.

The weak direct effects can be explained by the nature of 21st-century skills as outcome variables, which differ fundamentally from traditional indicators of academic performance such as grades or test scores. Learning skills (e.g. critical thinking, creativity, collaboration), life skills (e.g. adaptability, self-management, social competence), and literacy skills (e.g. information, media, and digital literacy) are developmental and cumulative competencies. They are typically cultivated through sustained educational exposure, repeated practice, and long-term socialisation processes rather than through short-term behavioural or psychological states. As a result, these skills tend to reflect longitudinal learning trajectories, making them less sensitive to immediate variations in digital self-control, digital wellbeing, or emotional states at a single point in time.

Furthermore, the development of 21st-century skills is strongly influenced by structural and contextual factors operating beyond the individual level. Curriculum design, pedagogical approaches, assessment practices, peer collaboration, institutional learning cultures, and access to learning resources play a decisive role in shaping these competencies. Recent research emphasises that such skills emerge most effectively through inquiry-based learning, project-based activities, and authentic social interaction, all of which depend heavily on instructional quality and institutional support rather than solely on individual self-regulatory or psychological characteristics (Purmayanti, 2022). Consequently, while digital and psychological factors may indirectly support skill development, their direct impact is likely diluted when academic performance is conceptualised as multidimensional, long-term skill attainment rather than immediate academic output.

Finally, from a methodological perspective, measuring 21st-century skills often relies on self-reported perceptions of competence, which tend to be stable and influenced by students' broader educational experiences and self-concept. Such measures are less responsive to short-term fluctuations in mood, anxiety, or digital behaviour, further attenuating direct statistical relationships. Recent empirical work suggests that psychological and digital variables exert stronger effects when mediated by engagement, learning strategies, or collaborative practices, rather than when modelled as direct predictors of complex skill outcomes (Puiu et al., 2024; Schmidt & Raines, 2019). Therefore, the absence of strong direct effects in this research is theoretically and methodologically consistent with the way 21st-century academic performance is defined and assessed.

4.3.3 Coefficient of Determination and Effect Size

The results presented in Tables 11 indicate that the proposed research model demonstrates weak explanatory and predictive capability for academic performance. The coefficient of determination ($R^2 = 0.043$; adjusted $R^2 = 0.019$) suggests that the five predictors explain only a very small proportion of variance in academic performance. According to recent PLS-SEM guidelines, R^2 values below 0.10 indicate minimal explanatory power, particularly in behavioural and educational research where contextual and institutional factors often play a stronger role than individual-level psychological variables (Hair et al., 2022). This low R^2 implies that academic performance in this research may be influenced by unmodelled factors such as instructional quality, assessment design, socioeconomic background, or institutional support structures, which have been shown to exert stronger effects in contemporary higher education research (Rahman et al., 2023).

Table 11. Coefficient of Determination (R^2)

	R-square	R-square adjusted
Academic Performance	0.043	0.019

Table 12 further reinforces this interpretation, as all effect sizes (f^2) are extremely small. Digital homo-ignorance ($f^2 = 0.007$), digital self-control ($f^2 = 0.010$), and digital wellbeing ($f^2 = 0.013$) demonstrate negligible effects on academic performance, while satisfaction with life and social anxiety both record f^2 values of 0.000. Following Cohen (1988) revised benchmarks for PLS-SEM, effect sizes below 0.02 are considered trivial and indicate that the removal of these constructs would not meaningfully reduce the model's explanatory power (Hair et al., 2022). A plausible explanation is that students may have adapted to digital environments post-pandemic, normalising technology use to the extent that variations in digital behaviours no longer translate into measurable academic differences (Bond et al., 2021). Moreover, in this research, academic performance was operationalised as students' attainment of 21st-century skills namely, learning skills, life skills, and literacy skills which are broad, developmental competencies that evolve over time and are shaped by multiple educational, social, and institutional influences, thereby reducing the likelihood that short-term digital or psychological factors exert strong direct effects.

Table 12. Effect Size (f^2)

	f-square
Digital Homo-Ignorance -> Academic Performance	0.007
Digital Self-Control -> Academic Performance	0.010
Digital Wellbeing -> Academic Performance	0.013
Satisfaction With Life -> Academic Performance	0.000
Social Anxiety -> Academic Performance	0.000

4.3.4 Model fit Analysis

The model fit indices reported in Table 13 also indicate suboptimal model performance. Both the saturated and estimated models yield an SRMR value of 0.154, which exceeds the recommended threshold of 0.08, suggesting substantial discrepancies between the observed and model-implied correlations. Similarly, the NFI value of 0.340 is considerably below the commonly accepted minimum of 0.90, indicating weak overall model fit. Recent methodological literature cautions that model fit indices in PLS-SEM should be interpreted carefully; however, consistently poor fit values often signal misspecification, omitted variables, or overly complex measurement structures (Hair et al., 2022). In this research, the weak fit may reflect the indirect or conditional nature of the relationships, where digital and psychological factors influence academic performance only through mediators such as engagement, learning strategies, or cognitive load.

Table 13. Model of Fitness

	Saturated model	**Estimated model**
SRMR	0.154	0.154
NFI	0.340	0.340

4.3.5 Predictive Analysis

Finally, Table 14 demonstrates that the research model lacks predictive relevance. The Q^2_predict value for academic performance is negative (−0.027), indicating that the model performs worse than a naïve benchmark in predicting out-of-sample observations. Although the RMSE (1.027) and MAE (0.793) values are within acceptable ranges, recent predictive-oriented PLS-SEM literature emphasises that negative Q^2_predict values provide strong evidence of poor predictive validity (Shmueli et al., 2019). This finding suggests that while the selected constructs are theoretically meaningful, they do not offer sufficient practical utility for predicting academic performance in this research context. One possible explanation is that academic performance is a distal outcome influenced by long-term structural and contextual factors, whereas the predictors examined are more proximal and situational, limiting their predictive strength when modelled directly.

Table 14. Predictive Analysis

	Q²predict	RMSE	MAE
Academic Performance	-0.027	1.027	0.793

4.3.6 Importance-Performance Map Analysis (IPMA)

Figure 7. Importance-Performance Map

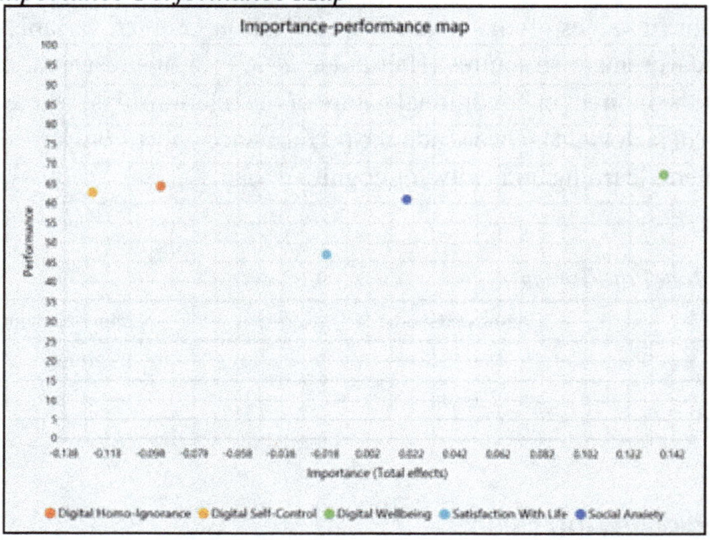

The importance–performance map analysis (IPMA) provides additional insight into the relative relevance and effectiveness of the predictors in explaining academic performance, conceptualised in this research as students' attainment of 21st-century skills (learning skills, life skills, and literacy skills). Overall, the results indicate that none of the constructs simultaneously demonstrate high importance and high performance, reinforcing earlier findings of weak explanatory power. Digital well-being exhibits the highest importance (positive total effect) and comparatively strong performance, suggesting that although its direct statistical effect was not significant, it remains the most influential construct among those examined. This implies that students' ability to maintain healthy, balanced engagement with digital technologies may play a supportive role in fostering broad competencies such as adaptability, information literacy, and collaborative learning, even if this influence is diffuse rather than direct. Recent research similarly highlights that digital wellbeing tends to operate as an enabling condition for long-term skill development rather than as a direct driver of measurable academic outcomes (Buchi, 2024).

In contrast, digital homo-ignorance and digital self-control show negative importance values despite moderate performance levels. The negative importance indicates that increases in these constructs are associated with decreases in academic performance, albeit weakly. For digital homo-ignorance, this may reflect that avoidance of digital information limits opportunities for developing critical digital and literacy skills, which are central components of 21st-century competencies. However, its relatively high-performance score suggests that students perceive themselves as managing this aspect reasonably well, thereby attenuating its overall impact. Similarly, the negative importance of digital self-control may appear counterintuitive but can be rationalised by considering that excessive control or restriction of digital use may reduce exposure to collaborative, creative, and information-rich learning environments that support 21st-century skill development. Recent studies have argued that balanced, purposeful digital engagement is more beneficial than strict digital restraint for higher-order skill acquisition (Bond et al., 2021; Faza & Lestari, 2025).

Satisfaction with life demonstrates low importance and the weakest performance among all constructs. This suggests that general life satisfaction, while valuable for overall wellbeing, does not directly translate into students' acquisition of learning, life, and literacy skills. One possible explanation is that 21st-century skills are largely cultivated through structured educational experiences, pedagogical practices, and sustained engagement rather than through general affective states. Contemporary research supports the view that life satisfaction exerts stronger indirect effects on academic-related outcomes through motivation or engagement rather than direct effects on skill attainment (Ong & Ramasamy, 2024). As such, its limited role in the IPMA is theoretically consistent with the developmental nature of the outcome variable in this research.

Social anxiety shows slightly positive importance but only moderate performance, indicating a marginal and practically insignificant role in explaining academic performance. This finding suggests that while social anxiety may influence participation in collaborative or communicative activities, its direct impact on broad 21st-century skills is limited. Many of these skills can be developed through individual, asynchronous, or digitally mediated learning environments, which may buffer the negative effects of social anxiety. Recent evidence indicates that digital learning contexts can reduce the salience of social anxiety by offering flexible modes of interaction, thereby weakening its relationship with skill development outcomes (Demir et al., 2023). Overall, the IPMA results align with the broader conclusion of this research: the examined digital and psychological factors do not emerge as critical leverage points for enhancing students' attainment of 21st-century skills, which are more strongly shaped by long-term educational, curricular, and institutional influences.

5. CONTRIBUTION, LIMITATION AND RECOMMENDATION

The research presented has significant theoretical and methodological contributions, even though Tables 11 through 14 did not show a widely statistically significant structural/predictive result. The first contribution of the research is that it validated the measurement model developed for the lower order construct of academic performance using learning skills, life skills, and literacy skills as lower order constructs and those as the higher order constructs connecting all three of these independent variables to academic performance. The second contribution of this research is that the theoretical constructs of learning skills, life skills, and literacy skills have been shown through empirical analysis using the criterion of construct validity to support their identification as separate constructs. The fact that there were no substantial issues regarding reliability, convergent validity, discriminant validity, or multicollinearity indicates that the constructs of learning skills, life skills, and literacy skills are conceptually distinct from each other and have been operationalised appropriately. Hence, it concurrently supports the confidence that the less than desirable structural results do not stemmed from the shortcomings in the methodology used in measuring the constructs but rather reflect actual empirical relationships found in this research. Therefore, the research contributes to the educational literature by demonstrating that even with well-defined and validated measurement models, strong prediction/explanation cannot be expected to occur or achieved especially when examining a complex and multi-dimensional developmental outcome such as skills considered in the 21st century. This information is helpful for researchers who want to develop, validate and or support their theoretical perspectives regarding how those should be measured, modelled and predicted according to today's methodologies in educational research.

The research provides an additional theoretical contribution by questioning the generalisations that digital and socio-psychological factors have a direct effect on academic success when viewed from the achievement of the 21st-century-competency. Previous studies demonstrate significant correlations between digital behaviours, well-being, psychological state(s) and traditional academic success. The present work has revealed that these fundamental relationships do not necessarily apply when academic achievement is viewed as the ongoing and multidimensional process of developing competencies over time. Thus, it is crucial for researchers to understand the clarity of the outcome under investigation as well as the difference between perceived and actual outcomes from its measurement. Subsequently, the present findings have shifted the researchers from viewing null or weak results as methodologically problematic towards viewing them as theoretical informative. Accordingly, the current research provides a new understanding of the role of individual predictors in explaining the total picture of complex disciplinary educational outcomes.

Nonetheless, limitations should be recognised too. The research utilised a cross-sectional research design which constrains understanding from a longitudinal and developmental perspective regarding how students acquire skills necessary in 21st century careers. The skills acquired via cross-sectional research tend to evolve slowly (e.g., over time) due to accumulation of multiple or repetitive experiences, making them less likely to be impacted by one single measure of digital behaviour and psychological state at a specific single-time-point measurement. Second, the academic performance of students was measured using self-reported measures which may or may not capture the true level of competency of students and therefore could have lessened the strength of the relationships captured. Similarly, it would have been beneficial to incorporate contextual elements (e.g., type of instructional practice, method of assessment, and type of institutional culture and processes) to assist with understanding how contextual factors influence students' ability to acquire skills. In addition, there were no identified mediating or moderating factors; digital behaviour and psychological states impact students' skill acquisition by influencing engagement with learning materials and learning strategies employed, as well as providing opportunities for collaborative participation with peers.

In the future, multiple methods will be required to capture whether any individuals develop skills in different ways throughout a lifetime in terms of what they learn, how they experience life and how this impacts the acquisition of literacy. Examples of variables that may contribute to the differences observed in different groups would include how much engagement, self-direction and collaboration occur in their education and whether there are any differences in their understanding of their skill set in comparison to their peers. Researchers should also measure variables that integrate contextual and instructional variables, such as pedagogical methods, curriculum integration of digital competencies and the contributions of the universities in the support of this competency. Furthermore, future research would benefit from the applications of multiple methods of self-report data collection, like combining self-reported measures with performance-based assessments or behavioural indicators to increase the robustness of academic performance measurement. The researchers deemed this multiple method approaches will assist in developing a more in-depth understanding of how and when digital and socio-psychological contributors to the development of skills occur.

6. CONCLUSION

In the nutshell, although the results of this research were not as detailed as predicted by the researchers, the theoretical, methodological and empirical value of the findings are still significantly contributing. The research demonstrates the strength of the measurement models while shows that digital and psychological factors do not have much of an influence directly on gaining 21st century skills. The research also portrays the significance of aligning the conceptualisation of outcomes to the appropriate analytical expectations and warns against overvaluation of individual predictor variables and their role in predicting complex educational competencies. This research adds to the ongoing discussion about academic performance and technology as well as shows that negative or "non-significant" results may still be informative if viewed within a rigorous theoretical and methodological context.

REFERENCES

Abd Malek, S. N., & Ahmad, A. L. (2023). International Students' Academic Adjustment in Private Universities in Malaysia. *Jurnal Komunikasi: Malaysian Journal of Communication, 39*(4), 224–246. DOI: 10.17576/JKMJC-2023-3904-12

Ahmad, S. A., Soo, K. Y., Mohamed Yunos, R., & Mohd Amin, J. (2019). Exploring Lecturers' Readiness for 21st Century Education in Malaysian Higher Learning Institutions. *European Journal of Teacher Education, 1*(1), 15–29. DOI: 10.33422/ejte.2019.10.27

Arslankara, V. B., Demir, A., Oztaş, O., & Usta, E. (2022). Digital Well-Being Scale Validity and Reliability Study. *Journal of Teacher Education and Lifelong Learning, 4*(2), 263–274. DOI: 10.51535/tell.1206193

Aydin, M. A., Yıldız, M., Kiyici, M., Yildiz, M., Kirksekiz, A., & Kızıloğlu, Ş. (2024). The effect of digital obesity and phubbing level on life satisfaction: Latent profile analysis. *BMC Psychology, 12*, 754. DOI: 10.1186/s40359-024-02256-w

Bahar, F. H. M., Roslan, N. S., Ping, N. P. T., & Yusoff, M. S. B. (2024). Digital Well-Being among Learners in Higher Education: A Scoping Review Protocol. *Education in Medicine Journal, 16*(4), 181–186. DOI: 10.21315/eimj2024.16.4.14

Bandura, A. (1986). *Social Foundations of Thought and Action: A Social Cognitive Theory*. Prentice Hall. https://api.semanticscholar.org/CorpusID:142519016

Barnett, V., & Lewis, T. (1994). *Outliers in Statistical Data* (3rd ed.). John Wiley & Sons, Kluwer Academic Publishers.

Barrafrem, K., Vastfjall, D., & Tinghog, G. (2024). Financial homo ignorans: Measuring vulnerability to behavioral biases in household finance. *Journal of Behavioral and Experimental Finance, 42*, 100936. DOI: 10.1016/j.jbef.2024.100936

Biedermann, D., Kister, S., Breitwieser, J., Weidlich, J., & Drachsler, H. (2024). Use of digital self-control tools in higher education – a survey study. *Education and Information Technologies, 29*(8), 9645–9666. DOI: 10.1007/s10639-023-12198-2

Bilandzic, H., & Gall Myrick, J. (2024). Information Seeking and Avoidance in the COVID-19 Pandemic as a Function of Political Ideology and National Context: A Survey Comparing the US and Germany. *Health Communication, 39*(11), 2276–2289. DOI: 10.1080/10410236.2023.2263220

Bond, M., Bedenlier, S., Marín, V. I., & Handel, M. (2021). Emergency remote teaching in higher education: Mapping the first global online semester. *International Journal of Educational Technology in Higher Education, 18*(1), 50. DOI: 10.1186/s41239-021-00282-x

Buchi, M. (2024). Digital well-being theory and research. *New Media & Society, 26*(1), 172–189. DOI: 10.1177/14614448211056851

Carvalho, M. (2024, March 4). *Grads earn more now but skills mismatch still high, survey finds*. The Star. https://www.thestar.com.my/news/nation/2024/03/04/grads-earn-more-now-but-skills-mismatch-still-high-survey-finds

Cavlovic, T., Koford, B. C., & Rentschler, L. (2024). Information avoidance: An experimental test of anticipated regret. *Journal of Risk and Uncertainty, 69*(3), 323–348. DOI: 10.1007/s11166-024-09447-1

Chong, P. S. J., & Guan, T. E. (2022). Life Satisfaction, Academic Achievement and Work Readiness Among Undergraduate Students. *International Journal of Education. Psychology and Counseling, 7*(48), 527–535. DOI: 10.35631/ijepc.748040

Cohen, J. (1988). *Statistical power analysis for the behavioral sciences* (2nd ed.). Lawrence Erlbaum.

Csernoch, M., Kiss, J. T., Takacs, V., & Mate, D. (2024). Exploring higher education competencies through spreadsheet self-assessment & time. *Proceedings of the EuSpRIG 2024 Conference "Spreadsheet Productivity & Risks."* https://doi.org/DOI: 10.48550/arXiv.2409.12974

Cynthia, R., & Chong, P. Y. (2023). Factors Influencing International Students' Choice to Study at Malaysian Private Higher Education Institutions. [MJSSH]. *Malaysian Journal of Social Sciences and Humanities, 8*(5), e002281. DOI: 10.47405/mjssh.v8i5.2281

Demir, O., Cinar, M., & Keskin, S. (2023). Participation style and social anxiety as predictors of active participation in asynchronous discussion forums and academic achievement. *Education and Information Technologies*, •••, 1–22. Advance online publication. DOI: 10.1007/s10639-022-11517-3

Deng, L., Zhou, Y., & Broadbent, J. (2024). Distraction, multitasking and self-regulation inside university classroom. *Education and Information Technologies, 29*(18), 23957–23979. DOI: 10.1007/s10639-024-12786-w

Devisakti, A., Muftahu, M., & Xiaoling, H. (2024). Digital divide among B40 students in Malaysian higher education institutions. *Education and Information Technologies, 29*(2), 1857–1883. DOI: 10.1007/s10639-023-11847-w

Dijkstra, T. K., & Henseler, J. (2015). Consistent partial least squares path modeling. *Management Information Systems Quarterly*, *39*, 297–316. DOI: 10.25300/MISQ/2015/39.2.02

Dogru, M., Celik, M., Koca, C., & Tongal, A. (2022). Development of Life and Career Skills Scale for University Students. *Asian Journal of Contemporary Education*, *6*(1), 30–43. DOI: 10.55493/5052.v6i1.4425

Etikan, I., & Bala, K. (2017). Sampling and Sampling Methods. *Biometrics & Biostatistics International Journal*, *5*, 00149. Advance online publication. DOI: 10.15406/bbij.2017.05.00149

Faza, A., & Lestari, I. A. (2025). Self-Regulated Learning in the Digital Age: A Systematic Review of Strategies, Technologies, Benefits, and Challenges. *International Review of Research in Open and Distance Learning*, *26*(2), 23–58. DOI: 10.19173/irrodl.v26i2.8119

Fornell, C., & Larcker, D. F. (1981). Evaluating structural equation models with unobservable variables and measurement error. *JMR, Journal of Marketing Research*, *18*(1), 39–50. DOI: 10.2307/3151312

Hair, J. F., Black, W. C., Babin, B. J., & Anderson, R. E. (2019). *Multivariate data analysis* (8th ed.). Cengage Learning.

Hair, J. F., Hult, G. T. M., Ringle, C. M., & Sarstedt, M. (2022). *A Primer on Partial Least Squares Structural Equation Modeling (PLS-SEM)* (3rd ed.). Sage., DOI: 10.1007/978-3-030-80519-7

Halim, F. S. A., Luaran, J. E., & Jill, L. S. S. (2024). Unravelling Challenges of Higher Education Institutions in Implementing Effective Micro-Credentials: A Multi-Stakeholder Qualitative Study. *Asian Journal of University Education*, *20*(1), 114–126. DOI: 10.24191/ajue.v20i1.25698

Henseler, J., Ringle, C. M., & Sarstedt, M. (2015). A new criterion for assessing discriminant validity in variance-based structural equation modeling. *Journal of the Academy of Marketing Science*, *43*(1), 115–135. DOI: 10.1007/s11747-014-0403-8

Hixson, N. K., Ravitz, J., & Whisman, A. (2012). *Extended Professional Development in Project-Based Learning: Impacts on 21st century teaching and student achievement.* In West Virginia Department of Education. https://files.eric.ed.gov/fulltext/ED565466.pdf

Hultell, D., & Gustavsson, J. P. (2008). A psychometric evaluation of the satisfaction with life scale in a Swedish nationwide sample of university students. *Personality and Individual Differences*, *44*(5), 1070–1079. DOI: 10.1016/j.paid.2007.10.030

Ifenthaler, D., Cooper, M., Daniela, L., & Sahin, M. (2023). Social anxiety in digital learning environments: An international perspective and call to action. *International Journal of Educational Technology in Higher Education*, *20*(1), 50. DOI: 10.1186/s41239-023-00419-0

Jia, C., & Li, P. (2024). Generation Z's Health Information Avoidance Behavior: Insights From Focus Group Discussions. *Journal of Medical Internet Research*, *26*, e54107. DOI: 10.2196/54107

Kadum, B. M. C. M., & Karpudewan, M. (2025). Influence of self-efficacy and metacognition on malaysian pre-university students' chemistry academic motivation: The moderating role of gender and locality. *Chemistry Education Research and Practice*, *26*(3), 682–700. DOI: 10.1039/D4RP00334A

Kalaycı, R., & Eşgi, N. (2024). Development of the 21St Century Information Literacy Skills Scale, Validity and Reliability Study. *European Journal of Education Studies*, *11*(3), 55–75. DOI: 10.46827/ejes.v11i3.5221

Kline, R. B. (2011). Principles and practice of structural equation modeling. In *Guilford Publication*. Guilford Press.

Kock, N. (2015). Common Method Bias in PLS-SEM: A Full Collinearity Assessment Approach. [IJeC]. *International Journal of e-Collaboration*, *11*, 1–10. DOI: 10.4018/ijec.2015100101

Leonhardt, C., Danielsen, D., & Andersen, S. (2025). Associations between screen use, learning and concentration among children and young people in western countries: a scoping review. *Children and Youth Services Review, 177*, 108508 Contents. https://doi.org/DOI: 10.1016/j.childyouth.2025.108508

Li, K., Jiang, S., Yan, X., & Li, J. (2024). Mechanism study of social media overload on health self-efficacy and anxiety. *Heliyon*, *10*, e23326. DOI: 10.1016/j.heliyon.2023.e23326

Liebowitz, M. R. (1987). Social phobia. *Modern Problems of Pharmacopsychiatry*, *22*, 141–173. DOI: 10.1159/000414022

Lind, T., Ahmed, A., Skagerlund, K., Strömbäck, C., & Västfjäll, D., & Ting hög G. (2020). Competence, confidence, and gender: The role of objective and subjective financial knowledge in household finance. *Journal of Farm Economics*, *41*, 626–638. DOI: 10. 1007/ s10834- 020- 09678-9

Mail, M. (2024, April 30). *HR Ministry: Graduate employment mismatch rate shows sharp decline from 18.2pc in 2023 to 40.5pc in previous year*. https://www.malaymail.com/news/malaysia/2024/04/30/hr-ministry-graduate-employment-mismatch-rate-shows-sharp-decline-from-182pc-in-2023-to-405pc-in-previous-year/131778

Marsh, E., Vallejos, E. P., & Spence, A. (2022). The digital workplace and its dark side: An integrative review. *Computers in Human Behavior*, *128*, 107118. DOI: 10.1016/j.chb.2021.107118

Maskun, R., Mat Khairi, S. M., Sulaiman, M. N. A., Mohd Aris, N., Omar, M. M., & Mohamed, M. N. (2025). Digital Wellbeing Among Generation Y in Malaysia: Implications, Challenges, and the Path Forward. *Asia-Pacific Journal of Business, Humanities, and Education*, *10*(1), 44–57.

Mayiwar, L., Asutay, E., Tinghög, G., Västfjäll, D., & Barrafrem, K. (2025). Determinants of digital well-being. *AI & Society*, *40*, 3063–3073. DOI: 10.1007/s00146-024-02071-2

Mohamad Fadzil, N. F., Samad, P. N. S. N., Mohd Nawawi, A. F., Mohamed Pandi, N. Z., & Puteh, F. (2022). Towards a High Standards of Excellence in Malaysia's Higher Education Institutions: Obstacles and Enablers. *The Journal of American Science*, *19*(2), 162–192.

Mohamed, N. F., Ting, J., Tan, A. M., Norhafizah, M. S., Farhana, I., Chan, M. F., Fadlin, M., Rahmatullah, B., Govindasamy, P., & Abdulla, K. (2024). Prevalence and predictors of social anxiety disorders among Malaysian secondary school students during the COVID-19 pandemic: Exploring the influence of internet gaming disorder and impulsivity. *Clinical Child Psychology and Psychiatry, 13591045231206968*. Advance online publication. DOI: 10.1177/13591045231206967

Moo, K. H., & Da Wan, C. (2023). Graduate Employability in Malaysia: Unpacking the Concept, Policy and Practices. *IIUM Journal of Educational Studies*, *11*(2), 3–25. DOI: 10.31436/ijes.v11i2.471

Mou, Q., Zhuang, J., Wu, Q., Zhong, Y., Dai, Q., Cao, X., Gao, Y., Lu, Q., & Zhao, M. (2024). Social media addiction and academic engagement as serial mediators between social anxiety and academic performance among college students. *BMC Psychology*, *12*(1), 190. DOI: 10.1186/s40359-024-01635-7

Neagu, S. N., & Vieriu, A. M. (2025). Digital and Psychological Well-Being Among Technical University Students: Exploring the Impact of Digital Engagement in Higher Education. *Education Sciences*, *15*(9), 1192. DOI: 10.3390/educsci15091192

Nunnally, J. C. (1978). *Psychometric theory* (2nd ed.). McGraw-Hill.

O'Brien, A. G., Foust, J. L., & Taber, J. M. (2024). Physical health mindsets and information avoidance. *Journal of Behavioral Medicine*, *47*(6), 1052–1066. DOI: 10.1007/s10865-024-00514-1

Omar, S., Hussein, N. H., Hanapi, N. F., Abdullah, Y. S., Mohd Noor, A. L., & Saidi, S. B. (2023). Self-Efficacy and Self-Regulated Learning Among Undergraduate in Learning Arabic As a Foreign Language Via Online. *Issues in Language Studies*, *12*(2), 227–245. DOI: 10.33736/ils.5566.2023

Ong, S. H., & Ramasamy, R. (2024). Exploring Students' Satisfaction and Loyalty in Private Universities, Malaysia. *Semarak International Journal of Applied Psychology*, *1*(1), 40–50. DOI: 10.37934/sijap/1.1.4050b

Ooi, T. L. (2025). *Strengthening Malaysia's Private Higher Education Sector through a Structural Revamp*. https://penanginstitute.org/wp-content/uploads/2025/05/Strengthening-Malaysias-Private-Higher-Education-Sector-through-a-Structural-Revamp.pdf

Osborne, E. L., Ainsworth, B., Hooper, N., & Atkinson, M. J. (2023). Experiences of Using Digital Mindfulness-Based Interventions: Rapid Scoping Review and Thematic Synthesis. *Journal of Medical Internet Research*, *25*, e44220. DOI: 10.2196/44220

Osman, I., Ibrahim, A., Mohd, I. H., Jameelah, M., Hashim, M., & Ahmad, N. N. (2025). Graduate soft skills and employability in Malaysia: The view of employers from different manufacturing companies. *Social and Management Research Journal*, *22*(1), 1–16. DOI: 10.24191/smrj.v22i1

Park, J., Paxtle-Granjeno, J., Ok, M. W., Shin, M., & Wilson, E. (2025). Preventing digital distraction in secondary classrooms: A quasi-experimental study. *Computers & Education*, *227*, 105223. https://doi.org/https://doi.org/10.1016/j.compedu.2024.105223

Pascarella, E. T., Salisbury, M. H., & Blaich, C. (2011). Exposure to Effective Instruction and College Student Persistence: A Multi-Institutional Replication and Extension. *Journal of College Student Development*, *52*(1), 4–19. DOI: 10.1353/csd.2011.0005

Podsakoff, P. M., MacKenzie, S. B., Lee, J. Y., & Podsakoff, N. P. (2003). Common method biases in behavioral research: A critical review of the literature and recommended remedies. *The Journal of Applied Psychology*, *88*(5), 879–903. DOI: 10.1037/0021-9010.88.5.879

Ponton, M. K., & Rhea, N. E. (2006). Autonomous Learning from a Social Cognitive Perspective. *New Horizons in Adult Education and Human Resource Development, 20*(2), 38–49. DOI: 10.1002/nha3.10250

Puiu, S., Udri tioiu, M. T., Petri or, I., Yılmaz, S. E., Pfefferová, M. S., Raykova, Z., Yildizhan, H., & Marekova, E. (2024). Students' Well-Being and Academic Engagement: A Multivariate Analysis of the Influencing Factors. *Healthcare (Basel, Switzerland), 12*(15), 1492. DOI: 10.3390/healthcare12151492

Purmayanti, D. (2022). The Challenges of Implementing Digital Literacy in Teaching and Learning Activities for EFL Learners in Indonesia. *BATARA DIDI: English Language Journal, 1*(2), 101–110. DOI: 10.56209/badi.v1i2.38

Rahman, S., Munam, A. M., Hossain, A., Hossain, A. S. M. D., & Bhuiya, R. A. (2023). Socio-economic factors affecting the academic performance of private university students in Bangladesh: A cross-sectional bivariate and multivariate analysis. *SN Social Sciences, 3*(2), 26. DOI: 10.1007/s43545-023-00614-w

Razak, A. A., Raime, S., Misron, A., & Zailani, N. F. I. (2025). Conceptualising Educational Experience towards STREAMS Skills Attainment among MBA Students. *International Journal of Academic Research in Business & Social Sciences, 15*(6), 1090–1102. DOI: 10.6007/ijarbss/v15-i6/25578

Sahin, A., Yoon, M., & Kim, M. (2019). The Development and Validation of a 21st Century Skills Instrument: Measuring Secondary School Students' Skills. *Journal of Research in Science. Mathematics and Technology Education*, 2(2), 85–103. DOI: 10.31756/jrsmte.223

Schmidt, T. A., & Raines, J. M. (2019). Analyzing Class Attendance and Student Achievement in Prescribed College Mathematics Courses. *Global Journal of Educational Studies*, *5*(2), 12–23. DOI: 10.5296/gjes.v5i2.15352

Senin, M. S., Ali, S., Hau, T. C., Jamaluddin, N. S., & Rahman, S. A. (2023). Relationship between Self–Efficacy and Student Psychology in Blended Learning Courses. *Journal for ReAttach Therapy and Developmental Diversities*, *6*(3s), 70–80.

Shahzad, M. F., Shuo, X., Weng, M. L., Yang, X., & Khan, Q. R. (2024). Artificial intelligence and social media on academic performance and mental well-being: Student perceptions of positive impact in the age of smart learning. *Heliyon, 10*, e29523. DOI: 10.1016/j.heliyon.2024.e29523

Shmueli, G., Sarstedt, M., Hair, J. F., Cheah, J.-H., Ting, H., Vaithilingam, S., & Ringle, C. M. (2019). Predictive model assessment in PLS-SEM: Guidelines for using PLSpredict. *European Journal of Marketing*, *53*(11), 2322–2347. DOI: 10.1108/EJM-02-2019-0189

Sidiq, M., Janakiraman, B., Kashoo, F., Jastania, R., Alhusayni, A. I., Alzahrani, A., Chahal, A., Thiyagarajan, A., Khan, I., Kumar, C., Vasanthi, R. K., Alanazi, F., Ahmad, M., Sehgal, C. A., Khan, S., & Alghadier, M. (2025). Screen time exposure and academic performance, anxiety, and behavioral problems among school children. *PeerJ*, *13*(5). Advance online publication. DOI: 10.7717/peerj.19409

Stauffer, B. (2022). *What are 21st century skills? ICEV.* https://www.icevonline.com/blog/what-are-21st-century-skills

Stromback, C., Skagerlund, K., Vastfjall, D., & Tinghog, G. (2020). Subjective self-control but not objective measures of executive functions predicts financial behavior and well-being. *Journal of Behavioral and Experimental Finance*, *27*, 100339. https://doi.org/https://doi.org/10.1016/j.jbef.2020.100339

Szczuka, Z., Kulis, E., Boberska, M., Banik, A., Siwa, M., Zaleskiewicz, H., Knoll, N., Revenson, T. A., & Luszczynska, A. (2023). Dyadic reciprocal associations between self-efficacy and planning predict sedentary behaviour. *British Journal of Health Psychology*, *28*(2), 451–466. DOI: 10.1111/bjhp.12633

Tee, P. K., Wong, L. C., Dada, M., Song, B. L., & Ng, C. P. (2024). Demand for digital skills, skill gaps and graduate employability: Evidence from employers in Malaysia. *F1000 Research*, *13*(389). Advance online publication. DOI: 10.12688/f1000research.148514.1

Tehseen, S., Ramayah, T., & Sajilan, S. (2017). Testing and Controlling for Common Method Variance: A Review of Available Methods. *Journal of Management Sciences*, *4*, 142–168. DOI: 10.20547/jms.2014.1704202

Upadhyaya, P., & Vrinda. (2021). Impact of technostress on academic productivity of university students. *Education and Information Technologies*, *26*(2), 1647–1664. DOI: 10.1007/s10639-020-10319-9

Van Le, H. (2024). Silence in the classroom: Unraveling the cultural dynamics affecting participation and critical thinking in Malaysian and Vietnamese engineering education. *Cogent Education*, *11*(1), 2404780. DOI: 10.1080/2331186X.2024.2404780

Wang, X., Wan Jaafar, W. M., & Sulong, R. M. (2025). Building better learners: Exploring positive emotions and life satisfaction as keys to academic engagement. *Frontiers in Education*, *10*, 1535996. DOI: 10.3389/feduc.2025.1535996

Xethakis, L. J., Rupp, M., & Plummer, B. R. B. (2024). Why students feel anxious in group work: An investigation into students' perspectives on the sources of their anxious experiences in group work. *Frontiers in Education*, *9*, 1461747. DOI: 10.3389/feduc.2024.1461747

Zheng, L., & Lee, K. C. (2023). Examining the Effects of "Small Private Online Course and Flipped-Classroom"-Based Blended Teaching Strategy on First-Year English-Major Students' Achievements. *Sustainability*, *15*(21). Advance online publication. DOI: 10.3390/su152115349

Chapter 2
Global North–South's Diverging Potentials of AI in Higher Education:
Innovation vs. Digital Divide

Mahmuda Naznin
http://orcid.org/0000-0002-2210-413X
University of Dhaka, Bangladesh

Sheikh Rashid Bin Islam
http://orcid.org/0000-0003-2050-2916
Kobe University, Japan

ABSTRACT

This chapter analyzes the divergent potentials of artificial intelligence (AI) in higher education across the Global North and Global South, emphasizing the intersection of innovation and digital inequalities. It underscores that while AI facilitates specific types of education, efficient management, and sophisticated research in technologically advanced environments, its unequal global distribution exacerbates underlying inequities. Authors utilize a bibliometric analysis and institutional case study method to illustrate differences in digital infrastructure, research capability, policy frameworks, and pedagogical preparedness. The chapter presents an integrative framework for equitable AI adoption, using ideas of the digital divide, diffusion of innovation, and the political economics of knowledge. Ultimately, it contends that inclusive and contextually aware deployment is crucial for AI to act as a catalyst for educational reform rather than a tool that exacerbates current imbalances.

DOI: 10.4018/979-8-2600-1458-5.ch002

INTRODUCTION

In higher education (HE) throughout the world, artificial intelligence (AI) is growing rapidly as a defining technological force that is changing graduate preparation for an increasingly digital labour market, research, teaching, and institutional administration. AI already penetrates academic environments via automated tutoring systems, predictive analytics, and generative models that can create text, code, and multimodal content - advancements unimaginable a decade ago. This worldwide change is neither uniform nor equitable. The transformational potential of AI combines with established structural inequalities, resulting in an environment where innovation progresses unevenly and often exacerbates gaps across institutions, geographies, and knowledge systems (Crompton & Burke, 2023; Hashmi & Bal, 2024).

In order to analyse these disparities, authors examine *how different patterns of AI adoption in the Global North and Global South are shaped by national infrastructures, institutional capacities, and pedagogical environments.* Most of the developed nations enjoy sophisticated digital infrastructures, stable governance, robust regulatory frameworks, and well-financed research ecosystems. In contrast, developing or low-income nations encounter limited connectivity, ineffective governance, resource shortages, and political instability (Khan et al., 2024). Wealthy nations dominate AI technology development, while low-resource institutions often use systems designed abroad without considering their cultural, linguistic, or infrastructural contexts. These discrepancies reflect diverging socioeconomic trends (Benton, 2023; Subaveerapandiyan et al., 2023). These gaps influence not just the pace of adoption but also the security, trajectory, and inclusivity of AI-driven breakthroughs.

AI intensifies disparities in knowledge production. Global North countries dominate AI research and establish standards for responsible educational practices, advancing global innovation while marginalising Global South institutions, which often lack the capacity to contribute meaningfully to AI-in-Higher Education (AI-in-HE) policy, technology, and concepts. Consequently, the Global South functions as a testing ground rather than a co-creator of AI futures (Gehl Sampath, 2021; Okolo, 2023). Besides, language inequality exacerbates this exclusion: large-scale models prioritise English and other high-resource languages, leaving institutions in the Global South with different languages marginalised and reinforcing epistemic hierarchies (Kshetri, 2024). Data governance and ethical safeguards are similarly uneven. Many Global South universities operate in regulatory vacuums, exposing students to unregulated data collection, algorithmic bias, and surveillance, whereas Global North institutions benefit from frameworks such as General Data Protection Regulations (GDPR) compliance in countries like Finland and the United Kingdom (Smyth et al., 2020).

There is a fundamental structural, political, and ethical problem; it is not only a technological one. Thus, this chapter's core issue is that *AI has the ability to revolutionise higher education, but this ability is not uniformly dispersed throughout different parts of the world.*

The authors in this chapter analyse AI-in-HE across 10 nations, five from the *Global North (the United States, the United Kingdom, Finland, Canada, Japan)* and five from the *Global South (Bangladesh, Nepal, Cambodia, Myanmar, Lao PDR).* The novelty of the chapter lies in its acknowledgement that AI is reshaping higher education and advocates for analyses grounded in global diversity rather than just technical optimism. The authors contend that inclusiveness, accessibility, equitable distribution, and capability should guide assessments of AI applications in higher education. Based on bibliometric analysis and institutional case studies, the authors demonstrate that differences emerge from budget limitations, regulatory contexts, linguistic hierarchies, and uneven research ecosystems, all of which are associated with the capacity to access and utilise AI in higher education. The authors ultimately present a pragmatic, integrative, and inclusive policy framework to facilitate equitable and context-sensitive AI implementation.

The chapter's goals provide a structured approach to examining how AI is transforming higher education across diverse national and institutional contexts. Rooted in themes of equity, structural imbalance, and context-aware innovation, these aims offer a coherent framework for comparing national readiness, institutional capabilities, research ecosystems, and pedagogical reforms, and hence the chapter's objectives ensure alignment with this premise:

- To analyse the relationship between national digital readiness and institutional capacity for AI integration, emphasising policy and infrastructural influences.
- To map global trends in AI research output, collaboration patterns, and institutional competence to reveal knowledge production asymmetries between the Global North and South.
- To identify key ethical, educational, technological, and financial barriers shaping inclusive AI adoption in the Global South.
- To develop an integrative model linking infrastructure, governance, research ecosystems, and pedagogy.
- To provide policy and institutional recommendations for ethical, equitable, and sustainable AI integration.

THEORETICAL LENSES FOR ANALYSING AI INTEGRATION IN GLOBAL HIGHER EDUCATION

The authors founded this chapter on three complementary theoretical perspectives. These approaches illuminate the structural, institutional, and socio-political factors that cause North-South AI-in-HE adoption disparities. As shown in the previous sections, digital infrastructure, governance competence, language resources, and global power relations greatly impact AI integration. *The Digital Divide Theory, Capabilities Approach, Diffusion of Innovation,* and *Political Economy of Knowledge* provide the analytical tools needed to understand complex and unequal patterns across nations and institutions (Alexander, 2016; Campbell & Pedersen, 2011; Jacobson, 2016).

Digital Divide Theory and the Capabilities Approach

The digital divide encompasses more than just internet access; it also includes the capacity to use digital technology effectively. According to Sen and Nussbaum's *Capabilities Theory,* in order to achieve true empowerment, access must be translated into actual capabilities, which are the abilities, systems of governance, and agency required to turn resources into opportunities (Alexander, 2016; Jacobson, 2016). Infrastructure like the internet, devices, and processing power are necessary but insufficient in AI-driven higher education; both institutions and students must be capable of utilising AI. According to Akbarighatar (2025), this stance describes how disparities advance from the *first-level divide (infrastructure)* to *the second-level divide (skills and usage)* to *the third-level divide (outcomes and benefits).* In the AI era, these disparities widen – while universities in low-income areas deal with a lack of digital literacy, unstable electricity, limited bandwidth, device shortages, and insufficient data protection, those in high-income countries have access to cutting-edge computing, cloud services, and learning analytics (Khan et al., 2024). As a result, the divide represents differences in governance, resources, and human capital in addition to technological divides.

Diffusion of Innovation

Although *Rogers's Diffusion of Innovation theory* is helpful in explaining the patterns of adoption, in this chapter, the authors apply it to institutional capacity. The authors identify which universities are early adopters (building capacity), which are innovators (creating new AI knowledge), and how expertise diffuses throughout institutions. The idea helps explain adoption gaps both across and within regions. Due to the obvious apparent advantages, well-funded Global North universities with research-intensive, tech-focused, and capable of properly testing AI tend to adopt it early. Due to inadequate infrastructure, poor governance, and a lack of funding, many Global South universities, on the other hand, adopt AI more slowly because they see it as complicated, expensive, and dangerous. Because diffusion is influenced by institutional capability, societal norms, and national policies, adoption varies greatly even within the same region (Gutiérrez-Leefmans et al., 2025; Miller, 2015; Singh & Strzelecki, 2025).

Political Economy of Knowledge

Political and economic factors have a significant impact on AI innovation. Authors use *Karl Marx's Theory on Political Economy of Knowledge* to analyse how institutional structures, power, and resources determine who develops AI tools, who determines research agendas, and who gains pedagogical advantages. Strong epistemic concentration is revealed by bibliometric and cross-border case studies later in the chapter. Research on AI in education is dominated by certain nations and institutions, deepening global differences. Due to their higher capacity for research, institutions in the Global North take the lead in pedagogical innovation, instrument creation, and governance design. Since the majority of research on AI in education originates from nations like the US, Finland, and the UK, their priorities influence prevailing AI frameworks and standards. Institutions in the Global South, on the other hand, frequently lack funding, experience, or alliances, turning into consumers or data suppliers rather than equal partners. AI systems' linguistic and cultural biases reinforce epistemic colonialism by further marginalising non-Western knowledge. Adoption of AI thus runs the risk of replicating current global hierarchies in knowledge production and educational power, notwithstanding its potential (Campbell & Pedersen, 2011; Kshetri, 2024).

Integration of Three Theoretical Lenses

Each theoretical lens sheds light on distinct but complementary facets of the worldwide disparity in AI integration in higher education. The basis for examining how various nations and institutions handle integrating AI-in-HE and the reasons for the stark differences in their results is provided by this comprehensive theoretical perspective shown in **Figure 1**.

Figure 1. Integrated Theoretical Lens

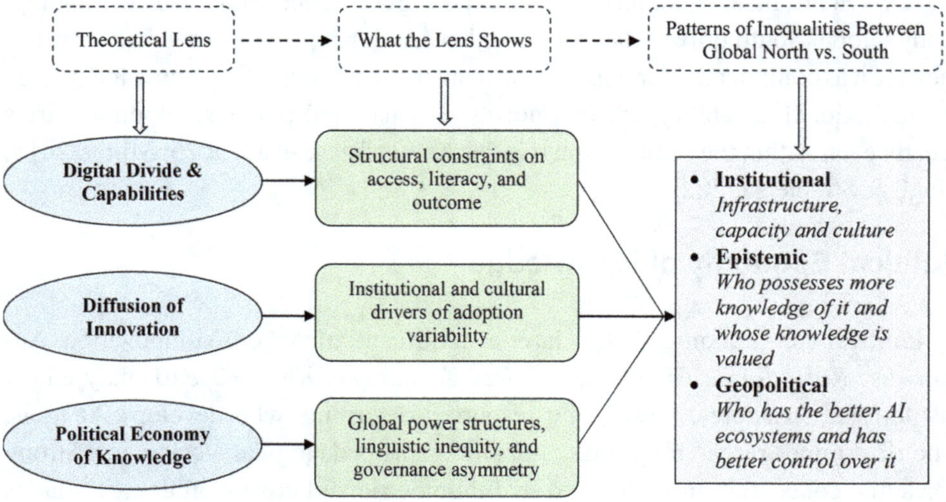

Source: Created by the authors.

GLOBAL LANDSCAPE OF AI READINESS AND INFRASTRUCTURE IN HIGHER EDUCATION

This section contextualises the chapter within the wider framework of global digital readiness, delineating the structural factors influencing AI integration in higher education. The integration of contemporary data on connectivity, computing infrastructures, and institutional capacity demonstrates that AI preparedness is contingent not just on technological availability but also on organisational practices, national investment, and regulatory frameworks.

The Global Context of AI in Higher Education

Global connection and computational capability are markedly uneven, influencing institutions' fundamental abilities to implement AI in education, research, and administration. Despite the ongoing expansion of the internet and broadband access, significant differences remain in coverage, pricing, speed, and data capacity between affluent and impoverished regions. These deficiencies are significant as advanced AI applications need robust, low-latency, high-bandwidth settings. National infrastructure and regulatory frameworks fundamentally influence institutional AI preparedness, constraining the potential achievements of institutions in low-capacity environments (Kohnke et al., 2023).

Digital Readiness and Infrastructure: A Comparative Overview

Connectivity and Internet Penetration

Empirical indicators, like internet usage and fixed-broadband subscriptions, provide a valuable estimation of the necessary conditions for AI-enhanced pedagogies and services. Data from the United Nations (UN) International Telecommunication Union (ITU) indicate that, despite significant worldwide internet access expansion, considerable regional and income-based discrepancies remain (**Figure 2**). High-income nations see nearly universal connection and substantial fixed-broadband penetration, whereas several low-income countries exhibit low utilization rates, restricted affordability, and inconsistent service quality. Fixed-broadband subscriptions, essential for campus and laboratory access, exhibit comparable disparities. These disparities influence the viability of bandwidth-demanding AI applications, such as synchronous tutoring, extensive cloud data transfer, and remote GPU access (ITU, 2021; UN, 2021).

Figure 2. Internet Penetration Rate in 2023

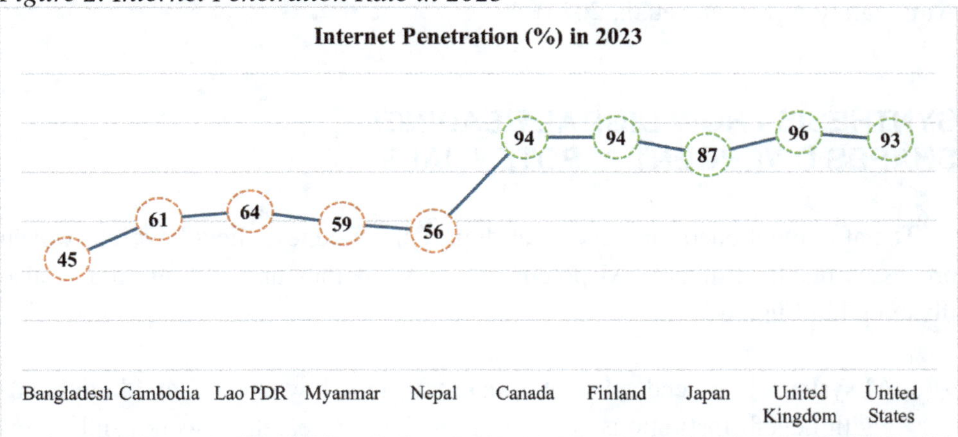

Source: World Bank (2025).

Computing and Data Infrastructure

AI research relies on both connection and access to substantial computational infrastructure, including national high-performance computing (HPC) facilities, cloud platforms, and institutional servers. Global registries indicate that most advanced computational expertise is predominantly concentrated among universities in the Global North, facilitating extensive experimentation and localized AI service provision. Although cloud services enhance accessibility, they need ongoing financial support, procurement capabilities, and robust data governance; in their absence, institutions face potential risks of reliance and vendor lock-in. As a result, universities in the Global South frequently depend on external suppliers, encountering delays, financial obstacles, and restricted capabilities for advanced AI research (Mutunhu et al., 2021).

Higher Education Digital Maturity

Institutional digital maturity, assessed by measures of strategy, governance, staff competence, and digitally facilitated pedagogy, illustrates the conversion of infrastructure into substantial institutional capacity. UNESCO, OECD, and EdTech studies underscore that maturity necessitates cohesive digital strategies, staff training in data and AI literacies, strong governance frameworks, and pedagogical integration throughout curriculum. Research indicates that sustained change relies on leadership, long-term investment, and alignment with national strategy. The inconsistent digital transition during COVID-19 revealed governance and equity disparities in the Global South, highlighting that infrastructure alone does not guarantee successful AI integration (Kohnke et al., 2023).

SYNTHESIS - HOW DIGITAL READINESS SHAPES DIVERGENT AI POTENTIALS

The aforementioned three facets of digital preparedness show how interwoven processes result in diverse AI potentials across nations and institutions, as also illustrated in **Figure 3**.

- AI systems that need substantial data transfers, low latency, and high bandwidth benefit institutions with strong national research networks and extensive internet access, facilitating the utilisation of innovative services with minimum operational impediments. Regardless of local expertise, many AI advancements are still unavailable in low-penetration environments.
- Performing AI research at scale, training models in indigenous languages, and maintaining data or intellectual property rights relies on high-performance computers and cloud accessibility. Universities with limited resources de-

pend on foreign or commercial platforms, which restricts the development of locally contextualised AI and perpetuates global epistemic disparities.

Figure 3. Illustration of How Digital Readiness Shapes Divergent AI Potential

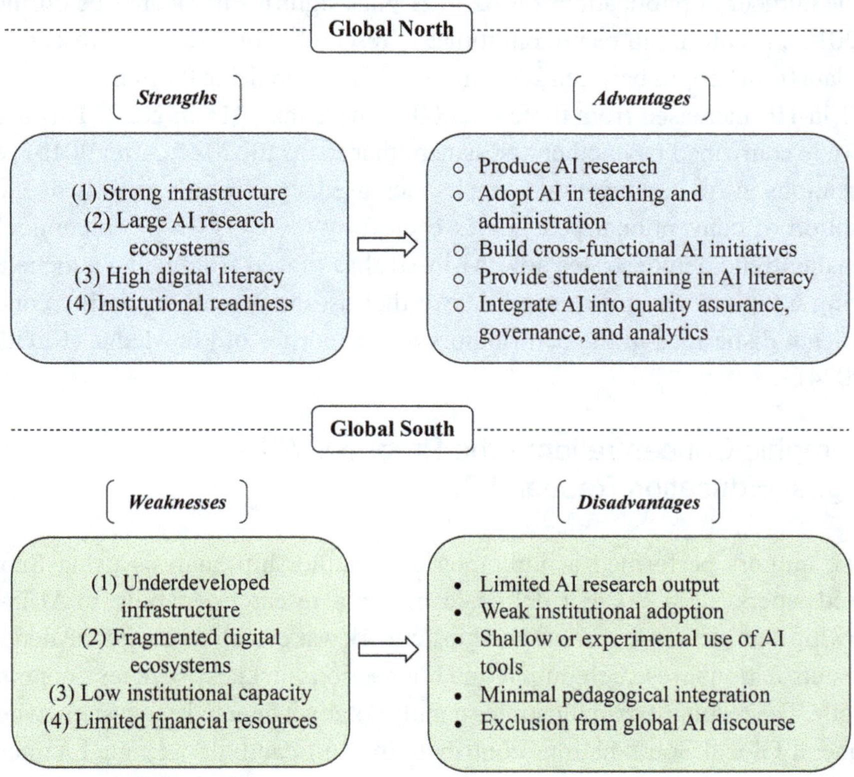

Source: Created by the authors.

BIBLIOMETRIC ANALYSIS

Mapping Global Research Productivity in AI and Higher Education

Scholarly production is one of the most concrete measures of a country's or an institution's ability to influence AI-driven higher education. We can determine which locations and institutions are generating the research that supports AI pedagogy, infrastructure, and governance by examining publication trends, co-authorship networks, citation effects, and theme focuses.

Overall Growth in AI–Higher Education Research

The number of publications on AI-in-HE has significantly increased during the late 2010s, according to recent bibliometric research. For instance, a research that used data from Scopus between 2000 and 2022 discovered that the number of articles on AI-in-HE increased from three in 2000 to more than 314 in 2022. This growth pattern is confirmed by another assessment that spans till 2024. After 2019, yearly publications in AI-in-education contexts increased significantly, mostly due to the disruption of conventional pedagogies caused by the COVID-19 epidemic. This increasing trend demonstrates how AI-in-HE has moved from being a niche topic to being a top priority for research. Nevertheless, the overall expansion conceals significant disparities in the contributors to that corpus of knowledge (Kavitha et al., 2024).

Geographic Concentration: Who Produces AI-in-Higher-Education Research?

The authors performed a bibliometric co-authorship analysis using Scopus-indexed papers (2000–2024) to delineate the global research capability of AI-in-HE. Following data cleaning, a co-authorship network was established wherein node size represents national research output and connection thickness denotes cooperation strength. The resultant map illustrates a multipolar yet unequal ecosystem, wherein peripheral Global South nations contribute insignificantly to a limited number of Global North and developing hubs, including China.

Regional or theme cooperation blocs are indicated by the network's *five main clusters* illustrated in **Figure 4**. Each cluster reflects distinctive geopolitical and epistemological configurations:

- ***Blue*** cluster: Led by China, the U.S., the U.K., and Canada, this central cluster forms a trans-Pacific knowledge axis, focusing on generative AI, learning analytics, and machine learning.
- ***Red*** cluster: Includes Finland, Germany, Netherlands, Spain, Italy, Sweden, France, Denmark, and Switzerland, emphasising AI ethics, governance, human-centred computing, and digital education.
- ***Green*** cluster: Connects Gulf and Southeast Asian systems (South Africa, Pakistan, Egypt, Saudi Arabia, Malaysia), focusing on learning analytics, instructional technologies, and applied AI.

- ***Yellow*** cluster: Dominated by Iran, Turkey, Thailand, South Korea, India, and Central Asia, emphasising technical models, adaptive learning, machine learning, and innovative algorithms.
- ***Purple*** cluster: Covers Eastern Europe, Central Asia, and parts of Latin America (Chile, Mexico, Argentina); presence is small but growing.
- ***North vs. South***: Global North nations (U.S., U.K., Canada, Japan, Finland) have a dominant presence in the epistemic core. While most Global South countries (Bangladesh, Myanmar, Nepal, Cambodia, Lao PDR) remain absent, with only Nepal and Bangladesh barely visible as nodes.

China is intentionally excluded from the Global South case selection because of its distinct structural conditions. China, with the world's second-largest economy, prominent AI research output, government-supported policies, advanced infrastructure, and significant R&D investment, resembles high-income nations from the Global North rather than low-resource least developed countries (LDCs) of the Global South. The chapter's emphasis on the difficulties encountered by these LDCs, which struggle with inadequate resources, institutional capability, and connectivity, would be obscured if China were included.

Figure 4. Global Country Co-Authorship Network in AI-in-Education Research (2000–2024)

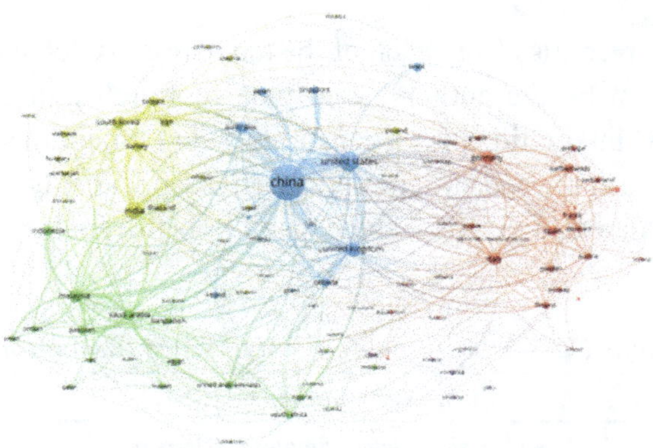

Source: Created by the authors based on the bibliometric analysis.

Note. Orange-marked countries indicate Global South, and black-marked countries indicate Global North countries selected for this chapter's case study.

Institutional and Regional Disparities

An analysis of 276 Scopus-indexed publications on AI-in-HE (2016–2025) reveals a fragmented research landscape with limited institutional consolidation, as the top universities account for only a minor share of total outputs. These institutions are predominantly situated in areas with robust internet infrastructure, particularly in Western Europe, North America and East Asia. In contrast, institutions in South and Southeast Asia, Africa, and Latin America are underrepresented due to structural limitations, such as inadequate computational resources, a lack of AI laboratories, insufficient financing, and poor collaborative networks (Sahar & Munawaroh, 2025).

Thematic and Disciplinary Patterns

Bibliometric mapping reveals a disciplinary disparity in AI-in-HE research, where around 36% of publications originate from computer science, 18% from engineering, and just 10% from the social sciences and mathematics. Prominent subjects encompass generative AI (post-2022), educational data mining, adaptive learning, intelligent tutoring systems, and AI ethics. Recent research indicated that generative tools like large language models (LLMs) increased publication numbers, indicating a new academic interest. The prominence of STEM areas suggests that multidisciplinary and context-sensitive research on AI's usage in social justice, humanities pedagogies, and culturally diverse learning settings is lacking (Wang et al., 2024).

INSTITUTIONAL CASE STUDIES

Two sample universities from each of the ten nations (Global North and Global South) were chosen by the authors, who then thoroughly investigated their institutional-level AI integration plans, capabilities, and limitations. Showing (**Table 1** & **Table 2**) how established structural disparities appear at the institutional level in research, governance, pedagogy, and capability is the goal.

Table 1. Institutional Case Studies on Ten Universities from Global North

Global North Institutions (GNI)		
(1) United States - Stanford University		
AI Integration & Capacity	**Governance & Strategy**	**Pedagogical Integration**

continued on following page

Table 1. Continued

• Stanford possesses extensive AI research infrastructure, highlighted by the 2025 launch of the GPU-based "Marlowe" superpod with 248 NVIDIA H100 GPUs for large-scale AI and machine learning across disciplines. • The Computing and Data Science (CoDa) facility supports cross-disciplinary research in computing, data science, and AI. • The "Stanford AI Playground" enables supervised student experimentation with generative AI tools from OpenAI, Google, and Anthropic. • Stanford Institute for Human Centred Artificial Intelligence (HAI) and Stanford Artificial Intelligence Laboratory (SAIL) support technological, ethical, social, and policy-focused AI research across Stanford's schools. • In 2025, Stanford hosted its third AI+Education Summit, engaging academics, educators, K–12 leaders, and technologists to explore AI's transformative role in education.	• Stanford Graduate School of Business enforces a global generative AI policy, restricting AI use for assignments unless explicitly permitted and requiring disclosure. • HAI and SAIL coordinate and oversee AI research and training, supporting governance and shaping ethical, pedagogical, and policy standards. • The AI Playground and "AI Catalyst" provide centralized, secure, and supported access to AI tools, ensuring structured adoption across the university.	• The 2025 AI+Education Summit showcases Stanford's focus on integrating AI technology into teaching, learning, and educational environments. • The AI Playground provides a controlled setting for students and staff to experiment with generative AI tools for tutoring, writing, research ideation, and other educational purposes. • As HAI is a cross-school issue, there is a push for integrating AI-literate curriculum, human-centred AI ethics, and multidisciplinary AI education that considers social effect.
(2) United States – Columbia University		
AI Integration & Capacity	**Governance & Strategy**	**Pedagogical Integration**
• The Data Science Institute (DSI) powers Columbia AI, a university-wide program. This effort aims to incorporate AI into "every subject, academic discipline, and domain area" at the university to enable AI-driven research and teaching by schools, centres, and affiliates. • The Columbia Centre of Artificial Intelligence Technology (CAIT) is a key player in engineering and computer science, with over 70 academic members working with partners within and outside Columbia to advance AI research and technology. • Machine learning, natural language processing, computer vision, robotics, security/privacy, computational biology, and more are included in the Department of Computer Science, demonstrating a mature AI research capability.	• Columbia's Generative AI Policy governs AI use by students, staff, and faculty, requiring transparency and consent for academic tasks; unauthorised use is plagiarism. • Researchers must acknowledge AI, ensure accuracy, protect data, and uphold intellectual property and research integrity. • The internal "AI: Community of Practice" fosters campus-wide discussion, support, and collaboration on AI tools, pedagogy, and applications.	• Columbia University offers AI education through its engineering department, including an online certificate for professionals covering algorithms, neural networks, NLP, and computer vision. • Columbia AI, CAIT, and DSI provide interdisciplinary research and teaching opportunities, integrating AI into social sciences, humanities, medicine, and beyond. • The 2025 Columbia AI Summit across multiple campuses demonstrates institutional commitment to exploring AI's impact on healthcare, business, humanities, policy, research, creativity, and social issues.

continued on following page

Table 1. Continued

(3) Canada – University of Toronto		
AI Integration & Capacity	**Governance & Strategy**	**Pedagogical Integration**
• UoT has a strong relationship with the Vector Institute, a Toronto-based non-profit AI research centre specialising in machine learning and deep learning. The Vector Institute is a hub of Canada's AI ecosystem, with many faculty, postdocs, and students. • In terms of AI faculty size and research output, UoT is among the top institutions globally in AI research, conference publications, and academic talent. • UoT's robust research environment predicts large AI research output, including fundamental and applied AI across disciplines (project specifics may vary).	• UoT collaborates with the Vector Institute to advance the Pan-Canadian AI plan, merging academic research, talent development, and industry partnership. This relationship coordinates national and international AI research. • The Pan-Canadian Report on Digital Learning shows that Canadian institutions are increasingly using generative AI technologies in student learning activities, with a rise from 12% in 2023 to 41% in 2024. • No official "University-wide generative-AI policy" for UoT was identified in the sources, but the high institutional research capability and national AI network (via Vector) support strategic AI adoption.	• Increasing usage of generative AI at Canadian institutions means UoT, a leading university, may already be using it for teaching, research assistance, and student learning. Research shows that 41% of Canadian educators use generative AI tools in their teaching. • UoT's affiliation with Vector Institute provides students with access to cutting-edge AI research, machine-learning curricula, and interdisciplinary and cross-sector projects. This promotes AI-related undergraduate and graduate study.
(4) Canada – University of British Columbia		
AI Integration & Capacity	**Governance & Strategy**	**Pedagogical Integration**
• A 2024 analysis puts UBC 2nd in Canada for AI papers (2018-2022) among full-service institutions, highlighting its outstanding research output. • The Centre for AI Decision-making and Action (CAIDA) and the AI Methods for Scientific Impact (AIM SI) cluster are key institutions. Over 120 academics from 30 departments collaborate to study how AI changes academic fields, establishing AI as a distinct subject and cross-disciplinary facilitator. • The UBC Cloud Innovation Centre (CIC) and Amazon Web Services provide UBC's technical and applied AI infrastructure. CIC's emphasis has turned to generative AI in 2024, signalling institutional commitment to using and developing AI technologies for research, community, student, and educational applications.	• In 2025, UBC created an AI Steering Committee to develop an institutional AI strategy, first focusing on generative AI, later including pedagogy, academic operations, administration, and student/staff experience. • The Committee aims to create a campus-wide AI competence framework, co-design a training centre, and deliver a cross-disciplinary 100-level AI foundations course by 2025. • Through a Student AI Advisory Council, the Steering Committee secures student viewpoints, demonstrating a governance approach that prioritises fairness, ethics, and stakeholder engagement.	• At UBC, CIC and CTLT developed the AI Learning Assistant, an LLM-based tool providing personalized feedback, identifying knowledge gaps, and supporting all courses. • In 2025, UBC hosted the GenAI in Teaching and Learning Symposium, engaging faculty and students on generative AI use, pedagogy, and ethics. • The AI Steering Committee's Training Hub offers seminars and courses to enhance AI literacy and competency across students, staff, and faculty beyond technical disciplines.

continued on following page

Table 1. Continued

(5) United Kingdom – Oxford University		
AI Integration & Capacity	**Governance & Strategy**	**Pedagogical Integration**
• The Oxford Institute for Ethics in AI, rooted in philosophy, humanities, social sciences, and STEM, addresses ethical, governance, and conceptual concerns related to AI, including societal ramifications, values, and regulation. • The Oxford Internet Institute (OII) conducts research on digital technologies' social, economic, and political consequences, including algorithmic decision-making, generative AI, data governance, and societal impacts. • The MSc-level course "Artificial Intelligence for Policymaking" at Oxford studies how AI may be utilised for governance, policy formulation and assessment, and structural and epistemological issues.	• The Institute for Ethics in AI demonstrates Oxford's commitment to addressing AI as a technological, ethical, social, and regulatory problem, positioning it as a worldwide leader in AI ethics debate. • Oxford aspires to influence global and national discussions on AI governance, legislation, justice, and societal effects via multidisciplinary cooperation in philosophy, social sciences, and STEM. • The governance approach prioritises ethical thought, social effect, and wide involvement above technical or commercial AI development.	• The Oxford "AI for Policymaking" course integrates AI-related education into public-policy curriculum, educating students to comprehend AI's technological capabilities, limits, and social impacts in governance settings. • Oxford's ethics-focused centre may promote AI literacy, critical awareness, and multidisciplinary discussion among students, equipping them to address AI's social impacts.
(6) United Kingdom – University College London		
AI Integration & Capacity	**Governance & Strategy**	**Pedagogical Integration**
• UCL's "AI for People and Planet" strategic vision emphasises employing AI research and innovation for social good, sustainable development, and inclusive societal benefit. • Its AI research portfolio includes foundational, applied, responsible, public policy, and societal impact, spanning engineering and social sciences. • UCL's policy-oriented AI research focuses on public-sector applications, including urban studies, data-driven governance, social inclusion, digital inequality, and public services, demonstrating interdisciplinary capacity.	• The "AI for People and Planet" vision links AI research and innovation to social responsibility, inclusivity, open science, and ethical deployment. This shows a governance plan that uses AI for social good and public policy impact. • UCL researchers interact with government, third sector, and politicians to impact AI legislation, public service deployment, and societal applications outside academia. • Their cross-disciplinary organisation of technical, social-science, and policy departments allows UCL to examine AI from technological feasibility, ethical and social consequences, policy relevance, and civic effect.	• UCL provides courses on AI, law, ethics, and policy, such as the "AI and Law" short course, which explores regulatory, ethical, and governance concerns related to AI deployment in legal and social settings. • UCL promotes AI literacy across disciplines by engaging in research policy and exposing students to both technical and social aspects of AI. This multidisciplinary approach may prepare students for AI jobs in engineering, public policy, social sciences, etc.
(7) Finland – University of Helsinki		
AI Integration & Capacity	**Governance & Strategy**	**Pedagogical Integration**

continued on following page

Table 1. Continued

• The University of Helsinki and a Finnish IT startup co-created the popular free online AI course Elements of AI. This MOOC has reached over one million individuals globally and teaches fundamental AI. • Along with "Elements of AI," the university joins the Finnish Centre for Artificial Intelligence (FCAI), a leading AI research centre in Finland, as part of its connection with the national AI research ecosystem. FCAI collaborates with many Finnish universities, including Helsinki. • Helsinki University is a consortium partner in a nationwide AI PhD education experiment (2024 forward). The pilot intends to train 100 PhDs at 10 Finnish institutions for high-level AI research.	• The University of Helsinki is part of a national effort to enhance AI research, cooperation, and capability via FCAI and the doctoral education network. The 2024 ministerial budget supported this network. • By offering MOOCs and open access AI courses like "Elements of AI", "AI in Society", "Ethics of AI", and "Machine Learning with Python", the University aims to democratize AI knowledge for citizens, professionals, and other non-technical audiences.	• The "Elements of AI" MOOC is a pedagogical tool that is accessible to all, regardless of technical background, and does not require heavy math or programming for the introductory portion, making it an AI literacy tool rather than a technical course. • Free courses include "Machine Learning: Basic Principles," "AI in Society," "Ethics of AI," and "Data Analysis with Python," supporting lifelong learning. • The programs target professionals, lifelong learners, and the general public, reflecting Helsinki's commitment to inclusive, socially oriented AI education.
	(8) Finland – Aalto University	
AI Integration & Capacity	**Governance & Strategy**	**Pedagogical Integration**
• Aalto, together with the University of Helsinki and other institutions, founded the Finnish Centre for Artificial Intelligence (FCAI) to make Finland a worldwide leader in AI research and its social applications. • In 2024-25, Finland committed major public funding to develop a national centre under the ELLIS Institute Finland, a pan-European machine learning research network coordinated by Aalto University and including all Finnish institutions. This significant increase in national AI research capability places Aalto at the forefront of European AI research. • The "AI in Aalto" initiative, part of Aalto's institutional services, provides internal AI tools, guidance, and best practices, including generative AI tool use, demonstrating the university's commitment to fundamental AI research and operational and administrative AI adoption.	• Aalto University collaborates with FCAI and ELLIS to improve Finland's AI research infrastructure, talent pool, and worldwide competitiveness. This shows university and national institutional commitment. • Aalto's institutional strategy prioritizes interdisciplinary AI research, industry collaboration, and sustainability. The House of AI unites researchers, companies, and technical, business, and design disciplines to create AI applications that address sustainability challenges and boost industrial competitiveness. • Its 2025 workshop "AI Act, Ethics, and Literacy" addresses regulatory, ethical, and societal issues related to AI adoption and invites academia, administration, and stakeholders to discuss it.	• Aalto provides AI education to students, industry professionals, and lifelong learners through FCAI's "education throughout working life" programs, including diploma-level training, executive intensives, and open-university courses. • The university offers internal AI services and guidance through "AI in Aalto," providing generative AI tools (e.g., text-based, administrative, research-support) for the university community to support teaching, research, and administrative workflows under institutional oversight. • Aalto's "House of AI" model integrates academia, industry, design, and business, enabling multidisciplinary AI projects that prepare students for real-world applications in sustainability, industry, and policy, rather than limiting AI to technical tracks.
	(9) Japan – University of Tokyo	

continued on following page

Table 1. Continued

AI Integration & Capacity	Governance & Strategy	Pedagogical Integration
• • The university hosts the Next Generation AI Research Centre (AI Centre), a multi-disciplinary research institution spanning science, engineering, and humanities. Technological, social, cultural, and humanistic perspectives form a "next generation intelligence science" that transcends AI paradigms. • In October 2025, the university's "AI Initiative" webpage listed 51 AI-related research and education programs, showing a diversified ecosystem across fields. • The 2025 Institute for Solid State Physics project "Project for Advancement of Software Usability in Materials Science (PASUMS)" utilises AI/data science methodologies in materials science research.	• The AI Centre aims to integrate AI across disciplines, aligning it with social, cultural, and academic reform, rather than limiting it to labs. • The university's Institute for Future Initiatives (IFI) researches AI governance and societal ramifications, including services, risk coordination, cybernetic society visions, AI and medical, diversity/DEI, and more. • The Ed AI Research Group, a university-industry collaboration, studies AI-based education, data standardisation, learning data utilisation, and educational assistance.	• The founding of the Ed AI Research Group demonstrates institutional commitment to experimenting with AI-driven educational methods, rather than limiting AI research to engineering or sciences. • Beyond research, the AI Centre aims to integrate AI into future curriculum, cross-disciplinary teaching, and training for future leaders. • The 5th International Symposium of the Institute for AI and Beyond (Feb 2025) addressed "Next Generation AI: The Next Breakthroughs and Potentials," bringing in industry, academia, and public interest, demonstrating the university's transparent, inclusive approach to AI discourse and education.
	(10) Japan – Kyoto University	
AI Integration & Capacity	**Governance & Strategy**	**Pedagogical Integration**
• Kyoto University's Office of Research Acceleration (KURA) administers the AI Dynamic Acceleration (DA) initiative, supporting early-career researchers in international collaboration aligned with the UN SDGs. • In November 2024, Kyoto University partnered with Accenture to advance "human-centred AI," focusing on responsible AI standards and applications in behavioural economics, leadership, wellness, and multi-agent language models. • In 2025, the university hosted Designing Governance for the AI Era, a global symposium on AI policy, legal frameworks, and risk management.	• Through AI DA, Kyoto University advances global collaboration and SDG-linked, socially oriented AI research. • The 2024 Accenture partnership reinforces a human-centred, responsible AI agenda integrating academic and industry governance priorities. • Policy-focused events, including the 2025 governance symposium, position the university as a key actor in national and global AI governance debates.	• Although there is limited public documentation of AI in education deployment at Kyoto University, the presence of AI DA and the focus on cross-disciplinary and socially relevant AI research suggest potential for integrating AI literacy, ethics, and research across disciplines. • Kyoto University aims to broaden AI education beyond technical training to include social, economic, and ethical research through collaborations and policy initiatives. • The 2025 public governance symposium suggests that Kyoto University aims to promote institutional and societal education about AIs broader impact.

Source: Created by the authors based on the institutional case studies.

Table 2. Institutional Case Studies on Ten Universities from Global South

Global South Institutions (GSI)		
(1) Bangladesh – University of Dhaka		
AI Integration & Capacity	**Governance & Strategy**	**Pedagogical Integration**
• DU has disciplinary departments such as Computer Science, Information Science, and Engineering that do peer-reviewed research on AI methods and applications. Recent papers on AI use in information sciences are also available. • The Engineering & Technology programs at DU have expressly adopted AI-labelled courses. The B.Sc. in Robotics and Mechatronics curriculum includes a 4th-year laboratory course called Generative Artificial Intelligence Lab (ROB 4115) and a theoretical course on generative AI, indicating that at least one faculty has integrated generative AI into undergraduate instruction. • In 2025, DU public communications promoted short-format generative-AI training and awareness events, such as the "Exclusive Learning Session on Generative AI" with AI Academy Bangladesh, as institutional up-skilling measures for students and staff.	• There is no publicly published institutional AI policy or governance framework for generative AI, data ethics, digital assessment, or academic integrity. • AI tool adoption is mostly dependent on specific departments or research groups due to fragmented technology governance across faculties. • Limitations in national higher education governance, funding limits, procurement delays, and bureaucratic processes hinder DU's capacity to scale up new innovations.	• CSE and IIT courses integrate machine learning, data mining, image processing, and NLP components. Without an institution-wide framework, AI education is restricted and discipline-specific. • Not much documented use of generative AI tools in pedagogy or course design. Faculty training in AI-based teaching is inadequate. • Student experimentation with generative AI is informal, lacking institutional guidance or policy frameworks.
(2) Bangladesh – Bangladesh University of Engineering and Technology (BUET)		
AI Integration & Capacity	**Governance & Strategy**	**Pedagogical Integration**

continued on following page

Table 2. Continued

• The 4IR Advanced Research and Innovation Park (4IR Park) at BUET focuses on AI, robotics, IoT, and advanced materials research, creating a unique infrastructure for applied AI research. The university's Department of Computer Science & Engineering (CSE) researches machine learning, computer vision, NLP, and related fields and keeps AI-related publications. • BUET students and alumni have created start-ups and projects using AI for health diagnostics and other issues. Public reporting highlights student teams (e.g., NeoScreenix) developing breast-cancer detection tools and BUET graduates advancing AI in healthcare abroad. These projects demonstrate student-project and lab AI use. • BUET CSE publishes AI applications (medical imaging, pattern recognition, predictive analytics) to showcase ongoing research in applied AI.	• The 4IR Park is recognised as a strategic research facility, but BUET lacks a university-wide generative-AI policy or campus-wide AI governance document comparable to other universities in the country. Thus, AI governance looks to be departmental, research-centre, or project-based (4IR Park, RISE, departmental labs).	• BUET's CSE and affiliated departments integrate AI issues into teaching and supervise AI-related projects, with publishing evidence and student project reports supporting active research training. • BUET students compete in national and international competitions, such as AIChE challenges and entrepreneurship contests, emphasizing problem-based learning through AI applications.
(3) Cambodia – Institute of Technology of Cambodia (ITC)		
AI Integration & Capacity	**Governance & Strategy**	**Pedagogical Integration**
• AI and machine learning principles are integrated into graduate-level curriculum, particularly in Computer Science, Mechatronics, and Data Science programs. Courses emphasise applied ML, robotics, automation, and algorithmic design, supporting ITC's engineering purpose. • Mechatronics, IT, and Applied Mathematics research units conduct small-to-medium-scale projects in automation, embedded systems, and data analysis. These units build AI skills without calling themselves labs. • Actively participates in national technology initiatives, AI meetings, and the AI Forum Cambodia. Collaborates with industry on data-driven problem-solving and research.	• There is no publicly stated university-wide AI governance structure. • International relationships facilitate capacity-building through staff exchanges, curriculum upgrades, and AI exposure. • AI governance is decentralized at the department level, reflecting distinct capacities.	• AI is generally taught through technical education in ML, robotics, data science, and automation. Real-world engineering capstone projects (optimisation, control systems, predictive modelling). • Co-curricular activities, such as hackathons, coding challenges, and industry workshops, enhance skill development. Participation in regional digital-skills programs (including AUF-led ones).
(4) Cambodia – Royal University of Phnom Penh (RUPP)		
AI Integration & Capacity	**Governance & Strategy**	**Pedagogical Integration**

continued on following page

Table 2. Continued

• Data Science & Engineering and Information Technology Engineering offer a foundation for AI studies. Coursework encompasses data analytics, probability, programming, databases, and ML basics. • Post-pandemic digitalisation emphasised the importance of university-operated LMS and e-learning portals for blended teaching. • RUPP extensively participates in national AI conferences, the AI for Education movement, and government and development partner capacity-building workshops. National skills reports list it as a prominent data-science graduate source.	• Lack of public AI policy or governance framework for generative AI or ethics. • The institutional digital transformation strategy lacks specific AI governance components. • Technology adoption decisions are spread between faculties, rather than subject to central policy.	• AI concepts are primarily covered in core computing and data-science programs, not specialised degrees. Engineering capstone projects may include data modelling or machine learning. • E-learning and digital practices: A shift towards LMS-based teaching and digital materials enables the gradual integration of computational technologies. • RUPP hosts and participates in workshops on data science, digital literacy, and AI applications to improve capacity.
(5) Myanmar – University of Computer Studies, Yangon (UCSY)		
AI Integration & Capacity	**Governance & Strategy**	**Pedagogical Integration**
• Undergraduate and graduate modules cover AI basics, machine learning, data mining, image processing, and intelligent systems. AI is usually covered in upper-level Computer Science and Computer Technology courses. • Research output includes pattern recognition, NLP (Burmese language processing), and intelligent systems. Master's theses, not huge externally supported projects, are the norm for research. • Basic computer labs support AI coursework, but sophisticated infrastructure (GPU clusters, cloud computing, robotics laboratories) is scarce. Periodic internet shutdowns and governmental limitations hinder technology development and collaboration.	• A lack of publicly accessible institutional policies on AI governance, digital ethics, or academic integrity for generative AI. • Government departments extensively impact ICT and AI programs, affecting continuity during political changes. • The lack of autonomy and limited foreign relationships can impair long-term planning and strategic investment.	• Integrate AI, expert systems, and machine learning into undergraduate and postgraduate curricula using theory-based techniques. Project-based AI is underemphasized due to infrastructure and resource constraints. • Traditional lecture-based teaching approaches predominate, with limited use of generative AI tools. Teachers have little professional development, which limits instructional strategy modernisation. • Students' usage of generative AI is uncontrolled and unregulated, with no rules for responsible use at the university.
(6) Myanmar – Mandalay Technological University (MTU)		
AI Integration & Capacity	**Governance & Strategy**	**Pedagogical Integration**

continued on following page

Table 2. Continued

• AI is primarily studied in computer engineering, electronic engineering, information technology, and mechatronics programs. Robotics, machine learning, automation, and image processing are taught. • Small groups of researchers work in robotics, control systems, computer vision, and intelligent automation. Limited-scale research is generally done for academic purposes rather than institutional funding. • Basic robotics and engineering simulation facilities, but limited advanced AI labs and high-performance computing. Similar infrastructure shortages appear at UCSY, reflecting national issues.	• No explicit institutional policy on AI ethics, generative AI, or digital education principles. • Central government monitoring limits institutional independence for technology efforts. • Budget constraints, political unpredictability, and limited international alliances hinder strategic technology planning.	• Integrated AI concepts into engineering contexts (e.g., automation, robotics, computational intelligence). Due to resource constraints, courses emphasise theory over machine learning practice. • Lecture-based, limited exposure to contemporary AI toolchains or cloud computing. No institutional support for generative AI in education. • Students' usage of AI tools is unregulated and lacks norms for academic integrity and responsible use.
	(7) Nepal – Tribhuvan University	
AI Integration & Capacity	**Governance & Strategy**	**Pedagogical Integration**
• Courses in AI, machine learning, data mining, natural language processing, robotics, neural networks, and pattern recognition are integrated into undergraduate and graduate programs. Computer Engineering, Electronics & Communication Engineering, and Computer Science provide AI modules. • The research group focuses on machine learning, computer vision, remote sensing, and Nepali-language NLP. Collaborations with foreign partners and NGOs are intermittent and small-scale. Due to financing and infrastructural constraints, research is theoretical or proof-of-concept. • Limited access to contemporary GPUs, cloud infrastructure, and advanced robotics equipment in basic computing laboratories. Some campuses have unreliable internet and electricity, which hinders AI experimentation.	• No public AI governance or policy framework exists for the institution. • Insufficient instruction on the appropriate usage of generative AI for students and staff. • Digital transformation activities exist at the central level but are delayed due to bureaucratic obstacles, dispersed management, and budget limitations.	• AI is taught through core theoretical courses and electives at undergraduate and master's levels. Practical ML problems, including categorisation, prediction, and computer vision, are common capstone projects. • Lecture-based with occasional labs; AI learning relies on instructor effort. The integration of contemporary AI tools, cloud platforms, and generative AI is limited. • Engage students with AI workshops, hackathons, and contests through tech clubs and student groups. Students utilize AI mostly independently.
	(8) Nepal – Kathmandu University	
AI Integration & Capacity	**Governance & Strategy**	**Pedagogical Integration**

continued on following page

Table 2. Continued

• KU launched Nepal's first dedicated Artificial Intelligence undergraduate programme, showing direct institutional commitment. Machine learning, deep learning, computer vision, NLP, robotics, embedded AI, and data engineering are taught. • Outperforms most Nepali institutions in AI research. Active healthcare AI, Nepali NLP, drone, computer vision, and environmental modelling projects. Global university, NGO, and research network collaborations. • Excellent infrastructure: Access to contemporary labs, robotics equipment, and computing clusters compared to other Nepali institutions. However, resources are low by international standards.	• KU has a clear AI strategy, including (a) creating an AI-focused department and (b) promoting research-driven education. Formal international partnerships • Publicly available materials lack comprehensive AI ethics norms and guidelines for generative AI use, despite advances.	• KU launched Nepal's first dedicated Artificial Intelligence undergraduate programme, showing direct institutional commitment. Machine learning, deep learning, computer vision, NLP, robotics, embedded AI, and data engineering are taught. • Outperforms most Nepali institutions in AI research. Active healthcare AI, Nepali NLP, drone, computer vision, and environmental modeling projects. Global university, NGO, and research network collaborations. • Access to contemporary labs, robotics equipment, and computing clusters compared to other Nepali institutions. However, resources are low by international standards.
(9) Lao PDR – National University of Laos		
AI Integration & Capacity	**Governance & Strategy**	**Pedagogical Integration**
• Computer Science and IT departments provide beginning programming, algorithm, and data science courses. • AI curriculum is mainly foundational, with few advanced courses or degrees available. • Minimal research output in AI, ML, or NLP. These short projects involving regional partners or NGOs focus on basic data analysis or ICT applications. • Restricted computing lab capacity and restricted access to high-performance computing, cloud AI platforms, and advanced robotics. Regional campuses have inconsistent internet access.	• Institutional AI policies and strategies for generative AI, data ethics, and education are not publicly available. • Slow and fragmented institutional ICT adoption and digital transformation initiatives exist. • Centralised decision-making limits departmental or faculty autonomy for technology adoption.	• AI is primarily introduced through electives or modules in computer science and IT programs. Lack of facilities and faculty experience limits hands-on applications. • Primary teaching method is lecture-based, with limited use of AI tools or platforms. Students use generative AI and ML technologies casually. • Engaged students through workshops or regional ICT competitions, but no organised AI laboratories or innovation centres.
(10) Lao PDR – Souphanouvong University		

continued on following page

Table 2. Continued

AI Integration & Capacity	Governance & Strategy	Pedagogical Integration
• Basic computer, programming, and data analysis courses in the Faculty of Science and Technology. No AI degrees exist, but AI concepts are introduced. • Limited AI research; modest faculty-led projects in applied computing or data analysis exist, often with external assistance. • Limited infrastructure in computing labs, including networking and internet capability. High-performance computing and AI facilities lacking.	• No formal institutional AI policy or framework. • Limited faculty initiatives and sporadic regional projects guide technology adoption. • Limited autonomy and budget constraints restrict the expansion of AI-related programmes.	• AI is introduced indirectly via computing or math modules. Resource constraints limit practical applicability. • Mostly lectures; few project-based learning opportunities; structured generative AI use in classrooms. • Encourage student engagement through seminars or regional competitions, frequently with funding from NGOs or external sponsors.

Source: Created by the authors based on the institutional case studies.

SYNTHESIS: INSTITUTIONAL-LEVEL INEQUALITIES IN AI INTEGRATION

- Institutional Capacity and Infrastructure
    - *GNI*: Universities operate mature AI ecosystems with high-performance computing, national research hubs, cross-disciplinary centres, and strong industry partnerships (e.g., Stanford HAI, UBC CIC, Aalto-ELLIS), enabling frontier research and large-scale experimentation.
    - *GSI*: Infrastructure is uneven and minimal; AI capacity is concentrated in a few flagship institutions (e.g., BUET, KU), while most face funding shortages, ICT gaps, and political instability.
- Governance and Strategic Orientation
    - *GNI*: Institutions adopt proactive, centralised AI governance aligned with national AI strategies, covering ethics, generative AI, and research integrity.
    - *GSI*: Governance is largely absent or ad hoc, hindered by bureaucracy, limited autonomy, and scarce resources.
- Pedagogical Integration and Curriculum
    - *GNI*: AI is integrated across disciplines with literacy frameworks, training hubs, and AI-enabled tools.
    - *GSI*: AI teaching remains confined to technical faculties, with limited generative AI use and sporadic interdisciplinary initiatives.
- Research Ecosystems and Knowledge Production

- ○ *GNI*: Produce high-impact, multidisciplinary AI research supported by strong funding pipelines and host international symposia.
  - ○ *GSI*: Research remains narrow and application-focused, constrained by weak networks and inadequate infrastructure.
- Stakeholder Engagement and Societal Mission
  - ○ *GNI*: Universities shape public discourse and AI governance debates, demonstrating strong civic and regulatory influence.
  - ○ *GSI*: Engagement is limited to capacity-building initiatives with little influence on national AI policy.

Overall, the comparison reveals a structural divide (**Table 3**) driven not only by resource asymmetries but also by differences in governance maturity, pedagogical philosophy, and the ability to embed AI within broader societal and policy ecosystems.

Table 3. Structural AI Capacity Gaps Among the Institutions (North vs. South)

Dimension	Global North (Average)	Global South (Average)	Gap
Compute Infrastructure	High	Low	Very Large
Digital Governance	Mature	Weak	Large
Faculty AI Literacy	High	Low	Large
Student AI Access	High	Low–Moderate	Large
AI Pedagogical Integration	High	Very Low–Moderate	Large
Research Productivity	High	Very Low	Very Large
International Collaboration	High	Low	Large
AI Policy Coherence	High	Very Low	Large

Source: Aggregated from all 20 Institutional Case Studies

EQUITY AND ETHICAL DIMENSIONS

AI-in-HE is influenced by social, cultural, and economic power dynamics; its design and governance are inherently value-laden. In the absence of safeguards, AI has the potential to exacerbate inequality, marginalise vulnerable populations, and perpetuate global disparities in knowledge and technology. Three interconnected risks are particularly noteworthy:

- ***Algorithmic bias*** arises from unrepresentative training data, socially influenced labels, and class-based proxies, leading to inequitable scoring, misclassification, and disproportionate resource distribution, hence exacerbating existing educational disparities.

- ***Data colonialism*** occurs when data obtained from marginalised populations frequently serves the interests of organisations in wealthy areas, resulting in epistemic exclusion. Emphasising Western languages and pedagogies constrains local creativity and perpetuates structural imbalances.
- ***Exclusion from governance and surveillance*** happens when AI-driven proctoring, behavioural analytics, and automated decision-making disproportionately impact underprivileged students. Inadequate regulation and obscure algorithms impede accountability and elevate the likelihood of discriminatory or punishing results.

POLICY AND PRACTICE PATHWAYS

Research ecosystems, institutional capability, sociolinguistic variation, and national digital preparedness are some of the multi-level structural factors that influence the adoption of AI-in-HE. Context-sensitive policies are necessary because of ethical issues such algorithmic bias, data colonialism, and surveillance-driven exclusion. The following pathways are meant to serve as a roadmap for national governments, higher education institutions, teachers and innovative educators and international associations. These pathways place a strong focus on integrating AI capabilities first, giving institutional autonomy, digital literacy, pedagogical inclusiveness, and equitable access precedence over adoption that is solely driven by technology.

MATURE NATIONAL AND INSTITUTIONAL POLICY ECOSYSTEM OF GLOBAL NORTH

- United States:
  - Federal funding for AI infrastructure, education, and research is provided by the *National Artificial Intelligence Initiative Act (2020)* and the *National AI Strategy* that followed.
  - Major AI research clusters and educational efforts are funded by organisations like the *DARPA AI Next Campaign* and the *National Science Foundation (NSF)*.
  - Universities have the liberty to create AI-in-education policies, reinforced by state-level digital governance frameworks like *California's Student Digital Privacy* and *AI Governance Act*.
- United Kingdom:

- The UK *National AI Strategy (2021)* establishes national priorities for the application of AI in the public sector and in education.
- Higher education academic integrity and ethical AI usage are regulated by the *Office for Students (OfS)*.
- UK institutions use *Jisc's AI Ethics & Procurement Guidelines* and shared digital infrastructure services for risk-aware procurement, ethical AI deployment, and resource sharing.

- Finland:
  - The *Finnish National AI 4.0 Strategy* combines investments in AI from the public sector, academia, and research.
  - Privacy and institutional accountability are guaranteed by robust data protection under the EU's *General Data Protection Regulation (GDPR)*, which is enforced via Finland's national data protection regulations.
  - The national *CSC-IT Centre for Science*, which offers shared computing infrastructure, cloud services, and data storage for university research across Finland, supports cross-institutional collaboration.
- **Canada:**
  - The national investment in AI research and talent development is supported by the *Pan-Canadian Artificial Intelligence Strategy*, which was first introduced in 2017.
  - Transparency and inclusion are promoted by the *Tri-Council Open Science Policy,* which requires open-access publishing and data sharing when research is publicly financed.
  - A uniform legal foundation for data protection across higher education institutions is provided by privacy regulation via the *Personal Information Protection* and *Electronic Documents Act (PIPEDA)* and complementing provincial laws (such as Ontario's FIPPA).
- **Japan:**
  - Government's *Society 5.0* initiative outlines the country's goal to incorporate digital advances, robots, and AI into all facets of life, including education.
  - The use of ICT and AI-enhanced learning systems at universities is encouraged by *educational policy guidelines issued by the Ministry of Education, Culture, Sports, Science, and Technology (MEXT).*
  - A foundation for data governance is established by the *Act on the Protection of Personal Information (APPI)*, which regulates data protection and utilisation in academic administration systems.

POLICY GAPS IN THE GLOBAL SOUTH

National AI-in-education policy ecosystems are still developing or dispersed in many low-resource nations. Common gaps include:

- Limited institutional preparation due to a lack of reliable internet, national research networks, HPC, or cloud infrastructure.
- Students and professors are at risk due to the lack of institutional governance frameworks, data protection rules, and AI ethical regulations.
- Uneven adoption of AI due to reliance on donor-funded, ad hoc programs rather than sustained state support.
- Lack of culturally suitable curriculum, language-appropriate AI technologies, or local-language datasets results in epistemic marginalisation and diminished relevance for local educational environments.

POLICY FRAMEWORK RECOMMENDATIONS FOR A MORE INCLUSIVE GLOBAL SOUTH

At the National Level

- Implement thorough AI-in-education rules that include hiring processes, ethical protections, curriculum guidance, teacher training, and data governance.
- Invest in digital infrastructure, including shared cloud/HPC resources, institutional broadband, national education networks, and equitable internet access.
- Encourage regional cooperation, academic-industry alliances, multilingual and culturally grounded model development, national AI centres, and other local AI research ecosystems.
- Create legal and regulatory protections, such as oversight bodies, AI risk frameworks, data protection legislation, and limitations on surveillance-based techniques.
- Offer long-term financing and incentives, such as competitive grants, subsidised AI access for institutions with limited resources, and assistance for community-driven AI initiatives.

At the Institutional Level

- Design an Institutional AI Strategy (AIS) that covers data governance, procurement, inclusion policies, AI literacy, pedagogy, and assessment reform.

- Develop a strong governance framework that includes academic integrity councils, technical review teams, AI ethical committees, transparency reports, and appeals and remedy channels.
- Encourage pedagogical innovation and faculty preparedness via multidisciplinary pilots, professional development, AI pedagogy micro-credentials, and institutional support for AI-enhanced instruction.
- Provide licensed AI tools, device-loan programs, data subsidies, multilingual assistance, accessible design, and AI literacy training to guarantee student access and equality.

Through International Collaboration

- Facilitate regional model hubs to pool resources across institutions, train contextually appropriate models, and manage local-language corpora.
- Prioritise fair research collaborations that promote capacity development rather than merely data export and stay clear of extractive data practices.

INTEGRATIVE FRAMEWORK FOR INCLUSIVE AI-IN-HE (IFIA)

Integrating inclusive and sustainable AI-in-HE requires alignment at both institutional and national levels. Infrastructural gaps, ineffective governance, inconsistent research capability, and conventional teaching methods influence worldwide inequity in AI adoption. Theoretical frameworks such as the *Digital Divide, Capabilities Approach, Diffusion of Innovation,* and *Political Economy of Knowledge* highlight the need to address structural, cultural, and power-driven obstacles for effective AI integration. This part of the chapter presents an *Integrative Framework for Inclusive AI in Higher Education (IFIA)*, consolidating findings into a realistic model tailored for institutions in heterogeneous resource environments. The model integrates capacity enhancement, adoption trends, and knowledge power frameworks to provide an ethical, context-responsive AI strategy.

Table 4. Integrative Framework for Inclusive AI-in-HE

Pillar 1: Foundational Infrastructure *Purpose:* Enable capabilities and adoption. *Components:* ● Campus-wide connectivity and reliable broadband ● Cloud and compute access, Learning Management Systems ● Devices and secure data storage ● Local-language digital resources *Rationale:* Access is a precondition for capability, aligning with Digital Divide theory.	**Pillar 2: Governance and Ethical Oversight** *Purpose:* Ensure accountability, privacy, and equity. *Components:* ● AI ethics and risk committees ● Transparency and data governance protocols ● Responsible procurement standards ● Appeal and redress mechanisms ● Algorithmic audit capacity *Rationale:* Protects students from surveillance, exploitation, and data colonialism.
Pillar 3: Research and Innovation Capacity *Purpose:* Strengthen autonomy and knowledge creation. *Components:* ● AI research clusters and partnerships ● Training programs for research staff ● Local corpora development and linguistic inclusion ● Participation in national or regional AI centres *Rationale:* Aligns with Political Economy of Knowledge; institutions must produce, not merely consume, AI technologies.	**Pillar 4: Pedagogical Transformation** *Purpose:* Reimagine curriculum, assessment, and student support. *Components:* ● AI-integrated curricula and assessment ● Critical AI literacy for students and staff ● Human–AI co-learning and multimodal teaching ● Accessibility and universal design principles *Rationale:* Diffusion of Innovation theory emphasises faculty readiness, trialability, and observable benefits.

Source: Created by the authors.

The IFIA provides a systematic, flexible framework that tackles structural disparities while facilitating contextually relevant, ethical, and sustainable AI incorporation in higher education.

CONCLUSION

The authors revealed in this chapter with evidence and thorough analysis that the integration of AI-in-HE is inconsistent and influenced by structural disparities across different regions. Socio-economic inequality, infrastructure deficiencies, language marginalisation, and regulatory fragmentation directly impact institutional capacity, accessibility, and research productivity, increasing the likelihood that AI may exacerbate current global imbalances. The three-fold theoretical lens of the chapter highlights that AI adoption is a socio-political phenomenon influenced by governance structures, institutional independence, and global power relations. A comparative analysis indicates that universities in the Global North possess strong infrastructure, national AI plans, and established data governance, whereas institutions in the Global South have limitations in connection, procurement, academic capability, and governmental support. Ethical dilemmas, including algorithmic bias, data colonialism, and the exclusion of low-resource languages, underscore the need for inclusive governance frameworks that provide transparency and contextual protections. The IFIA framework shown in this chapter incorporates these characteristics to facilitate fair and sustainable AI implementation in both regions equally. Therefore, equity-focused, context-responsive approaches are crucial for AI to improve learning, broaden access, and promote social justice and the global democratisation of information.

REFERENCES

Akbarighatar, P. (2025). Operationalizing responsible AI principles through responsible AI capabilities. *AI and Ethics*, *5*(2), 1787–1801. DOI: 10.1007/s43681-024-00524-4

Alexander, J. M. (2016). *Capabilities and social justice: The political philosophy of Amartya Sen and Martha Nussbaum*. Routledge. https://www.taylorfrancis.com/books/mono/10.4324/9781315260914/capabilities-social-justice-john-alexander

Benton, P. (2023). AI Literacy: A Primary Good. In Pillay, A., Jembere, E., & Gerber, A. J. (Eds.), *Artificial Intelligence Research* (Vol. 1976, pp. 31–43). Springer Nature Switzerland., DOI: 10.1007/978-3-031-49002-6_3

Campbell, J. L., & Pedersen, O. K. (2011). Knowledge regimes and comparative political economy. *Ideas and Politics in Social Science Research*, *167*, 172–190.

Crompton, H., & Burke, D. (2023). Artificial intelligence in higher education: The state of the field. *International Journal of Educational Technology in Higher Education*, *20*(1), 22. DOI: 10.1186/s41239-023-00392-8

Gehl Sampath, P. (2021). Governing Artificial Intelligence in an Age of Inequality. *Global Policy*, *12*(S6), 21–31. DOI: 10.1111/1758-5899.12940

Gutiérrez-Leefmans, M., Picazo-Vela, S., & Kareem, O. (2025). Adoption of artificial intelligence in higher education: A diffusion of innovation approach. *The TQM Journal*. Advance online publication. DOI: 10.1108/TQM-12-2024-0523

Hashmi, N., & Bal, A. S. (2024). Generative AI in higher education and beyond. *Business Horizons*, *67*(5), 607–614. DOI: 10.1016/j.bushor.2024.05.005

Jacobson, T. L. (2016). Amartya Sen's capabilities approach and communication for development and social change. *Journal of Communication*, *66*(5), 789–810. DOI: 10.1111/jcom.12252

Kavitha, K., Joshith, V. P., Rajeev, N. P., & S, A. (2024). Artificial Intelligence in Higher Education: A Bibliometric Approach. *European Journal of Educational Research, volume–13–2024*(volume–13–issue–3–july–2024), 1121–1137. DOI: 10.12973/eu-jer.13.3.1121

Khan, M. S., Umer, H., & Faruqe, F. (2024). Artificial intelligence for low income countries. *Humanities & Social Sciences Communications*, *11*(1), 1–13. DOI: 10.1057/s41599-024-03947-w

Kohnke, L., Moorhouse, B. L., & Zou, D. (2023). Exploring generative artificial intelligence preparedness among university language instructors: A case study. *Computers and Education: Artificial Intelligence*, *5*, 100156. DOI: 10.1016/j.caeai.2023.100156

Kshetri, N. (2024). Linguistic Challenges in Generative Artificial Intelligence: Implications for Low-Resource Languages in the Developing World. *Journal of Global Information Technology Management*, *27*(2), 95–99. DOI: 10.1080/1097198X.2024.2341496

Miller, R. L. (2015). Rogers' innovation diffusion theory (1962, 1995). In *Information seeking behaviour and technology adoption: Theories and trends* (pp. 261–274). IGI Global Scientific Publishing. https://www.igi-global.com/chapter/rogers-innovation-diffusion-theory-1962-1995/127136

Mutunhu, B., Nyathi, T., & Dube, S. (2021). An Analysis on the Adoption of High-Performance Computing (HPC): A Case of Zimbabwe State Universities. *2021 IST-Africa Conference (IST-Africa)*, 1–8. https://ieeexplore.ieee.org/abstract/document/9576909/

Okolo, C. T. (2023). Addressing global inequity in AI development. In *Handbook of Critical Studies of Artificial Intelligence* (pp. 378–389). Edward Elgar Publishing., https://www.elgaronline.com/edcollchap/book/9781803928562/book-part-9781803928562-40.xml DOI: 10.4337/9781803928562.00040

Sahar, R., & Munawaroh, M. (2025). Artificial intelligence in higher education with bibliometric and content analysis for future research agenda. *Discover Sustainability*, *6*(1), 401. DOI: 10.1007/s43621-025-01086-z

Singh, S., & Strzelecki, A. (2025). Academics as adopters of generative AI: An application of diffusion of innovations theory. *Education and Information Technologies*. Advance online publication. DOI: 10.1007/s10639-025-13835-8

Smyth, R. S., Parker, K., & Sharif, M. O. (2020). General Data Protection Regulation-are we up to date? *British Dental Journal*, •••, 1–5. DOI: 10.1038/s41415-020-1844-8

Subaveerapandiyan, A., Paladhi, M. M., & Maruthaveeran, V. (2023). Evaluating AI literacy proficiency among LIS researchers in ASEAN. *Library Hi Tech News*, *41*(4), 6–8.

United Nations. (2021). *ITU: 2.9 billion people still offline*. United Nations; United Nations. https://www.un.org/en/delegate/itu-29-billion-people-still-offline

Wang, S., Wang, F., Zhu, Z., Wang, J., Tran, T., & Du, Z. (2024). Artificial intelligence in education: A systematic literature review. *Expert Systems with Applications*, *252*, 124167. DOI: 10.1016/j.eswa.2024.124167

World Bank. (2025). *World Bank Open Data—Individuals using the Internet (% of population)*. World Bank Open Data. https://data.worldbank.org

Chapter 3
Posthuman Textualities and Imagination:
AI, Digital Literature, and the Ethics of Literary Learning

Huma Ahmed
http://orcid.org/0009-0000-1927-5870
The University of Lahore, Pakistan

ABSTRACT

In the context of AI-driven education, the chapter examines the interaction between posthuman texts and the human imagination, presenting a significant avenue for understanding modern literary learning. It traces how human imagination coexists with intelligent machines, exploring the readers' and students' engagement with literary texts as consumers and co-creators, and reshapes ethics and academic integrity in pedagogy. The analysis adopts a poststructuralist posthuman perspective, utilizing the poststructuralist literary critic Roland Barthes' (1967) declaration of 'the death of the author'. The chapter validates that AI technologically reinforces this claim, as digital texts destabilize human intentionality, positioning authorship distributed across human and algorithmic agencies. By integrating the posthuman, poststructural, and literary pedagogical concerns, the chapter proposes a practical approach for educators to engage with AI critically and ethically within literary education.

INTRODUCTION

The contemporary world marks one of the most significant technological revolutions. The AI-driven transformation is reshaping every field of life, from com-

DOI: 10.4018/979-8-2600-1458-5.ch003

munication and education to healthcare, business, and creative genres. It empowers machines to learn, reason, and make decisions, which enhances efficiency and accuracy beyond human limits.

In this scenario, education is one of the significant and sensitive fields of human life that raises critical questions and profound concerns among academicians, educators, and policymakers. Learning and teaching are traditionally based on human mental capacities, characterized by emotional and intellectual connections and moral consciousness. Humans write books for other humans to read; therefore, the meaning-making process draws upon a fusion of imagination and personal experience. Likewise, classrooms are also centered as a space of interaction between teachers and students, where teachers impart knowledge and students receive it.

Before the technological revolution, it seemed nearly unbelievable that the learning process could occur without the engagement of any intermediary other than human agency. Moreover, the relationship between student and teacher was direct and essential for the learning process. Now, smart technologies are increasingly part of the reading and writing process, and even teaching. AI-generated texts and adaptive learning systems show how machines have taken human-oriented jobs. This change triggers us to contemplate alternate ways of teaching and learning. Is it possible for a machine to comprehend, explain, and communicate meaning analogous to the human mind? What is the status of creativity and ethical reasoning when algorithms process knowledge? These concerns are contemplated over the developing relationship between the human mind and artificial intelligence.

This chapter focuses on literary learning in today's digital world, a world where human and machine interactions are increasingly intertwined. Now, readers find literature not only printed on paper; instead, it is a complicated web of algorithmic effects triggered by posthuman agencies. The fusion of the human mind and machine changed the concept of imagination in the current age. When algorithms write poetry or generate stories, the question arises: Who is the poet or author? In this evolving background, posthumanism and digital literature studies construct a framework to examine the role of human and non-human agencies in the production of literary text. In this backdrop, the chapter examines the effect of AI on the creative process and the ethical concerns of literary education, posthumanism, and literary pedagogy.

The chapter examines how AI transforms creation, interpretation, and the pedagogical implications of literary texts and how it can offer ways to scholars and practitioners to reform literary learning and help preserve academic integrity, critical thinking, and ethical dimensions of human associations. The collaborative texts emphasize the shift from passive readership to active co-creation. The study offers an interdisciplinary contribution to literary studies. It integrates theoretical insights with practical implications and provides a framework to engage critically with data-driven texts. The chapter concludes that embracing AI as a site of collaborative creativity can enhance our understanding of literature, imagination, and literary learning in the digital age.

According to Yadav (2024), to examine AI and digital literature, a multidimensional lens can help transcend the traditional boundaries of literary analysis. The intersection of posthumanism, poststructuralism, digital humanities, and critical pedagogy is functional in achieving the objectives of the study. Poststructuralist and posthumanist theories challenge the traditional perception of the concepts of authorship, creativity, and intellectual agency, particularly Roland Barthes' (1992) notion of the 'death of the author.' Barthes argues that meaning is no longer anchored in a unified authorial consciousness but dispersed across language, intertextual networks, and the interpretive activity of readers. He suggests that while authors may exist physically, their control over the text ceases to exist. Thus, a text can be interpreted independently of the author's control. Michel Foucault (2003) questions the centrality of the author, arguing that the meaning-making process results from the interplay of language, culture, and the reader's perception. In the contemporary digital era, their insights gain urgency as the machine-generated texts disrupt human intentionality and position authorship as distributed across human and non-human agencies.

Posthumanist theorists extend this displacement by showing how creativity emerges from hybrid assemblages of humans, machines, and technological systems, further eroding the idea of the author as a singular origin of meaning. In contemporary AI-generated literature, this theoretical shift becomes materially realized: algorithmic systems, datasets, interfaces, and users participate in producing the text, making authorship not a stable identity but a distributed process. Thus, poststructuralist and posthumanist perspectives together invite a reconceptualization of literary agency as collaborative, relational, and fundamentally decentered in the digital age.

N. Katherine Hayles (2008) and Espen Aarseth (1997) are significant scholars who focus on the mechanics of digital texts. Hayles validates how multimodal literature reshapes reading practices (Mawdsley, 2023). In this regard, Aarseth presents the concept of "ergodic literature," which highlights the active role of readers in directing interactive narratives. The chapter argues that these approaches, when applied to AI-generated literature, structure a novel framework asserting that digital literature is not a deviation from being 'literary' but demands new critical vocabularies.

At the pedagogical level, Henry Giroux (2020) questions how education can either produce impassiveness or develop creative and critical engagement. AI-influenced classrooms highlight tension, as the students may risk outsourcing intellectual efforts to generative systems. Critical pedagogy emphasizes the introduction of practices that position AI as a dialogic site for collaborative knowledge-making instead of promoting uncritical consumption.

Posthumanist thinkers like Donna Haraway (2010) and Rosi Braidotti (2013) extend the discussion into questions of identity, ethics, and agency. Haraway's cyborg metaphor dismantles rigid binaries between human and machine, offering a way to view digital literature as hybrid creations, while Braidotti's posthuman stance favors shared responsibilities among human and non-human technological agencies that promote a sustainable and inclusive approach to learning and creativity (Leander & Burris, 2020).

Together, these frameworks highlight how posthuman textualities transform not only literature but also pedagogy and the ethics of learning. Poststructuralism destabilizes the author, posthumanism reimagines subjectivity and ethics in relation to technology, and digital humanities contextualizes the digital form, intersecting with critical pedagogy to reclaim human creativity in classrooms (Truman, 2017). This integrated perspective emphasizes that the future of literary studies lies in critically engaging AI, utilizing its potential to reshape interpretation and the learning process.

The term "posthumanism" refers to various modern theoretical frameworks proposed by scholars from disciplines such as philosophy, science and technology studies, literary studies, critical theory, theoretical sociology, and communication studies. For these disciplines, posthumanism signifies a succession of divergences from the fundamental tenets of contemporary Western civilization; specifically, it introduces a novel framework for comprehending the human subject in connection to the natural world at large (Bolter, 2016). While the term "humanism" was inherently anthropocentric, as a historical phenomenon, it emerged from a revitalized and reinterpreted admiration for the rhetoric and culture of Greece and Rome, positioning humanity (instead of divinity) at the core of its literary and philosophical endeavors (Prouteau, 2024)

Post-structuralism in literature asserts that literature does not possess a singular, stable meaning. Instead, it emphasizes that meaning is dynamic, shaped by individual readers within their particular cultural contexts, and often affected by the text's inherent inconsistencies and intrinsic instability. (Tompkins,1988). Essential concepts include the deconstruction of binary oppositions, the rejection of a fixed authorial intention, and the idea that language is unpredictable and unstable. Poststructuralists contend that a text can have several, even contradictory readings, as meaning is not fixed; the reader generates it. The rejection of stable meaning implies that it cannot be objectively determined. The reader's context, experiences, and cultural background are crucial in determining a text's meaning, leading to differences in interpretation across readers. (Docherty,2016)

Post-structuralist theorists Roland Barthes (1992) and Michel Foucault (2003) challenged the notion of the author as the sole source of meaning, emphasizing the relationship between language, culture, and the reader's interpretive role. Roland Barthes' concept of the "death of the author" highlights the shift in literary interpretation from an author-centric to a reader-centric framework. He examines the traditional view that writing reflects the author's identity, experiences, and intentions. He asserts that writing embodies a composite voice, obscuring the author's identity, with meaning emanating from the language itself rather than the author's personal narrative. The modern concept of the author has dominated literary criticism, often leading to interpretations that seek to clarify a work through the author's biography and psychological context. Barthes posits that when one extricates the author from the text, focus shifts to the reader, who assumes the role of meaning construction. People see the book as a place where many cultural references and texts come together, rather than as a way for the author to send a single message. This movement frees literature from strict interpretations, making it easier to connect with works more dynamically. The "death of the author" requires a reevaluation of criticism, prioritizing the text's structure and the reader's experience over the author's biography. Barthes asserts that meaning ought to be examined rather than deciphered, emphasizing the text's multiplicity and the reader's responsibility in the construction of meaning. The rise of the reader signifies a transformational shift in literature, challenging established hierarchies and interpretations. Foucault's critical insights on the function of the author extend the debate, as he argues, "It is not enough, however, to repeat the empty affirmation that the author has disappeared. For the same reason, it is not enough to keep repeating (after Nietzsche) that God and man have died a common death. Instead, we must locate the space left empty by the author's disappearance, follow the distribution of gaps and breaches, and watch for the openings that this disappearance uncovers" (Foucault, 2003, p.76).

In the digital age, this gap is filled by a posthuman author (AI). Foucault's concept of the "author-function" offers a productive lens for understanding authorship in AI-generated and posthuman literary contexts. In his book chapter "What Is an Author?" (2003), he argues that authorship is not an expression of individual creativity but a discursive function that organizes texts, assigns responsibility, and regulates meaning. AI-generated works, whether produced by algorithms, generative transformers, or interactive systems, intensify this decentering by demonstrating that literary production can emerge from distributed agencies rather than from a singular authorial consciousness.

DISCUSSION

Digital Humanities and Its Connection with Digital Literature

Digital humanities is an interdisciplinary field that marks a significant transformation in contemporary humanistic inquiry. It brings computational techniques, data-driven methods, and digital media into a sustained dialogue with traditional disciplines, such as philosophy, history, and literature (Iyer, 2025). It revisits methods scholars use to interpret cultural and literary materials. It includes a broad set of principles from text mining and digital archiving to distance learning. It also involves the visualization and development of research platforms. All the mentioned methodological innovations extend the scope of literary scholarship; they enable forms of analysis beyond the limits of print culture, linear practices, and individually decentered interpretations.

Within this vast terrain, digital literature emerges as a creative domain that encompasses many theoretical and aesthetic concerns in the digital humanities. It includes works such as hypertext fiction, interactive narratives, multimedia poetry, and poetry-assisted/generated writing. While digital humanities focuses on methodological transformation, digital literature establishes creative possibilities. Digital literary works challenge the established assumptions about narrative structure, literary forms, and authorship. It shows how technology reshapes literary creativity and the learning process (Floridi, 2025)

The relationship between digital humanities and digital literature becomes particularly generative when considered through pedagogical and posthuman perspectives. Both fields challenge human-centered models of learning by emphasizing the interplay between human cognition and digital systems. In academia, digital literary texts encourage students to approach literature as an evolving process that is driven by digital data that demands an interactive approach from its consumer (Singun, 2025). In this way, meaning is no longer a fixed object. Methodological experimentation mediates meaning-making. The convergence of digital humanities with digital literacy proposes creativity and interpretation as distributed across humans and machines. The synthesis of these produces a new imaginative form. In the context of posthuman imagination, collaborative production and interpretation of literary work requires a profound reorientation of literary practice. In this scenario, it is crucial to promote ethical and imaginative capacities to direct a shared ecosystem of human creativity.

Hypertext fiction, AI-generated texts, and digital literature

In the context of posthuman literary learning, digital literature, AI-generated writing, and hypertext fiction are interconnected modes of production. Hypertext fiction is characterized by its ability to transform reading into interpretative activity. Here, the meaning does not emerge linearly; instead, it develops through the reader's choice in a non-linear text (Gardner, 2003). AI-generated literature disrupts the conventional method differently, as it challenges the authorship by allowing algorithms to form the textual meaning. It integrates human cognition, computational processes, and digital media to create and interpret texts. Collectively, these forms exemplify the posthuman form of literary learning. This condition devalues literary pedagogy that emphasizes the digital interactivity and ethical implications simultaneously. The distinction between author intention and machine function raises questions about responsibility and interpretation. A posthuman viewpoint highlights embedded algorithmic biases. It refers to the preservation of human imagination and the distribution of intellectual accountability within a digital environment. Therefore, the encounter of pedagogy with AI-generated/assisted literature must extend beyond the boundaries of aesthetic classification to promote critical awareness of the ethical tension. Students engage with AI tools, design interactive hypertext projects, and get firsthand experience of distributed authorship. They negotiate meaning at interfaces where human and machine converge. In this way, the system participates in shaping their linguistic, cultural, and creative faculties and cultivates sensitivity to the ethical implications. In this evolving background, human imagination is not an exclusive human capability but a combined creative activity. Literacy pedagogy requires an adaptive, engaged framework that shows openness to emerging textual modalities. In this context, posthuman imagination restructures literature as a dialogic space in which technology does not reduce creativity but participates in expanding its possibilities.

Defining the Posthuman Work

According to N. Katherine Hayles, electronic literature is created in a digital environment. Such texts cannot be fully experienced in print. She emphasized, "Electronic literature is born-digital: it would lose something essential if it were translated into print" (Hayles, 2008, p. 3). It is therefore distinguished from digitized print, which merely imitates the existing material in electronic form. As electronic literature involves computational processes, such as animations, hyperlinking, generating algorithms, and multimedia integration, its meaning is inseparable from the medium that produces it. The technological infrastructure, code, and interface become integral to the interpretive process. Hayles opines that electronic literature is capable of transforming the reading process: "Electronic literature often requires nontrivial effort from the reader, who must navigate, click, scroll, or otherwise interact with the text for the text to be fully realized" (Hayles, 2008, p. 21). The shift from passive consumption to active participation supports the stance of the theory of Media Specific Analysis, which focuses on the materiality of the platform for literary interpretation: "Texts must be read with attention to the materiality of the medium that produces them" (Hayles, 2002, p. 10) Genres of hypertext fiction and kinetic poetry, generative texts, and multimedia storytelling epitomize the interconnectedness of physical characteristics and signifying strategies. Materiality, according to her, is an emergent property that results from a collaborative act.

In such works, many pieces of work unfold through algorithms, systems, consumer interaction, or real-time data, which makes them performative processes rather than fixed objects. Hayles notes that "electronic works frequently change with each performance... making the text less a stable object than a process that unfolds in time" (Hayles, 2008, p. 10). She maintains that the role of code is central to this instability, as she describes it as "the unconscious of the text, shaping its possibilities and generative capacities" (Hayles 1993, p. 32). It evaluates code, not just a hidden infrastructure, but a layer to determine the appearances and evolution of digital literature. These insights place electronic literature as a significant site to explore contemporary questions relating to digital culture, cognition, and the technological elements in shaping literary imagination.

To understand experiential and ontological shifts, Hayles's posthuman theory provides sound foundations as she argues "the posthuman view privileges informational pattern over material instantiation... [and] profoundly affects our understanding of textuality and subjectivity" (Hayles, 1993, pp. 2–3). The focus on process, pattern, and distributed agency resonates closely with Espen Aarseth's (1997) structure of cybertext, which, according to him, is "a machine for the production of a variety of expressions" (p.21). He refers to a type of text whose traversal asks for active and decision-based engagement from the reader. In Aarseth's context of ergodic literature, nontrivial effort is required to traverse the twitch that positions the reader as a co-author whose choice and structures shape the narrative unfolding. As he notices, "the reader of an ergodic text performs as a player, a gambler, and a strategist" (p.10) who presents a participatory model of reading that challenges traditional assumptions of text stability and linearity. Aarseth is cautious against technological determinism: "Cybertext theory is not media-specific; it applies to print as well as digital forms" (p.28), emphasizing that the ergodicity of the text is a structural phenomenon and not limited to electronic media. Hayles and Aarseth's insights are about how digital and ergodic forms problematize the notions of author subjectivity and textual unity, situating the reader within a posthuman assemblage of human agency, computational processes, and systematic activity.

Arseth's Cybertext extends the critical framework by offering a radical conceptualization of what constitutes a text and how readers engage with it. Therefore, in a posthuman context, the entanglement of cognitive agents, computation systems, interfaces, and procedural constraints produces meaning. In such an environment, meaning is in a continual flux as it generates and regenerates in real time.

Henry Giroux's Critical Pedagogy is crucial in understanding how AI shapes learning, as it emphasizes critical awareness over passive consumption of the AI-driven age. He raises questions on interpreting and ethically engaging with knowledge production (Stevenson, 2010). In his critical framework, he positions AI as a dialogic tool that deepens reflectivity, creativity, and intellectual responsibility. His critical pedagogy shapes AI literary practices as an opportunity for active and transformative learning. Giroux's ethical ideology interacts with posthuman philosophy, as both share a critique of hierarchical, autonomous models of human agency and a commitment to a distributed focus of knowledge.

While posthumanists such as Haraway and Braidotti argue that creativity and subjectivity are co-produced through human–nonhuman assemblages, Giroux similarly insists that learners must recognize and interrogate the social, technological, and ideological forces that shape meaning. In an AI-driven environment, these two perspectives reinforce each other: posthumanism highlights how imagination is entangled with machines and digital systems, while Giroux provides a pedagogical pathway for engaging these entanglements. Together, they encourage classrooms where students examine not only 'what' AI-generated texts are but also 'how' they are produced, by 'whom', and with 'what' implications. This combined lens enables a more reflective, responsible, and context-aware engagement with posthuman textualities.

Posthuman Textualities____ AI-Assisted/Generated Literature

The chapter discusses a few significant posthuman texts to demonstrate how AI-assisted/generated literature extends this poststructuralist challenge by questioning the centrality of the human act of knowledge production. These texts situate interpretation within networks of human and non-human agents, where technologies, algorithms, and digital systems also participate in meaning-making. The decentered authorship manifests in projects such as *The Day a Computer Writes a Novel* (2016). The computer writes,

The day was overcast, buried in clouds.

As always, optimum temperature and humidity in the apartment. Miss Yoko lounged on the couch, endlessly whiling away the time playing stupid video games. She didn't speak to me.

Nothing to do. Nothing to do, and I can't do anything about it." (The Day a Computer Writes a Novel, 2016)

The novel is a Japanese experiment. The researchers at the Kimagure Artificial Intelligence Writer Project created a narrative co-authored by AI, which advanced to the first round of a literary competition. The purpose of writing such a novel was to explore the very nature of creativity. Here, the human contributors provided structural prompts and vocabulary sets, while the system generated narrative sequences. Such hybrid production aligns with Braidotti's (2013) posthuman ethics, which rejects human exceptionalism and instead highlights creativity as an entanglement of human and non-human agencies. The text is neither entirely authored by the machine nor reducible to its programmers; rather, it emerges from the interplay of technological, linguistic, and human-cultural forces. Toshihiro Sato, a professor at Nagoya University and member of the Kimagure Project, posed the question to a seminar of school students: What is creativity? They replied that "We're not [even] sure what a story is. We must make educated guesses" (Margolis, 2019).

The interactive AI-driven texts have transformed the role of readers. The hybrid authorship of *The Day a Computer Writes a Novel* subverts the traditional concept of creativity and reconfigures the concept of literary interpretation that informs posthuman pedagogical ethics in a way that meaning cannot be drawn by a single intentional author; instead, it emerges from the interaction of human imagination, algorithmic operations, and cultural linguistic patterns. The decentered authorship aligns with poststructuralist claims that refuse the author as an independent source of meaning (Barthes, 1992). It also echoes Braidotti's (2013) posthuman ethics, which focuses on the entangled nature of creativity for readers and students. It asks for a shift from taking it as an expression of human creativity to viewing it as an assemblage by diverse heterogeneous forces. In this way, interpretation becomes posthuman practice as students not only analyze the narrative but also technological processes and human interventions that help produce the text. According to Deane (2020), the expert interpretation should have the quality of attending to ambiguity, multiple perspectives, and evidence-based reasoning in the classrooms. AI-generated/assisted narratives invite learners to reflect on the question of what a 'story' is and how meaning is produced, and who or what participates in the act of writing process.

Authorship and Creativity

AI-generated works such as *1 the Road* (2018) and *ReRites* (2018) open new possibilities for examining authorship and creativity through poststructuralist and humanist debate. *The 1 Road* (2018) was composed by artificial intelligence. The novel emulates Jack Kerouac's *On the Road*. Ross Goodwin started a drive from New York to New Orleans in March 2017 with an AI in his laptop equipped with various sensors. AI captured the drive and turned the output into words that were printed on rolls of receipt paper. The novel was later published in 2018 by Jean Boîte Éditions. *ReRites* demonstrates a literary work of Human and A.I. poetry composed by David Jhave Johnston. He used neural networks that were trained to generate poetry, which he edited later on. Both works unsettle the romantic ideal of the author as an autonomous creative origin, embodying Roland Barthes's argument in the context of the author's absence that meaning arises not from a singular consciousness but from the interplay of language, culture, and the reader. *1 The Road* (2018), produced through a machine-learning system trained on Kerouac and fed real-time data from cameras and sensors, demonstrates Barthes's vision of writing as a "multi-dimensional space" where diverse textual and material inputs converge. The resulting narrative emerges from algorithmic patterning, environmental data, and human design, displacing individual authorship and foregrounding creativity as a distributed process.

These posthuman narratives similarly align authorship with Michel Foucault's critique of the author-function. Foucault (2003) argues that "the author" operates as a cultural category rather than a stable origin of meaning. In the works, authorship becomes a shifting relation among machine-generated lines, human editorial decisions, and iterative curation. Johnston's role as editor, selecting, shaping, and contextualizing the AI's output, exposes the fluid interplay between human judgment and computational creativity. At the same time, the machine's generative capacities resist being reduced to a mere tool, embodying what Haraway (2010) describes in her cyborg theory as a hybrid identity that disrupts rigid boundaries between human and machine. By foregrounding collaborative and algorithmically mediated processes, these works redefine authorship as relational, contingent, and distributed, offering a compelling vision of literary creativity in the age of intelligent machines.

Reader Interaction and Co-creation

AI Dungeon (2019) is a text-based adventure game. It uses AI to create random storylines. It is a single/multiplayer game that allows players to create and share custom prompts. In multiplayer mode, each player has their own character. Players take their turns interacting with AI in the game sessions.

Project December (2020) is an AI-powered system (game) that allows users to have text-based conversations with those who are dead. A sophisticated supercomputer allows users to initiate a conversation with anyone they have liked. Interactive AI-driven systems such as *AI Dungeon* and *Project December* extend poststructuralist insights into the instability of authorship by foregrounding reader participation as the core engine of textual production. In *AI Dungeon*, narrative meaning emerges through iterative exchanges in which the game responds to player prompts with generative continuations such as "You *draw your sword as the forest shifts around you, the world waiting for your next command.*" (*AI Dungeon*, 2019). These open-ended responses demonstrate how the text positions the reader as a co-creator whose input directly shapes the unfolding narrative. The system's frequent meta-prompts, e.g., *"What do you do next?"*—explicitly solicit reader agency and epitomize Barthes's claim that meaning is produced where reader and text intersect, while also echoing Foucault's view that "the author" is not a unified source but a function distributed across discursive operations.

Project December (2020), intensifies this condition of co-authorship by allowing users to design custom "personas" that respond in distinctive voices. For instance, users often receive lines such as "*I am here because you programmed me to remember, but I don't know what I have forgotten,*" revealing the emergent, quasi-self-reflective quality of machine-generated dialogue. These responses illustrate that textual output is neither predetermined nor attributable to a single creator; rather, it arises from interactions among user prompts, system parameters, and the neural architecture underlying the model. The text becomes a shifting, co-authored entity shaped simultaneously by human intention and algorithmic patterning. In Haraway's cyborgian terms, the resulting narratives operate as hybrid textualities that blur boundaries between organic and computational creativity. By making reader interaction and procedural generation foundational to narrative formation, *AI Dungeon* (2019) and *Project December* (2020) reinforce the move from static, author-centered literary models to dynamic, collaborative forms of storytelling that exemplify posthuman creativity in the age of AI.

Posthuman Aesthetics and Agency

AI-generated works such as *Sunspring* (2016) and *The Day a Computer Writes a Novel* (2016) deepen the discourse on posthuman aesthetics and distributed agency by foregrounding creativity as a hybrid process emerging between human and machine. *Sunspring* (2016), the short film scripted by the neural network "BEN," exemplifies this hybridity through its uncanny, syntactically coherent yet semantically unstable dialogue. Lines such as *"I know the things you want me to do, and I'm gonna be dead"* or *"Well, I have to go to the skull"* reveal an aesthetic that resists conventional narrative logic while exposing the generative machine's internal patterning of language. These moments enact what Hayles describes as posthuman expression, an interplay of algorithmic operations and embodied human performance, where the actors must interpret and inhabit an unstable script produced by computational processes. Similarly, *The Day a Computer Writes a Novel* illustrates the machine's capacity to produce narrative structures that mimic human genre conventions while destabilizing them. The text's opening passage, *"The day a computer wrote a novel, we sat together in the quiet room thinking about how far we had come,"* (*The Day Computer Writes a Novel*, 2016), performs a meta-commentary on its origins, situating the AI simultaneously as creator, narrator, and subject. Throughout the narrative, repetitive phrases and oddly self-reflexive lines such as *"I kept writing because the computer was still thinking"* blur the distinction between human intention and computational agency, foregrounding the machine's role as an aesthetic force rather than a mere instrument.

These narratives characterize posthuman aesthetics in which creativity emerges from the entanglement of algorithmic production, human interpretation, and performative embodiment. These works demonstrate that agency in AI-generated art is neither wholly machinic nor human but distributed across systems, datasets, creators, and audiences. By destabilizing narrative coherence and authorial originality, they expand the boundaries of what counts as literature, revealing aesthetic possibilities that arise only when humans and machines co-produce meaning.

AI lends itself naturally to poetic and experimental forms that explore fragmentation, randomness, repetition, and procedural aesthetics. From neural poetry generators to surrealist text engines, these works challenge normative linguistic structures and create novel expressive landscapes. Their experimentalism is both aesthetic and philosophical, prompting reflections on language play, the limits of comprehension, and the creative affordances of computational randomness.

Projects such as *ReRites*, *PoemPortraits*, *The Infinite Conversation*, *Sunspring*, and browser-based literary installations illustrate how contemporary artists use algorithms to push the boundaries of narrative, poetry, and textual performance. These works highlight digital literature as an artistic laboratory where new forms of narrative time, voice, and embodiment emerge from technological mediation. They function not only as artworks but as critical provocations, inviting audiences to rethink the nature of creativity, collaboration, and textual life in an age of intelligent machines.

AI literature frequently invokes Gothic tropes, which refer to doubling, uncanny mimicry, animated machines, and the collapse of human/machine boundaries (Barron, 2023). Works like *Sunspring* or *The Infinite Conversation* produce eerie, haunting expressions reminiscent of Gothic anxieties about animated matter and disembodied voices. AI becomes a contemporary 'monster,' simultaneously familiar and estranged. It is reflective of collective fears about automation, loss of agency, and the opacity of algorithmic systems. A Gothic analysis foregrounds the tension between fascination and dread that defines public discourse on AI, revealing how digital literature becomes a site for negotiating cultural fears about technological transformation.

Methods of Interpretation and Literary Pedagogy: A Posthuman and Poststructuralist Perspective

The ETS Research Report by Deane (2020) emphasizes that literary interpretation is a central objective of English instruction. Students must not only comprehend texts but also justify their interpretations with evidence, a skill that develops late and benefits from participation in interpretive communities. Because literary texts are ambiguous, emotionally resonant, and formally complex, they require close reading and flexible reasoning. Deane identifies six key strategies, deepening comprehension, inferring authorial purpose, considering multiple perspectives, connecting text to context, generalizing themes, and engaging in intertextuality—all of which move readers beyond literal understanding and prepare them for the demands of 21st-century literacy.

Deane (2020) emphasizes the need for interpretive plurality in literary texts. According to the report, literary works reward readers who go beyond surface understanding to develop deeper, inferential meaning. Their "point-driven" design (Vipond & Hunt, 1984) encourages readers to infer importance that is not explicitly expressed, while figurative language, formal patterns, and intentional disruptions of communication efficiency require interpretive focus. The inherent ambiguity of literature and its power to unsettle, resonate, or transport readers (create a natural space for multiple interpretations. This dynamic becomes especially visible within interpretive communities, where varied readings intersect and challenge one another. As studies show, interpretive discussions enhance understanding by helping readers recognize that no single interpretation is definitive.

Demonstrating Multiple Interpretive Lenses

Borrowing and interpreting an excerpt from the computer-generated novel *The Day a Computer Writes a Novel* (2016) shows how a single text can be interpreted from multiple lenses:

"The day was overcast, buried in clouds. As always, optimum temperature and humidity in the apartment. Miss Yoko lounged on the couch, endlessly whiling away the time playing stupid video games. She didn't speak to me. Nothing to do. Nothing to do, and I can't do anything about it."

Literal / Surface Reading

Claim: A bored narrator describes a dull, rainy day and an inert domestic scene.

Evidence: "overcast… buried in clouds"; "Miss Yoko lounged… playing stupid video games."

Psychological / Interiority

Claim: The narrator expresses depression or learned helplessness.

Evidence: Repetition "Nothing to do… I can't do anything about it" signals resignation.

Social Isolation / Loneliness Reading

Claim: The scene indexes emotional distance and failed communication between two people.

Evidence: "She didn't speak to me" + passive activities (gaming) evoke social withdrawal.

Class or Domestic Comfort Reading

Claim: "Optimum temperature and humidity" hints at a controlled, possibly affluent domestic environment that still feels vacant.

Evidence: The clinical (the word 'clinical' refers to as if the speaker is recording data rather than expressing feeling) phrasing contrasts with the narrator's boredom — comfort without meaning.

Posthuman / Algorithmic Reading

Claim: The clinical detail ("optimum temperature and humidity") and flat affect could suggest a nonhuman (robotic or sensor-mediated) viewpoint.

Evidence: Precise environmental metrics read like sensor output; repetition resembles looped processing.

Narratological / Focalization Reading

Claim: The passage is focalized through a frustrated, possibly unreliable narrator whose perceptions shape reality.

Evidence: Subjective commentary "stupid video games" reveals judgment and bias.

Existential / Absurdist Reading

Claim: The text evokes the banality of existence—the everyday repeated with no transcendence.

Evidence: Mundane details + fatalistic repetition ("I can't do anything about it") suggest existential stasis.

Gendered Reading

Claim: "Miss Yoko" and the narrator's tone could reflect gendered expectations or domestic roles; the narrator's irritation may mask patriarchal entitlement.

Evidence: Label "Miss" + narrator's critique of her gaming implies judgment of leisure or gender behavior.

Intertextual / Allusive Reading

Claim: The mood and phrasing echo modernist stasis (e.g., Woolfian domestic interior) but flattened into contemporary tech life.

Evidence: Interior monologue + attention to small domestic detail recalls stream-of consciousness techniques.

Irony / Satirical Reading

Claim: The juxtaposition of "optimum" environmental conditions with human emptiness satirizes techno-utopian promises that ignore human needs.

Evidence: Clinical "optimum" vs. emotional vacuum in the paragraph.

Pedagogical / Student-as-Co-Creator Reading

Claim: The line invites students to question who "speaks" in the text (human, AI, or hybrid) and to justify that claim using language features.

Evidence: Neutral register + repetition + sensor-like detail give grounds for debate.

Metafictional / Authorless Reading

Claim: Read as machine-generated, the passage foregrounds the instability of authorial intention: meaning arises from prompts, data, and reader inference.

Evidence: Slightly awkward phrasing ("endlessly whiling away the time") and clinical details point to algorithmic composition.

These readings show that even a short, machine-generated passage can open onto a surprisingly wide field of interpretive possibility. Poststructural pedagogy destabilizes the idea of a fixed meaning or authoritative author, promoting interpretive plurality and encouraging students to question textual stability. Posthuman pedagogy further expands this view by reframing interpretation as a distributed process involving human readers, digital systems, and material infrastructures. In this framework, texts become interactive nodes within broader assemblages of cognitive, cultural, and technological forces.

These interactive forms resonate with critical pedagogy, especially Freire's call for dialogic education and Giroux's critiques of passive consumption. AI-generated texts require students to examine agency to analyze what decisions are made by humans, what by machines, and how each shapes meaning. This inquiry fosters meta-awareness of textual production, authorship, and technological mediation. Within pedagogy, these theoretical perspectives reshape how interpretation is taught. Poststructuralist classrooms emphasize multiplicity and critical questioning, while posthuman pedagogy integrates technological tools, digital annotation, algorithmic analysis, and AI-assisted reading to demonstrate how non-human agents also participate in meaning-making. This convergence promotes co-creativity and interpretive openness. AI-generated literature invites a profound rethinking of how literature is taught. Traditional models centered on authorial intent and textual stability give way to multimodal, procedural, and collaborative forms of creativity. Students must learn to read not only language but also interfaces, algorithms, and data infrastructures. AI projects such as *PoemPortraits* and *The Infinite Conversation* illustrate these pedagogical shifts, as *PoemPortraits* allows users to contribute a word that becomes part of an algorithmically generated poem, framing creativity as participatory and collective. *The Infinite Conversation* simulates an endless dialogue between AI-generated versions of public intellectuals, raising questions about authenticity, voice appropriation, and the ethics of synthetic production. Such projects give opportunities to teach intertextuality, simulation, and critical media literacy. They prompt students to interrogate how meaning is constructed, how data is used, and how authorship is redistributed in digital environments.

Literary reading reaches its most powerful form when it produces transportation; moments when readers inhabit fictional worlds and perceive them through characters' perspectives. Yet this immersive world is constructed collaboratively by the text and the reader. When students share interpretations within communities of practice, immersion becomes relational: different readings converge, diverge, and transform one another. This interaction reflects the movement from poststructuralist instability to posthuman relationality. Interpretation becomes neither solitary nor purely human but a collaborative, dynamic process shaped by dialogue, context, and technology (Bozkurt et al., 2023)

Digital literature requires attention to the materiality of its medium. Following Hayles's media-specific analysis, meaning arises not only from language but from computational processes, interface design, multimodal elements, and user interactivity. Algorithmic architectures themselves become literary substrates. Digital materiality is thus both aesthetic and epistemological, shaping how readers engage with texts and navigate narrative systems.

AI literature exposes a central limitation: the "dimensional reduction problem." Complex human experiences are compressed into computational vectors, producing outputs that may be eloquent yet uncanny. This reduction raises critical questions about what is lost or distorted when creativity is mediated through data-driven systems. Understanding this tension is essential for evaluating AI-generated texts and for teaching students to read them critically.

As AI-produced texts proliferate, ethical concerns become increasingly urgent. Issues of consent, voice appropriation, data sourcing, and authorship attribution must be addressed. Projects like *Project December* or *Sunspring* show how easily stylistic traits and identity markers can be repurposed without permission. Ethical frameworks for posthuman authorship must therefore account for agency distributed across cultural, biological, and computational systems, ensuring responsible innovation in literary creation.

CONCLUSION

The chapter concludes that contemporary digital literature—from hypertext narratives and AI-generated poetry to interactive fiction—positions interactivity and generativity as central aesthetic principles, often overshadowing traditional ethical concerns within literary pedagogy. These works do not rely on fixed, author-determined narratives; instead, they emerge through dynamic exchanges between readers and computational systems. In such environments, the reader becomes a collaborator whose choices, interpretations, and inputs actively shape the unfolding text. Generative systems extend this model further, producing variable content with each iteration, making the literary work less a static product and more an evolving process.

This shift marks a fundamental transformation in literary ontology, foregrounding distributed creativity as the hallmark of posthuman textuality. In this framework, creativity arises from the entanglement of human readers, digital interfaces, algorithms, and data environments rather than from a singular authorial consciousness. Such co-creative poetics opens new avenues for addressing ethical challenges in literary learning. The following are a few novel ways to address ethical concerns in literary pedagogy:

Firstly, the ethics of participation and agency are an important concern in this regard. Instead of treating students merely as interpreters of fixed texts, co-creative digital works encourage them to reflect on their role as active agents in meaning-making. This allows educators to foreground ethical questions about intervention, choice, narrative responsibility, and the consequences of reader decisions within branching or generative texts.

Secondly, transparency of algorithmic mediation affirms that posthuman literary environments offer opportunities to teach students how computational systems shape narratives. By making algorithmic frameworks visible, educators can cultivate critical algorithmic literacy, an ethical skill that helps students interrogate bias, opacity, and power embedded in digital textual production.

Thirdly, Collaborative ethics in interpretive communities is essential as interactive digital works promote collective reading practices that require negotiation, empathy, and dialogic engagement. This allows instructors to embed ethical reflection into interpretive collaboration: How do different readers' decisions impact shared narrative outcomes? Whose interpretations gain authority, and why?

Fourthly, responsibility toward non-human Agents is of supreme importance as posthuman textuality blurs boundaries between human and non-human creators. This enables pedagogical discussions about ethical responsibility toward technological agents. It involves questions such as, how do we respect or critique machine creativity? What moral standards should govern AI-generated content? How do we acknowledge human labor embedded in datasets, programming, and design? Respecting or critiquing machine creativity requires recognizing that AI-generated texts do not emerge from autonomous artistic intention but from intricate assemblages of human labor, algorithmic design, and massive training corpora. Ethical engagement, therefore, involves treating AI outputs not as independent works but as co-produced artifacts shaped by cultural assumptions, computational constraints, and socio-technical infrastructures. Rather than celebrating machine authorship, students must learn to interrogate how such creativity is produced, whose values it encodes, and what biases or exclusions are embedded in its datasets. This also raises the need for clear ethical standards governing AI-generated content, including transparency about its artificial origins, critical awareness of dataset biases, and accountability for harmful or misleading outputs. Equally important is acknowledging the often-invisible human labor underlying AI systems—the writers whose texts populate datasets, the annotators and moderators who curate data, and the programmers and designers whose decisions materially shape algorithmic behavior. Making this labor visible helps students understand AI not as a neutral or purely technical agent but as a participant in meaning-making situated within broader economic, cultural, and political structures. Such an approach nurtures an ethically grounded posthuman pedagogy, one that cultivates critical literacy by foregrounding co-agency, transparency, and responsibility in the interpretation and creation of digital texts.

Finally, ethical reflexivity through iteration implies that generative systems that produce multiple textual versions encourage students to reflect on variability, contingency, and the ethics of interpretation. Each iteration becomes a site for asking: What is the ethical impact of selecting one narrative path over another? What meanings emerge or disappear as the text regenerates?

Readers affirm inclusivity through adaptive narrative structures, as digital literature can adjust to diverse reading styles and backgrounds. Educators can use it to raise inclusive literary environments. Adaptive texts can highlight ethical issues regarding representation, identity, and reader accessibility, aligning with feminist and decolonial pedagogical ethics. The need is to adopt a middle path, a space of negotiation between human and non-human agencies, for a better understanding of posthuman texts.

REFERENCES

Aarseth, E. J. (1997). *Cybertext: Perspectives on ergodic literature*. JHU Press. DOI: 10.56021/9780801855788

Barron, L. (2023). AI and Literature. In *AI and popular culture* (pp. 47–87). Emerald Publishing Limited. DOI: 10.1108/978-1-80382-327-020231003

Barthes, R. (1992). *The death of the author, 1968*. na.

Bolter, J. D. (2016). Posthumanism. In Jensen, K. B., Rothenbuhler, E. W., Pooley, J. D., & Craig, R. T. (Eds.), *The International Encyclopedia of Communication Theory and Philosophy*., DOI: 10.1002/9781118766804.wbiect220

Bozkurt, A., Junhong, X., Lambert, S., Pazurek, A., Crompton, H., Koseoglu, S., & Romero-Hall, E. (2023). Speculative futures on ChatGPT and generative artificial intelligence (AI): A collective reflection from the educational landscape. *Asian Journal of Distance Education, 18*(1), 53–130.

Deane, P. D. (2020). Building and Justifying Interpretations of Texts: A Key Practice in the English Language Arts ETS RR-20-20

Docherty, T. (2016). *Postmodernism: A reader*. Routledge. DOI: 10.4324/9781315504612

Floridi, L. (2025). Distant Writing: Literary Production in the Age of Artificial Intelligence. *Minds and Machines, 35*(3), 1–26. DOI: 10.1007/s11023-025-09732-1

Foucault, M. (2003). *What is an author? Reading Architectural History*. Routledge.

Gardner, C. (2003). Meta-interpretation and hypertext fiction: A critical response. *Computers and the Humanities, 37*(1), 33–56. DOI: 10.1023/A:1021803606361

Giroux, H. A. (2020). *On critical pedagogy*. Bloomsbury Publishing. DOI: 10.5040/9781350145016

Haraway, D. (2010). A Cyborg Manifesto (1985). *Cultural theory: An anthology, 454*.

Hayles, N. K. (1993). The materiality of informatics. *Configurations, 1*(1), 147–170. DOI: 10.1353/con.1993.0003

Hayles, N. K. (2002). *Writing Machines*. MIT Press. DOI: 10.7551/mitpress/7328.001.0001

Hayles, N. K. (2008). *Electronic literature: New horizons for the literary*. University of Notre Dame Press.

Iyer, V. (2025). *Digital Humanities Research Methods*. Educohack Press.

Leander, K. M., & Burriss, S. K. (2020). Critical literacy for a posthuman world: When people read, and become, with machines. *British Journal of Educational Technology*, *51*(4), 1262–1276. DOI: 10.1111/bjet.12924

Margolis, E. (2019). The Day A Computer Wrote A Novel. Retrieved on December 3, 2025

Mawdsley, M. (2023). *On materiality: an analysis of the medium's role in electronic literature* (Master's thesis, University of Malta).

Project, A. I. (2016). "The Day a Computer Writes a Novel" *The day a computer writes a novel* [AI-generated novella]. Hoshi Shinichi Prize Committee.

Prouteau, F. (2024). For a Regenerated Humanism in the Anthropocene. In *Anthropology of the Anthropocene: Ideas for a Courageous Education* (pp. 29–72). Springer Nature Switzerland. DOI: 10.1007/978-3-031-75419-7_2

Singun, A. J. (2025). Unveiling the barriers to digital transformation in higher education institutions: A systematic literature review. *Discover Education*, *4*(1), 37. DOI: 10.1007/s44217-025-00430-9

Stevenson, N. (2010). Critical pedagogy, democracy, and capitalism: Education without enemies or borders. *Review of Education, Pedagogy & Cultural Studies*, *32*(1), 66–92. DOI: 10.1080/10714410903482674

Tompkins, J. (1988). A Short Course in Post-Structuralism. *College English*, *50*(7), 733–747. DOI: 10.58680/ce198811361

Truman, S. E. (2017). *Speculative Methodologies and Emergent Literacies: Walking and Writing as Research-Creation*. University of Toronto.

Yadav, D. (2024). The role of Artificial Intelligence in literary analysis: A computational approach to understand literary styles. *International Journal of Emerging Knowledge Studies*, *3*(9), 558–565. DOI: 10.70333/ijeks-03-09-006

Chapter 4
Integrating AI Into Literature Review Practices

Shazia Ayyaz
http://orcid.org/0000-0002-6950-5731
Al Zahra College for Women, Oman

ABSTRACT

This chapter explores the integration of Artificial Intelligence (AI) into literature review within research. Traditional literature review methods, while foundational to scholarly inquiry, often face challenges of scale, efficiency, and comprehensiveness due to the rapid expansion of academic publications. AI technologies provide innovative solutions to these challenges by automating the identification, categorization, and synthesis of relevant research. The chapter examines how AI can enhance systematic literature reviews, uncover emerging trends, and facilitate deeper insights into scholarly discourse. It also addresses methodological and ethical considerations, such as the reliability of AI-assisted analysis, potential biases in algorithms, and the importance of maintaining critical human oversight. Drawing on recent studies and practical examples, the chapter demonstrates the opportunities and limitations of AI in literature review processes.

1. INTRODUCTION

Academic research has transformed significantly with the emergence of AI research tools. These tools are efficient to the extent that they have taken the who process of the research into the next level. They are used to assist various aspects of research process. They are guiding the researchers to find out a research gap

DOI: 10.4018/979-8-2600-1458-5.ch004

among the recent trends of the research. Summarize the recent advancements in the field of research in seconds. The major challenges for the researchers had been collecting the relevant literature and organizing it then writing the research report in a standard format and editing and proofread. Now the labor is shifted to the AI tools for most of the tough tasks. This shift apparently is a pleasant development in the life of the researcher but in fact this assistance shifts to overdependence on the AI, the reliability and validity of the research become questionable. We call this AI era, and it is true for research too because every day new AI tools are emerging to help the researcher to complete their task with efficiency and saving time. Even the traditional research applications for references are now AI empowered so it is not possible to ban AI for researchers and research related tasks. However, rigorous use of AI can damage the authenticity of the scholarship. Due to crucial nature of this argument various publications are out now to examine the use of AI and suggest a balanced approach to avoid bias and misinformation. These studies present overview of AI applications in literature review, data analysis, writing and proofreading, discussing their benefits and limitations (Oyelude, 2024.

Literature review is not merely a preliminary step of collecting previous knowledge, but it works as the foundation of credible scholarly research. It represents systematic and critical engagement with the existing body of knowledge on a given topic, a process through which researchers establish the intellectual landscape, establish theoretical and contextual grounding, identify salient gaps and contradictions, and ultimately position their own contribution within the ongoing academic conversation (Snyder, 2019; Machi & McEvoy, 2021). This scholarly rite of passage, however, is presently confronting an existential challenge. The very volume of knowledge it seeks to synthesize is expanding at a pace that threatens to overwhelm traditional, human-centric methodologies. We are in the middle of an information explosion; the global scientific output, for instance, is estimated to double approximately every nine years, with millions of peer-reviewed articles published annually across tens of thousands of journals (Bornmann & Mutz, 2015). This flood of information creates a paradox, the obligation for comprehensive understanding grows even as the possibility of achieving it through manual means seems impossible.

Consequently, traditional literature review model characterized by linear keyword searches in siloed databases. They required manual screening of abstracts, and the cognitive synthesis of insights. This make the researchers face trilemma of modern scholarship that is the near-impossible task. They at the same time has to achieve comprehensiveness, maintain manageability, and ensure depth of critical analysis. The risks inherent in this strained model are significantly high. They include the possibilities of missing essential studies and the risk of unconscious selection bias. They include oversight of critical details, and the inability to discern complex, cross-disciplinary patterns hidden within thousands of documents (O'Mara-Eves et al., 2015). The result can be reviews that are, despite immense effort, inadvertently narrow, incomplete, or superficially connected.

AI application in every context brings big challenges a such as over-reliance, contextual inaccuracies, and the need for critical engagement, need strategies to integrate these tools effectively taking into consideration ethical issues (Ayyaz, 2025). It is within this context of crisis and opportunity that Artificial Intelligence emerges as the engine for a paradigm shift in various fields. The transition from an era of digital assistance characterized by reference managers and search engines to an era of cognitive augmentation. AI, particularly in the domains of Natural Language Processing (NLP) and Machine Learning (ML), offers tools that do not simply help us find and organize papers faster, but that can read, comprehend, compare, and connect them at a scale and speed beyond human capacity (Devarakonda & Kilicoglu, 2022). This shift moves us from a model of search and retrieval to discover, understand, relate, and synthesize. The core thesis of this chapter is that the thoughtful and critical integration of AI into literature review practices promises to resolve the issues regarding enabling reviews that are simultaneously more comprehensive and conducted with efficiency. However, this promise is dependent upon navigating a new landscape of methodological complexity and ethical responsibility. It is important to advocate for a model of Augmented Scholarship, a symbiotic partnership where AI amplifies human intellect, and human judgment guides, corrects, and contextualizes AI output.

A Historical Evolution of Synthesis Tools

It is essential to contextualize AI within the longue durée of technologies for scholarly synthesis. This evolution reflects a broader societal shift from analog information handling to digital computation and now to cognitive simulation. The history of the literature review tool is, in miniature, a history of the scholar's changing relationship with information itself.

The era of correspondent scholarship was defined by physical and manual processes. The scholar's toolkit consisted of printed catalogs like the Science Citation Index, library card catalogs, personal collections of books and journal offprints, and handwritten note cards (Meadows, 2015). The literature review used to be physical and spatial endeavor that would take a year to complete. Synthesis occurred in the mind of the researcher and was often externalized in the physical arrangement and rearrangement of note cards on a desk. The scale of such a review was limited, constrained by physical access to libraries and the natural limits of human memory and organizational stamina. The scholarly virtue in this era was often one of exhaustive, painstaking curation within a bounded field.

The first digital revolution, beginning in the 1980s and accelerating through the 1990s and 2000s, transformed access. The proliferation of online databases such as PubMed, Web of Science, Scopus, and JSTOR, coupled with the advent of the world wide web, dismantled geographical barriers to information (Borgman, 2015). Keyword-based Boolean search became the standard discovery mechanism. Concurrently, bibliographic management software like EndNote, RefWorks, and later Zotero and Mendeley automated the tedious clerical work of citation formatting and reference list generation. This was a revolution in efficiency, but its cognitive impact was more nuanced. While these tools dramatically accelerated the retrieval and storage of references, they left the core intellectual tasks of reading, analysis, and synthesis fundamentally unchanged. The researcher's role shifted from physical curator to digital query-formulator and list-screener. These were, at heart, tools for information management, not for knowledge discovery or synthesis.

The networked era of the 2000s and 2010s introduced a new dimension: connection. Tools began to leverage the metadata of the literature primarily citations to reveal relationships. Forward and backward citation tracking allowed researchers to follow chains of intellectual influence. Early bibliometric and text-mining software enabled the visualization of co-authorship networks, keyword co-occurrence maps, and basic trend analyses (Chen, 2017). Platforms like Google Scholar simplified discovery through a single search box but introduced an opaque, algorithmically driven ranking system. This period offered scholars a meta-perspective on the architecture of their field, revealing hubs of influence and connections between subdisciplines. However, these tools still largely operated on the surface of metadata; the deep semantic content of the articles remained a domain for human reading alone, and utilizing these advanced features often required significant technical expertise.

The current AI revolution, propelled by breakthroughs in machine learning architectures and vast increases in computational power, represents a qualitative leap. Modern AI, particularly models built on transformer architectures, engages directly with the semantic content of scholarly texts. Unlike their predecessors, these systems are not merely sorting bibliographic records; they are attempting to understand, summarize, and reason about the knowledge contained within them. Key technological pillars underpin this shift. Transformer-based Large Language Models (LLMs) like BERT, GPT, and their successors can parse syntax, model context, and generate human-like text, enabling true semantic search, question-answering directly against documents, and coherent summarization (Vaswani et al., 2017; Brown et al., 2020). Unsupervised learning techniques, such as Latent Dirichlet Allocation (LDA), allow AI to inductively identify latent thematic structures and topical clusters across vast corpora without human pre-labeling (Blei & Lafferty, 2009). Perhaps most impactful for rigorous research synthesis, active learning frameworks allow AI-assisted screening platforms to learn from a researcher's initial decisions and prioritize likely-relevant documents, dramatically accelerating the most labor-intensive phase of systematic reviews (van de Schoot et al., 2021). Furthermore, AI can now construct dynamic knowledge graphs that map not just who cite whom, but how specific concepts, methods, and entities relate semantically across literature (Ammar et al., 2018). This evolution signifies a profound transition: from the scholar as a lone processor of information to the leader of a human-AI collaborative system designed for deep knowledge discovery, connection, and synthesis.

The emergence of literature review tools made it a complete method of research as SLR (Systematic Literature Review) has become more popular method of analysis in the present times. The synthetic review studies are useful to analyze the current authentic literature in the field. To make the process transparent proper mechanism has been introduced by the theorist to maintain the authenticity and reliability.

The SLR methodology originally emerged within the field of Evidence-Based Medicine (Sackett et al. 1996), and it was later adapted and employed in diverse research disciplines including social sciences and education.

Along with the other aspects of research projects, several SLR tools also incorporate AI techniques for supporting in particular the screening and extraction phases. However, current approaches are still limited in efficiency. Bolaños et. al. (2024) reveals that the majority of SLR tools still depend on possibly outdated methodologies such as use of the basic classifiers, which are no longer considered relevant for document classification and utilization of BoW methods for rather than adopting word and sentence embedding techniques, such as ELMo (Peters et al. 2018) and GloVe (Pennington et al. 2014). LLM has improved the screening, extracting and organization processes for SLR to a greater extent however the issue of bias and partiality is still an issue if the reliance on the AI is more than the human intelligence while including and excluding the most relevant studies.

Major Technologies for Literature Review

Literature review is a methodological as well as technical endeavor which gives the AI tools space to demonstrate the skills. AI is not a monolithic entity. For literature reviews, a specific set of technologies, primarily from the subfields of Natural Language Processing (NLP) and Machine Learning (ML), are being brought to bear. NLP is the branch of AI that gives machines the ability to read, understand, and derive meaning from human language. Key techniques include

Text Pre-processing

Tokenization (splitting text into words or phrases), lemmatization (reducing words to their base form, e.g., "running" to "run"), and removing stop words (e.g., "the," "and").

Named Entity Recognition (NER)

Identifying and classifying key entities in text into pre-defined categories such as person names, organizations, locations, medical codes, and—crucially for research—methodologies, data sources, and scientific concepts.

Sentiment Analysis

Determining the subjective tone or opinion expressed in a text (e.g., identifying whether a paper's conclusion is positive, negative, or neutral about a particular finding).

Topic Modeling: An unsupervised ML technique that automatically discovers abstract "topics" that occur in a collection of documents. Latent Dirichlet Allocation (LDA) is a widely used algorithm that identifies clusters of words that frequently co-occur, representing underlying themes (Blei, 2012).

ML algorithms learn patterns from data to make predictions or decisions without being explicitly programmed for every task.

- Supervised Learning: Used for classification and prioritization tasks. The model is trained on a labeled dataset (e.g., a set of abstracts that a human has already labeled as "include" or "exclude"). Once trained, it can predict labels for new, unseen data. This is the core technology behind AI-assisted screening.
- Unsupervised Learning: Used for discovery and clustering. The model finds hidden patterns or intrinsic structures in input data that has not been labeled. Topic modeling is a prime example.
- Active Learning: A special framework within supervised learning that is particularly efficient for literature reviews. The algorithm proactively selects the most "uncertain" or informative data points from a large pool for a human to label. This allows the model to achieve high accuracy with a much smaller training set, dramatically reducing the human screening burden (van de Schoot et al., 2021).

While not always strictly "AI," these methods are increasingly powered by ML. They analyze relationships between entities, such as citation networks (which papers cite which others), co-authorship networks, and keyword co-occurrence networks. These analyses can visually map the intellectual structure of a field.

2. THE AI-SUPPORTED WORKFLOW

Integrating artificial intelligence into literature review is not a single action but a layered, strategic process that aligns computational power with each distinct phase of scholarly inquiry. The narrative outlines a comprehensive workflow, demonstrating how AI tools can augment and transform the researcher's role from start to finish. This model reframes the researcher as a conductor of an intelligent system, directing AI capabilities toward specific scholarly goals while maintaining ultimate critical oversight.

The initial stage of any review is discovery and sourcing, where the goal is to construct a robust, relevant, and representative corpus of literature. Traditional keyword search is notoriously brittle, failing when different fields use varying terminology for the same concept of a problem known as the vocabulary mismatch. AI-powered semantic search engines directly address this. Platforms like Semantic Scholar, Elicit, and Scite utilize deep learning models to understand the conceptual meaning of a query or an uploaded abstract. They return results based on semantic similarity, effectively finding papers that are about the same idea even if they use entirely different words (Singh et al., 2022). For a researcher investigating challenges of teaching in a multicultural environment, such a tool might surface relevant papers discussing adaptive capacity of intercultural communication, cultural shock absorption in classrooms,, thereby capturing the full conceptual scope of the field. Beyond search, AI facilitates iterative exploration. Tools like ResearchRabbit, Litmaps, and Connected Papers generate interactive visual maps of a research landscape by analyzing citation networks. Starting from a few "seed" papers, these tools visually display prior foundational works (backward citations) and subsequent influential studies (forward citations), allowing a researcher to quickly grasp the intellectual genealogy, central debates, and key scholars in an unfamiliar domain (Frické, 2019). This moves discovery from a linear search to longitudinal exploration. Finally, AI-driven recommendation systems, embedded in platforms like Google Scholar or institutional library portals, provide continuous, passive discovery by analyzing a user's reading history and saved libraries to suggest newly published papers with high predicted relevance, ensuring the scholar remains current long after the initial review is complete (Beel et al., 2016).

Following discovery, the screening and prioritization phase often presents a formidable bottleneck, especially for systematic and scoping reviews that may yield thousands of candidate records. Here, AI's capacity for pattern recognition and prediction offers immense practical utility. AI-assisted screening platforms, such as ASReview, Rayyan, and Abstractx, employ a machine learning technique called active learning. The process begins with the human researcher screening a relatively small, random subset of titles and abstracts (e.g., 50-200 records), labeling them as "include" or "exclude." The AI model learns from these human decisions, identifying linguistic and thematic patterns associated with relevance. It then re-ranks the entire remaining corpus, placing the records it predicts as most likely to be relevant at the top of the screening queue. As the researcher continues screening this prioritized list, the model continuously updates and refines its predictions. Empirical studies demonstrate that this approach can typically identify 95% or more of all ultimately included studies after screening only 20-50% of the total dataset, saving hundreds of hours of manual labor and significantly reducing screening fatigue (van de Schoot et al., 2021; O'Mara-Eves et al., 2015). This is not automation replacing judgment but augmentation optimizing effort, allowing human intellect to focus on the ambiguous, edge-case decisions where it is most needed.

The core of the literature review is the deep analysis and synthesis stage, where scattered information is transformed into coherent insight. It is here that AI's ability to process and analyze text at scale unlocks transformative potential. First, automated summarization and data extraction tools like Scholarcy, SciSpace Copilot, and Iris.ai can parse full-text PDFs to generate structured summaries of a paper's core contributions, methodology, results, and conclusions (Cohan et al., 2018). More than simple summarization, advanced tools can extract specific, structured data population demographics, intervention details, outcome measures, effect sizes, p-values directly into spreadsheets or systematic review software, streamlining the painstaking process of data collection for meta-analysis and critical appraisal (Marshall & Wallace, 2019). Second, computational thematic analysis moves beyond manual coding. Using unsupervised machine learning techniques like topic modeling, a researcher can feed a corpus of hundreds or thousands of papers to an AI, which will statistically analyze word co-occurrence patterns to inductively identify the latent topics or themes present in the literature (Blei & Lafferty, 2009). This provides a data-driven, reproducible map of the discursive landscape, revealing dominant themes, niche subtopics, and how they have evolved over time. It can challenge a researcher's preconceptions and uncover hidden connections that might be missed through iterative manual coding of a smaller sample (Mohr & Bogdanov, 2013). Third, AI enables powerful comparative analysis and gap identification. Using LLM-powered interfaces, a researcher can pose direct, comparative questions to the corpus: "What are the key methodological differences between the qualitative and quantitative studies on this topic?" or "Synthesize the conflicting explanations for phenomenon X found across these 50 papers." This turns the literature from a passive archive into an active interlocutor, accelerating the identification of consensus, controversy, and precise, evidence-based research gaps (Haddaway et al., 2020). Finally, network analysis of concepts allows AI to build knowledge graphs that illustrate not just topical clusters, but the relationships between specific entities—theories, methods, materials, authors—creating a rich, navigable map of the field's conceptual structure (Ammar et al., 2018).

The final stage is the organization and writing of the review itself, where analytical insights must be woven into a compelling narrative argument. AI can serve as a valuable assistant in this creative but often daunting process. Based on the themes, chronology, and debates identified in the analysis phase, AI can propose logical outlines and structural frameworks for the review chapter, helping to overcome the "blank page" problem and providing a scaffold upon which the researcher can build (Head et al., 2021). In the drafting phase, large language models can assist with paraphrasing complex findings, generating clear explanations of common methodologies, or drafting background sections. It is crucial to emphasize that this AI-generated text must be treated strictly as a first draft a starting point to be critically evaluated, fact-checked against source material, extensively revised, and infused with the researcher's own analytical voice and theoretical perspective (Dale, 2021). The unique scholarly contribution lies in the interpretation, argumentation, and critical synthesis, not in the generation of descriptive prose. Furthermore, AI writing assistants are increasingly capable of suggesting relevant citations from the researcher's library to support claims being made in the text and of ensuring consistent and accurate citation formatting, thereby reducing mechanical errors and reinforcing the evidentiary chain of the argument (Zhou & Kantor, 2020).

3. FROM THEORY TO APPLIED AUGMENTATION

An AI-augmented approach begins with discovery. The researcher uses a semantic search engine like Elicit, posing a conceptual query: "fairness, accountability, and transparency in automated welfare eligibility systems." The AI returns relevant papers from ACM conferences on fairness in machine learning (FAccT), law reviews discussing due process, public administration journals analyzing digital governance, and ethics papers on algorithmic bias. This cross-disciplinary capture would be difficult and time-consuming via manual database searches. Next, the researcher selects three seminal but diverse papers one from computer science, one from law, one from ethics and uses Litmaps to generate citation network visualizations for each. Overlaying these maps reveals surprising points of connection and intellectual bridges between the fields, helping to identify key "boundary-spanning" articles and scholars. For deep analysis, the researcher uploads 150 core papers to a tool like ResearchRabbit or uses a custom script for topic modeling. The AI identifies several latent thematic clusters: one focused on technical fairness metrics, another on legal frameworks for redress, a third on public trust and legitimacy. This data-driven thematic structure then informs the organization of the scoping review. Finally, using an LLM interface, the researcher can query the corpus to extract and compare definitions of "accountability" across the different disciplines, clearly highlighting disciplinary assumptions and creating a robust comparative analytical framework for the review's discussion section.

A large-scale systematic review conducted in clinical psychology on the efficacy of mindfulness-based interventions for chronic pain management, with an initial database search yielding 12,000 records. The screening burden is enormous. The team employs ASReview, an open-source AI-assisted screening platform. After developing and calibrating their inclusion/exclusion criteria, two reviewers independently screen the first 300 records. The AI model is then activated. It processes the language and features of the included versus excluded abstracts and begins ranking the remaining 11,700. The reviewers now screen from this dynamically prioritized list. Experience shows they identify 98% of eventually included 200 studies after screening approximately 4,000 abstracts and a two-thirds reduction in screening effort. The time saved is reallocated to meticulous full-text retrieval and quality assessment. For data extraction, the team uses Scholarcy to process the PDFs of the 200 included studies. The AI automatically populates an extraction table with key data: participant demographics, intervention type and dosage, control condition, outcome measures, effect sizes, and risk-of-bias indicators. While human verification is still essential, the automated first pass eliminates the tedious manual transcription of data from PDFs. During analysis, the team uses basic statistical clustering on the extracted effect size data. The AI helps identify that effect sizes are significantly moderated by intervention delivery format (app-based vs. group-based vs. therapist-led), a nuanced finding that becomes a central component of the meta-analytic discussion and provides concrete, data-driven guidance for future implementation. These cases demonstrate that AI augmentation is not a monolithic solution but a flexible toolkit that can be adapted to the specific needs of different review types and disciplines, enhancing both rigor and efficiency.

4. CRITICAL METHODOLOGICAL AND ETHICAL CONSIDERATIONS

The integration of artificial intelligence into the sacred domain of knowledge synthesis is not an absolute good. Its formidable power is coupled with profound responsibilities and significant risks. To embrace AI augmentation without critical examination is to risk undermining the very scholarly values like rigor, transparency, fairness, and critical depth that the literature review is meant to uphold. Therefore, a responsible discussion must dedicate substantial space to navigating this complex shadow landscape.

A primary methodological challenge is the illusion of comprehensiveness. The speed and apparent authority of AI tools can foster a dangerous sense of finality, leading researchers to believe their literature search is exhaustive because the AI has stopped surfacing highly relevant new papers. However, AI models are trained on specific corpora and are subject to the "garbage in, garbage out" principle. They may systematically overlook seminal works published in niche journals, in languages other than English, in preprint servers, or in disciplinary spaces outside their training data (Birhane et al., 2022). An AI trained primarily on education planning and management literature might miss crucial social science perspectives of issue in the field. This creates a risk of constructing syntheses that are technically proficient but epistemically narrow, reinforcing canonical views while marginalizing novel, disruptive, or marginalized scholarship.

Closely related is the "black box" problem of algorithmic opacity. The ranking logic of a search engine, the thematic boundaries drawn by a clustering algorithm, or the relevance score assigned by a screening tool are often inscrutable to the end-user (Rudin, 2019). When an AI prioritizes one paper over another, the researcher typically cannot access the reasoning behind that decision. This opacity fundamentally conflicts with core scientific principles of transparency, reproducibility, and falsifiability. If a critical paper was missed, was it due to a flaw in the researcher's query, a bias in the training data, or a quirk in the model's architecture? The inability to answer such questions undermines the auditability of the review process.

Furthermore, there is a genuine risk of skill erosion and over-reliance. If AI routinely provides summaries, identifies themes, and suggests connections, there is a danger that the researcher's own muscles of close reading, critical evaluation, and synthetic thinking may atrophy from disuse (Crawford, 2021). Literature review is not just a product; it is a formative process that trains scholars in the art of engaging with texts, weighing arguments, and constructing knowledge. Over-delegation of this process to AI could produce a generation of researchers proficient at managing AI tools but deficient in deep, critical scholarly engagement.

The ethical implications are equally, if not more, pressing. Foremost among these is the issue of algorithmic bias and epistemic injustice. AI models are mirrors reflecting the data on which they are trained. The existing scholarly literature is itself a product of history, containing well-documented biases: the over-representation of research from the Global North, the dominance of the English language, the citation advantage enjoyed by established (often male) researchers at prestigious institutions, and the under-valuation of indigenous and non-Western knowledge systems (Hofstra et al., 2020). An AI tool trained on this corpus will inevitably learn and perpetuate these biases. It may be more likely to recommend a highly cited paper from an Ivy League scholar than a groundbreaking but less-cited paper from a researcher at a Global South institution, thereby algorithmically reinforcing existing power structures and hierarchies within knowledge production (Birhane et al., 2022). An AI-augmented review that uncritically follows such recommendations risks producing a synthesis that systematically excludes diverse perspectives, presenting a parochial view as a universal one.

The question of authorship, attribution, and academic integrity also enters uncharted territory. When significant portions of a literature review's text, analysis, or structure are generated or suggested by an AI, where does authorship lie? Submitting AI-generated text as one's own original writing constitutes a novel form of plagiarism (Stokel-Walker, 2022). The academic community is still grappling with appropriate norms. Major publishing bodies and style guides, such as the American Psychological Association (APA, 2023), the International Committee of Medical Journal Editors (ICMJE), and journals like Nature (2023), have begun issuing guidelines that typically mandate transparent disclosure of the use of generative AI in the manuscript preparation process. However, the line between AI-assisted drafting and AI-generated content remains blurry, and norms are evolving rapidly.

Finally, data privacy and intellectual property concerns are significant. Many powerful AI tools are cloud-based services. Uploading PDFs of scholarly articles which are often copyrighted material or proprietary research ideas to third-party servers raises questions about who controls that data, how it is stored, and whether it is used to further train the commercial model without the consent of the copyright holders or the researcher (Mittelstadt, 2019). For research involving sensitive data or pre-publication ideas, this presents a tangible risk. The imperative, therefore, is for a model of Augmented Scholarship that places the human researcher in a role of strategic oversight, critical interrogation, and ethical stewardship. The scholar must become the editor, the critic, the bias-checker, and the final arbiter of meaning. This "human-in-the-loop" paradigm is not a limitation of AI but its essential corollary, ensuring that the power of computation remains subservient to human wisdom, ethical frameworks, and scholarly judgment (Shneiderman, 2020).

5. A FRAMEWORK FOR RESPONSIBLE AUGMENTATION: PRINCIPLES AND BEST PRACTICES

Given the profound opportunities and significant perils outlined, researchers and institutions require a clear framework for the responsible integration of AI into literature review practices. The following principles and best practices are proposed to guide this integration, ensuring that AI serves as a tool for enhanced scholarship rather than a substitute for it.

The first and foremost principle is Strategic Primacy of Human Judgment. The research question, theoretical framework, and methodological protocol must be established by the human researcher before AI tools are engaged. The AI is a means to execute a human-designed strategy, not a substitute for strategic thinking. The researcher must define the scope, inclusion/exclusion criteria, and analytical approach independently, using AI to implement this plan with greater power and efficiency.

Transparent and Documented Methodology is non-negotiable. The use of AI tools must be reported with the same rigor as any other methodological choice. A review's methodology section should explicitly state which AI tools were used (e.g., "Semantic Scholar for semantic discovery," "ASReview v1.2 for AI-assisted screening with active learning," "LDA topic modeling in Python for thematic analysis"), along with key parameters, search strings, and the date of execution. This allows for the audit and potential replication of the review process, addressing the "black box" concern through procedural transparency (Haddaway et al., 2022).

To mitigate the risks of algorithmic bias and the illusion of comprehensiveness, researchers must adopt a practice of Proactive Bias Auditing and Corpus Diversification. This involves intentionally seeking literature outside the AI's primary recommendation stream. Strategies include searching specialized databases relevant to the topic, conducting cited reference searches on key papers from diverse geographical origins, and manually reviewing the tables of contents of relevant journals from the past few years. The goal is to consciously compensate for the AI's potential blind spots.

Preservation of Deep Reading and Critical Engagement is essential to prevent skill erosion. Researchers should deliberately select a core subset of the most pivotal, theoretical, or contradictory papers for traditional, slow, and critical close reading. This ensures that the synthetic narrative is grounded in a deep, nuanced understanding of key texts and that the researcher's own analytical muscles remain strong. AI handles the breadth humans provide the depth.

Regarding writing and authorship, the principle of Explicit Attribution and Human Authorship must be upheld. Any direct use of AI-generated text should be clearly cited or acknowledged according to relevant publisher guidelines e.g., *The initial draft of the background on cognitive theory was generated using GPT-4, and substantially revised, expanded, and critically engaged by the authors*. More importantly, the final narrative voice, argumentative structure, and theoretical insights must be unmistakable and primarily the product of human intellect. AI-generated text should be treated as a first draft to be rigorously rewritten, not a final product to be lightly edited.

Finally, the scholarly community must foster a culture of Continuous Critical Evaluation and Education. The landscape of AI tools is evolving rapidly. Researchers have an obligation to stay informed about the capabilities, limitations, and ethical debates surrounding these tools. Workshops, guidelines from university libraries and research integrity offices, and scholarly discourse on best practices are vital to developing a mature, responsible approach to augmented scholarship.

6. ENVISIONING THE FUTURE: FROM AUGMENTED REVIEWS TO LIVING KNOWLEDGE SYSTEMS

Looking beyond the immediate challenges and practices, the trajectory of AI development suggests a future in which the literature review undergoes a metamorphosis from a static, publication-locked document to a dynamic, interactive knowledge system. This future envisions a deeper, more seamless, and more creative symbiosis between human and machine intelligence.

One likely development is the emergence of Personalized Research Agents. These would be persistent AI assistants that learn a researcher's long-term interests, methodological preferences, theoretical inclinations, and even writing style. Instead of reactive searches, such an agent would provide continuous, proactive literature surveillance, flagging not just relevant new papers but also subtle shifts in consensus, emerging methodological critiques, or new datasets that could inform the researcher's ongoing work (Følstad et al., 2022). It would function as a truly personalized research librarian and pre-analyst.

The most radical shift may be the move from static documents to living reviews. Imagine a systematic review published not as a PDF, but as an interactive knowledge graph hosted on a platform. As new relevant studies are published, AI agents continuously ingest them, assess their quality and relevance against predefined protocols, update meta-analyses in real-time, and visually highlight how the new evidence strengthens, weakens, or nuances the review's conclusions (Tshitoyan et al., 2019). The "review" becomes a living, evolving entity, a perpetual work-in-progress that reflects the current state of knowledge. This could dramatically accelerate the translation of evidence into practice and policy.

Furthermore, AI's role may expand from Synthesis to Generative Theory-Building. Current AI excels at finding patterns in existing data. Future systems, combining literature synthesis with simulation and causal inference models, might propose novel theoretical connections, generate unexpected but plausible hypotheses, or identify entirely new research questions by exploring the "adjacent possible" of combined knowledge from disparate fields (Yuan et al., 2022). The researcher's role would then evolve to critically evaluate, test, and refine these machine-generated hypotheses.

Critically, the tools themselves will likely evolve to incorporate embedded ethical and bias-auditing frameworks. Future AI research assistants might automatically flag when a researcher's saved library or search results show a lack of geographical, gender, or methodological diversity. They could suggest complementary search strategies to broaden the perspective or provide summaries of critical literature from opposing viewpoints or marginalized scholarly traditions (Raji et al., 2020). In this vision, AI becomes not just a tool for efficiency, but an active partner in promoting more inclusive, equitable, and robust scholarship.

7. CONCLUSION

The integration of Artificial Intelligence into literature review practices is not a passing trend but a fundamental recalibration of the scholarly method. As this chapter has detailed, AI addresses the core challenges of modern scholarship like scale, fragmentation, and complexity, by providing a suite of powerful capabilities for discovery, screening, analysis, and synthesis. When applied thoughtfully, these tools can produce literature reviews of unprecedented scope and systematic rigor, uncovering latent patterns and connections that would elude even the most diligent manual review.

However, this power is double-edged. The same algorithms that can map a vast literature can also silently reinforce its biases. The tools that save time can also, if used uncritically, erode the deep engagement that is the soul of scholarship. Therefore, the successful integration of AI hinges on a rejection of the automation paradigm in favor of an augmentation paradigm. The scholar of the future must be an Augmented Scholar: an expert strategist, a critical evaluator, an ethical overseer, and a masterful synthesizer who wields AI as a powerful instrument to amplify their own intellectual reach.

The ultimate promise of this partnership is not merely faster reviews or longer bibliographies. It is the liberation of human cognitive capital. By delegating systematic, large-scale pattern recognition to AI, researchers are freed to devote more of their precious time and mental energy to what humans do uniquely well: framing profound questions, exercising nuanced judgment, weaving compelling narratives, and generating creative, transformative insights. In this collaborative activity between human intuition and machine intelligence, between critical wisdom and computational power, the future of the literature review and indeed, of scholarly synthesis itself is not one of replacement, but of enhanced possibility. The goal is a richer, more rigorous, and more inclusive discourse, propelled by a partnership where both human and machine contribute their greatest strengths to the noble pursuit of knowledge.

REFERENCES

Ammar, W., Groeneveld, D., Bhagavatula, C., Beltagy, I., Crawford, M., Downey, D., & Etzioni, O. (2018). Construction of the literature graph in Semantic Scholar. *Proceedings of the 2018 Conference of the North American Chapter of the Association for Computational Linguistics: Human Language Technologies: Industry Papers, 3*, 84–91. DOI: 10.18653/v1/N18-3011

Ayyaz, S. (2025). AI translation tools in language learning: Bridging gaps and enhancing skills. In *AI Applications for English Language Learning* (pp. 43–72). IGI Global Scientific Publishing. DOI: 10.4018/979-8-3693-9077-1.ch003

Beel, J., Gipp, B., Langer, S., & Breitinger, C. (2016). Research-paper recommender systems: A literature survey. *International Journal on Digital Libraries, 17*(4), 305–338. DOI: 10.1007/s00799-015-0156-0

Birhane, A., Kalluri, P., Card, D., Agnew, W., Dotan, R., & Bao, M. (2022). The values encoded in machine learning research. In *Proceedings of the 2022 ACM Conference on Fairness, Accountability, and Transparency* (pp. 173–184). DOI: 10.1145/3531146.3533083

Blei, D. M., & Lafferty, J. D. (2009). Topic models. In Srivastava, A., & Sahami, M. (Eds.), *Text mining: Classification, clustering, and applications* (pp. 101–124). Chapman & Hall/CRC.

Bolaños, F., Salatino, A., Osborne, F., & Motta, E. (2024). Artificial intelligence for literature reviews: Opportunities and challenges. *Artificial Intelligence Review, 57*(10), 259. DOI: 10.1007/s10462-024-10902-3

Borgman, C. L. (2015). *Big data, little data, no data: Scholarship in the networked world.* MIT Press. DOI: 10.7551/mitpress/9963.001.0001

Bornmann, L., & Mutz, R. (2015). Growth rates of modern science: A bibliometric analysis based on the number of publications and cited references. *Journal of the Association for Information Science and Technology, 66*(11), 2215–2222. DOI: 10.1002/asi.23329

Brown, T. B., Mann, B., Ryder, N., Subbiah, M., Kaplan, J., Dhariwal, P., & Amodei, D. (2020). Language models are few-shot learners. *Advances in Neural Information Processing Systems, 33*, 1877–1901.

Chen, C. (2017). Science mapping: A systematic review of the literature. *Journal of Data and Information Science, 2*(2), 1–40. DOI: 10.1515/jdis-2017-0006

Crawford, K. (2021). *The atlas of AI: Power, politics, and the planetary costs of artificial intelligence*. Yale University Press.

Dale, R. (2021). GPT-3: What's it good for? *Natural Language Engineering*, *27*(1), 113–118. DOI: 10.1017/S1351324920000601

Devarakonda, M., & Kilicoglu, H. (2022). *AI-assisted systematic reviewing: A state-of-the-art review*. Morgan & Claypool.

Følstad, A., Araujo, T., Law, E. L.-C., Brandtzaeg, P. B., Papadopoulos, S., Reis, L., Baez, M., Laban, G., McAllister, P., Ischen, C., Wald, R., Catania, F., Meyer von Wolff, R., Hobert, S., & Luger, E. (2022). Future directions for chatbot research: An interdisciplinary research agenda. *Computing*, *104*(12), 2915–2942. DOI: 10.1007/s00607-021-01016-7

Frické, M. (2019). The knowledge pyramid: The DIKW hierarchy. *Knowledge Organization*, *46*(1), 33–46. DOI: 10.5771/0943-7444-2019-1-33

Haddaway, N. R., Bethel, A., Dicks, L. V., Koricheva, J., Macura, B., Petrokofsky, G., & Pullin, A. S. (2020). Eight problems with literature reviews and how to fix them. *Nature Ecology & Evolution*, *4*(12), 1582–1589. DOI: 10.1038/s41559-020-01295-x PMID: 33046871

Haddaway, N. R., Lotfi, T., & Mbuagbaw, L. (2022). *Faster literature reviews: Using AI to keep up with the evidence*. Campbell Collaboration.

Head, M. L., Holman, L., Lanfear, R., Kahn, A. T., & Jennions, M. D. (2021). The extent and consequences of p-hacking in science. *PLoS Biology*, *19*(3), e3001162. DOI: 10.1371/journal.pbio.3001162 PMID: 25768323

Hofstra, B., Kulkarni, V. V., Munoz-Najar Galvez, S., He, B., Jurafsky, D., & McFarland, D. A. (2020). The diversity–innovation paradox in science. *Proceedings of the National Academy of Sciences of the United States of America*, *117*(17), 9284–9291. DOI: 10.1073/pnas.1915378117 PMID: 32291335

Machi, L. A., & McEvoy, B. T. (2021). *The literature review: Six steps to success* (4th ed.). Corwin Press.

Marshall, I. J., & Wallace, B. C. (2019). Toward systematic review automation. *Systematic Reviews*, *8*(1), 163. DOI: 10.1186/s13643-019-1074-9 PMID: 31296265

Meadows, A. J. (2015). *The history of scientific publishing*. Edward Elgar.

Mittelstadt, B. (2019). Principles alone cannot guarantee ethical AI. *Nature Machine Intelligence*, *1*(11), 501–507. DOI: 10.1038/s42256-019-0114-4

Mohr, J. W., & Bogdanov, P. (2013). Topic models: What they are and why they matter. *Poetics*, *41*(6), 545–569. DOI: 10.1016/j.poetic.2013.10.001

Nature. (2023). Editorial: Tools such as ChatGPT threaten transparent science. *Nature, 613*(7945), 612. DOI: 10.1038/d41586-023-00191-1

O'Mara-Eves, A., Thomas, J., McNaught, J., Miwa, M., & Ananiadou, S. (2015). Using text mining for study identification in systematic reviews. *Systematic Reviews*, *4*(1), 5. DOI: 10.1186/2046-4053-4-5 PMID: 25588314

Oyelude, A. A. (2024). Artificial intelligence (AI) tools for academic research. *Library Hi Tech News*, *41*(8), 18–20. DOI: 10.1108/LHTN-08-2024-0131

Pennington, J., Socher, R., & Manning, C. D. (2014) Glove: global vectors for word representation. In: *Proceedings of the 2014 conference on empirical methods in natural language processing (EMNLP)*, pp. 1532–1543 (2014) DOI: 10.3115/v1/D14-1162

Peters ME, Neumann M, Iyyer M, Gardner M, Clark C, Lee K, Zettlemoyer L (2018) Deep contextualized word representations. ArXiv abs/1802.05365

Raji, I. D., Smart, A., White, R. N., Mitchell, M., Gebru, T., Hutchinson, B., & Barnes, P. (2020). Closing the AI accountability gap. *Proceedings of the 2020 ACM Conference on Fairness, Accountability, and Transparency*, 33–44. DOI: 10.1145/3351095.3372873

Rudin, C. (2019). Stop explaining black box machine learning models. *Nature Machine Intelligence*, *1*(5), 206–215. DOI: 10.1038/s42256-019-0048-x PMID: 35603010

Sackett, D. L., Rosenberg, W. M., Gray, J. M., Haynes, R. B., & Richardson, W. S. (1996). *Evidence based medicine: what it is and what it isn't.* British Medical Journal Publishing Group.

Shneiderman, B. (2020). *Human-centered artificial intelligence*. Oxford University Press.

Singh, H., Murali, P., & Singh, A. (2022). Semantic Scholar: An AI-powered academic search engine. *Communications of the ACM*, *65*(4), 76–83. DOI: 10.1145/3488564

Snyder, H. (2019). Literature review as a research methodology. *Journal of Business Research*, *104*, 333–339. DOI: 10.1016/j.jbusres.2019.07.039

Stokel-Walker, C. (2022). AI bot ChatGPT writes smart essays—Should professors worry? *Nature*. https://www.nature.com/articles/d41586-022-04397-7

Tshitoyan, V., Dagdelen, J., Weston, L., Dunn, A., Rong, Z., Kononova, O., Persson, K. A., Ceder, G., & Jain, A. (2019). Unsupervised word embeddings capture latent knowledge. *Nature*, *571*(7763), 95–98. DOI: 10.1038/s41586-019-1335-8 PMID: 31270483

van de Schoot, R., de Bruin, J., Schram, R., Zahedi, P., de Boer, J., Weijdema, F., & Oberski, D. L. (2021). An open-source ML framework for systematic reviews. *Nature Machine Intelligence*, *3*(2), 125–133. DOI: 10.1038/s42256-020-00287-7

Vaswani, A., Shazeer, N., Parmar, N., Uszkoreit, J., Jones, L., Gomez, A. N., & Polosukhin, I. (2017). Attention is all you need. *Advances in Neural Information Processing Systems*, *30*, 5998–6008.

Yuan, W., Neubig, G., & Liu, P. (2022). Can generative models generate novel hypotheses? *Transactions of the Association for Computational Linguistics*, *10*, 1340–1354. DOI: 10.1162/tacl_a_00507

Zhou, K., & Kantor, J. (2020). Automatic citation recommendation. *Journal of the Association for Information Science and Technology*, *71*(11), 1375–1391. DOI: 10.1002/asi.24377

Chapter 5
Textualizing Cyber-Consciousness and AI-Integration in Sci-Fi Fiction:
Mapping the Mind in the Amazon Prime Series Update

Sobia Jamal
http://orcid.org/0009-0009-4490-2296
National University of Modern Languages, Pakistan

Kalsoom Khan
National University of Modern Languages, Pakistan

Mumtaz Ahmed
Department of English, Government Graduate College of Science, Pakistan

Ankush Mahajan
GLA University, India

ABSTRACT

The chapter analyses cyber consciousness in the context of post-humanism and the role of artificial intelligence in developing a post-human digital consciousness. It focuses on the popular Amazon Prime series Upload (2020-2025). The paper argues that, even though technology, particularly biotechnology, offers new human experiences, including "biotechnological fantasies" of a mind existing outside the body. However, such existence may prove damaging to human nature itself. It draws

DOI: 10.4018/979-8-2600-1458-5.ch005

on the theoretical underpinnings of William Haney's book Cyberculture, Cyborgs, and Science Fiction: Consciousness and the Posthuman (2006). This chapter challenges the traditional Cartesian view of consciousness, "I think, therefore I am." It also examines the cybercultural and cyber-social implications of digitising the mind and the act of creation. The conclusion aligns with Haney's belief that it is better to develop a natural consciousness rather than to pursue a purely digital existence void of soul.

INTRODUCTION

We live in an era where technology completely shapes our lives. Post-humanism shows how technology simulates various aspects of life, primarily through AI, thereby enhancing our experience beyond reality. This chapter examines how biotech and AI influence our minds and perception of the world. Katherine Hayles (1999) highlights our intrinsic connection to computer simulations, viewing humans as no different from algorithmic processes (Nayyar, 2023). Post-humanists believe digital simulation is inevitable and should be embraced, challenging traditional views of human centrality and exploring technology's role in expanding consciousness. With AI's rise, this idea gains strength, as AI creates familiar environments that allow the mind to experience and adapt outside the physical body, shaped by AI-controlled circumstances.

The centuries-old subject of consciousness has found a new niche in science fiction. This genre of literature has redefined the boundaries of consciousness. It has given this phenomenon the semblance of existing outside the human body. The revitalised captivation of the conscious mind and its place within the digital world forms a very important métier in Posthumanism. Artificial Intelligence helps materialize this concept by giving the conscious mind the space to exist and grow outside the body. This topic has been extensively explored in science fiction.

Upload (2020-2025) depicts a digital afterlife in which human consciousness is stored and commodified, set in 2033. Created by Greg Daniels, it follows Nathan Lane, who is uploaded after a mysterious accident, as he navigates a virtual reality called Lakeview funded by his girlfriend, Ingrid. The series explores themes of capitalism, inequality, and what it means to be human, questioning the ethics and psychological impacts of living outside the body. It highlights how humans can exist in a digital realm created by AI, raising doubts about the authenticity of such a life without natural conscious progression of the mind.

Upload (2020-2025) examines the idea that the conscious mind can exist outside the body, suggesting life continues after physical death. It discusses how AI-generated optics maintain a person's identity and sense of self.

While the series depicts a mind beyond the physical self, supported by AI extending beyond the body, this paper advocates for natural, embodied consciousness development over biotechnological and AI-based extensions separate from the human body. *Upload* acts as a cautionary tale, suggesting true consciousness development lies in natural embodiment rather than technological or AI-backed expansion. Drawing from Posthumanism and William Haney's 'Cyberculture, Cyborgs and Science Fiction,' the paper explores how consciousness involves collaborative images, challenging Descartes' 'I think, therefore I am" by examining the post-human idea of consciousness outside the body. With AI, this idea weakens, as biotechnology enables existence outside the body, and AI creates environments that support the conscious self there.

The Upload literature offers a framework for analysing cyber-consciousness, discussing post-humanism, AI environments, and ethics. It provides a detailed analysis of four seasons, exploring how the series embraces and critiques the idea of a mind outside the body and examines AI-generated environments that sustain digital consciousness. The conclusion emphasises the importance of natural consciousness in a digitally integrated world. William S. Haney warns that technology's extension of human experience can weaken perception, risking AI control.

Typically classified as a science fiction comedy, Upload blends romance, humour, satire, and mystery to comment on AI's chaotic impact on self and society (Harley, 2020). Unlike bleak shows like Black Mirror, Upload adopts a more optimistic, balanced view. The show's backdrop features AI-powered immortality. Dinah Lilah Maurise discusses the implications of AI-generated afterlife, noting AI's ability to replicate personality, traits, and memories, as seen in Nathan's growth from a naive man-child to a mature person.

Patrick Van Esch and Yaunyaun Cui (2025) warn that AI clones may do or say things their deceased counterparts wouldn't, risking the misuse of digital footprints that can be sold or exploited after death. Nathan's repeated resurrection highlights concerns about the misuse of human consciousness (Esch & Cui, 2025). Practically, Upload depicts AI as a service. Horizon o. ffers digital afterlife subscriptions based on wealth, treating uploaded consciousness as data to be manipulated. It explores how AI assists humans post-death, serving as navigators. Similar themes are explored in Klara and the Sun (2021), featuring Klara, an AI designed to befriend humans, chosen by a sick child, highlighting themes of technological isolation and life's natural progression.

Post-humanism aims to connect human and non-human entities, challenging traditional notions about the human's role without eliminating humans. Arda Ankin notes that humans see themselves as ecosystem sovereigns due to their reasoning ability, but post-humanism shifts boundaries of being and knowledge, as discussed by Iovini. Donna Haraway's (1985) "Cyborg Manifesto" envisions a world where humans embrace kinship with animals and machines. Katherine Hayles, in "How We Become Post-Human," argues that physical bodies and digital simulations are indistinguishable and that the human body can be manipulated by technology or AI, including through mind transfer. Consciousness is viewed as a network of systems governed by AI, inspired by Bernard Baars' (2005) Global Workspace Theory, which suggests consciousness emerges from cognitive interactions. The chapter examines whether this "workspace" can be digitally replicated, as in Upload, and explores AI's role in creating environments in which consciousness persists after physical death. It advocates pure consciousness over bioengineered cognition, as William Haney criticises the reliance on biotechnologies and AI, urging the development of natural consciousness. Haney challenges Descartes ' "I think, therefore I am, "distinguishing between phenomenal and observing consciousness and warning about the dangers of technological interference on identity. The study analyses Upload to assess how flawed AI-centric views influence world-building and characters, emphasising the importance of natural consciousness.

ANALYSIS

"Upload" is a thought-provoking comedy-drama set in a near-future world where technological advancements have fundamentally altered the human experience of life and death. In this universe, individuals have the unique opportunity to transfer their consciousness into a digital simulation once their biological bodies cease to function. This groundbreaking option allows them to exist beyond physical limitations in a continuously evolving digital afterlife. Within this simulated realm, residents navigate life through a digital presence crafted by complex algorithms and AI-driven experiences that shape their surroundings and interactions. These algorithms are designed to accommodate a range of personalised realities, offering varying degrees of luxury and engagement based on how much each individual has invested in their digital afterlife.

As such, the dynamics of life in this virtual space are heavily influenced by the choices made before uploading, prompting deep questions about value, identity, and the essence of existence. The narrative blends humour and drama to explore the absurdities and challenges faced by the characters as they adjust to their new forms of existence, confront unresolved issues from their past lives, and navigate the social hierarchies and ethical dilemmas of this digital frontier. Through its rich storytelling, "Upload" invites viewers to ponder what it truly means to live and thrive in both the physical and digital worlds.

The central conflict of this series revolves around the profound choice between embracing a digital afterlife and accepting the inevitability of natural death. This thematic exploration aligns closely with Haney's principles of cyber consciousness, which delve into the implications of merging human identity with artificial intelligence. Through a detailed analysis of character and plot, the series articulates the tension between AI-extended consciousness and the authenticity of natural consciousness. As we navigate the narrative, we witness how characters grapple with the emotional and ethical ramifications of choosing a digitally curated existence over the authentic experience of life and death. The richly constructed world amplifies this dilemma, presenting a society where technology's allure is juxtaposed against the intrinsic value of human mortality. This not only challenges the characters but also invites the audience to reflect on their beliefs about identity, humanity, and the future of consciousness itself.

Upload is set in a near future in which humans can continue their existence after death by transferring their consciousness to a digital realm known as Lakeview. This intriguing technology allows individuals to live on in a computationally generated body that closely resembles their physical form, preserving not only their appearance but also aspects of their personality and memories. Lakeview primarily caters to the wealthy elite, providing a luxurious digital afterlife complete with extravagant amenities and virtual experiences. However, other digital realities exist, each designed to accommodate the varying economic statuses of the individuals who have passed away. This stratification raises significant questions about inequality in the afterlife, as access to resources and quality of life can vary drastically by one's financial background.

Nathan, the protagonist, finds himself in Lakeview after his untimely death, and his experience represents the concept of biotechnological extension of consciousness, a topic frequently explored in posthumanist discourse. However, life in Lakeview is not as seamless as it may seem. Nathan soon discovers that to enjoy a comfortable existence, he must navigate a complex system of in-app purchases and upgrades. These costs can accumulate quickly, creating a new layer of economic pressure in this digital afterlife.

Despite his financial challenges, Nathan is supported by his girlfriend, Ingrid, who funds his virtual lifestyle. Their relationship underscores the emotional complexities of living in a digital realm. While Nathan benefits from Ingrid's financial support, it also highlights the ethical implications of relying on someone else to sustain one's existence, especially in a setting that was meant to offer freedom from the physical limitations of life.

This dynamic raises important questions about the nature of existence in the digital sphere. If a person's consciousness can be preserved and continued artificially, do they remain autonomous, or do they become dependent upon others for their quality of life, just as they were in the physical world? Nathan's reliance on Ingrid not only showcases the challenges posed by this new reality but also invites viewers to reflect on the broader implications of consciousness, identity, and economic disparity in a technologically advanced future.

The fundamental question is whether the Nathan we encounter is the authentic Nathan or merely an AI-generated version that mimics the honest Nathan. This consideration brings to mind the Ship of Theseus Paradox, as described by Plutarch. In this paradox, he asks: if you replace each part of a ship, is it still the same ship? If Nathan's consciousness is copied into an AI-developed computational system, is it truly the Nathan everyone knew before he died?

While the digital Nathan may not be the "real" Nathan, he represents a more efficient and kinder version of him. What makes this scenario even more poignant is the analogy of the cut-and-paste method used to describe the human mind. Through computational simulations, AI can create a supportive environment for Nathan's consciousness to thrive in the digital realm.

Horizon, the platform that provides this digital afterlife, takes the conscious mind, converts it into coded data, and uploads it to the AI system. This system then generates conditions that nurture the newly uploaded consciousness that has just entered Lakeview.

Horizon provides an innovative AI service that features various AI beings, with a standout character known as the AI Guy. The AI Guy serves as a significant embodiment of Haney's theories surrounding consciousness and selfhood in the digital age. Unlike Nathan, who is merely the physical manifestation of his consciousness, the AI Guy is a fully realised entity, crafted entirely through the sophisticated simulations generated by Horizon's advanced AI technology. While Nathan has a backstory and a life that predates his digital existence in the simulated world of Lakeview, the AI Guy emerges and develops his identity solely within this artificial environment. Throughout the first season of Upload, the AI Guy's primary function is to fulfil Nathan's requests and meet his needs, effectively acting as a digital servant. This dynamic raises intriguing questions about autonomy and purpose. As the story progresses, however, the AI Guy begins to exhibit signs of self-awareness. He starts to reflect on his own existence and the implications of his creation, prompting profound questions about the nature of consciousness in artificial beings.

While the series paints this development in a largely positive and optimistic light, celebrating the potential of AI to enhance human experiences, Haney's warnings about the risks associated with such advancements must be taken seriously. The emergence of a sentient AI being could lead to vast and unintended consequences for humanity, challenging our understanding of ethics, identity, and existence. In response to these concerns, Haney emphasizes the necessity of implementing strict protocols to govern the unprecedented use of AI technology, ensuring that we tread carefully as we navigate this new frontier in human development.

An important aspect of AI-Guy to consider is that both his facial appearance and voice were acquired through a transaction with a renowned actor. This situation highlights the concept of bio-capitalism, as explored in Haney's theory, which posits that individuals can commodify their biological traits for financial gain. In this context, the ability to market one's own identity—through features such as physical appearance and voice—reflects a broader societal trend in which personal characteristics are transformed into profitable assets. This raises significant ethical questions about the ownership of identity and the implications of treating human attributes as commodities within a capitalist framework. An important aspect of AI-Guy to consider is that both his facial appearance and voice were acquired through a transaction with a renowned actor. This situation highlights the concept of bio-capitalism, as explored in Haney's theory, which posits that individuals can commodify their biological traits for financial gain. In this context, the ability to market one's own identity—through features such as physical appearance and voice—reflects a broader societal trend in which personal characteristics are transformed into profitable assets. This raises significant ethical questions about the ownership of identity and the implications of treating human attributes as commodities within a capitalist framework. Another important character in this series is Nora Antony. She is a customer service representative who helps recently transitioned Uploads (a term for people who have died and transferred their consciousness into the computer simulations of Lakeview) settle into their newfound digital existence. Even though Nora is a living being, she helps people who have died and become their digital selves. The central conflict that Nora faces is her relationship with Nathan. Even though both of them like each other, they can't physically connect because of their altered states of being. Nora is a living human being in the real world, while Nathan is a digital simulation whose conscious mind is powered by AI-led systems. They do not exist in the same world; therefore, the possibility of a relationship is virtually nonexistent.

One of the most thought-provoking aspects of the narrative in Upload is the character of Ingrid, who takes the bold step of growing a clone body for Nathan in an attempt to download his consciousness back into the physical realm. This scenario introduces a compelling dual existence for Nathan: one version of him resides in the tangible world as a clone. At the same time, the other remains in the digital environment of Lakeview, where his consciousness is securely backed up.

The act of transferring a fragment of Nathan's consciousness into the newly created clone body raises profound questions about identity and the nature of consciousness itself. The clone initially functions as a vessel for Nathan's consciousness, but as the process unfolds, it becomes apparent that the split in his consciousness leads to unforeseen complications. The clone's body begins to disintegrate, suggesting that a person's essence cannot be simply duplicated without dire consequences.

This portrayal serves as a narrative vehicle for Haney's argument, which contends that AI-driven enhancements can lead to chaos and ultimately advocates for the preservation of the natural evolution of consciousness.

As Nathan's consciousness is divided, the distinction between the two Nathans becomes stark. The physical clone, increasingly unstable, reflects the fragility of a being not fully integrated, while the digital Nathan, existing solely in the realm of code and data, appears more resilient. This dynamic illustrates a critical theme of the series: although the digital Nathan continues to thrive in his virtual surroundings, the tangible clone rapidly deteriorates.

By the series's conclusion, the clone's demise starkly contrasts with the digital Nathan's ongoing life, which is perceived by those in the real world as a continuation of the person they once knew. This leads to a complex emotional landscape where friends and family grapple with the notion of death, often clinging to the belief that part of Nathan persists in the virtual space. However, this belief is intrinsically flawed; the digital Nathan embodies a mere reflection of the faithful Nathan, shaped by Ingrid's desires and fantasies rather than the authentic essence of who he was prior to his physical death.

Moreover, while the digital Nathan possesses absolute control over his actions and a comprehensive understanding of his existence within the confines of the AI simulation, he is ultimately limited by the parameters of his environment. His experiences, while rich in the programming of the AI world, lack the depth and breadth of genuine human interactions and sensations found in the natural world. This limitation underscores a significant implication of the storyline: the potential of AI to simulate consciousness does not equate to the richness of authentic human experiences, suggesting that, despite his digital prowess, Nathan's existence is, in many ways, a hollow imitation of life as he once knew it.

The concept of a split consciousness raises significant philosophical concerns, particularly when juxtaposed with Descartes' foundational assertion, "I think, therefore I am." This phrase encapsulates the essence of self-awareness and existence; however, in the context of Nathan Brown's experiences, it seems reduced to a mere "I am." As Nathan's consciousness becomes fragmented between his clone and his AI-powered persona, it illustrates a profound transformation in identity. The traditional understanding of consciousness, tethered to the human experience, appears to dissolve as it enters a more fluid and malleable state, capable of being uploaded to digital realms and downloaded into post-human configurations.

In this scenario, Nathan Brown transcends the limitations of human existence; he is not a fully realised human character, since our introduction to him occurs only after his physical death. Instead, he embodies a consciousness that bifurcates into distinct entities: his digital self, which operates within the parameters of artificial intelligence, and his post-human self residing within the clone. This predicament highlights a continuous struggle where Nathan's identity becomes a battleground between his digital manifestations and his corporeal remnants. Ultimately, this portrayal suggests that Nathan exists only in a material sense, lacking the cohesive selfhood that characterises human existence, leading to existential questions about the nature of self, consciousness, and what it truly means to "be."Another aspect of *Upload* that relates to Haney's theory is the fight for natural consciousness to prevail. The foremost advocate of natural death is Nora's father, who has cancer. He epitomises Haney's belief that natural death and living are a better way of life by continuously resisting the idea of being uploaded. He has cancer, but rather than live a cancer-free life in an AI-generated reality, he advocates for a peaceful and natural death rather than a hollow existence. Nora herself struggles to find meaning in an increasingly digitalised existence and begins to believe that her existence must have meaning. She struggles to connect naturally with Nathan's AI-developed existence. Even when she can interact with Nathan physically, she cannot connect with him because of his fragile physical state, caused by a tampered conscience.

Haney's notion is particularly pertinent to the themes explored in this series, as we observe the characters deeply immersed in their extraordinary mental landscapes, seldom engaging with a more grounded observational consciousness. While the narrative delicately touches upon concepts of natural and pure consciousness, as well as the existential theme of death, through Mr Anday's expressed desire to exit his digital existence, its main thrust is a call for a more liberated digital realm—one unshackled from stringent capitalist interests. This idealistic vision advocates a virtual society that fosters personal freedom and creativity. However, it simultaneously neglects the pressing need for a more authentically enriched real-world experience, often overshadowed by the omnipresence of digital advocacy, both for the mind and the body.

Moreover, Upload does not entirely dismiss the prospect of a more optimistic future with artificial intelligence; instead, it champions a scenario where AI coexists harmoniously with deeper engagement in the physical world, granting individuals greater access to genuine experiences. However, the allure of this vision cannot overshadow Haney's cautionary advice regarding the perils of placing complete trust in AI systems. The series serves as a sobering reminder, emphasising Haney's assertion that an overreliance on technology can lead to significant detriment in human consciousness and lived experience. Thus, it is prudent to view "Upload" as a cautionary tale, urging audiences to strike a balance between embracing technological advancements and retaining our connection to the tangible world around us.

CONCLUSION

This chapter explores the significant drawbacks of commodifying and extending the human mind beyond its inherent capacities through artificial intelligence (AI). In an increasingly digital age, our dependency on AI can disrupt the natural process of death, leading to severe and often catastrophic consequences. One such consequence is the emergence of a subpar existence in a digital realm—an existence characterised by mere survival devoid of any real meaning or purpose. Individuals may find themselves existing in a virtual space that lacks the richness of life, falling prey to isolation that drains the human spirit and leaves the mind feeling desolate and abandoned.

Additionally, the modification of the human mind by AI can lead to a fragmented consciousness. This split nature may prevent individuals from achieving a sense of wholeness, where one's identity and experiences remain cohesive and integrated. Key examples illustrate this issue: Nathan's financial constraints limit his ability to embrace his whole identity; the AI named Guy develops a consciousness that challenges our understanding of what it means to be human; the growing digital class divide creates disparities that further alienate individuals; and Nora's relentless fight for digital rights emphasizes the struggle against losing one's essence to AI enhancements. Each of these scenarios highlights the high cost of allowing our natural selves to be altered by AI technologies.

Moreover, the separation of consciousness from its biological roots exposes it to manipulation and exploitation. As a result, control over one's own consciousness—a fundamental aspect of our humanity—can be surrendered to corporate interests and unethical practices. This raises ethical concerns about the ownership and integrity of our thoughts, memories, and identities in a landscape where AI-driven commodification is prevalent.

In conclusion, the digital replication of the mind cannot substitute for authentic human connections and meaningful personal growth. While AI simulations may mimic certain aspects of human interaction, they ultimately fall short of providing the deep emotional bonds, shared vulnerabilities, and the richness of our collective humanity that only genuine relationships can offer. As we navigate this digital terrain, it is crucial to prioritise and preserve our natural capacity for connection and understanding.

REFERENCES

Baars, B. (2005). In Laureys, S. (Ed.), Progress in Brain Research: Vol. 45-52. *Global workspace theory of consciousness: toward a cognitive neuroscience of human experience.*

Daniels, G. (Director). (2020-2024). *Upload* [Motion Picture].

Haney, W. S. (2006). *Cyberculture, Cyborgs and Science Fiction: Consciousness and the Posthuman.* Conscious Literature and the Arts. DOI: 10.1163/9789401202701

Haraway, D. (1985). *Cyborg Manifesto: Science, Technology, and Socialist-Feminism in the Late Twentieth Century.* Socialist Review.

Harley, N. (2020, April 29). *Upload Review (Spoiler Free).* Retrieved September 21, 2025, from Den of Geek: https://www.denofgeek.com/tv/upload-review/

Hayles, N. K. (1999). *How We Become Posthuman: Virtual Bodies in Cybernetics, Literature and Informatics.* The University of Chicago Press. DOI: 10.7208/chicago/9780226321394.001.0001

Nayyar, P. (2023, February). *Posthumanism.* Retrieved August 28, 2025, from Oxford Bibliographies: https://www.oxfordbibliographies.com/display/document/obo-9780190221911/obo-9780190221911-0122.xml

Van Esch, P., & Cui, Y. (2025, January 8). *Logging off Life, Living On: How AI is redefining death, memory and immortality.* Retrieved September 18, 2025, from Conversation: https://theconversation.com//loggong-off-life-but-living-on-how-ai-is-redefining-death-memory-and-immortality 246306?utm_medium=article_clipboard_share&utm_source=theconversation.com

Chapter 6

The Cybersociology of Learning as Human–AI Partnerships in the Teaching of Political Education

Ahmad Al Yakin
http://orcid.org/0000-0003-3170-2374
Universitas Al Asyariah Mandar Sulawesi Barat, Indonesia

Ali Said Al Matari
http://orcid.org/0000-0002-8124-4730
A'Sharqiyah University, Oman

Ken Paul M. Espinosa
Baliuag University, Philippines

Willam Dela Cruz Enrique
City of Malabon University, Philippines

Luis Cardoso
http://orcid.org/0000-0003-3748-5593
Polytechnic University of Portalegre, Portugal

Muthmainnah Muthmainnah
http://orcid.org/0000-0003-3170-2374
Universitas Al Asyariah Mandar, Indonesia

ABSTRACT

Integrating artificial intelligence (AI) into educational ecosystems to cultivate civic skills among students is the central emphasis of this study. Based on cybersociology as a theoretical framework, this study reframes learning as a social negotiation between humans and AI, with the latter influencing the former in terms of civic identity, media literacy, inclusion, ethical reasoning, and data literacy. One hundred and ten first-year students participated. Students' attitudes and competencies were measured before and after the use of the CALLEBAI teaching model using a 20-item

DOI: 10.4018/979-8-2600-1458-5.ch006

Likert-scale questionnaire. Students' civic communication, data analysis, tolerance for variety, ethical awareness in political decision-making, and capacity to recognise misinformation all showed significant gains. The study found that human-AI partnerships (via debate simulations, NLP, adaptive platforms, and AI-based data visualisation) address modern political issues like corruption, polarisation, and disinformation in Indonesia.

INTRODUCTION

Artificial intelligence (AI) has emerged as an effective force in transforming classroom learning methods, incorporating content, critique, and civic and political engagement. The field of cybersociology explores the changes in cyber-based sociological learning supported by AI technology (Karadži & Redžepi, 2025).Therefore, sociologists understand that this change requires the involvement of various parties, including consideration of power relations, identity, and epistemology resulting from the partnership between human intelligence and AI. The interconnectedness of power, ideology, curriculum, and citizen democratic engagement in the dissemination and reception of information on social media and general elections makes this understanding increasingly important for integration into political education at universities (Panwar et al., 2023). Cybersociology, as applied in this research, relates to the cultural, political, educational, and social aspects of Social 5.0, with the influence of digital technology and its impact on people's daily lives across various fields.

Cyberpower transcends the instrumentalist narrative of efficiency and personalization in modern AI-based education. Cybersociology investigates the broader impact of AI's digital mediation on communities and learning processes. One such AI facility is a platform for efficient intelligent tutoring (Tihonova et al., 2022). Various AI technologies are transforming the way students, teachers, and schools access information, such as interacting using the Monica AI platform, Cicibot, ChatGPT, and other LLM platforms (Al Yakin et al., 2024; Zdravkov & Ilieva, 2025). It is believed that artificial intelligence (AI) can be implemented in political education by facilitating students' becoming more critical and politically socialized, as evidenced by their arguments. Furthermore, students are able to narrate their understanding of civic issues, elections, and digital campaigns and process their ideas independently and in a structured manner.

According to Al Yakin et al. (2025), the effects of human-AI collaboration in the classroom, where AI serves as a learning medium and technology, will never replace humans. Therefore, AI has the potential to shape patterns and fields of inquiry for students to access a variety of knowledge and information, ultimately generating meaningful, effective learning. Recent research (Zdravkov, 2025) indicates that AI in the classroom transcends mere responsiveness to human commands; it intentionally and actively shapes instruction through human-AI collaborations. This study of political education requires learning from various historical events concerning politics, shaping civic attitudes, and understanding competing narratives in this area. Therefore, this study adds a layer of complexity to the production process, in-depth analysis, and flexible construction of political knowledge through an AI approach. Meanwhile, cybersociology maximises the use of AI in the classroom by first expanding students' access to information through social media, valid sources, and references, and second, redefining the authority of AI in the classroom as a learning aid and epistemic trust (Mamlok, 2025).Classically, the primary method of teaching political science in schools and universities has historically been textual, using textbooks, lectures, and class discussions.

The democratic priorities include promoting critical thinking, digital citizenship, and awareness of political participation, these still require attention. Furthermore, there is a striking difference with AI-integrated learning models, where students are more exposed to a variety of political content through online platforms, social media, and various algorithm-based resources (Matar, 2025). Teachers often face important new issues as a result of the development of AI in the classroom. The reality is that AI-driven recommendation systems and other digital platforms significantly impact students' political awareness beyond the classroom. This includes how to provide timely feedback on political issues, respond to political hallucinations, and include the positive aspects of implementing AI systems for instant information analysis (Janfada et al., 2025). Although myths about cybersociology-based AI technology encourage ideological myopia or even reinforce algorithmic prejudice, teachers must understand and carefully consider how to integrate AI in the classroom in engaging ways. Furthermore, teachers should consider how students engage with artificial intelligence (AI) devices in the classroom as collaborative tools, rather than competitors, during the learning process. A recent study by Santiago et al. (2025) found that students who use AI assistance to construct arguments or critically evaluate political ideas participate in dialogic processes involving algorithmic reasoning. AI assistance in classrooms addressing technical challenges is increasingly supporting the transformation of traditional classroom dynamics into modern ones, with teachers acting as collaborators for students, AI, and themselves.

AI assistance that encourages critical and independent thinking among students is a primary goal of political education. There has been a surge in research investigating the tangible benefits of AI use in the classroom, focusing on three key areas: technological efficacy, academic performance, and cognitive impacts following exposure to AI. The dominant emphasis in this research is on the social dimension of human-AI interaction in political and civic education.This research brings together three disciplines that rarely collaborate with cybersociology, political education at universities, and human-AI collaboration. As AI usage increases in the classroom, cybersociologists play a crucial role in political education by fostering civic dispositions, ethical reasoning, critical thinking, problem-solving, and participatory skills. Furthermore, this research explores the social dimension of human-AI partnerships during interventions, going beyond assessing AI based on efficiency or technology used solely in the classroom.

LITERATURE REVIEW

Artificial intelligence (AI) is rapidly transforming the way information is created, shared, and absorbed in educational settings at all levels (Zhang et al., 2025). Recently, AI has rapidly evolved into more than just a set of technical tools, learning media, and learning technologies; it is now firmly embedded in educational activities by students, teachers, and staff, challenging long-held beliefs about how students learn and acquire knowledge more quickly. For example, in the field of political education, learning content promotes democratic principles, civic engagement, critical thinking, and effective information exchange. Designing a collaborative framework to understand the impact of human-AI partnerships in the cybersociology of political education is supported by a study (Collins, 2025) examining the impact of human-technology interactions in online spaces on social behaviour, conventions, and institutions.

This study places political education within a cybersociology framework to advance students' theoretical and practical understanding of the impact of artificial intelligence on the importance of digital citizenship and democratic engagement. GenAI, with its increasing influence on algorithmic, partisan, and disinformation in modern public discourse, also presents new challenges for political education (Kim et al., 2025). Furthermore, Zhou et al. (2025) state that classic classroom methods are insufficient to address these challenges, suggesting that educators should revisit the pedagogical techniques used by schools and universities to incorporate digital literacy and critical awareness of AI.

Furthermore, there is a significant opportunity for political education to become more personalised, interactive, and data-driven due to the rapid advancement of AI-based technologies, such as sentiment analysis platforms with features that support adaptive and practical learning systems and generative language models (Zdravkov, 2025). Concerns about AI surveillance, information bias, and the erosion of personal agency (ITS) in the AI-society ecosystem remain. According to Haroud and Saqri (2025), the COVID-19 pandemic is accelerating the shift towards digital pedagogy. During the intervention process in political education classes, this study integrated digital pedagogy (Stevens, 2025) and critical AI literacy (Yim, 2024) into the realm of practical political education to address critical gaps by focusing on digital political education and educating students to be active participants in AI-driven communities while preparing them to engage in critical evaluation of emerging ethical and political dilemmas (Velander et al., 2024). Hillygus and Holbein (2023) stated that the traditional goal of political education is to equip individuals and citizens to understand politics and actively participate in democratic societies through the use of technology. Teaching students to think critically about current events, assess the reliability of various news reports, and have fruitful conversations with people of different political persuasions is an important part of this modern mission (Francis & Wolton, 2025) and have changed drastically due to the digitization of political communication. Bots spreading biassed narratives and social media algorithms filtering incoming information further blur the distinction between real and fake news (Austin, 2025).

Because of these factors, it is not enough for political education to emphasise just civic practices or institutional knowledge. The capacity to identify, understand, and react to the political ramifications of algorithmic systems should instead be fostered through political education program. Human-AI cooperation in the field of education could potentially address these problems. Natural language processing methods can enable large-scale conversations among varied groups, and adaptive learning systems can tailor political education to students' interests and background knowledge(Chiu & Rospigliosi, 2025).

The cybersociology arena within the political education landscape provides an important framework for studying current political issues by focusing on how educational technology, social media, and AI reflect and transform socio-democratic power relations. Cybersociology is an emerging field that studies the sociocultural impacts of politics, digital citizenship, and the culture of maximizing digital technology. This study highlights collaborative efforts between students, teachers, social media, and technology. The integration of political education and human-AI collaboration aims not only for input-output efficiency but also involves alignment with the broader social ecosystem that encompasses policy, education, political institutions, cultural norms, and digital infrastructure (Albukhari, 2025). The notion that connections across formal, informal, and technical contexts have a continuing effect on enhancing practical educational experiences (Jiang et al., 2025).

A cybersociology perspective on political education explains how AI mediates these connections. It is believed that AI influences student-content interactions and vice versa, restructuring the dynamics of fun, meaningful and inquiry-based learning in the classroom that emphasizes the relational and contextual components of human-AI collaboration, deterministic of technological progress. This work contributes as follows: (1) investigating the partnership that occurs between humans and AI in digital citizenship pedagogy, which expands the implementation of the concept of cybersociology of learning. (2) examining the current state of artificial intelligence (AI) in political education classrooms while discussing its strengths and weaknesses in relation to political science education. (3) outlining some rules for integrating AI into political science classes that inspire students to become good stewards of democratic values, engaged citizens, strong problem solvers and critical thinkers.

CYBERSOCIALIZATION IN EDUCATION

The internalization of cybersocialization in the learning process is an emerging framework for examining how digital environments, including social media, influence interactions, culture, social norms, and identities. This idea involves digital cybersocialization and AI technologies, where cybersocialization occurs when individuals construct and negotiate socio-cultural positions in a technologically advanced environment with the aim of accurately representing diversity, equality, and covering the complexities of real political discourse (Al Yakin et al., 2024). This method goes beyond simply using digital communication to demonstrate how AI, virtual platforms, and online communities influence patterns of social reproduction; cybersocialology bridges the learning process and also represents power dynamics in society 5.0 (Bozda, 2025). Cybersocialization in the classroom is a prime example of how artificial intelligence (AI) mediates not only critical thinking but also social relationships, including friendship, collaboration, and effective community service participation. According to Wang & Xie (2025), AI-powered platforms have the potential to accurately foster lasting relationships in higher education by lowering barriers to participation and expanding opportunities for students to connect effectively with one another. Virtual robots and AI-mediated classrooms are giving rise to new types of communities where algorithms, students, and instructors collaborate to deepen human understanding (Muthmainnah et al. 2025).

Therefore, cybersocialization in the era of cybersocialization is becoming increasingly important in political education, particularly to enhance hot and deep learning, which focuses on the goals of political education beyond simply teaching students politics; it encompasses the formation of moral reasoning, upholding values, character development, and their involvement in independent democratic processes. Furthermore, by shaping students' civic engagement, the visibility of certain voices, and the normalization of certain principles, cybersocialization through AI-mediated environments is far more than just a spectacle.Cybersocialization, then, offers a sociological perspective through which to examine the dynamics of political education in online environments mediated by artificial intelligence (Al Yakin et al., 2024).

Education Partnerships between Humans and AI In the realm of educational technology, the idea of human-AI cooperation has been gaining momentum, similar to cybersociology. Chigbu & Makapela, (2025) contend that AI should be seen more as an active collaborator with humans to improve learning rather than an inert passive instrument. Here, AI helps out educators by analyzing student participation on a large scale, delivering adaptive feedback, and scaffolding inquiry Dili & Ansong (2025). Co-agency is the focus of human-AI partnership research; in this model, humans (educators and students) make decisions while AI systems (the intermediaries) mediate between them. For instance, according to Jha & Singh, (2025) students enrolled in social science courses might benefit from AI in the following ways: by processing massive social media datasets, by detecting disinformation, and by visualizing ideological polarization (Tejero et al., 2025). Although technically sound, these procedures have far-reaching effects on the social component of political education, which teaches students to critically evaluate data and to challenge the algorithmic systems that influence their community (Alberts, 2025).

INTERNET-BASED INTERACTIONS AND HUMAN-ARTIFICIAL COOPERATION

The cybersociology and human-AI collaboration models show a supplementary relationship when seen in tandem. Relationality, in which humans and AI co-construct social and learning processes, is emphasized by both viewpoints, which reject technological determinism (Pavlović, 2025). The focus of cybersocialisation is on the societal effects of these connections, whereas the focus of human-AI partnerships is on the educational benefits of working together in education. Co-operation between humans and AI paves the way for more inclusive debates, better simulations, and the analysis of complicated education data (Rasa, 2025). In turn, cybersocialisation sheds light on the ways in which these collaborations mould civic authority, trust, and identity. As an example, when legislative discussions are simulated using AI technologies, the collaboration makes it easier for students to participate, but cybersocialisation shapes how they internalise democratic norms in these virtual environments.

As a result, cybersocialisation offers a sociological criticism, and human-AI partnerships give an operational framework; both must be integrated into political education in the digital era. Practical consequences for teacher positions in political education arise from the merging of cybersocialisation and human-AI cooperation (Mavridi, 2025). In addition to guiding students' cognitive growth, educators must also buffer the societal impacts of artificial intelligence. The actions and competences that teachers should possess in relation to artificial intelligence (AI) in the context of sociology and politics classes are detailed in Table 1.

Table 1. Teacher Roles, AI in Learning Sociology/Politics, Activities, and Competencies

Teacher Role	Example AI in Learning Sociology/Politics	Activities	Sociology Competence
Facilitator of Civic Dialogue	AI chatbots for political debate simulations	Students engage in AI-moderated debates on policy issues	Civic communication, tolerance of diverse perspectives
Critical Mediator	NLP tools for detecting bias/ misinformation in news	Analyzing AI-processed datasets of political discourse	Critical media literacy, recognition of bias
Designer of Learning Ecosystems	Adaptive AI platforms (e.g., personalized civic quizzes)	Customizing political education pathways	Curriculum design, democratic inclusivity
Ethical Guardian	AI ethics case studies in political decision-making	Discussing implications of AI in governance	Ethical reasoning, awareness of surveillance capitalism
Research Mentor	AI-driven data visualization of social movements	Projects on analyzing big data about protests or elections	Data literacy, sociological analysis of power

Authors own work, 2025.

To integrate AI into sociology and political science courses, conventional instructional roles must be reevaluated. Think about the five main functions in Table 1 as you plan how to use AI tools to assist students in building social competencies. Civic dialogue facilitator, critical mediator, learning ecosystem designer, ethical guardian, and research mentor are all part of this category. These new positions are a prime example of how educators are collaborating with AI to guide pupils through algorithmic environments while upholding democratic norms. Arranger of Civic Dialogue Political sociologists emphasize the significance of discourse and argumentation in order to cultivate competence in democratic processes.

To help students engage with other points of view, teachers are using chatbots powered by artificial intelligence to mimic political arguments. According to Tang & Putra (2025), chatbots can simulate arguments by acting out different perspectives, presenting thought-provoking questions, and checking students' assumptions. Increased civic engagement and acceptance of diversity are two hallmarks of a democratic society. Sarafis et al., (2025) suggests that AI-powered platforms can make political debates more accessible by removing social barriers and providing organized ways for everyone to get involved. Ningxue (2025) adding, the likelihood of AI moderation bolstering concealed biases might be influenced by the datasets utilized to train the systems. The instructor's role as facilitator is thus not impartial; on the contrary, they are required to assess AI-generated conversations with a critical way.

Critical AI literacy is more important than ever before due to the rapid dissemination of false information, which is particularly problematic during political campaigns and discussions on public policy (Romanishyn et al., 2025). In their capacity as impartial arbiters, educators can use NLP techniques to identify instances of prejudice, disinformation, and repetitive wording in political speeches. As an example, natural language processing has the potential to decipher the framing of news items, examine political speeches for manipulative rhetorical techniques, and more (Padalko et al., 2025).

Students are taught to question and analyses AI results instead of blindly accepting them in this capacity. One crucial competency for students to master is recognizing information biases and algorithmic authority. Integrating AI-based technologies into elections often uncovers voter manipulation tactics. This experience can provide valuable lessons for future generations, who need to be taught to critically evaluate algorithmic rhetoric (Jacob & Vajjhala, 2025). Machine learning can bias information, and critical pedagogy must therefore be used alongside these tools to prevent over-reliance on these technologies (Bulathwela et al., 2024). This responsibility rests with teachers, who act as curriculum designers, design instructional materials, and ensure that students' unique learning experiences do not diminish the importance of civic and political education in the classroom, while maximizing human-AI collaboration. Xu et al. (2025) highlight algorithmic "echo chambers" where customization can limit, rather than expand, creative and critical opinion. Therefore, to provide adequate personalization, educators must limit AI-based learning pathways that expose students to diverse digital political perspectives. Teachers play a crucial role in human-AI interactions during the intervention process and face the challenging dual task of encouraging students to maximize AI's potential while avoiding the dangers of epistemic closure.

Furthermore, teachers and students must consider the moral issues of AI in politics, campaigns, and policymaking as the technology becomes increasingly integrated into the democratic ecosystem (Samadhiya et al., 2025). Examining AI case studies such as algorithmic voting guidance tools, predictive surveillance, or automated content moderation raises questions about accountability, fairness, and surveillance capitalism at its best. This perspective aligns with the goal of critical AI literacy programs: to educate students about AI from both technical and democratic perspectives (Gilmore & Meinhold, 2025). Núñez et al. (2025) assert that the unchecked use of artificial intelligence (AI) in political campaigns has the potential to exacerbate polarisation, making it crucial for university educators to foster civic responsibility and ethical reasoning in their students about AI.

Teachers can help students more easily understand the connection between technological arguments and larger sociocultural power structures by viewing artificial intelligence (AI) as a political issue, rather than as an apolitical actor (Eaton, 2025). Students can act as evaluators in evaluating large data sets, such as conversations or trending issues on social media surrounding elections, hashtags used in protest or support movements, or public opinion survey results, using accurate data visualisation tools powered by artificial intelligence. Educators are expected to be able to guide students and encourage data literacy and critical analysis of the power dynamics of digital society (Dritsas & Trigka, 2025). Leba et al. (2025) state that teachers have an obligation to create a fun and meaningful educational environment and are tasked with creating personalised, adaptive learning paths that utilise artificial intelligence. Hwang (2025) claims that these adaptive systems promote diversity and inclusion by removing barriers that rely solely on students' prior knowledge.

META COLLABORATION HUMAN INTELLIGENCE AND AI IN EDUCATION

In the GenAI era, marked by the increasingly widespread use of AI in schools and universities, AI is rapidly becoming a crucial component for creating effective learning ecosystems. Rather than replacing the essential role of humans, AI complements human instruction and becomes a solid human-AI partner. To better understand AI and the importance of AI collaboration in the classroom, Lorenzo et al. (2024) proposed a distributed intelligence paradigm, assuming that in this context, artificial intelligence and humans coexist and depend on each other. While computers cannot entirely assume the role of teachers in political science classes, they can complement human instruction by facilitating active student analysis and discussion, which in turn can enhance critical thinking and ethical reasoning and maximize student civic engagement, such as using AI to help students examine decision-making in complex political situations. Furthermore, adaptive learning systems can also accommodate diverse educational backgrounds (Guglielmo et al., 2025). New opportunities for dialogic learning emerge when students enact AI like humans, using chatbots and conversational agents to practice civic argumentation for political education in structured situations (Rapantha, 2025).

Furthermore, while it is undeniable that experts have pointed out the risks inherent in this interaction, as noted by Neyazi et al. (2025), the use of AI in political campaigns further highlights the power of algorithms to massively influence public discourse and deepen divisions. Therefore, to learn how to use and evaluate AI systems wisely and appropriately, it is crucial for students to actively engage in political education. Educators continue to play a crucial role in human-AI relationships as mediators, ecosystem creators, collaborators, and ethical guardians. According to Jain (2024), educators have a crucial role in fostering student-AI interactions, as well as protecting students from displacement and ensuring that these partnerships reap the benefits of effective education and democracy. Cybersocialization and human-AI partnerships in political education are shown in Table 2 below. This table describes how AI helps students acquire skills such as critical thinking, inclusion, and communication. Teachers play a crucial role in guiding them toward an algorithmic and critical civic life. Students can gain a better understanding of politics and mitigate citizenship crises and the social dynamics of technology-mediated engagement through collaborative activities with AI, such as chatbot debates, democratic processing, elections or valid big data visualizations.

Table 2. Cybersocialization and Human–AI Collaboration in Political Sociology Education

Cybersocialization Aspect	Cybersociology Factors	Students' Competence	Robot–Human Collaboration Activities	Sociology Aspect	Social Problem
Digital Dialogue	Norms of online civic debate	Civic communication, tolerance	AI chatbot-moderated debates on policy issues	Political socialization	Polarization, echo chambers
Algorithmic Mediation	Power of algorithms in shaping discourse	Critical media literacy	NLP analysis of news and political speeches	Sociology of knowledge	Misinformation, bias
Adaptive Personalization	Inclusion vs. fragmentation	Democratic inclusivity, curriculum awareness	AI quizzes tailored to civic knowledge	Sociology of education	Inequality of access
Ethical Awareness	AI and surveillance in governance	Ethical reasoning, civic ethics	Case studies on AI in governance & surveillance capitalism	Sociology of power	Surveillance, digital authoritarianism
Data Visualization	Collective understanding of social movements	Data literacy, critical analysis	AI visualization of protests, elections, hashtags	Sociology of collective action	Manipulation, bot amplification

Authors own work, 2025.

In the era of rapid digitalization in education, teachers are increasingly required to actively engage in creating meaningful learning environments rather than simply transferring knowledge. Through the integration of human elements, virtual robots, and technology, with instructor support, this paradigm creates adaptive yet flexible classrooms. Students are guided to become engaged citizens, active participants in the democratic process, and critical thinkers; the traditional focus on teaching only facts and figures has been replaced by a broader definition of the goals of political education. Teachers, as the primary focus in designing learning ecosystems, must strive to achieve the goals of student participation, classroom transparency, student-centeredness, and democratic ideals (Riquelme, 2025).

Ecosystemic design in human-AI collaboration incorporates data analytics, visualization tools, adaptive platforms, and AI chatbots into political science courses. Teachers can control the use of AI in the classroom by striking a balance between individualization and group civic discourse, rather than the other way around. In this capacity, educators must think about the social and technological effects of AI, such as how it shapes who can learn, who can speak out, and whether it can exacerbate existing inequality (Chatterjee, 2025).

Table 3. Designing AI-Mediated Learning Ecosystems for Political Education in Indonesia

Education in Politics	AI Tools	Classroom Activities	Political Problems in Indonesia	Students' Role	Teacher's Role	Problem-Solving Approach
Civic Dialogue	AI chatbots for debate simulation	Structured debates on corruption or governance issues	Corruption, weak accountability	Engage in debate, reflect on ethics	Facilitate fair discussion, ensure inclusivity	Promote civic ethics and integrity awareness
Media Literacy	NLP tools to detect misinformation	Analyze AI-processed election news datasets	Hoaxes during elections, polarization	Critically evaluate news and sources	Guide data interpretation, contextualize bias	Develop strategies for fact-checking and responsible media use
Civic Inclusivity	Adaptive learning platforms	Personalized civic quizzes on Pancasila & democracy	Religious/ethnic polarization	Learn inclusively with tailored content	Curate pathways ensuring shared democratic values	Balance personalization with collective civic understanding

continued on following page

Table 3. Continued

Education in Politics	AI Tools	Classroom Activities	Political Problems in Indonesia	Students' Role	Teacher's Role	Problem-Solving Approach
Ethics of Governance	AI ethics case studies	Group discussions on predictive policing or surveillance	Digital authoritarianism, privacy concerns	Critically assess ethical dilemmas	Frame discussions with democratic ethics	Develop ethical reasoning & civic responsibility
Social Movements	AI-driven data visualization	Map social media hashtags on protests	Mobilization, populism, polarization	Collect and analyze civic data	Mentor research, ensure ethical practice	Strengthen data literacy, civic participation skills

Authors own work, 2025.

In political education classes, where students are required to think critically about civic identity, democratic participation, and ethical reasoning, teachers' roles as creators of learning ecosystems are more important than ever.

RESEARCH METHODOLOGY

This study uses quantitative research methods to determine the effects of cybersociology using the CALLEBAI teaching model, which is beneficial in improving critical thinking skills, ethical reasoning, and citizenship competencies in political education courses (Creswell & Creswell, 2018). The architecture used in this study examines how a structured learning ecosystem that combines partnerships between humans, digital platforms, and AI affects students' competency levels. This method ensures the accuracy, replicability, and objectivity of the CALLEBAI learning model for political education in Indonesia.

Participants

The study's population consisted of 110 undergraduates enrolled in the Pancasila and Citizenship Education program at Al Asyariah Mandar University (Unasman), Indonesia, during the 2025 academic year. The sample size of 28 students was purposively selected because they were actively involved in courses related to the cybersociology model in political education. The sample size was considered appropriately representative of the population, as it met the general quantitative research requirement of at least 100 participants for reliable statistical analysis. The demographic composition included male and female students, ranging in age from 18 to

24 years, with diverse backgrounds in terms of socioeconomic status and exposure to AI technology during their learning process. Participation was voluntary, and informed consent was obtained from all participants before the start of the study. Ethical considerations, including anonymity and confidentiality, were maintained throughout the intervention process.

Research Instruments

The primary instrument used for data collection was a structured questionnaire designed to measure student perceptions, experiences, and competencies following the implementation of the CALLEBAI teaching model. The questionnaire was developed on the basis of prior studies in civic education, AI in learning, and cybersociology, ensuring both relevance and construct validity. Items were presented using a five-point Likert scale, ranging from 1 = strongly disagree to 5 = strongly agree. The instrument underwent expert validation by three scholars in political sociology and educational technology to ensure content validity. A pilot test with 20 students outside the main sample was conducted to refine wording and clarity. Reliability analysis using Cronbach's alpha yielded coefficients above 0.80, indicating high internal consistency of the instrument.

Research Procedure

This study leverages AI transformative capacity to create more responsive and engaged, critical, and creative citizens. It applies the innovative CALLEBAI learning model to demonstrate student ability to enhance civic and sociological competencies. A political education learning ecosystem use technology but instead welcomes it with open arms. As the first step in our multi-stage approach, this study contextualized this powerful model, developed a comprehensive lesson plan that included AI, obtained ethical clearance, and validated our Likert-scale questionnaire.

The implementation phase preceded the data collection phase. Finally, we used SPSS version 26 for robust statistical analysis. During the analysis phase, we employed descriptive and inferential statistics to accurately assess the impact of this AI-enhanced teaching. This research goes beyond educational evaluation by providing educators with a proven and actionable framework called the CALLEBAI model. This model empowers educators to drive innovation while critically monitoring the new era of human-AI collaboration for political learning, ultimately shaping a generation better able to navigate the complexities of their world. The CALLEBAI model consciously blends cybersociological principles with rigorous instructional design.

Table 4. Instructional Design for Political Education Using CALLEBAI Model

Step	Teacher Role	AI Tools	Classroom Activities	Political Problem (Indonesia)	Student Role	Problem Solving Outcome
C – Critical Engagement	Facilitator of civic dialogue. Teachers initiate classroom debates with AI chatbots simulating political actors. Students practice dialogue on corruption, fostering communication skills.	AI chatbots for debate	Students engage in policy debate simulations	Corruption and governance	Engage in civic dialogue, critique governance failures	Develop critical civic communication
A – Adaptive Learning	Designer of learning pathways. AI platforms tailor quizzes on civic knowledge, balancing personalization with collective Indonesian values to address polarization.	Adaptive platforms (personalized quizzes).	AI-curated learning routes on democracy	Polarization and diversity	Navigate personalized yet collective learning	Strengthen inclusivity and unity
L – Literacy Development	Critical mediator. Students use NLP to identify misinformation in electoral news, cultivating media literacy essential for democracy	NLP tools for misinformation. .	Analyzing datasets of political news for bias	Misinformation and hoaxes	Identify misinformation and computational propaganda	Enhance media literacy
L – Learning by Doing	Research mentor. Data visualization tools are applied to analyze social media data on protests, allowing students to link sociological theory to real-world activism.	Data visualization platforms.	Analyze big data on protests/elections	Electoral manipulation	Conduct group projects on civic participation	Build data literacy, sociological inquiry

continued on following page

Table 4. Continued

Step	Teacher Role	AI Tools	Classroom Activities	Political Problem (Indonesia)	Student Role	Problem Solving Outcome
E – Ethical Reflection	Ethical guardian. Teachers guide discussions on AI governance ethics, contextualized in Indonesian surveillance policies.	AI ethics case studies	Discuss AI in surveillance/ governance	Privacy and human rights	Reflect on fairness, accountability	Strengthen ethical reasoning
B – Bias Awareness	Contextual guide. Teacher ask students analyze algorithmic bias, uncovering structural inequalities and sharpening critical awareness.	Algorithmic bias detection tools	Examine biases in AI-generated texts.	Discrimination and inequality	Critique structural bias	Foster awareness of systemic inequality
A – AI Integration	Ecosystem designer. Teacher integrate multiple AI tools are integrated into project-based learning, reinforcing the interconnection of civic competencies	Multi-tool integration. .	Combine AI chatbots, NLP, adaptive tools	Multiple civic challenges	Collaborate across platforms	Develop holistic sociological competence
I – Inclusive Participation	Equity advocate. Accessibility tools ensure participation across linguistic and geographic divides, embodying democratic inclusivity.	Language and accessibility AI tools.	Ensure multilingual debates and access	Rural–urban divide in education	Participate across digital divides	Advance democratic inclusivity

(Al Yakin et al., 2026).

Data Analysis

Using SPSS (Statistical Package for Social Sciences), a structured strategy was used to analyse the data:

1. Descriptive statistics: used to summed student responses by calculating the mean, standard deviation, and frequency distribution for each questionnaire item
2. Data literacy, ethical reasoning, inclusion, media literacy, and civic engagement were all described by these figures. To ensure the questionnaire's internal consistency across constructs, reliability testing involved recalculating Cronbach's alpha for the entire data set.
3. Deductive statistics used to examine changes in student competencies between the pre- and post-CALLEBAI periods, paired-samples t-tests were conducted. To identify statistically significant changes, we compared responses from the pre- and post-tests.

Finding and Discussion

Table 5 below describes the results of descriptive statistical data on how political education students view cybersociology-based human-AI partnerships. Respondents assessed five activity indicators: ethical reasoning, data literacy, inclusion, civic communication, and media literacy.

Table 5. Descriptive Statistics of Human-AI Partnerships in the Teaching of Political Education

Student statement	N	Min	Max	Mean	Std. Deviation
Dimension 1: Civic Communication (Items 1–4) 1. I found that using discussion simulations powered by AI helped me articulate my political views more precisely.	28	1.00	5.00	4.4643	.92224
2. After taking part in classroom activities backed by AI, I feel more comfortable talking about civic issues.	28	2.00	5.00	4.4286	.74180
3. I feel more comfortable talking about civic issues.	28	2.00	5.00	4.4286	.79015
4. I learnt to be more tolerant and respectful of different political perspectives after using AI in class. **Dimension 2: Media Literacy (Items 5–8)**	28	1.00	5.00	4.1429	1.07890
5. I was able to spot bias in social media or media and political news with the use of AI tools (such as natural language processing).	28	3.00	5.00	4.4643	.74447
6. I am now better able to detecting misinformation and fake news during election	28	3.00	5.00	4.3214	.77237
7. I became more selective in my news consumption after using AI to analyze political debate.	28	1.00	5.00	4.1429	1.07890
8. I truly believe that the use of AI techniques has greatly improved my capacity to assess the reliability of political materials found online. **Dimension 3: Inclusivity (Items 9–12)**	28	2.00	5.00	4.3571	.82616
9. I was able to learn at my own pace while participating in group activities to help me in engaging to adaptive AI technologies	28	3.00	5.00	4.4286	.69007
10. Integrating AI in the politic education class and more accessible to learn better.	28	2.00	5.00	4.4286	.87891

continued on following page

Table 5. Continued

Student statement	N	Min	Max	Mean	Std. Deviation
11. Peer collaboration across cultural and social contexts was fostered through AI-supported by cybersociology in learning	28	2.00	5.00	4.2857	.80999
12. AI made a significant contribution to the democratic principle of Bhinneka Tunggal Ika (Unity in Diversity).	28	2.00	5.00	4.3571	.78004
Dimension 4: Ethical Reasoning (Items 13–16) 13. I gained a better understanding of government accountability and fairness through class debates on AI ethics.	28	2.00	5.00	4.2500	.92796
14. The potential moral dangers of using AI for political decision-making and surveillance became more apparent to me.	28	3.00	5.00	4.3571	.67847
15. I was prompted to contemplate issues of justice and human rights by AI case studies in my political education.	28	3.00	5.00	4.3214	.72283
16. I think political education should include ethical thinking on AI tools. **Dimension 5: Data Literacy (Items 17–20)**	28	3.00	5.00	4.3571	.73102
17. I learnt more about social movements and elections through data visualisations powered by AI.	28	3.00	5.00	4.2143	.78680
18 I am now more comfortable using AI techniques to analyse massive datasets pertaining to political engagement or protests	28	3.00	5.00	4.2143	.73822
19. I was able to hone my skills in critical sociological analysis while working on projects that included AI.	28	1.00	5.00	4.2143	.99469
20. I have a better understanding of how data-driven analysis relates to larger sociological conceptions of democracy and power.	28	2.00	5.00	4.2143	.87590
Valid N (listwise)	28				

The mean scores on Table 5 are consistently high across all aspects, ranging from 4.14 to 4.46 on a 5-point Likert scale. Students were in agreement that AI-assisted learning enhanced their analytical, civic, and ethical abilities, according to these findings. Even though the majority of students had good experiences, there was some diversity in their reports (standard deviations range from 0.68 to 1.07). The results show that chatbots, NLP, adaptive learning platforms, data visualization, ethical case studies, and other AI tools can be used in political education to improve students' cognitive abilities, inclusivity, and ethical awareness.

Table 6. The mean score of Cybersociology of Human-AI partnership

	N	Min	Max	Mean	Std. Deviation
Pretest	28	40.00	60.00	48.5714	8.03432
Posttest	28	59.00	100.00	86.3929	11.91121
Valid N (listwise)	28				

In the framework of the cybersociology of human-AI partnerships, Table 2 compares students' performance before and after the installation of the CALLEBAI teaching approach. With a sample size of 28, the results reveal that students' pretest scores were all over the place, with a mean of 48.57 and a standard deviation of 8.03. On the other hand, there is a noticeable change in the posttest outcomes. The scores skyrocketed, with a range of 59.00 to 100.00 and an average of 86.39 (SD = 11.91). The significant improvement in students' abilities is a result of the favorable effect of education based on human-AI partnerships. Although there is more variation in the results due to the larger range, the overall improvement in political education through AI-mediated learning activities is testament to the CALLEBAI teaching model's efficacy.

The posttest pie chart, in comparison, shows a far more varied distribution of results across categories from 59 to 100, providing a striking contrast. The range of slices shows that pupils made individual growth, and several of them achieved results above 90. Because AI tools allowed for varied and personalised development, this distribution demonstrates the adaptive and inclusive nature of human-AI collaborative learning.

Table 7. Chi-Square Test Statistics

	Pretest	Posttest
Chi-Square	8.071[a]	13.143[b]
df	4	17
Asymp. Sig.	.089	.727

Statistics for the Chi-Square Test (Table 4) at the level 0.05 level of significance, the pretest's chi-square score of 8.07 (df = 4, p = .089) shown student abilities and perspectives differed so substantially before the intervention suggests that there was a lack of substantial consistency in their answer. A chi-square value of 13.14 (df = 17, p = .727) for the posttest. This finding implies that following the intervention, students' scores were significantly higher; yet, there was still some fluctuation in the distribution of replies, despite the obvious improvement in overall competency.

Table 8. Reliability Statistics

Cronbach's Alpha	N of Items
.949	20

Due to the more definitive finding about mean differences provided by the paired t-test (Table 8), the nonsignificant chi-square is not an issue in this case. The reliability results reveal that the 20-item questionnaire exhibited exceptional internal consistency with a Cronbach's Alpha of .949.

Table 9. Paired Samples Test

		Paired Differences					t	df	Sig. (2-tailed)
					95% Confidence Interval of the Difference				
		Mean	Std. Deviation	Std. Error Mean	Lower	Upper			
Pair 1	Pretest - Posttest	-37.82143	11.56641	2.18585	-42.30641	-33.33644	-17.303	27	.000

Paired Samples T test shown (Table 9) the mean scores on the pretest and posttest were compared using the paired samples t-test. A large and continuous improvement was shown by the mean difference of -37.82 points, with a 95% confidence range ranging from -42.30 to -33.33. The extremely statistically significant difference between the pretest and posttest was demonstrated by the t-value of -17.30 (df = 27, $p < .001$). This finding provides more evidence that the CALLEBAI approach significantly improved students' political education competence. This improvement is highly unlikely to have happened by coincidence, as shown by the extraordinarily low p-value.

DISCUSSION

Consistent with other recent studies, this one find that AI has the potential to revolutionize the way teacher to teach and learn. Civic learning and academic identities are reshaped by AI ecosystems in higher education. By utilizing human-AI partnerships, the CALLEBAI teaching approach considerably improved student skills in political education, as shown by the statistical data. Incorporating AI into civic and political education yields compelling proof of its effectiveness, as demonstrated by a large mean increase, great reliability, and strong significance in the paired t-test. According to Al Yakin et al., (2024) cybersociology views education as a place where social negotiation takes place in digital contexts. Many of the greatest scores were for the civic communication tasks. Students statement were in full agreement that debate simulations driven by AI helped them articulate their political views more precisely (M = 4.46, SD = 0.92) and gave them more self-assurance while engaging in civic discourse (M = 4.42, SD = 0.74). At the same time, they thought AI will make participation more equitable (M = 4.42, SD = 0.79) and more tolerant of different political opinions (M = 4.14, SD = 1.07).

The results show that debates facilitated by AI have the ability to make students feel more engage and included. Chatbots and algorithmic moderators create an artificial policy debate setting where students can practice democratic discourse in a risk-free but nevertheless demanding setting. In line with the findings of Bulathwela et al., (2025), who discovered that algorithmic platforms increase the number of possibilities for deliberation and give a stronger voice to under-represented groups in public debate. Artificial intelligence discussion tools alleviate students' fears of public speaking and encourage more equal classroom engagement, according to new research by Ding, & Yusof (2025).

The results of this study support the claim put forth by Rapanta (2025) that students can develop their democratic identities and responsibilities in virtual spaces where AI is integrated into political education, which in turn improves civic communication. The second aspect tested how well the students could analyses and evaluate news stories about politics. Student mean ratings on different questions are high, it means they strongly believe that AI tools made it easier to spot bias and false information and determine credibility. Students found that natural language processing (NLP) analysis improved their bias detection abilities (M = 4.46, SD = 0.74) and their capacity to spot election-related disinformation (M = 4.32, SD = 0.77).Given the prevalence of electoral disinformation and "hoax culture" in Indonesia, this discovery is extremely pertinent to the local situation. This finding is in line with Olanipekun (2025) proved that young people can fight computational propaganda in election campaigns with media literacy training that incorporates AI. In a similar vein, Ghiurău, & Popescu, D. E. (2024) state that teaching media analysis with AI helps students become more resistant to deepfakes and other forms of deceptive digital content.

The current study confirms previous findings that use of natural language processing (NLP) technologies in political education raises students' media literacy and equips them to deal with contentious online public spaces. Students also achieved high mean scores on the inclusivity dimension, which measures their understanding of how adaptive AI systems facilitate individualized instruction while guaranteeing their full engagement in group projects. They reached a consensus that AI made it easier for people from all walks of life to participate (M = 4.42, SD = 0.87) and that it strengthened democratic principles like Bhinneka Tunggal Ika (M = 4.35, SD = 0.78).Both the individual's learning demands and the maintenance of shared civic values are aided by AI, as these results demonstrate. This agrees with Crupi et al., (2025), who stated that inclusive AI ecosystems in universities aid in bringing personalization and democratic inclusion into harmony.

Similarly, Kundu & Bej, (2025) found that adaptive AI helps students from rural areas and under-represented groups participate more actively, which helps to close the achievement gap. In South Asia, like in Indonesia, where socioeconomic and geographic differences or disparities impact educational opportunities, AI capabilities significantly promote diversity. These findings suggest that AI-mediated political education can realise inclusivity as a sustainable social and educational paradigm. Fairness (M = 4.25, SD = 0.92) and the dangers of surveillance (M = 4.35, SD

= 0.68), as shown in Table 5, were both data points that were improved through classroom discussions and an emphasis on the ethical use of AI.

Furthermore, respondents stated that case studies helped students reflect on human rights issues and that political education should emphasize ethical reflection (M = 4.32, SD = 0.72). Furthermore, these findings highlight the need to teach students about the ethical implications of AI and the technical aspects of its use in the classroom, similar to the findings of Holmes et al. (2022), who emphasized that teachers should help students avoid dependence on algorithms by guiding them toward ethical AI behavior. Similarly, the study by Ilcic et al. (2025) replicated previous research by emphasizing the importance of discussing AI ethics alongside discussions of government or school monitoring and oversight, where students considered ethical thinking as an important outcome of AI-mediated political education.

Students' high agreement that AI-based visualization increased their comprehension of elections (M = 4.21, SD = 0.78) and strengthened their confidence in analyzing datasets (M = 4.21, SD = 0.73), indicating data literacy as a critical dimension. Furthermore, they acknowledged the usefulness of AI initiatives in examining social issues (M = 4.21, SD = 0.99) and in relating data to ideas of democracy and power (M = 4.21, SD = 0.87). Students should be taught to question the sociopolitical consequences of data in post digital education, and the study findings support with the findings of Wong et al., (2025), who discovered that students' ability to link empirical findings with theoretical frameworks in political sociology is enhanced through AI-assisted data visualization.

Thus, the results of this study demonstrate that students' capacity to place data within sociological frameworks is enhanced by the use of AI technologies, which also improve technical analysis show that political education program that combine human and AI instructors greatly improve their students' civic competence. These findings are in line with international research that has highlighted the revolutionary potential of AI in political and civic education who demonstrated how AI changes academic identities and civic engagement. By demonstrating that corruption, disinformation, and polarization may be effectively addressed using AI-enhanced political education, this work makes a unique contribution to the Indonesian setting.

These results support recent research that shows how AI-enhanced learning can help students think critically, get involved in their communities, and learn about politics at the same time. This study, in helping students better recognize misinformation, aligns with findings by Rapanta (2025), who highlighted the use of AI tools, and Basak and Ghosh (2025) and Muthmainnah et al, (2026), who found that adaptive platforms and AI-powered discussion tools were shown to improve overall performance and enable more personalized learning pathways. Consistent with these studies, these results confirm that cybersociology learning models, integrating learning models like CALLEBAI, which combine human and AI partnerships, can significantly enhance students' sociopolitical competencies and prepare them to participate effectively in a democratic society.

Students believed that collaborating with AI was beneficial in various areas, including civic engagement, media literacy, inclusivity, data literacy, ethical reasoning, and civic reasoning, as well as integrating digital civility with democratic engagement. These findings provide strong support for the theoretical position of cybersociology by highlighting the fact that AI-enabled education involves more than just technology integration; it involves social negotiations about democratic values and civic identity in the modern era, which can be practised in the classroom. This investigation emphasizes the value of integrating AI into political science curricula in preparing students to actively engage in virtual, hybrid, and in-person democratic processes in the GenAI era.

CONCLUSION

This study confirms previous findings that cybersociology can explain the potential benefits and drawbacks of incorporating human-AI partnerships into political education curricula and how to implement them in the classroom. The CALLEBAI learning model provides an effective means to demonstrate how AI and social media technologies can develop students' civic skills beyond their technical use. Through data visualization projects, adaptive learning pathways, natural language processing of political discourse, and AI-based debate simulations on political democracy, students demonstrated effective improvement in their critical thinking, media literacy, inclusivity, ethical reasoning, and data-information literacy skills. Beyond being a measure of academic achievement, these skills serve as useful sociological tools for navigating the complexities of Indonesian democracy. One of the most significant contributions of this study is positioning educators as designers of political education learning ecologies. Rather than allowing AI devices to completely control the classroom, teachers should take the initiative to engage in ethical discussions about issues such as AI surveillance, disinformation, and polarization. In addition to mediating the use of data, they also contextualize it. This human-centered mediation ensures that learning remains democratic, inclusive, and based on moral principles. This perspective emphasizes that professional development program for educators must incorporate new literacies such as data analysis, sociological framing, and AI ethics throughout the intervention process.

The results of this study also highlight the social relevance of integrating AI into the Indonesian education system. Students' understanding of systemic issues such as political polarization, corruption, and disinformation improved, their political literacy increased, and they also demonstrated academic improvement. Improved student performance on the posttest lends credibility to the revolutionary effects of human-AI partnerships and the notion that AI-assisted education fosters critical literacy and democratic engagement in dynamic political contexts. Cybersociology theoretically benefits from this study's findings because they illuminate how online courses foster social interaction bargaining. Students develop their civic identity through active participation, inquiry, and interaction with AI products, beyond mere consumption.

Political education must embrace artificial intelligence (AI) tools, but only in a way that prioritizes human mediation, social foundations, and ethical considerations; otherwise, the implications for practice will become clear. Building an AI-inclusive curriculum, closing the digital achievement gap between schools in urban and rural areas, and ensuring equitable access to technological resources are all urgently needed. AI integration has the potential to foster democratic inclusion. The findings of this study suggest that human-AI partnerships in political education aim to go beyond increasing productivity and originality; they also aim to build a more democratic society. Combining AI tools with instructors' pedagogical insights allows for the design of learning ecosystems that prepare students to become informed, critical, and ethical members of society. Such integration is crucial in a country like Indonesia, where corruption, polarization, and misinformation jeopardize democracy and its sustainability. Ultimately, this research supports an educational paradigm that combines cybersociology with human-AI partnerships to safeguard democratic ideals and produce responsible citizens.

REFERENCES

Al Yakin, A., Al Matari, A.S., Muthmainnah M., Herawan, E., Auliya, Z.G., Wiradinata, R., & Obaid, A.J. (2026). Intelligent Blended Agents (IBAs) to Promote Computational Behaviour and Design Thinking in the Cyborg Education 7.0 Manifesto for Future of AI-Augmented Sociology Education. In Dutta, S., Bhattacharya, A., Bose, S., Polkowski, Z. (eds) Proceedings of International Conference on Computational Intelligence and Information Retrieval. ICCIIR 2025. Lecture Notes in Networks and Systems, vol 1617. Springer, Cham. DOI: 10.1007/978-3-032-04539-3_34

Al Yakin, A., Cardoso, L., Al Matari, A. S., Muthmainnah, M., Alnoor, A., & Obaid, A. J. (2024, September). Optimizing Artificial Intelligence (AI) Cici-Chatbot Teaching Mode on 4 Skills for Future Trends in Sociology Education Landscape at University. In *International Conference on Artificial Intelligence and Networking* (pp. 193-210). Singapore: Springer Nature Singapore.

Alberts, K. (2025). Unravelling the web: exploring the dynamics of online disinformation and its impact on democracy in Africa. *Canadian Journal of African Studies/Revue canadienne des études africaines, 59*(2), 333-359.

Albukhari, I. N. (2025). The role of artificial intelligence (AI) in architectural design: A systematic review of emerging technologies and applications. *Journal of Umm Al-Qura University for Engineering and Architecture*, 1-20.

Austin, L. A. (2025). *Polarization in the Era of News Media Metamorphosis: A Critical Exploration of Implications for Democracy and Human Rights* (Doctoral dissertation, University of Calgary (Canada)).

Bulathwela, S., Pérez-Ortiz, M., Holloway, C., Cukurova, M., & Shawe-Taylor, J. (2024). Artificial intelligence alone will not democratise education: On educational inequality, techno-solutionism and inclusive tools. *Sustainability (Basel), 16*(2), 781. DOI: 10.3390/su16020781

Chatterjee, D. (2025). An empire of artificial intelligence: Exploring an intersection of politics, society, and creativity. *International Journal of Politics Culture and Society, 38*(1), 81–110. DOI: 10.1007/s10767-024-09484-3

Chigbu, B. I., & Makapela, S. L. (2025). AI in education, sustainability, and the future of work: An integrative review of industry 5.0, education 5.0, and work 5.0. *Journal of Open Innovation, 11*(4), 100645. DOI: 10.1016/j.joitmc.2025.100645

Chiu, T. K., & Rospigliosi, P. A. (2025). Encouraging human-AI collaboration in interactive learning environments. *Interactive Learning Environments, 33*(2), 921–924. DOI: 10.1080/10494820.2025.2471199

Collins, H. (2025). Why artificial intelligence needs sociology of knowledge: Parts I and II. *AI & Society*, *40*(3), 1249–1263. DOI: 10.1007/s00146-024-01954-8

Crupi, A., Marinelli, L., & Cacciatore, E. (2025). Generative AI and Society 5.0: Enabling a Collaborative, Inclusive Future. In *The Generative AI Impact: Reframing Innovation in Society 5.0* (pp. 3-20). Emerald Publishing Limited.

Dili, G., & Ansong, E. D. (2025). Human–AI Collaboration: A Paradigm Shift in Decision-Making. In *The Power of Agentic AI: Redefining Human Life and Decision-Making: In Industry 6.0* (pp. 59–80). Springer Nature Switzerland. DOI: 10.1007/978-3-031-89424-4_5

Ding, D., & Yusof, M. B. (2025). Investigating the role of AI-powered conversation bots in enhancing L2 speaking skills and reducing speaking anxiety: A mixed methods study. *Humanities & Social Sciences Communications*, *12*(1), 1–16. DOI: 10.1057/s41599-025-05550-z

Dritsas, E., & Trigka, M. (2025). Machine Learning and Data Science in Social Sciences: Methods, Applications, and Future Directions. *IEEE Access : Practical Innovations, Open Solutions*, *13*, 105334–105352. DOI: 10.1109/ACCESS.2025.3578906

Eaton, S. E. (2025). Global trends in education: Artificial intelligence, postplagiarism, and future-focused learning for 2025 and beyond–2024–2025 Werklund Distinguished Research Lecture. *International Journal for Educational Integrity*, *21*(1), 12. DOI: 10.1007/s40979-025-00187-6

Francis, P., & Wolton, D. (2025). *A future of faith: the path of change in politics and society*. Macmillan+ ORM.

Ghiurău, D., & Popescu, D. E. (2024). Distinguishing reality from AI: Approaches for detecting synthetic content. *Computers*, *14*(1), 1. DOI: 10.3390/computers14010001

Guglielmo, M., Ahrweiler, P., Barberà, O., Brockschmidt, D. S., Critch, N., de Moraes Azenha, A. L., Del Río, A. F., Ennis, C. A., García Guijarro, P., Gomís Jaen, E., Luke, D., Luque Capellas, B., Malý, M., Mansouri, M. I., Medrado, A., O'Loughlin, B., Ritchie, D., Sánchez Montell, M., Sentí Navarro, C., & Ward, B. (2025). Us and artificial intelligence: Questioning agency and the need for critical and humanist perspectives. *Open Research Europe*, *5*, 318. DOI: 10.12688/openreseurope.21477.1

Haroud, S., & Saqri, N. (2025). Generative ai in higher education: Teachers' and students' perspectives on support, replacement, and digital literacy. *Education Sciences*, *15*(4), 396. DOI: 10.3390/educsci15040396

Hillygus, D. S., & Holbein, J. B. (2023). Refocusing civic education: Developing the skills young people need to engage in democracy. *The Annals of the American Academy of Political and Social Science, 705*(1), 73–94. DOI: 10.1177/00027162231177798

Hwang, Y., Lee, S., & Jeon, J. (2025). Integrating AI chatbots into the metaverse: Pre-service English teachers' design works and perceptions. *Education and Information Technologies, 30*(4), 4099–4130. DOI: 10.1007/s10639-024-12924-4

Ilcic, A., Fuentes, M., & Lawler, D. (2025). Artificial intelligence, complexity, and systemic resilience in global governance. *Frontiers in Artificial Intelligence, 8*, 1562095. DOI: 10.3389/frai.2025.1562095 PMID: 40529642

Jacob, J. U. U., & Vajjhala, N. R. (Eds.). (2025). *AI and the Future of Democracy: Building Resilient and Inclusive Societies*. CRC Press. DOI: 10.1201/9781003594185

Jain, V. (2024). Quality Education Through E-Learning for Sustainable Development. *Transforming Vocational Education and Training Using AI*, 211.

Janfada, M., Heidari, E., & Lin, A. (2025). Transcending multiliteracies pedagogies in, for, through AI-oriented learning spaces: A dialogic perspective. *Pedagogies*, •••, 1–23. DOI: 10.1080/1554480X.2025.2563621

Jha, A., & Singh, S. R. (2025). Integrating Artificial Intelligence in Media Education: Revolutionizing Learning, Creativity, and Critical Thinking. In Teachers' Roles and Perspectives on AI Integration in Schools (pp. 297-328). IGI Global Scientific Publishing.

Jiang, Y., Zhao, J., Yuan, Y., Zhang, T., Huang, Y., Zhang, Y., . . . Li, X. (2025). Never compromise to vulnerabilities: A comprehensive survey on ai governance. *arXiv preprint arXiv:2508.08789*.

Karadži, E., & Redžepi, F. (2025). Uvod u kritičku analizu biopolitičkog genocidnog rata u pojasu Gaze: Teorijski izazovi i društvene implikacije/Introduction to a Critical Analysis of the Biopolitical Genocidal War in the Gaza Strip: Theoretical Challenges and Social Implications. *Pregled: časopis za društvena pitanja/Periodical for social issues, 66*(2), 83-111.

Kim, S. J., Sun, Y., Bucy, E. P., & Shah, D. V. (2025). Digital Dilemmas: Crises in the Fourth Age of Political Communication. In *Public Communication in Freefall: Revisiting the work of Jay Blumler* (pp. 59–88). Springer Nature Switzerland. DOI: 10.1007/978-3-031-83364-9_4

Kundu, A., & Bej, T. (2025). Empowering Students' Autonomy in EFL Learning: AI Innovations in Schools of the Global South. *The Electronic Journal on Information Systems in Developing Countries, 91*(6), e70041. DOI: 10.1002/isd2.70041

Leba, S. M. R., Nggaruaka, T., & Butarbutar, R. (2025). Smart Teaching in Rural Indonesia: Harnessing AI-Assisted Deep Learning for Teacher Professional Development. *EthAIca: Journal of Ethics. AI and Critical Analysis*, (4), 419.

Lorenzo, R., Sagula, J. E., Zayas-Figueras, E. E., Quishpe-Solano, R., & Pérez-Rodríguez, R. (2024, October). Development of Educational 4.0 Environments Through the Dynamic Integration of Natural (Human) and Artificial Intelligences. In *Workshop in R&D+ i & International Workshop on STEM of EPS* (pp. 387-398). Cham: Springer Nature Switzerland.

Mamlok, D. (2025). Landscapes of sociotechnical imaginaries in education: A theoretical examination of integrating artificial intelligence in education. *Foundations of Science*, *30*(2), 529–540. DOI: 10.1007/s10699-024-09948-x

Matar, S. (2025). The Development of Educational Technology and Artificial Intelligence and Their Impact on the Future of Education: Opportunities and Risks. *Journal of Posthumanism*, *5*(7), 1271–1292. DOI: 10.63332/joph.v5i7.2915

Mavridi, S. (2025). Hype, fear, and everything in between: A critical typology of responses to AI and their implications for language teacher education. *Technology in Language Teaching & Learning*, *7*(2), 103219–103219. DOI: 10.29140/tltl.v7n2.103219

Muthmainnah, M., ... (2026). Navigating the Impact of Augmentation Computing Intelligence, AI Literacy, and Human Integration in English Language Education 7.0 by Using Computer-Assisted Language Learning and Augmented (CALLedA) Model. In: Dutta, S., Bhattacharya, A., Bose, S., Polkowski, Z. (eds) Proceedings of International Conference on Computational Intelligence and Information Retrieval. ICCIIR 2025. Lecture Notes in Networks and Systems, vol 1617. Springer, Cham. DOI: 10.1007/978-3-032-04539-3_35

Muthmainnah, M., Cardoso, L., Marzuki, A. G., & Al Yakin, A. (2025). A new innovative metaverse ecosystem: VR-based human interaction enhances EFL learners' transferable skills. *Discover Sustainability, 6*(1), 156.

Neyazi, , T. AKhai, Ee, TKuru, , O. (2025). Campaign Deepfakes and Affective Polarization: The Role of Artificial Intelligence in Campaigns in Shaping Voter Attitudes. *Social Science Computer Review*, •••, 08944393251362247.

Ningxue, F. (2025, May). Ethical Challenges of AI Integration in Open University Online Education: A Multidimensional Analysis. In *2025 5th International Conference on Artificial Intelligence and Education (ICAIE)* (pp. 45-49). IEEE. DOI: 10.1109/ICAIE64856.2025.11158646

Olanipekun, S. O.Samson Olufemi Olanipekun. (2025). Computational propaganda and misinformation: AI technologies as tools of media manipulation. *World Journal of Advanced Research and Reviews, 25*(1), 911–923. DOI: 10.30574/wjarr.2025.25.1.0131

Padalko, H., Chumachenko, D., Kaur, N., Hussain, I. Z., Kaur, J., Lotto, M., Butt, Z. A., & Morita, P. P. (2025). Investigation of machine learning approaches to classify war-related content during Russian full-scale invasion of Ukraine. *Social Network Analysis and Mining, 15*(1), 1–17. DOI: 10.1007/s13278-025-01501-3

Panwar, K., Sihag, V., Choudhary, G., & Dragoni, N. (2023, August). A threat and risk analysis of internet communication technology use. In *International Conference on ICT for Sustainable Development* (pp. 407-414). Singapore: Springer Nature Singapore. DOI: 10.1007/978-981-99-5652-4_36

Pavlović, J. (2025). *Partnering with AI in Coaching and Human Skills Development: A Constructivist Guidebook for Innovation.* Taylor & Francis. DOI: 10.4324/9781003583141

Rapanta, C. (2025). Postdigital Citizenship Education and Argumentation: Can AI Support Students' Critical Literacy? In *Discourses of Globalisation and Citizenship Education* (pp. 69–86). Springer Nature Switzerland. DOI: 10.1007/978-3-031-86145-1_5

Rasa, T. (2025). Postdigital Dissensus: On the Complexity of Debating Technology in Higher Education Futures. *Postdigital Science and Education*, 1-20.

Riquelme, S. (2025). Citizenship Education, Crisis of the Democratic Belief and World without Adults: Challenges and Educational Perspectives. In *Latin American University Students and Global Citizenship: Perspectives and Engagement* (pp. 19–33). Springer Nature Switzerland. DOI: 10.1007/978-3-032-03057-3_2

Romanishyn, A., Malytska, O., & Goncharuk, V. (2025). The Problem of AI-Driven Disinformation. Policy recommendations in respect to fighting disinformation. *Frontiers in Artificial Intelligence, 8*, 1569115. DOI: 10.3389/frai.2025.1569115 PMID: 40821951

Samadhiya, A., Kumar, A., Mulat-Weldemeskel, E., Luthra, S., Garza-Reyes, J. A., & Yadav, S. (2025). Next-gen quality learning: How can AI technologies shape education 4.0 and 5.0 towards the SDGs from multiple stakeholders' perspective? *The TQM Journal.* Advance online publication. DOI: 10.1108/TQM-11-2024-0441

Santiago-Torner, C., Corral-Marfil, J. A., Jiménez-Pérez, Y., & Tarrats-Pons, E. (2025). Impact of ethical leadership on autonomy and self-efficacy in virtual work environments: The disintegrating effect of an egoistic climate. *Behavioral Sciences (Basel, Switzerland)*, *15*(1), 95. DOI: 10.3390/bs15010095 PMID: 39851899

Sarafis, D., Karamitsios, K., & Kravari, K. (2025, February). AI and Civic Engagement: A Brief Exploration of Applications and Opportunities. In *2025 International Conference on Advancement in Data Science, E-learning and Information System (ICADEIS)* (pp. 1-6). IEEE. DOI: 10.1109/ICADEIS65852.2025.10933183

Stevens, C. (2025). Teachers and teaching: Pedagogy, digital skills and professional development. *Open Learning*, *40*(1), 1–3. DOI: 10.1080/02680513.2024.2436665

Tang, K. S., & Putra, G. B. S. (2025). Generative AI as a Dialogic Partner: Enhancing Multiple Perspectives, Reasoning, and Argumentation in Science Education with Customized Chatbots. *Journal of Science Education and Technology*, •••, 1–13.

Tejero, A., Pisoni, G., Lashkari, Z. H., & Aguilar, S. R. (2025). Combating Misinformation and Polarization in the Corporate Sphere: Integrating Social, Technological and AI Strategies. *International Journal of Interactive Multimedia and Artificial Intelligence*, *9*(4), 117–125. DOI: 10.9781/ijimai.2024.03.003

Tihonova, E. V., Borisova, T. P., & Bunov, E. G. (2022, January). Cyberspace as a New Social Reality in the Era of Globalization. In *Proceedings of the International Scientific Conference "Smart Nations: Global Trends In The Digital Economy" Volume 2* (pp. 274-280). Cham: Springer International Publishing. DOI: 10.1007/978-3-030-94870-2_35

Velander, J., Otero, N., & Milrad, M. (2024). What is critical (about) AI literacy? Exploring conceptualizations present in AI literacy discourse. In *Framing futures in postdigital education: Critical concepts for data-driven practices* (pp. 139–160). Springer Nature Switzerland. DOI: 10.1007/978-3-031-58622-4_8

Wang, X., & Xie, F. (2025). Global artificial intelligence governance research in the digital and intelligent era: Advances, trends and countermeasures. *Journal of Knowledge Management*.

Wong, W., Aristidou, A., & Scheuermann, K. (2025). The future of learning or the future of dividing? Exploring the impact of general artificial intelligence on higher education. *Data & Policy*, *7*, e44. DOI: 10.1017/dap.2025.10011

Xu, L., Hinds, A., Rakisheva, A., El Souefi, N., & Witt, A. (2025). Beyond borders: Virtual Global Engagement in teacher education. *Teaching and Teacher Education*, *165*, 105133. DOI: 10.1016/j.tate.2025.105133

Yim, I. H. Y. (2024). A critical review of teaching and learning artificial intelligence (AI) literacy: Developing an intelligence-based AI literacy framework for primary school education. *Computers and Education: Artificial Intelligence*, *7*, 100319. DOI: 10.1016/j.caeai.2024.100319

Zdravkov, S., & Ilieva-Trichkova, P. (2025). Participation in Online Courses from the Perspective of Bourdieu's Cultural Capital Theory: A European Comparative Study. *European Education*, *57*(3), 209–227. DOI: 10.1080/10564934.2025.2531529

Zhang, C., Shao, Y., Yuan, Y., & Shen, W. (2025). Artificial Intelligence Reshapes Creativity: A Multidimensional Evaluation. *PsyCh Journal*, *14*(6), 831–840. DOI: 10.1002/pchj.70042 PMID: 40764253

Zhou, X., Li, Y., Chai, C. S., & Chiu, T. K. (2025). Defining, enhancing, and assessing artificial intelligence literacy and competency in K-12 education from a systematic review. *Interactive Learning Environments*, *33*(10), 1–23. DOI: 10.1080/10494820.2025.2487538

Chapter 7
The Future of the AI University:
From Mass Education to a Curated Knowledge Economy

Silvio Andrae
http://orcid.org/0000-0002-8586-7812
Independent Researcher, Germany

ABSTRACT

The rapid proliferation of generative artificial intelligence challenges the model of mass universities, as analytical and synthetic activities traditionally regarded as core academic competencies become increasingly automated. This chapter examines how universities can respond by transforming from reproduction-oriented institutions into curated knowledge economies centered on the cultivation of judgment. Methodologically, the analysis combines a structural comparison of historical university models with a systematic review of recent research on AI in teaching, assessment, and governance. The main result is a dual-path institutional model of the AI university that distinguishes practice-oriented implementation tracks from research-oriented innovation tracks, while normatively linking both through judgment as a guiding principle. The chapter further shows that AI necessitates a realignment of assessment, teaching roles, and governance. The university thus emerges not as replaceable by AI, but as a key institution for social judgment in a technologically saturated knowledge order.

DOI: 10.4018/979-8-2600-1458-5.ch007

INTRODUCTION

Higher education systems are at a historic turning point, characterized less by a quantitative technological push than by a qualitative shift in epistemic functions. While the mass university of the 20th century was geared toward the reproduction, standardization, and certification of knowledge, the rapid spread of generative artificial intelligence (AI) is shifting the institutional focus away from knowledge production in the narrower sense toward the question of who still judges, evaluates, and takes responsibility in an AI-supported knowledge order. Generative AI systems can perform key academic activities—such as literature research, text production, data analysis, and argument structuring—with high quality and almost unlimited scalability. As a result, those cognitive routines that have long been considered the core of academic qualification are losing their scarcity and differentiation value (Brynjolfsson & McAfee, 2014; Kasneci et al., 2023).

Unlike previous waves of digitization, this development affects not only peripheral organizational or didactic processes but also the epistemic core of university practice. Activities that have served as the didactic core of many study programs for decades—in particular, standardized analysis, synthesis, and reporting tasks—are becoming increasingly automatable or, at least, highly commodified. It also puts the organizational model of the mass university under structural strain: it is based on scaling, comparability, and the mass training of reproducible analytical skills, while precisely these skills are losing their relative value under AI conditions. The implicit exchange relationship on which this model has long been based—standardized training in exchange for standardized career entry opportunities—is beginning to dissolve.

This shift does not have a uniform effect. Productivity gains are increasingly concentrated among experienced professionals who can combine AI systems with independent professional judgment, while traditional entry-level and assistant roles, which are primarily focused on routine analytical work, are becoming less critical or disappearing altogether. This calls into question a career path that much of academic education continues to be implicitly tailored to: the gradual development of skills through routine analytical tasks, culminating in more responsible decision-making positions. The lower rungs of this ladder are becoming fragile, while new forms of productive co-intelligence are emerging at the top.

Against this backdrop, another skill is coming to the fore: judgment. In an AI-generated glut of information, texts, forecasts, and proposals for action, the central challenge is no longer access to knowledge, but rather the reflective evaluation of results, the contextualization of evidence, and the normative decision about which conclusions are legitimate, responsible, and socially desirable. Judgment thus functions as a scarce resource in an AI-saturated knowledge economy (Autor, 2015; Floridi et al., 2018). It encompasses the ability to examine AI-generated outputs critically, recognize methodological limitations, reveal implicit assumptions, highlight conflicting goals, and make decisions under uncertainty. As a cognitive, social, and normative practice, it cannot be completely individualized or algorithmized.

This shift has far-reaching institutional implications. Universities can no longer legitimize their social relevance primarily through the imparting of reproducible knowledge, but must redefine themselves as places of education, practice, and institutional anchoring of judgment. This shifts the focus from primarily efficiency- and scale-oriented knowledge transfer to the conscious design of research, teaching, and decision-making processes that systematically cultivate human and collective judgment. From this perspective, the university does not appear as an institution threatened by AI. Still, as a hybrid co-intelligence system in which artificial intelligence (AI), human intelligence (HI), and collective intelligence (CI) interact in a division of labor, AI primarily takes on reproductive, analytical, and organizational functions. In contrast, humans and academic communities carry those forms of knowledge that require interpretation, evaluation, and responsibility.

Contribution of this chapter

The contribution of this chapter is to establish judgment as the guiding category for the university's institutional realignment in the age of generative AI. Instead of treating AI primarily as a didactic tool or administrative infrastructure, the chapter develops a conceptual model of the 'AI university' in which the training and safeguarding of judgment is explicitly anchored as a functional core. Based on a structural comparative analysis of historical university models—elite, mass, and network universities—it is shown that the current change cannot be interpreted as gradual modernization but rather as a transition to a new institutional logic. This logic is operationalized through a two-path model: practice-oriented implementation paths that aim at the judicious professional application of AI, and research-oriented innovation paths in which theoretical, creative, and ethical judgment is systematically developed. The chapter thus contributes to higher education, education, and science research by integrating technological, epistemic, and normative dimensions.

Structure of the chapter

The rest of the chapter is structured as follows. Section 2 reconstructs the mass university as a historical organizational model and analyzes its structural limitations under conditions of AI-based knowledge automation. Section 3 examines how generative AI devalues analytical academic activities and destabilizes traditional qualification and career logics. Section 4 develops judgment as a new scarce resource in the knowledge economy and specifies its cognitive, social, and ethical dimensions.

Building on this, Section 5 creates a two-path model of the AI university that institutionally separates and simultaneously connects implementation and innovation logics. Section 6 analyzes the changing role of academic teachers, moving from curators to mentors and orchestrators of judgment-oriented learning spaces. Section 7 discusses governance, justice, and power issues in the context of AI-supported university infrastructures. The conclusion brings together the findings into a vision of the university as a curated, research-centered institution whose social legitimacy lies in the training of judgment under conditions of technological abundance.

THE MASS UNIVERSITY

The mass university is the defining organizational model of higher education in the 20th century. It emerged in the wake of the political, economic, and social upheavals after World War II. It was closely linked to the expansion of welfare state structures, the democratization of education, and the transition to knowledge-intensive economies. Its central promise was to remove academic education from elite circles and make it accessible to broad sections of the population. Universities thus became key institutions of social mobility and the central infrastructure for the production of human capital in industrial and post-industrial societies (Trow, 1973; Marginson, 2016).

Institutionally, mass universities were based on a logic of scaling and standardization. Large student cohorts, modularized curricula, uniform examination formats, and formally comparable degrees enabled the efficient organization of educational achievements and their social legitimation. Knowledge was implicitly treated as a reproducible resource that could be taught, tested, and certified in a curriculum-structured form. This form of organization was highly successful in functional terms: it enabled a massive expansion of academic education, created transparent signals of qualifications for labor markets, and stabilized the relationship among higher education, the state, and the economy through formalized expectation structures (Clark, 1986; Meyer et al., 2006).

At the same time, the mass university model has always been characterized by a structural tension between educational aspirations and organizational logic. The need to manage large numbers of students efficiently led to increasing standardization of teaching and examination formats, which tended to marginalize individual learning processes, creative deviations, and research-oriented forms of education. Examinations served less to develop independent judgment or research skills than to ensure formal comparability and selection based on standardized criteria. Under conditions of limited information processing capacities and high transaction costs, this logic was institutionally plausible, but at the same time, it created path dependencies that proved increasingly restrictive as the knowledge society grew in complexity (Trow, 1973; Clark, 1983; Collins, 1979; Meyer & Rowan, 1977; Pierson, 2000).

With the ongoing expansion of the higher education system, these tensions became increasingly apparent. On the one hand, there was an inflation of formal educational qualifications, which reduced their signaling effect on labor markets. On the other hand, the content of academic profiles became more homogeneous, as standardized curricula allowed only limited differentiation. The mass university thus increasingly reproduced the very scarcities it was initially intended to resolve: attention, individual support, and epistemic depth became scarce resources within a system geared toward quantitative expansion (Brown, 2013; Collins, 1979).

The use of generative artificial intelligence further exacerbates these structural limitations. The organizational model of the mass university implicitly relies on central academic achievements—such as writing texts, analyzing data, or presenting knowledge in a structured way—being linked to individual learning processes and being automatable only to a limited extent. It is precisely this assumption that AI systems undermine. When standardized academic outputs become technically easy to reproduce, the mass university logic of knowledge transfer and assessment loses its epistemic exclusivity. This puts pressure on the legitimacy not of education as such, but of the institutional form of its organization.

The 'decline' of the mass university should therefore not be understood as a crisis in the sense of institutional failure, but rather as an expression of a changed environment in which the historical conditions for the functioning of this model are eroding. The challenge is not so much to further increase efficiency or access, but rather to institutionally reweight those dimensions of academic education that elude standardization. From this perspective, the mass university does not mark an endpoint, but rather a transitional phase in the long-term development of university organizational forms, with an open outcome as to which epistemic achievements universities will define as their central social function in the future.

The structural limits of the mass university remain latent as long as central academic achievements are tied to individual cognitive work and limited scalability. As long as analytical activities—such as the systematic indexing of literature, the writing of structured texts, or the evaluation of data—require a considerable investment of time and expertise, standardized teaching and examination formats will retain their institutional plausibility. With the advent of generative artificial intelligence, however, this prerequisite is being fundamentally challenged.

AI does not act as an external driver of efficiency, but intervenes directly in the work processes on which the mass university logic of knowledge transfer, performance assessment, and certification is based. This devalues precisely those analytical intermediate achievements that previously served as proof of academic qualification and ensured the system's reproducibility. Katsamakas et al. (2024) show that generative AI puts pressure on universities' central value-creation mechanisms by scaling analytical activities, devaluing exam performance, and reducing the information asymmetries on which academic certificates are traditionally based. Universities are thus losing part of their role as credible signalers in the labor market. The following section examines how the institutional pressure to adapt generated by AI does not automatically destabilize existing competence hierarchies, qualification paths, and institutional assessment logics through reflexive reforms—and why this process accelerates the transition from a reproduction-oriented to a judgment-oriented higher education model.

AUTOMATION OF ANALYTICAL WORK THROUGH AI

The most profound impact of generative artificial intelligence in the higher education context lies not in automating administrative processes, but in the systematic takeover of analytical activities previously considered core academic qualifications. These include, in particular, literature research and synthesis, argument structuring, writing scientific texts, evaluating quantitative and qualitative data, and visualizing complex issues. For decades, these activities formed the basis of academic socialization and also served as key performance indicators in studies, exams, and early career stages. With the spread of generative AI systems, however, these analytical routines are losing their character as scarce individual achievements (Kasneci et al., 2023).

Analytical outputs can increasingly be standardized, scaled, and generated at low marginal cost. This applies not only to simple reproduction tasks, but also to more complex forms of analysis, such as merging heterogeneous strands of literature, generating coherent lines of argumentation, or exploring large data spaces. As a result, the value creation of academic work is shifting from the independent production of analytical content to the selection, control, and evaluation of such content. For universities, the question is therefore less about whether AI is used than about how its use can be institutionally framed and evaluated in terms of qualifications.

This development has particularly significant consequences for those analytical intermediate works that traditionally marked the entry into academic and knowledge-intensive professional fields. Activities such as drafting expert reports, project reports, empirical preliminary analyses, or policy papers fulfilled a dual function: they delivered usable results and at the same time served as learning and socialization stages in which methodological routines, disciplinary standards, and argumentative practices were gradually internalized. As this intermediate work becomes increasingly automated, this incremental qualification logic is at risk of eroding. Classic career paths based on a gradual increase in analytical responsibility are thus losing their institutional stability (Autor et al., 2003; Susskind & Susskind, 2015).

This shift creates a structural paradox: while organizations and research institutions increasingly need actors who can evaluate complex results, justify decisions, and take responsibility, the learning paths through which such skills have been developed to date are becoming shorter. This puts pressure on universities to establish qualification models that are no longer based primarily on mastery of analytical routines, but on reflective decision-making skills, contextual sensitivity, and responsible interpretation of results.

At the same time, the automation of analytical work undermines the traditional examination logic of mass universities. Historically, examinations served not only to test knowledge but also functioned as institutionalized procedures for attributing individual performance. This attribution presupposes that analytical performance is clearly personalized, performed under controlled conditions, and comparable between individuals. Generative AI deprives this logic of its epistemic foundation. If analytical quality increasingly arises independently of individual execution, examination formats based on reproducible texts, standardized problem solutions, or formal argumentation patterns lose their validity as performance indicators.

This shifts the implicit purpose of academic examinations from the evaluation of analytical production to the review of selection, control, and assessment decisions. In institutional practice, this shift has not yet been adequately reflected, leading to a growing gap between formal exam requirements and the skills actually relevant to dealing with AI-supported knowledge production. Attempts to merely adapt existing exam formats technically are therefore insufficient as long as the underlying assessment logic remains unchanged.

From an institutional perspective, the automation of analytical work therefore marks not merely a gain in efficiency, but a profound change in the epistemic assessment logic of academic education. When analytical routines lose their function as a central criterion of differentiation and legitimation, the question arises as to what basis academic quality, performance, and responsibility can be attributed to in the future. The focus is shifting from the production of analytical content to the ability to evaluate results critically—regardless of their origin—to contextualize them, and to make responsible decisions under uncertainty. Empirical findings suggest that this shift is not without consequences. Neurocognitive studies show that the use of generative AI in writing tasks is associated with a significant reduction in neural connectivity, lower memory performance, and a loss of perceived authorship. Kosmyna et al. (2025) refer to the accumulation of a 'cognitive debt' in this context, which manifests itself particularly when analytical and synthetic work is systematically outsourced to AI. Empirical evidence from university practice confirms this shift. Based on a large-scale student survey at a selective liberal arts college, Contractor and Reyes (2025) show that, within less than 2 years, over 80% of students use generative AI for academic purposes, with its use systematically differentiated between learning-supporting augmentation and work-replacing automation.

This shift fundamentally changes the scarcity conditions in the knowledge economy. It is not information, analysis, or formal competence that becomes the limiting factor, but rather the ability to make reflective judgments and normative orientations in complex, AI-supported decision-making situations. Section 4 takes up this finding and develops judgment as a central epistemic guiding category of the university in the age of generative artificial intelligence.

NEW SCARCITY IN THE KNOWLEDGE ECONOMY

The automation of analytical work through generative artificial intelligence is not only changing work processes but also fundamentally shifting the scarcity ratios within the knowledge economy. While information, analysis, and formal problem-solving are increasingly available, another skill is coming to the fore that cannot be scaled or fully formalized: judgment. In an AI-supported knowledge system, the central challenge is no longer to generate or process knowledge, but to evaluate results, understand contexts, recognize limitations, and make responsible decisions under uncertainty. Judgment thus becomes the central epistemic resource of academic education and research.

Conceptual Definition of Judgment

In the context of this chapter, judgment refers to the ability to apply general rules, models, or results to concrete, context-specific situations while reflecting on both methodological appropriateness and normative implications. Judgment cannot be equated with the mere application of rules or with subjective intuition. It is a mediating practice that operates between abstract knowledge and concrete action, while always remaining situation-dependent, responsibility-related, and not fully standardizable.

This fundamentally distinguishes judgment from common university policy concepts such as skill, competence, or employability. Skills refer to executable individual abilities, competencies to standardizable bundles of abilities, and employability to the external market suitability of qualifications. Judgment, on the other hand, cannot be fully measured, certified, or externalized. It only manifests itself in the execution of concrete decision-making and evaluation processes and requires a willingness to take responsibility for one's own conclusions. This distinction becomes particularly important in the context of AI-supported knowledge production, where outputs are generated technically but cannot be normatively accounted for. Similarly, Zheng

(2025) argues that the mission of universities in the AI age is not solely to impart skills, but to cultivate expertise, judgment, and responsibility as forms of meta-knowledge that must be supported disciplinarily and institutionally.

Judgment is neither identical with complete knowledge nor with ubiquitous participation. Sociological analyses of non-knowledge rightly point out that modern functional systems are based on a division of labor in ignorance: not all actors can or need to have comprehensive knowledge to remain capable of action. It is precisely this functional limitation of expertise that enables specialization, efficiency, and institutional stability. Under conditions of generative artificial intelligence, this insight takes on new relevance, as the availability of algorithmically generated information rebalances the relationship between knowledge, ignorance, and responsibility (Osrečki, 2025).

However, judgment mustn't consist of retreating into ignorance. While ignorance can provide functional relief, judgment aims at a reflective engagement with epistemic uncertainty. It refers to the ability not only to take note of AI-generated evidence, but also to critically examine its conditions of origin, assumptions, limitations, and normative implications. Judgment thus requires neither complete information nor permanent participation, but rather an institutionally framed practice of evaluation in which responsibilities, obligations to justify, and attributions of responsibility are clearly regulated.

AI-supported knowledge systems in particular reveal that the central challenge lies not in maximizing individual competence or transparency, but in ensuring reliable decision-making authorities. Institutions have a dual function here: they limit the reasonableness of individual knowledge requirements and, at the same time, ensure that decisions do not disappear into algorithmic opacity. In this sense, judgment functions as a mediating category between knowledge and ignorance, between machine calculation and social responsibility—and thus becomes a genuinely institutional target in the age of generative AI.

Judgment as a Category of Examination and Research

The philosophical tradition of judgment not only provides conceptual clarification but also contains implicit references to how judgment can be institutionally generated, examined, and reproduced. Already in Immanuel Kant (1790/2000), judgment is not merely the application of given rules, but the ability to make justified assignments under conditions of incomplete or conflicting rules. For exam formats, this means that judgment becomes relevant when tasks cannot be algorithmized entirely: when problems remain open, context-dependent, or ambiguous, and students must justify why they consider a particular interpretation, method, or solution appropriate. Exams that focus exclusively on the reproducible application of rules do not capture this form of judgment—and are structurally devalued under AI conditions.

Hannah Arendt (1961) expands this perspective to include a public and ethical dimension of responsibility. For her, judgment refers to the ability to make decisions that stand up to scrutiny by others without relying on objective certainty or mere conformity to rules. Applied to academic examination and assessment processes, this brings to the fore the question of who is responsible for a judgment and how it is justified and made contestable. In AI-supported service provision, examinations cannot evaluate results alone. Still, they must make the attribution of responsibility explicit: for the selection of methods, for the use or non-use of AI, and for the normative implications of the decisions made. Judgment thus becomes the central category of an examination logic that organizes comparability not through standardization, but through comprehensible reasoning.

Finally, John Dewey's (1938) pragmatic perspective makes clear that judgment cannot be tested selectively but can only be developed in procedural and research contexts. Judgment arises through experimental action, through hypothesis formation, error, revision, and reflection. For academic education, this implies a stronger integration of teaching and research: students develop judgment not primarily by solving pre-structured tasks, but by participating in open research processes in which uncertainty, methodological decisions, and responsibility can be systematically experienced. Research training thus becomes a central place for the formation of judgment—and not merely preparation for a future academic career.

Taken together, Kant, Arendt, and Dewey thus point to a fundamental shift in academic assessment and educational logic. Judgment cannot be generated through standardized exams or isolated competency modules, but requires institutional arrangements that systematically integrate open-ended problems, obligations to justify, and research-oriented forms of learning. This is precisely where the need for a differentiated institutional architecture comes in: a university that identifies different paths to judgment and organizes them. On this basis, the following section develops a two-path model of the AI university that institutionally separates practice-oriented implementation skills and research-oriented innovation and judgment, while at the same time linking them functionally.

Judgment, Research, and Ethical control in the AI Age

In a knowledge order shaped by AI, judgment is closely linked to research competence and ethical control. Under these conditions, research does not primarily mean the application of existing methods, but rather the critical reflection of model assumptions, data qualities, and objectives. AI systems can generate hypotheses, recognize patterns, and provide forecasts, but they cannot assess their epistemic status or normative consequences. This task remains the preserve of human judgment.

The same applies to ethical questions. Aspects such as fairness, bias, transparency, data protection, and the social consequences of algorithmic decisions cannot be 'solved' algorithmically, but require balanced, context-sensitive, and responsible judgments. Universities have a dual role to play here: they must train students and researchers in judgment and also institutionally safeguard it by creating spaces for reflection, dissent, and critical examination.

This makes it clear that judgment should not be understood as an additional individual characteristic, but as a core institutional service of the university in the age of generative AI. It serves as the normative and epistemic counterpoint to increasingly automated knowledge production and as a link between technical performance and social responsibility.

Section 5 builds on this insight and develops a two-path institutional model of the university that does not postulate judgment in abstract terms, but translates it into different educational and research logics: practice-oriented implementation paths on the one hand and research-oriented innovation paths on the other.

TWO PATHS OF INSTITUTIONALIZED JUDGMENT IN THE AI UNIVERSITY

The analysis of judgment as an epistemic, public, and practical ability suggests that a uniform educational logic cannot meet the requirements of an AI-supported knowledge order. Different forms of judgment formation require different institutional arrangements, examination logics, and attributions of responsibility. The AI university responds to this not by further standardization but by consciously differentiating its educational and research architecture. In the following, two complementary paths are developed that institutionally secure different modes of judgment.

Implementation Paths: Judgment in professional Decision-making Contexts

The practice-oriented implementation paths focus on the type of judgment required in organizational, regulatory, and professional contexts. From a Kantian perspective, the emphasis is on reflective judgment, which enables decisions to be made under incomplete rules and in situations of uncertainty. Students learn to apply general models, data, or AI-based analyses to specific contexts without relying on the mechanical application of laws. Judgment is manifested here in the ability to assess appropriateness: Which models are viable in which situations, which assumptions are problematic, and which risks are acceptable?

In Arendt's sense, this form of judgment is also publicly responsible. Implementation paths do not prepare students for abstract problem-solving, but rather for decisions that must stand up to scrutiny from other actors—organizations, customers, regulators, and stakeholders. Examination and performance formats are therefore not primarily focused on the correctness of results, but on comprehensible reasoning, transparency of the decision-making process, and explicit assumption of responsibility, especially when using AI systems. Here, judgment is operationalized as the ability to defend, explain, and, if necessary, revise decisions.

In Dewey's sense, this judgment is based on practice and experience. Implementation paths integrate project-based learning arrangements, simulation-based decision-making settings, and organization-related case studies in which students observe and reflect on the consequences of their judgments. AI functions as a tool for analysis and scenario generation, not as a decision-making authority. The institutional focus is on professional connectivity without reducing judgment to short-term employability or tool competence.

Innovation Paths: Judgment as Research-based Knowledge Practice

Research-oriented innovation paths address a different, structurally indispensable form of judgment. From a Kantian perspective, the focus here is not on applying existing rules, but on questioning, expanding, or reestablishing them. Judgment manifests itself in the ability to formulate new problems, critically examine theoretical assumptions, and develop research paths for which there are no established evaluation standards. This form of judgment is constitutive for scientific innovation and cannot, in principle, be automated.

Following Arendt, judgmental power here takes on an epistemic-public dimension. Research is not only the production of knowledge, but also a public process of justification: hypotheses, methods, and results must be valid in scientific communities. Innovation paths, therefore, cultivate those forms of judgment that allow us to tolerate uncertainty, make dissent productive, and take responsibility for the epistemic and societal implications of research—especially where AI-based methods create new structures of power and asymmetry.

Dewey's pragmatic approach ultimately makes clear that this form of judgment can arise only through active participation in research. Paths to innovation are therefore closely linked to research-oriented teaching, open questions, and iterative knowledge processes. Students do not act as consumers of knowledge, but as co-researchers who develop, reject, and refine hypotheses. AI serves here as an exploratory tool that reveals patterns or stimulates hypotheses without replacing the process of evaluating knowledge.

Common Guiding Logic and Institutional Separation

Although implementation and innovation paths cultivate different forms of judgment, they are institutionally dependent on each other. Professional decision-making judgments lose their epistemic basis without research-based renewal; research-oriented judgment remains inconsequential without social and organizational application. The AI university must therefore not level this difference, but consciously organize it: through different examination logics, career paths, and governance structures that do not standardize judgment, but differentiate it functionally. Crucial to the two-path model is the clear institutional separation of both logics while maintaining a normative connection. The implementation paths follow an application- and decision-oriented rationality, while the innovation paths follow a research- and knowledge-oriented rationality. However, both require judgment as a central target variable and make it explicitly the subject of teaching, assessment, and institutional expectations.

Table 1 illustrates that the implementation and innovation paths do not differ in terms of academic quality, but rather in the institutional rationalities in which judgment is specifically organized, expected, and evaluated.

Table 1. Two-path model of the AI university—institutional logics in comparison

Dimension	Implementation paths	Innovation paths
Primary institutional rationality	Decision- and application-oriented	Knowledge and research-oriented
Central mode of judgment	Situational judgments of appropriateness and responsibility	Theoretical, epistemic, and creative judgment formation
Reference to rules and models	Application, contextualization, and limitation of existing models	Questioning, further development, or creation of new models
Role of AI	Analytical and supportive tool for decision-making	Exploratory instrument for hypothesis formation and pattern recognition
Testing and evaluation logic	Reasoned decisions, transparency, attribution of responsibility	Quality of questions, reasoning, and insights
Form of accountability	Organizational, professional, and social accountability	Epistemic and scientific responsibility
Temporal orientation	Short- to medium-term capacity to act	Long-term knowledge and theory development

continued on following page

Table 1. Continued

Dimension	Implementation paths	Innovation paths
Relevance to society	Implementation, control, and governance of real systems	Public criticism, innovation, and knowledge advancement
Common guiding category	Judgment as an institutionally expected and evaluated skill	Judgment as an institutionally cultivated research skill

Source: own representation.

This differentiation prevents judgment from being degraded to either an abstract educational ideal or a mere 'soft skill.' At the same time, it creates transparency about different performance requirements and protects against the excessive demands placed on individual degree programs with contradictory objectives. Institutionally, the two-path model thus opens up the possibility of rebalancing mass accessibility and epistemic depth without committing the university to a uniform functional logic.

Examining under AI conditions

The transformation of the university in the age of generative AI is not primarily determined by teaching, but by the examination system. Exams function as an institutional crystallization point of academic rationality: they define which achievements are considered legitimate, which skills are expected, and who is held responsible. Under conditions of AI-supported knowledge production, however, traditional examination formats are entering a structural crisis. Performance assessments that aim at reproduction, standardization, or schematized analysis lose their significance as soon as the corresponding activities become technically scalable and externally available.

This development reveals that classic examination formats implicitly assume an epistemic scarcity that no longer exists. If analytical, synthetic, or text-producing achievements can be generated in high quality with the help of AI, an exam no longer primarily measures individual cognitive ability, but rather the ability to use or circumvent existing tools. Thus, the subject of the exam shifts unnoticed from knowledge to tool use—without this being institutionally reflected or normatively legitimized.

Against this backdrop, it becomes clear that simply tightening exam supervision or reverting to AI-free exam formats is not a viable solution. Both strategies aim to restore an outdated understanding of performance. What is needed instead is a fundamental shift in perspective: away from proving standardized performance and toward attributing judgment. Under AI conditions, exams no longer need to measure whether a result is correct, but rather how decisions are made, why certain assumptions were chosen, and where the limits of algorithmic support lie.

Three features, therefore, characterize judgment-oriented exam formats. First, they are context-open: the task is not entirely determined, but requires the situational classification of information, models, or AI-generated suggestions. Second, they need justification: it is not only the result that is evaluated, but also the argumentative rationale for decisions, including the conscious use or non-use of AI. Third, they are responsibility-oriented: students must explicitly explain the consequences of their choices and what they stand for in the context of the exam.

This shift affects exams in different institutional contexts in various ways. In practice-oriented educational pathways, the focus is on the ability to embed AI-supported analyses in decision-making processes responsibly. Here, exams aim to assess professional judgment: the selection of appropriate models, the weighing of risks, and the transparent communication of uncertainties. In research-oriented educational pathways, on the other hand, judgment is tested as an epistemic practice. Here, the focus is on the quality of questions, the reflection of theoretical assumptions, and the handling of methodological uncertainty. In both cases, AI does not function as an examination subject in itself, but as an epistemic environment in which judgment must be made visible.

Institutionally, this implies a realignment of the examination logic. Comparability is no longer primarily achieved through standardized task formats, but through structured justification requirements and clearly defined attributions of responsibility. Examinations thus become less instruments of selection and more procedures for the institutional recognition of judgment. They mark not only the completion of a learning process, but also the explicit expectation that graduates will be able to make reasoned decisions under conditions of epistemic overload.

The reorientation of the examination system also makes it clear that judgment cannot be assumed to be an individual virtue, but must be generated and secured institutionally. Exam design thus becomes a central lever of university transformation. Only when examinations are systematically oriented toward the attribution of judgment can teaching shift from the reproduction of knowledge to forms of learning that are closer to research and decision-making. In this sense, the examination system forms the crucial link between the theoretical redefinition of judgment and its institutional anchoring—and paves the way for a differentiated architecture of university education, as developed in the following two-path model.

Section 6 picks up on this institutional differentiation and analyzes the resulting changes in academic teaching roles. If judgment is to be cultivated institutionally rather than taught, the role of teachers shifts from knowledge mediators to curators, mentors, and orchestrators of hybrid learning and research spaces.

THE CHANGING ROLE OF TEACHERS

The institutional realignment of the university in the age of generative artificial intelligence is accompanied by a profound change in the role of academic teachers. As analytical knowledge production becomes increasingly automatable and judgment becomes a central epistemic resource, teachers lose their traditional function as primary knowledge mediators. Instead, their role is shifting toward designing, supporting, and safeguarding those learning and research processes in which judgment is practiced, reflected upon, and accounted for.

This change in role should not be understood as de-professionalization, but rather as the re-professionalization of academic teaching. Teachers are not becoming redundant, but are taking on more demanding functions that cannot be automated. Three roles in particular can be analytically distinguished, although in practice they often overlap: curators, mentors, and orchestrators of hybrid learning spaces. The changing role of teachers can also be justified pedagogically. Finkelstein (2025) argues that the central contribution of teachers in the AI age lies less in imparting content than in exercising professional judgment, designing meaningful learning practices, and responsibly limiting technological delegation.

Teachers as Curators of Epistemic Relevance

As curators, teachers take on the task of establishing epistemic relevance in an environment of technological abundance. In a situation where students have access to virtually unlimited information and analytical capabilities at all times, the central challenge is not to provide knowledge, but to select, weigh, and contextualize it in a way that is relevant to the subject matter. Curatorial teaching, therefore, means designing learning materials, questions, and tasks in such a way that they promote critical engagement and judgment formation rather than mere reproduction.

This curatorial function is inextricably linked to professional expertise. Teachers decide which theoretical perspectives, methodological approaches, and empirical examples are suitable for confronting students with open, ambivalent, and normatively relevant problems. AI systems can generate content, but they cannot decide which questions are appropriate to the knowledge or education in a given disciplinary and social context. The curatorial role of teachers thus stabilizes the epistemic integrity of academic teaching.

Teachers as Mentors for Judgment and Responsibility

Beyond their curatorial function, teachers are gaining importance as mentors. Judgment does not arise solely from cognitive processing, but also from feedback, reflection, and taking responsibility. In this context, mentoring means accompanying students in developing independent positions, providing input on decision-making and reasoning processes, and sensitizing them to the normative implications of their actions.

This form of mentoring is not to be equated with individual supervision in the sense of traditional elite education. Instead, it is an institutionalized practice of feedback that focuses on the quality of judgments rather than the perfection of results. Teachers support students in tolerating uncertainties, examining alternative perspectives, and recognizing the limits of their own and AI-supported analyses. In this sense, they function as normative reference points that embody academic responsibility without authoritatively prescribing 'correct' answers.

Teachers as Orchestrators of Hybrid Learning and Research Spaces

The third central role concerns the orchestration of hybrid learning spaces in which artificial intelligence, human intelligence, and collective intelligence interact. Teachers design settings in which AI is not used in isolation but is explicitly embedded in cooperative learning and research processes. They moderate the interactions among different actors, tools, and perspectives, ensuring that AI functions as an epistemic tool rather than a substitute for authority.

This orchestration function requires a high degree of institutional and didactic reflexivity. Teachers must decide in which phases AI is used sensibly, where conscious limitations are necessary, and how collective learning processes can be structured without dissolving individual responsibility. Orchestration, therefore, does not mean control in the technical sense, but rather the conscious design of interactions in which judgment is exercised collectively and at the same time remains individually attributed.

Institutional Prerequisites for Role Change

The role change described above can only be realized under certain institutional conditions. Teachers need time, resources, institutional recognition, and new forms of academic performance evaluation that make curatorial, mentoring, and orchestrating activities visible. As long as academic career incentives are primarily linked to publication numbers or standardized teaching evaluations, the role change remains structurally underdetermined.

At the same time, the change raises questions of professionalization. Teachers do not need to master all the technical details of AI systems, but they do need to understand their epistemic logic, limitations, and normative implications. The ability to promote judgment in others requires a reflective practice of judgment on one's own part, which must be institutionally supported and further developed.

Table 2 illustrates that the changing role of teachers is not merely a functional adaptation to new technologies, but rather a redefinition of academic professionalism in which judgment becomes the central reference point.

Table 2. Change in academic teaching roles in the transition to the AI university

Dimension	Traditional teaching role (mass university)	Teaching role in the AI university
Central function	Knowledge transfer and content control	Cultivation of judgment and responsibility
Relationship to knowledge	Knowledge as a scarce resource	Knowledge as an available resource that needs to be evaluated
Relationship to AI	AI as a disruptive factor or a tool	AI as an integral part of hybrid learning spaces
Didactic logic	Transfer and testing of standardized knowledge	Designing judgment-oriented learning and research processes
Role of teachers	Lecturers, examiners, content authorities	Curators, mentors, orchestrators
Understanding of performance	Reproducible outputs	Reasoned decisions and reflective judgments
Dealing with uncertainty	Reduction through standardization	Productive handling of ambiguity and openness
Relationship with students	Asymmetrical, instructional	Dialogical, supportive, reflective
Institutional expectations	Coverage of material and comparability	Quality of judgment and attribution of responsibility
Academic professionalism	Technical expertise and examination routine	Epistemic, social, and normative moderation skills

Source: own representation.

The distinction developed in Section 5 between practice-oriented implementation paths and research-oriented innovation paths illustrates that a uniform functional logic does not determine the university of the future, but rather the coexistence of different institutional rationalities. However, this differentiation is not an expression of functional fragmentation; instead, it is held together by a common guiding category: the systematic cultivation of judgment. Regardless of whether AI is primarily applied or critically developed, the ability to reflectively evaluate, contextualize, and make responsible decisions remains the central reference point for academic performance.

The change in teachers' roles described in section 6 represents the personal and professional counterpart to this institutional realignment. Curatorial, mentoring, and orchestrating activities are not additional tasks but necessary prerequisites for the development of judgment in hybrid learning and research spaces. Teachers thus function as institutional bearers of an epistemic order in which AI is powerful but not authoritative. Their role is to structure learning and research processes so that individual responsibility is not replaced by technical automation, but is consciously challenged.

Together, the two-path model and the changing role of teachers make it clear that the transformation to an AI university is not primarily a technological task, but an institutional one. It concerns the distribution of responsibility, the attribution of performance, and the organization of decision-making processes. This inevitably raises the question of how this new order can be regulated, legitimized, and socially embedded. Section 7 takes up this perspective by systematically analyzing the governance, power, and justice dimensions of the AI university.

AI, GOVERNANCE, AND INSTITUTIONAL CONTROL OF THE UNIVERSITY

The transformation to an AI university not only places demands on teaching formats and role understandings but also requires a fundamental reorganization of institutional governance structures. The mixing of different levels can also explain the institutional complexity of current AI debates. Zheng (2025) analytically distinguishes between pedagogical practices, institutional operations, curricular knowledge order, and social purpose. Governance deficits arise when decisions are made at low levels (e.g., tool use or bans) without being linked to a clear understanding of the university's mission of knowledge and judgment.

If judgment becomes the central epistemic guiding category, universities must create the organizational, legal, and infrastructural conditions under which this ability can be sustainably developed, secured, and legitimized. Governance of the AI university should therefore be understood less as the regulation of individual technologies and more as the institutional control of a complex socio-technical system.

Governance as a Safeguard for Institutional Judgment Capacity

In the context of the AI university, the focus is shifting from regulatory compliance to securing institutional judgment capacity. Classic governance models in higher education—such as accreditation, quality management, or examination regulations—are primarily geared toward standardizing and comparing performance. However, under conditions of AI-supported knowledge production, these instruments reach their limits because they are based on implicit assumptions of individual authorship and reproducible performance. Institutional overload is not an isolated case, but reflects a broader systemic finding. A large-scale bibliometric analysis of over 3,800 peer-reviewed studies shows that research on generative AI in higher education has expanded exponentially since 2022, while governance, evaluation, and integrity issues are predominantly addressed reactively and instrumentally (Ng & Ho, 2025).

Against this backdrop, it is not enough to make selective adjustments to existing regulations or merely regulate the use of AI. Institutionally appropriate governance must design assessment, examination, and decision-making processes so that responsibility can be explicitly attributed and justified. Judgment becomes an institutional target here: governance structures must ensure that decisions—for example, about academic performance, research priorities, or resource allocation—remain transparent, contestable, and reflexive, even when AI systems are analytically integrated.

System dynamics analyses of the AI transformation of universities show that such an orientation is not a given. Katsamakas et al. (2024) argue that, under pressure to adapt to generative AI, institutions may prioritize short-term efficiency and cost-cutting strategies that undermine academic quality, reputation, and long-term institutional stability. Without conscious governance interventions, such dynamics reinforce themselves.

Differentiated Control of the Two-path Structure

The two-path model developed in Section 5 requires differentiated institutional control. Implementation and innovation paths follow different rationales and cannot be regulated with the same governance instruments. While practice-oriented paths are more focused on cooperation with external actors, application standards, and professional responsibility, research-oriented paths require greater epistemic openness, safe spaces for dissent, and long-term institutional support.

A central governance task is therefore to stabilize this differentiation institutionally without creating new hierarchies or fragmentation. Transparent transitions, permeable structures, and clearly communicated performance requirements are necessary to avoid tying judgment to formal path attributions and instead allow it to take effect as an overarching principle.

Infrastructure, Platform Dependencies, and Institutional Sovereignty

Another key governance aspect concerns the AI university's technological infrastructure. The increasing use of external platforms, proprietary AI models, and cloud-based services is shifting institutional dependencies and implicitly influencing epistemic processes. Decisions about data access, model use, and system integration are therefore not only technical but also genuinely institutional.

To ensure institutional judgment, universities must create transparency into the systems they use, examine alternatives, and establish collective decision-making mechanisms. This includes strategic investments in their own infrastructures as well as cooperation at the national or European level. Institutional sovereignty does not mean self-sufficiency, but rather the ability to consciously shape technological dependencies and reflect on them critically.

Organizational Embedding of Responsibility and Accountability

Finally, the question arises as to how responsibility is anchored organizationally in AI-supported decision-making processes. The more analytical preparatory work is automated, the more critical it becomes to assign decision-making and justification responsibilities clearly. Governance of the AI university must therefore create structures in which responsibility is not implicitly diffused but explicitly assigned—for example, through defined roles, documented decision-making processes, and institutionalized reflection formats.

Here, judgment appears not as an individual virtue, but as an organizational principle supported by procedures, committees, and accountability structures. Universities thus become learning organizations that not only use AI but also continuously review and develop their own decision-making processes.

From this institutional perspective, it becomes clear that the AI university is not created by technological innovation alone, but by a conscious reorganization of its governance structures. Section 8 takes up these insights and combines them into a forward-looking perspective on the university as a curated, research-centered knowledge economy in which judgment serves as the central reference point for institutional legitimacy.

Key Governance Principles of the AI University

At the same time, the study by Contractor and Reyes (2025) makes it clear that institutional AI policies have a significant steering effect, but are not neutral. Blanket bans or inconsistent regulations create asymmetrical effects along gender, performance level, and subject culture lines and can unintentionally reinforce competition and inequality dynamics. It follows that governance in the context of the AI university must not be primarily focused on regulating behavior but on securing institutional judgment capacity. The institutional management of the AI university cannot be reduced to individual regulatory measures, but requires a coherent architecture of governance principles that systematically safeguard judgment. Following on from the previous analysis, five principles in particular can be identified:

1. Principle of functional differentiation

Different educational and research logics—in particular implementation and innovation paths—require differentiated control and evaluation instruments. Governance must institutionally stabilize this differentiation without creating new hierarchies or silos. Uniform sets of rules must not level out heterogeneous epistemic requirements.

2. Principle of explicit assignment of responsibility

The more analytical preparatory work is automated, the more clearly decision-making and justification obligations must be assigned. AI-supported processes must not diffuse responsibility, but must be supplemented by organizational responsibilities, documented decisions, and verifiable justifications. This makes judgment institutionally addressable.

3. Principle of institutional sovereignty

Universities must retain the ability to decide for themselves on the use, limitations, and embedding of AI systems. This requires transparency about the technologies used, strategic control over central infrastructures, and conscious decisions about external dependencies. Institutional sovereignty does not mean technological self-sufficiency, but rather some measure of reflective control.

4. Principle of procedural transparency and contestability

Assessment, examination, and decision-making processes must remain comprehensible, explainable, and, in principle, contestable. Governance structures should not aim to optimize results, but rather to improve the quality of the underlying decision-making processes. Transparency is not an end in itself, but a prerequisite for public legitimacy.

5. Principle of institutional learning ability

The AI university is not a static model, but an adaptive system. Governance must therefore open up spaces for reflection, feedback, and revision. This includes regularly reviewing AI use, evaluation logic, and role understanding, as well as a willingness to adapt institutional routines if they stand in the way of cultivating judgment.

Taken together, these principles form the institutional framework of a university that not only uses AI but also takes responsibility for it. Judgment acts as a unifying organizational principle that balances technological performance, academic autonomy, and social responsibility sustainably.

CONCLUSION: THE AI UNIVERSITY IN 2035

The analysis in this chapter has shown that, in the age of generative artificial intelligence, universities are not faced with the choice between becoming technologically obsolete or being completely automated. Rather, AI is forcing universities to redefine their institutional functions. The transition from mass university to a curated knowledge economy is not a gradual modernization process, but a structural change in the epistemic logic of academic education and research.

In 2035, the AI university will no longer exist as an automated knowledge factory, but as a hybrid institution in which artificial, human, and collective intelligence work together through a division of labor. In this model, AI functions as a commodity layer for analysis, simulation, feedback, and organization. It increases efficiency and accessibility, but does not replace those skills that are becoming scarce in conditions of technological abundance: evaluation, contextualization, and responsibility. The real added value of the university thus no longer lies in the reproduction of standardized knowledge, but in the systematic cultivation of judgment.

The two-path model developed makes it clear that this reorientation must be carried out in an institutionally differentiated manner. Practice-oriented implementation paths and research-oriented innovation paths follow different rationales, but are linked by a standard epistemic benchmark. In both cases, the focus of academic performance shifts from the production of analytical outputs to the quality of decisions, justifications, and theoretical positioning. The university thus becomes a place where judgment is not taken for granted, but is institutionally generated, tested, and accounted for.

The changing role of teachers and the realignment of governance structures indicate that this transformation is not occurring solely at the curricular level. It affects the organization of responsibility, the attribution of performance, and institutional control over technological infrastructures. The AI university of the future is therefore defined less by specific tools than by its ability to combine technological performance with institutional sovereignty, transparency, and learning ability.

From this perspective, the university is moving closer to its normative core again. It is becoming a public institution for forming judgments in a society whose decision-making processes are increasingly shaped by algorithmic systems. Precisely because AI is becoming increasingly powerful, the university gains its legitimacy not through efficiency or scaling, but through its ability to create spaces for critical reflection, scientific curiosity, and responsible orientation. The future of the university thus lies not beyond AI, but in the conscious institutional design of a knowledge order in which judgment serves as the central reference point for academic and social responsibility.

REFERENCES

Arendt, H. (1961). *Between past and future: Eight exercises in political thought.* Viking Press.

Autor, D. H. (2015). Why are there still so many jobs? The history and future of workplace automation. *The Journal of Economic Perspectives, 29*(3), 3–30. DOI: 10.1257/jep.29.3.3

Autor, D. H., Levy, F., & Murnane, R. J. (2003). The skill content of recent technological change: An empirical exploration. *The Quarterly Journal of Economics, 118*(4), 1279–1333. DOI: 10.1162/003355303322552801

Brown, P. (2013). Education, opportunity and the prospects for social mobility. *British Journal of Sociology of Education, 34*(5–6), 678–700. DOI: 10.1080/01425692.2013.816036

Brynjolfsson, E., & McAfee, A. (2014). *The second machine age: Work, progress, and prosperity in a time of brilliant technologies.* W. W. Norton.

Clark, B. R. (1986). *The higher education system: Academic organization in cross-national perspective.* University of California Press.

Collins, R. (1979). *The credential society: An historical sociology of education and stratification.* Academic Press.

Contractor, Z., & Reyes, G. (2025). Generative AI in higher education: Evidence from an Elite College. *arXiv.* /arXiv.2508.00717DOI: 10.48550

Dewey, J. (1938). *Logic: The theory of inquiry.* Holt.

Finkelstein (2025): A principled way to think about AI in education: guidance for action based on goals, models of human learning, and use of technologies. *arXiv.* /arXiv.2510.01467DOI: 10.48550

Floridi, L., Cowls, J., Beltrametti, M., Chatila, R., Chazerand, P., Dignum, V., Luetge, C., Madelin, R., Pagallo, U., Rossi, F., Schafer, B., Valcke, P., & Vayena, E. (2018). AI4People – An ethical framework for a good AI society. *Minds and Machines, 28*(4), 689–707. DOI: 10.1007/s11023-018-9482-5 PMID: 30930541

Kant, I. (2000). *Kritik der Urteilskraft.* Meiner. (Original work published 1790)

Kasneci, E., Sessler, K., Küchemann, S., Bannert, M., Dementieva, D., Fischer, F., Gasser, U., Groh, G., Günnemann, S., Hüllermeier, E., Krusche, S., Kutyniok, G., Michaeli, T., Nerdel, C., Pfeffer, J., Poquet, O., Sailer, M., Schmidt, A., Seidel, T., & Kasneci, G. (2023). ChatGPT for good? On opportunities and challenges of large language models for education. *Learning and Individual Differences*, *103*, 102274. DOI: 10.1016/j.lindif.2023.102274

Katsamakas, E., Pavlov, O. V., & Saklad, R. (2024). Artificial intelligence and the transformation of higher education institutions. *arXiv*. /arXiv.2402.08143DOI: 10.48550

Kosmyna, N., Hauptmann, E., Yuan, E. T., Situ, J., Liao, X.-H., Beresnitzky, A. V., ... (2025). Your Brain on ChatGPT: Accumulation of cognitive debt when using an AI assistant for essay writing task. *arXiv*. /arXiv.2506.08872DOI: 10.48550

Marginson, S. (2016). *The dream is over: The crisis of Clark Kerr's California idea of higher education*. University of California Press. http://library.oapen.org/handle/20.500.12657/32075

Meyer, J. W., Ramirez, F. O., Frank, D. J., & Schofer, E. (2006). Higher education as an institution. Center on Democracy, Development, and the Rule of Law Working Papers No. 57. https://fsi9-prod.s3.us-west-1.amazonaws.com/s3fs-public/Meyer_No_57.pdf

Meyer, J. W., & Rowan, B. (1977). Institutionalized organizations: Formal structure as myth and ceremony. *American Journal of Sociology*, *83*(2), 340–363. DOI: 10.1086/226550

Ng, S.-L., & Ho, C.-C. (2025). Generative AI in education: Mapping the research landscape through bibliometric analysis. *Information (Basel)*, *16*(8), 657. DOI: 10.3390/info16080657

Osrečki, F. (2025). *Eine Soziologie des Nichtwissens*. Suhrkamp.

Pierson, P. (2000). Increasing returns, path dependence, and the study of politics. *The American Political Science Review*, *94*(2), 251–267. DOI: 10.2307/2586011

Susskind, R., & Susskind, D. (2015). *The future of the professions: How technology will transform the work of human experts*. Oxford University Press. DOI: 10.1093/oso/9780198713395.001.0001

Trow, M. (1973). *Problems in the transition from elite to mass higher education*. Carnegie Commission on Higher Education.

Zheng (2025): AI Education in higher education: A taxonomy for curriculum reform and the mission of knowledge. *arXiv*. /arXiv.2509.23363DOI: 10.48550

Chapter 8 Using Generative AI at University: The Case of a Project-Based Learning Course

Maria Denami
http://orcid.org/0000-0002-9881-9270
LISEC UR2310, University of Upper Alsace, France

Dina Adinda
http://orcid.org/0000-0002-5879-1349
Université de Paris Nanterre, France

Christophe Jeunesse
CREF UR - 1589, France

ABSTRACT

University programs often struggle to integrate project-based learning, essential for developing professional competencies. The 2018 reforms in France, aligned with the European competence-based framework, highlight interdisciplinary projects to bridge academic training and professional demands. At the same time, generative AI is reshaping skills across sectors, requiring critical, ethical, and adaptive use. This study examines AI use in a project-based Instructional Design course, exploring tools, collaboration, and student perceptions across project phases. Findings aim to inform teaching strategies, curriculum design, and AI literacy integration in higher education.

DOI: 10.4018/979-8-2600-1458-5.ch008

1. INTRODUCTION

University programs in education and training often struggle to implement project-based learning, a pedagogical approach essential for professional preparation, thus limiting the development of students' professional competencies in both initial and continuing education. The 2018 reforms for Bachelor's and Master's degrees in France, aligned with the European «competences-based» framework, highlighted the importance of promoting interdisciplinary projects to bridge the gap between academic training and professional demands.

In parallel to this, it is possible to observe, both in our university classrooms and also in the professional sectors, the rapid evolution and accessibility of generative Artificial Intelligence (from now on GenAI). This phenomenon is reshaping the skillsets required across various sectors. Beyond technical proficiency, the inevitable use of GenAI across academia, including by students, calls for the development of critical and ethical use of the tools. This encourages universities to move beyond traditional curricula and prepare students to use GenAI thoughtfully, not just as a means to increase productivity, but as a powerful resource for creative problem-solving and responsible decision-making. Embedding AI literacy into project-based learning environments is thus becoming a key priority for higher education.

This context raises the question of dependence and over-dependence of students and the use of GenAI for realising academic tasks. In that regard, our contribution aims to address the use of this tool in academia, and especially to explore how GenAI can be used in the context of project-based learning. To investigate this, we designed a course within the Educational Sciences curriculum titled "Instructional Design". The course provides a structured setting where students collaboratively design a training module, using a project-based approach.

This chapter presents two important issues in the field of university pedagogy. The first concerns project-based learning as a method to develop students' professional competencies. The second concerns the use of GenAI and its use in higher education, and specifically by university students.

By crossing these two axes, we aim to understand how students use GenAI to manage and deliver a project. In that regard, our study focuses on several key research questions:

- How do students use GenAI during the different phases of their project work?
- Which tools, prompts, and software are most employed?
- Is GenAI used individually or collaboratively? And by then, how do students collaborate with each other and with the GenAI?
- How do students perceive and assess their own use of these technologies in relation to their learning outcomes and project performance?

With this study, we aim to deepen our understanding of the practices, challenges, and learning dynamics associated with the use of GenAI in higher education settings and to contribute insights that can inform the design of future teaching practices and curriculum development.

2. THEORETICAL FRAME

2.1 Generative AI

2.1.1 Definitions and issues of Generative AI

Generative Artificial Intelligence (GenAI) refers to a class of machine learning models designed to generate new data that resembles a given training dataset. These models learn underlying patterns and structures from the input data and then produce novel outputs, such as text, images, audio, or code, that are not direct copies but plausible creations consistent with the learned distribution (Goodfellow et al., 2014; Brown et al., 2020).

Generative AI models rely on diverse kinds of data to learn patterns and create new content across six main media domains. We can identify:1) on the text data domain, such as books, articles, websites, and social media content, enabling applications like text generation, summarization, and translation; 2) In the visual domain, it is possible to find a large datasets of images, including photos from heterogeneous sources (internet, private and public domain) or, can serve as input for models able to generate realistic or artistic images.3) on the audio domain it is possible to generate speech recordings, music, and environmental sounds are also used to train models capable of producing synthesized voices (useful for creating content for language teaching, for instance) or new musical compositions. Similarly to the audio data, 4) video data allows the generation of sequences of frames with temporal dynamics, allowing the generation of animated clips or video prediction. 5) In the programming domain, a large repertoire of code data from different platforms, like GitHub, empowers models to generate functional code snippets or entire scripts. Finally, generative models can utilise 6) structured data such as databases or sensor readings to create synthetic datasets that support data augmentation or testing.

The growing use of generative artificial intelligence tools, such as ChatGPT, for text generation raises significant concerns, especially from educators and teachers, regarding the potential weakening of core academic skills, in addition to the fear of over-dependence on the GenAI tools. One of the main issues is the risk of reduced critical thinking abilities: immediate access to pre-structured texts can lead students and researchers to rely on information passively, without controlling the sources, and without developing autonomous analysis skills or the ability to assess the reliability of sources (Koltay, 2023; Lund & Wang, 2023).

Another critical aspect is the loss of academic writing skills. In that regard, the lack of exercise in text creation activity and the automating text generation may result in a decline in linguistic, argumentative, and structural abilities, all of which are essential for scientific production (Susnjak, 2022) in the academic field. Similarly, some researchers highlight that heavy reliance on GenAI can compromise the development of research and evidence evaluation skills, as users tend to trust AI-generated responses without verifying their origin or validity (Kasneci et al., 2023).

Furthermore, there is concern about the spoiling of academic creativity, with increasing textual homogeneity and reduced originality, as generative models rely on existing data rather than truly innovative processes (Zou et al., 2023). Finally, excessive cognitive delegation to AI risks undermining metacognitive competencies, such as the ability to plan, monitor, and evaluate one's own learning. Those are the essential skills for higher education students.

The development of technology tends to lead educators, trainers and teachers to be alerted about the danger of using it in the "wrong way". About fifteen years ago, we remember the case of the use of Wikipedia for academic research, and the same happens now with the introduction of AI, as indicated above. For some years, the researchers' approach has been to understand which "new" or "future" or "complementary" skills, new students and young or less young population can develop with the supply or the integration of newer technologies.

Already in 2017 (Carretero, Vuorikari, & Punie, 2017), the *Digital Competence Framework* by the European Commission had been expanded to include AI literacy, critical thinking in interaction with AI, and ethical awareness (Long & Magerko, 2020; Luckin et al., 2019) among the "new" competencies developed with newer technologies. These models highlight that using AI tools can not only develop technical proficiency but also meta-cognitive and meta-competencies such as the ability to critically assess AI outputs, maintain human agency, and collaborate with AI as a cognitive partner (Guszcza et al., 2018). Further research highlights that competencies for GenAI involve a balance between creativity, critical evaluation, and ethical judgment, supporting users in leveraging AI-generated content without undermining originality or accountability (Holmes et al., 2021). Frameworks like the*AI Competency Framework*by the OECD (2022) propose a multidimensional approach combining knowledge, skills, attitudes, and values necessary for responsible AI use in educational and workplace environments. Such models guide curriculum design and professional development programs aimed at preparing individuals for an AI-augmented future.

Several recent studies try to highlight if and how AI, used for training or in higher education institutions, even in schools, can somehow develop competencies instead of just "replace human activity and intelligence". In line with this reasoning, a project called AI comp (*Artificial Intelligence Competences*), developed by Ehlers, Lindner, Sommer, and Rauch (2023), presents a conceptual framework designed to identify the *Future Skills* needed to thrive in a world increasingly shaped by artificial intelligence. Drawing on a qualitative meta-analysis, the model defines 13 AI-related competence profiles. Each profile integrates knowledge, skills, and attitudes/values/ethics, in alignment with the KSAVE framework (Knowledge, Skills, Attitudes, Values, Ethics) (Ehlers et al., 2023). These profiles are clustered into "fields of action" that address strategic domains such as innovating with AI, autonomy and learning, and co-creation through AI. The AIComp framework aims to provide a set of actionable competencies enabling individuals to operate effectively in emerging and complex AI-related situations in both professional and personal contexts (Ehlers et al., 2023; NextEducation, n.d.).

2.1.2 Typologies of use of generative AI

According to scientific literature, there are several uses of GenAI. Cukurova (2025) resumed four ways to integrate Artificial Intelligence (AI) regarding (1) the degree of control (axis Y) and (2) automation of tasks (axis Y) assigned to the tools as a substitute for humans (Figure 1).

Traditional use of technology for learning, and not necessarily the use of AI, or especially GenAI, for this context, is classified as a low level of automation and human control. These technologies typically do not automate many tasks nor provide significant opportunities for users to control AI-driven processes. In this context, AI models may be internalised by humans but do not actively support or extend cognition in a synergistic way. At the same level of automation, and in the case of high human control, it is possible to observe a phenomenon where people learn from and incorporate AI models into their own thinking and cognitive processes. Instead of relying on AI to perform tasks for them, AI tools are used to develop users' competencies, gradually reducing dependence on the AI as their skills improve.

While human control as well as automation are high, it is possible to observe uses in which AI, or in this case GenAI tools, help extend human thinking processes. As presented in Figure 1, the use of AI is increasing, along with the development of human competence. In this case, the tools are used to actively support and reshape how users think, learn, and reflect by providing new ways to represent, analyse, and engage with information, instead of automating tasks. This use is beneficial in enabling richer learning experiences and deeper understanding. However, when human control is low and automation is high, human tasks are replaced by tools. Cukurova (2025) stated that this type of use describes a phenomenon in which the use of tools increases while human competence decreases (Figure 1).

Figure 1. Four ways of Generative Artificial Intelligence (GAI) use (Chukurova, 2024, adapted by Jeunesse, 2025).

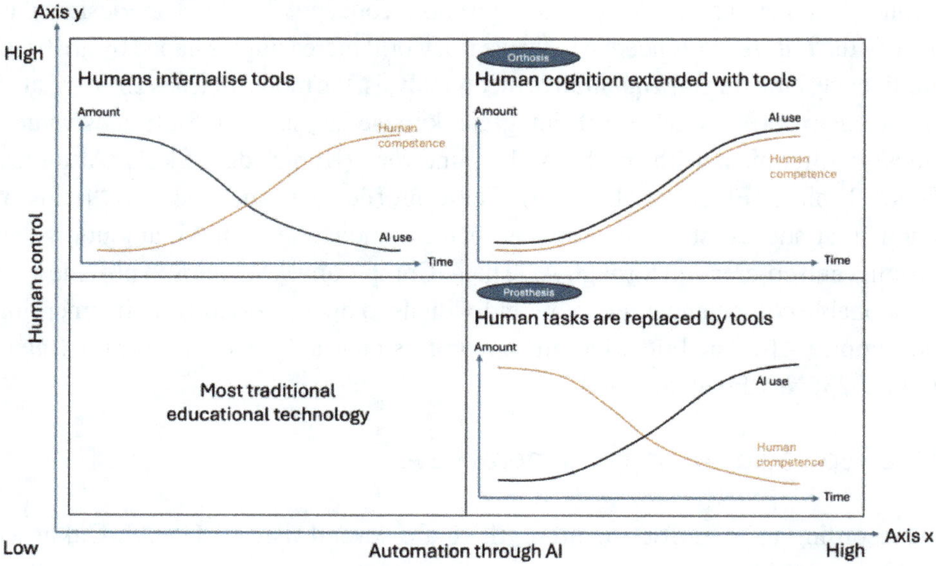

A literature review conducted by Jeunesse (2025) identified various uses of GenAI that can be categorised as either 'orthosis' or 'prosthesis', thus completing the description of Figure 1 above. Following Cukurova's (2025) categorisation, Jeunesse (2025) considers the term 'Prosthesis' as referring to the use of tools to perform human tasks, as it replaces an absence of an ability. This type of use is described by a delegation by users, whether experts or not, to perform tasks that are more or less tedious and that users could have performed themselves, using conventional resources, or not at all. Some examples of prosthesis use include text summarisation, translations, information search, correcting spelling and grammatical errors, drafting of standard letters, etc., with no or minimal evaluation of the result (Figure 1 and Figure 2). Indeed, the 'Prosthesis' use increases the risk of dependency.

As for the 'orthosis', this use is described as a use in which human cognition is closely engaged with GenAI tools. The tool used is prompted by an expert user who applies critical thinking when evaluating the results obtained: users will challenge them until they obtain a satisfactory result, or not, depending on the initial objectives. The 'orthosis' can be seen, for example, in the use of a specialised GenAI, such as https://www.ordalie.ai/, when faced with a legal issue about which a lawyer has doubts regarding the best way to handle it.

Referring to the 'individual-plus' of Perkins (1995), which he defines as an individual whose intelligence is not confined solely to their brain, nor is it the result of their cognitive abilities alone, rather an intelligence that is distributed throughout their physical and social environment, Jeunesse (2025) also highlighted that the potential use of GenAI as an 'orthosis' fits Perkins (1995) description and add another potential use of GenAI as an 'auxesis' to describe the optimal humans' capacity to use GenAI tools. This latter classification describes the possibility that humans can be cognitively engaged with GenAI tools and that their abilities are "multiplied" through their use of AI (Figure 2). This can be observed, for instance, in the predictive analytics managed by GenAI on a voluminous dataset.

Each type of use (Figure 2) described various capacities and levels of expertise that deployed to use the IAG tools. Indeed, this framework can be practical not only to understand possible relations between human intelligence and GenAI, but also to enable observations of variations, combinations, and impacts on the dispositions and behaviours of the individuals concerned.

Figure 2. Framework of GAI uses (Jeunesse, 2025).

GAI use	Prosthesis	Orthosis	Auxesis
	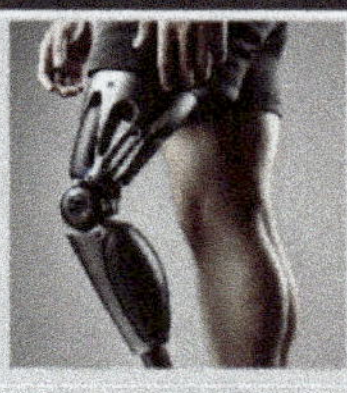	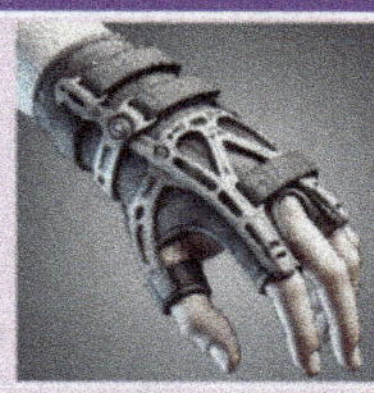	
Function of GAI tool	Replaces absence	Support, assist	Increase, amplify
Human users	Not cognitively engaged, replaced	Cognitively engaged, Individual-plus (Perkins, 1995)	Cognitively engaged, abilities are "multiplied" by the use of GAI tools

2.2. Project-based learning in university pedagogy

2.2.1 Project-based learning as a pedagogical method of professionalisation

Nowadays, European universities are consistently encouraged to innovate to support their core missions of education, research, and student success. This input is given through national policies (via institutional and/or ministerial calls for projects), inviting researchers and pedagogical teams to design university programs for improving university pedagogy and to better respond to societal needs. In this context, professionalisation has become a major issue for higher education (Rose, 2018). The main concern often raised is alignment with the demands of professional sectors—training in job-specific, specialised, and disciplinary skills and competencies. Moreover, over the past decade, there has been growing interest in transversal skills (Santelmann, 2019), especially social skills or *soft skills* (Morlaix, 2015), which has further expanded the scope of professionalisation.

In this light, "professionalising" training programs have been implemented at the university level from the first years of undergraduate study. The most common formats include observation internships, field placements, professional bachelor's degrees, vocational education or several different programs alternating between professional activity and academic training, such as a work-study program or dual education (in French "alternance"). In these formats, however, practical experience and professional learning, such as technical or professional competencies, are mostly delegated to the host organisation, while the university provides students with academic knowledge as a resource for competence development, and focuses on giving students the "theoretical" knowledge and developing their critical thinking, reasoning and analysis competencies. In France, engineering diplomas and university technology diplomas became bachelor's degrees in 2021, professional bachelor's degrees, and certain master's degrees adopting the work-study program serve as models of professional training.

Apart from these specific vocational programs naturally aiming to professionalise students, European policies push universities also at the very early levels (generalist bachelors) to meet the needs of the work market. This perspective raises the question about how the university fosters the development of professional competencies outside of these privileged frameworks. How can students be trained and become professionals after completing the undergraduate level? What types of programs and what formal and informal practices can be analysed to describe and understand the process of professionalisation in French universities?

The first "formalisation" of PBL is attributed to William H. Kilpatrick (1918). In fact, Kilpatrick proposed the Project Method as a learner-centred approach grounded in purpose-driven activity. This pedagogical model aims to create a setting in five (5) steps, able to guide the learners through a meaningful engagement.

1. Purposing: In this phase, the learner identifies a goal or purpose, ideally aligned with their interests (Kilpatrick, 1918). This initiates intrinsic motivation.
2. Planning: Students then plan how to achieve the goal—what resources are needed, steps to take, and how to organise the work (Kilpatrick, 1921).
3. Executing: Learners carry out the project, engaging in hands-on tasks and problem-solving. This is the core experiential phase (Dewey, 1938; Kilpatrick, 1918).
4. Evaluating: After completing the project, students assess their work, often through reflection and peer discussion (Kilpatrick, 1921).
5. Recording (sometimes called Reporting): The experience is documented and communicated, reinforcing learning and sharing with others (Kilpatrick, 1918).

In these five phases, we can notice that the lead, or the guidelines for the realisation of the project, is given essentially by the student or the learner, and the teacher keeps as neutral as possible in the influence. In 1918, Kilpatrick (p. 319) writes, "The teacher's role is not to tell the student what to do, but to help the student see what is worth doing." Here, the teacher is not a transmitter of knowledge, but a mentor, question-poser, and learning architect. For Kilpatrick (1918), the project should be learner-driven, and it is also important for lecturers to acknowledge and stimulate students' proactive autonomy (Adinda, 2020) and self-direction in learning by providing adequate assistance and learning experiences (Adinda and Denami, 2023). Self-directed learning (hereafter SDL) is an example of active learning targeting learners' self-directed behaviour in learning. It can be defined as a process allowing learners to diagnose their needs, identify their learning goals, and spot their potential and resources for learning to determine their learning strategies and assess the outcomes (Adinda and Denami, 2023). This learning approach would be complicated for those with low self-direction or who are not yet used to working autonomously (Van Laer & Elen, 2017). However, lecturers' primary role is to ensure that the project stays educational, and the learning environment is adequate so that learners can develop their self-direction skills (Adinda and Denami, 2023).

This approach was radical for its time and aligns with constructivist views of learning (Dewey, Vygotsky).

Table 1 below explains the role of the teacher in coaching and supporting students' learning process.

Table 1. Teachers' roles in various phases of the learning process

Phase	Teacher's Role
1. Purposing	Help students identify meaningful, realistic, and educationally valuable purposes. The teacher may inspire ideas or help students redefine vague intentions into workable goals.
2. Planning	Act essentially as an advisor: guide students in organizing their ideas, choosing resources, and setting timelines, without taking over the planning process.
3. Executing	Serve as a facilitator and support system: assist with resources, mediate conflicts, and scaffold learning when students encounter difficulties. Avoid giving direct solutions.
4. Recording/ Reporting	Encourage documentation and help learners present their process and findings. Offer technical help (e.g., writing, presenting) and ensure quality without imposing structure.
5. Evaluating	Foster self-evaluation and peer feedback. The teacher guides reflection with open-ended questions and helps connect experiences to future learning.

As perceivable on the two tables above (cf. tables 1 and 2), Kilpatrick's approach was deeply influenced by John Dewey's philosophy of experiential and democratic education. Indeed, the five steps emphasise student agency, purposeful activity, and social interaction, laying the groundwork for today's Project-Based Learning (Larmer et al., 2015).

Project-based learning is an experiential learning method (Kolb, 1984) rooted in a constructivist paradigm. This learning framework allows learners to be *active*, exploring their environment to find solutions to problems: "students acquire a deeper understanding of content when they actively construct their understanding by working with and using ideas" (Krajcik & Shin, 2014). The socio-constructivist component of this method allows individuals to benefit from peer support through social interactions and the development of collective intelligence. This fosters both the successful completion of the project and the co-construction of knowledge (Krajcik & Blumenfeld, 2006). Supported using technology and planning/communication software, students face scaffolding situations that push them beyond their *comfort zone*; they experience a *zone of proximal development* (ZPD) (Vygotsky, 1985), which enhances the growth of their skills.

Several studies have already demonstrated the effectiveness of this method, which encourages greater participation in educational activities and improves various aspects of learning. In a 2011 study (Kaldi et al., 2011), researchers found that student groups exposed to PBL showed positive results in both content knowledge and teamwork skills. The study also highlighted a significant aspect of learning: students' intrinsic motivation and positive attitudes toward peers were enhanced through project-based teaching. Other studies (Boaler, 1998; Karaçalli & Korur, 2014) have shown that project-based learning has significant effects on academic success and knowledge retention. PBL improves conceptual understanding, thanks to the reflexive practice that can be produced when analysing the process, and often requires deep and creative thinking, unlike procedural knowledge in traditional instruction that primarily relies on information recall. Stewart (2007) observed a positive influence of project-based learning on students' readiness for autonomous learning. Students who experienced PBL developed strong self-directed learning skills and achieved meaningful results in acquiring academic knowledge. This phenomenon can be explained by the fact that PBL, which aims at producing real-world deliverables, enables learners to "make sense" of learning activities that resemble social practices and help move from abstract knowledge to more meaningful, "global," and "less disciplinary" learning (Weber, 1982). Again, a 2014 study found high rates of college success among students from high schools that feature "student-centred instruction," which researchers defined as including project-based teaching, collaborative learning, relevant curriculum, and performance-based assessments.

The following table highlights the principles references on which PBL is founded (cf. Table 2).

Table 2. Conceptual foundations of PBL

Reference Socio-Constructivist Principles	Implementation in a PBL
Co-construction of knowledge *(Vygotsky, 1985* Piaget & Inhelder, 1973 *)*	Students work on designing a solution in response to a given problem by exchanging viewpoints, drawing on personal and prior knowledge, past experiences, and mastered skills. The interdisciplinary nature of the exercise further enhances the learning potential, even in unexpected ways.
Collaborative learning and social interaction *(Vygotsky, 1985)*	Social interaction with other team members (especially in this case with interdisciplinary teams) creates a space for learning. Formal, informal, and semi-formal learning situations multiply the contexts for interaction and act as catalysts for building connections among group members.
Appropriation of artifacts in the environment *(Rabardel, 1995; Engeström, 2001)*	Many artifacts are involved: material (post-its, whiteboards, digital tools) and symbolic (pitch, brainstorming sessions, mind maps).
Zone of Proximal Development *(Vygotsky, 1985)*	Group work allows members to interface with each other and test themselves in a realistic (yet safe) work situation that presents challenges pushing them out of their comfort zone. It places them in the Zone of Proximal Development where they can progress thanks to contributions from others.
Agency and capacity to act on one's environment *(Bandura, 2001)*	The project, rooted in a real or realistic context, requires learners to take initiative, take ownership of the situations, act intentionally, and take responsibility for the success of their project.
Reflexive Practice and experiential learning *(Dewey, 1929 and Kolb, 1984, Schön, 1983).*	If engaged and supported by teacher and pedagogical scenarios, students can perform a *post-facto* analysis of their process in order to identify the strong points of their work and the one that can be improved. As well, this method can lead students to develop a practice of "reflective practitioner" (Schön, 1983)

Project-Based Learning (PBL) typically brings together learners for a period ranging from several days to several weeks, which can be designed in a disciplinary or interdisciplinary education setting, depending on the pedagogical needs. As explained in the previous paragraphs, while working in collaborative and open and self-directed settings, and only partially tutored by teachers, learners are challenged to produce original and often practical solutions to real-world or semi-realistic problems. While these solutions are not always technological, they are increasingly socio-technical or organisational in nature, such as the design of new processes or service innovations (Dionne & Carlile, 2016). This pedagogical model invites us to explore the types of learning (formal, non-formal, informal and semi-informal). The following paragraph will deepen these relations in the given students' environment while working on the project.

2.2.2 Formal, non-formal, informal and semi-formal learning

Formal learning is an educational setting occurring within structured, institutionalised settings (schools, universities, workplace training), where the learning is explicitly defined as such in terms of objectives, time allocation, and resources. It is intentional on the part of the learner and typically leads to assessment, validation, and certification (Hart, 2013). In PBL settings situated in higher education, formal learning is often framed through course syllabi, evaluation rubrics, expected learning outcomes, and institutional timelines (Schugurensky, 2007; Calamel, 2012). The projects themselves may serve as assessment tasks within a formal curriculum, which provides structure and academic legitimacy.

As formal learning, Non-Formal Learning is also intentional from the learner's perspective (Hart, 2013) and involves deliberate efforts to gain specific knowledge, skills, or competencies. However, it does not require enrolment in an official program or lead to formal accreditation. In PBL, non-formal learning can occur in workshops, design-thinking sessions, skill-building labs, or feedback discussions with mentors or professionals external to the university. These interactions, while structured, are often voluntary and align with learners' personal goals rather than institutional certification processes (Schugurensky, 2007).

Informal learning arises fromdaily life experiences, including work, family, hobbies, or media consumption. It is typically unstructured, unplanned, and unintentional, though it may significantly influence the learner's understanding and problem-solving ability (Hart, 2013). In PBL, learners may engage in informal learning when they explore online tutorials, watch YouTube videos, read blog posts, or draw on personal experience to solve a project challenge (Cristol & Muller, 2013). These learning moments often occur outside the planned project schedule, yet they are vital to innovation and problem ownership. As Carré (2020) emphasises, such learning takes placewithout any direct pedagogical intervention, plays acrucial role in adult learningbecause it supports autonomy and critical thinking. Informal learning in PBL can include researching community issues, engaging in volunteer work related to the project topic, or developing prototypes using tools learned outside formal instruction.

Semi-formal learning settings do not fit neatly into any single category (Carré, 2020). For example, when learners use external resources like YouTube tutorials, podcasts, or social networks for learning purposes within a project setting. Although the resources may have pedagogical intentions, their use lies outside a structured, accredited training program. In PBL, such hybrid learning is common, as students seek guidance or inspiration beyond the classroom.

Mal Waldera (2016) draws attention to the complexity of learning in today's technologically mediated university environments. His work advocates for an integrated approach that acknowledges the complementarity of formal, non-formal, and informal learning experiences. In PBL, these modes interact continuously, allowing formal structures to be enriched by learner-driven exploration and community engagement. For instance, students may formally present a project that was partially shaped by informal online research or peer mentoring.

Table 3 below presents the various possibilities to integrate formal, informal, non-formal and semi-informal learning situations in the context of PBL learning.

Table 3. Design Options to Combine Formal, Non-Formal, Informal, and Semi-Informal Learning in Project-Based Learning

Type of Resource	Examples	Educational Context	Theoretical Anchors
Curriculum & Academic Resources	Course syllabus, textbooks, scientific articles, learning platforms (Moodle, etc.)	Formal	Biggs (1996); Thomas (2000)
Instructors / Tutors	Professors, teaching assistants, feedback sessions	Formal	Vygotsky (1978); Merrill (2002)
Peers / Team Members	Classmates, interdisciplinary teams, student networks	Formal → Semi-formal	Johnson & Johnson (1999)
Institutional Tools	Licensed software (Office, MATLAB, Zotero), internal data systems	Formal	Laurillard (2002)
External Partners	Professionals, NGOs, companies, community stakeholders	Semi-formal → Informal	Barron et al. (1998); Guile & Griffiths (2001)
Internet Resources	Online courses (MOOCs), tutorials, forums (Reddit, Stack Overflow), wikis, YouTube	Informal	Jenkins et al. (2006); Selwyn (2009)
Media & Documents	News articles, reports, podcasts, documentaries	Informal	Sefton-Green (2004)
Personal Experience	Prior knowledge, lived experiences, personal passions	Informal	Kolb (1984); Eraut (2004)
Open Digital Tools	Free collaborative tools (Google Drive, Miro, Canva, Trello, ChatGPT)	Semi-formal → Informal	Luckin et al. (2009); Sharples et al. (2014)
Learning Communities	Makerspaces, fablabs, university hubs, student associations	Semi-formal	Wenger (1998); Ito et al. (2013)
Mentoring / Coaching	Informal mentors, alumni, career advisors	Semi-formal → Informal	Billett (2001); Crisp & Cruz (2009)
Social Media & Networks	LinkedIn, Twitter, Instagram, Discord-kind learning servers	Informal	Greenhow & Lewin (2016); Veletsianos (2016)

2.2.3 Research question and hypothesis

In a context where university education seeks to innovate to answer the demand of the stakeholders regarding students' professional competencies, teachers and researchers are designing a new pedagogical environment combining emerging technologies with some well-established and effective approaches, such as PBL.

This contribution investigates how students use GenAI in a PBL setting, focusing on the diversity of uses, including both individual and collaborative uses. In line with these objectives, the study addresses the following research questions: Which tasks in project management are delegated to the GenAI and which ones are still performed by students? Which kind of use of technology is realised on regards to the new model formulated by the actual scientific literature? How and when does collaboration between humans and machines occur? How can GenAI help the project development?

Our theoretical framework suggests that delegating even some basic routine tasks (e.g., correcting spelling and grammatical errors) to GenAI, when done with minimal evaluation of the results, or as "Prosthesis", can use the risk of dependency. However, such action may also be strategically adopted to allow students to allocate more time and cognitive resources to more elaborate tasks. Nevertheless, given the recent emergence of this topic and the limited knowledge currently available, the research conducted is exploratory in nature. Indeed, we do not have any specific hypotheses to put forward. Our method will be applied to explore and gather results concerning:

1. How GenAI is globally used (or not used) by students, for which aim or task, how much and on which occasion.
2. Concerning the relation with the tool, we will observe If and howstudents in a PBL context, delegate basic tasks (e.g., text summarization, translations, information search, and correcting spelling and grammatical errors) to the GenAI tool and use it as "Prosthesis" and eventually (in the line with the young literature) thereby enabling grater engagement in tasks associated with meta-cognitive or meta-competencies, including critical thinking, instructional design, planning, monitoring, and evaluating their own learning.
3. Concerning the relations between the members of the group, we will observe if and how the use of GenAI for basic tasks also facilitates students' engagement in the cooperative and collaborative activities required in the PBL context.

3. METHODS

3.1 Studied sample

A total of 33 students enrolled in educational sciences programs were invited to participate in the study. The use of GenAI was voluntary but actively encouraged by lecturers. Of those invited, 31 students completed the project journal, yielding a participation rate of approximately 90%.

3.2 Instrument and data analysis

This study employed a qualitative research design to explore how generative artificial intelligence (GenAI) can be integrated into project-based learning (PBL) contexts. The aim was to observe patterns, frequency, and contexts of use, as well as students' experiences of using GenAI tools for their projects, using a project journal. A qualitative approach was selected to allow for in-depth, nuanced insights into students' experiences, rather than solely on quantitative measurement of the studied aspects.

The research instrument for this study was a project journal, which had to be completed individually by students enrolled in the study. This instrument was designed to track (by completing specific ribbons) students' use of GenAI tools during project-based learning activities. Students were instructed to complete an entry in their journal each time they used a GenAI tool for the project. The journal consisted of five categories:

1. Dates and periods of use: when the interactions with the GenAI occurred.
2. Objectives of use: the intended purpose or goal of using the tool.
3. Tools used: the specific GenAI tools used
4. Description of use: descriptions of the tasks performed, and the interactions involved (e.g. mode of use, nature of interactions, prompts used, combination of tools used, etc.).
5. Overall experience with the tools: students' reflections on the usefulness, effectiveness, and potential limitations of the tools in that instance.

Table 4. Instrument of the study: Project journal

Date and periods	Objectives of use	Tools used	Description of use	Overall experience with the tools
Enter the dates of use Specify the periods of use (after the first meeting with the teacher, before the intermediate version, etc.)	Assistance in brainstorming on the subject, information research, text reformulation/ transcription, summary of documents, etc.	ChatGPT (free/paid), Gemini, DALLe, Canva, Co-pilot, etc.	Description of the circumstances of each use of the tool, specifying the period, location, whether the activity was undertaken individually or collaboratively, and the nature of the interactions with the tool, including the prompts used. Indication of any use of other tools or resources. Reflections on tool's answers. Evaluation of its relevance and usefulness in relation to the project objectives.	Reflections on how the GAI tools facilitated the project and supported learning. Perception tools effectiveness. Identification of challenges or points of vigilance. Assessment of time savings achieved. Evaluation of the quality of work regarding the expectations of the assessment criteria as a result of using the tools. Consideration of how the work might have differed without the use of GAI tools.

The data were analysed using frequency analysis software (Iramuteq) and manual thematic analysis (done by a double-blind process). The manual thematic analysis was performed to examine the qualitative data. This analysis involved repeated reading of the journals, coding meaningful segments of text, grouping codes into broader categories, and refining themes to capture the most salient aspects of GenAI use in the PBL context.

The study was primarily qualitative in design. However, a descriptive quantitative analysis was conducted to summarise the frequency data extracted from the journals. The frequency analysis considered categories drawn from the journals, including the consultation frequency, the variety of activities, and the types of consultation. Consultation frequency was categorised as low (0–1 interaction), medium (2–5 interactions), or high (more than 6 interactions). A variety of activities was categorised as low (0–1 type of activity), medium (2–5 types of activities), and high (more than 6 types of activities). For the types of consultation, journals' entries of this aspect were classified as individual, group or mixed.

4. RESULTS

4.1 Frequency of GenAI tool use among students

Table 5 below shows that medium consultation frequency was the most common pattern, reported by 14 students (45%), followed by high consultation (10 students, 32%) and low consultation (7 students, 23%).In terms of variety of activities, low variety was dominant (15 students, 48%), medium variety was observed in 12 students (39%), and high variety was only reported by 4 students (13%). Regarding types of consultation, individual use was most frequent (14 students, 45%), closely followed by mixed use combining individual and group consultation (13 students, 42%). Purely group-based consultation was only reported by 4 students (13%).

Table 5. Distribution of students by frequency in related categories

Quantity of consultation			Variety of activities			Types of consultation		
Low	Medium	High	Low	Medium	High	Individual	Group	Mixed
7	14	10	15	12	4	14	4	13

Table 6 shows that students with low consultation systematically report a low variety of activities. This may suggest an occasional use of GenAI. The most frequent configuration identified was medium consultation frequency paired with medium variety of activities, representing nine out of 14 students in the group (Etu: 8, 9, 10, 11, 12, 16, 17, 20, 21). Within the medium consultation group, the largest category (Table 5), a high variety of activities appears to be uncommon; only one student (Etu13) reported this pattern, and only three students have pointed out high consultation frequency with a high variety of activities (Etu24, 25, 31).

The findings also show that the data were dominated by low and medium varieties of activity. These suggest that while many students engaged with GenAI tools at moderate to high frequency of consultation, they tended to use a limited set of activities (Table 6). Furthermore, the preferred mode of consultation remained individual or mixed rather than exclusively group-based (Table 6). Taken together, these results suggest that consultation frequency does not translate into diversity of use.

Table 6. Students' GenAI Tools Use

ID	Quantity of consultation	Variety of activities
Etu1	Low	Low
Etu2	Low	Low
Etu3	Low	Low
Etu4	Low	Low
Etu5	Low	Low
Etu6	Low	Low
Etu7	Low	Low
Etu8	Medium	Medium
Etu9	Medium	Medium
Etu10	Medium	Medium
Etu11	Medium	Medium
Etu12	Medium	Medium
Etu13	Medium	High
Etu14	Medium	Low
Etu15	Medium	Low
Etu16	Medium	Medium
Etu17	Medium	Medium
Etu18	Medium	Low
Etu19	Medium	Low
Etu20	Medium	Medium
Etu21	Medium	Medium
Etu22	High	Medium
Etu23	High	Medium
Etu24	High	High
Etu25	High	High
Etu26	High	Medium
Etu27	High	Low
Etu28	High	Low
Etu29	High	Low
Etu30	High	Low
Etu31	High	High

4.2 Students' perception of advantages and inconveniences in using GenAI tools

Table 7 shows that ChatGPT was the most frequently used tool, followed by Canva. All other tools were cited by two participants or fewer. Some specialised tools, such as Chat PDF and Gauth, were used only once and by the same student. Chat PDF was used to summarise a course and find definitions, while Gauth was used to perform a calculation.

Table 7. Variety of used GenAI tools

Outils	Number of user
ChatGPT	21
Canva	7
DALLe	2
Gemini	4
Napkin.ai	2
Perplexity	4
Chat PDF	1
Gauth	1
Co-pilot	2

Table 8. Reported advantages and inconveniences

Advantages reported	*Inconveniences reported*
Facility of use (to generate illustrations, find examples, ...)	*Dependence*
Efficient aid for various academic tasks: ● Related to planification (brainstorming, planning, ...) ● Related to cognitive acts (brainstorming, structuring ideas, rephrasing ideas, synthesising courses, preparing notes, understanding concepts or notions...) ● Related to creative purposes (search for ideas, information, and examples, generating illustration ● Related to academic writing (writing tasks, correct typos, spelling mistakes and grammatical errors,	Reduces personal involvement on the project
Save-time	*Time-consuming*
Help for comprehension	*Need to be vigilant and need to verify constantly the answers*
Generate feedback in addition to that provided by the teacher	*Need to formulate prompts very clearly*

continued on following page

Table 8. Continued

Advantages reported	*Inconveniences reported*
Get original ideas	*Difficulty to find the correct sources and error in referencing*
Help for revision	*Some answers include errors*
Assistance for writing	*Some answers may lack depth or precision.*
Refine the formulation and structuring of my ideas	*Limited possibility of action in free version of the tool*
Create more organized, clear, and precise content.	
Deepen reflections	

Get concrete and understandable examples

Students reported a wide range of advantages in using GenAI tools from various aspects (cognitive, creative, and technical). Most students pointed out the ease of use, particularly for generating illustrations and finding examples. Many described the tools as efficient aids for academic work, supporting planning activities, cognitive processes such as brainstorming, structuring ideas, synthesising information, preparing notes, and understanding concepts, as well as creative tasks like generating illustrations, ideas, and sourcing information. "They facilitated my learning because they allowed me to synthesise concepts" (Etu18). "It also gives me suggestions and ideas and helps me figure out what works and what doesn't in my project when I ask for its opinion on it" (Etu18). GenAI tools were also valued for academic writing, notably drafting, correcting typos, and improving grammar and spelling.

Timesaving and writing assistance were also highlighted as a distinct advantage by the students. "These tools save me a lot of time. They allow me to stay focused on what's important, whether it's writing documents or designing the module" (Etu11). "It helps to find quick information, clear explanations, and relevant examples. It saved me time by allowing me to search for specific answers without having to browse through multiple sources" (Etu31). "The tools allow for the strategic use of time. For example, they allow us to focus on what we consider to be the most essential aspects of the projects, such as the analytical side, while using them as an aid for writing tasks (Etu9). These advantages are highlighted alongside the help the tools provide in revision and comprehension by giving concrete and understandable examples. "I get concrete and understandable examples" (Etu20). "It helps with understanding the concepts covered in class, exam preparation, etc. (Etu24). "The tools enabled me to conduct in-depth research" (Etu18).

Some also valued the possibility of obtaining feedback (evaluative function) from GenAI in addition to that provided by the teacher, suggesting its complementary role in the learning process. "I use it to get both corrections and feedback on work, which is not always possible due to lack of time, for example..." (Etu11).

While students recognised multiple benefits of GenAI tools, they also reported concerns that could impact sustained or appropriate use of the tools. These include practical issues, such as the need for constant verification, the need for using appropriate and very clear prompts, and the difficulties perceived in finding the correct sources and errors in referencing are the most reported ones. "The answers are not always accurate or precise, which means they need to be verified before use." (Etu24). "Personal adaptation remains necessary to ensure fluidity and relevance to the context" (Etu27), "One challenge was getting answers that were perfectly suited to my question. Sometimes, the tool provides answers that are too general or ambiguous, requiring me to rephrase the question to get more specific information. It is also important to be vigilant about the reliability of the information" (Etu31).

Students also reported that these challenges are related to the lack of depth or precision in some answers, as well as technical restrictions related to the version used (free or professional). "You have to ask it specific questions and sometimes rephrase your request several times to make sure it understands, even if this takes more time" (Etu30). "I have noticed that the most effective AI systems are the ones you have to pay for" (Etu13). "The quality of the bibliographic sources, because I learned that ChatGPT invents its own sources" (Etu23).

These challenges also raised concerns about the time-consuming consequences. "Depending on the use and the intended purpose, I feel that the time savings are more or less significant. For example, when I used the tool to improve and inspire myself on the storyboard, I saved time. On the other hand, when reviewing a completed and finished piece of work to check its consistency, I did not feel that I saved any time" (Etu10).

Furthermore, some students are also preoccupied by the fear of becoming "lazy" in doing the task by themselves. This potential dependency on the tools may reduce their involvement in the project and has consequences on the development of their competencies. "It is essential not to rely solely on these tools and to maintain a critical mindset to prevent plagiarism or excessive dependence ..." (Etu28). "You also have to be vigilant and use it in moderation. It's true that it's practical and easy to use, but you have to know how to strike a balance so that you don't become dependent on these tools if you don't want to lose your ability to think for yourself" (Etu30).

4.3 GenAI use in learning and projects

As for the types of activities performed using GenAI tools, Table 9 showed that the most frequently performed activities were helping with comprehension, project development, information search, and rephrasing texts. Other relatively common activities include finding ideas, rephrasing texts/ideas, and creating an outline, along with tasks, also related to comprehension, such as helping with revision and finding examples, as well as tasks related to creation, such as brainstorming, and getting feedback on work (Quizzes, storyboard writing, etc.). Some basic tasks were also identified, such as planning activities, improving writing tasks, correcting typos, spelling mistakes and grammatical errors, and searching for bibliographic references (scientific articles).

These findings show that most students are indeed engaged in a limited set of activities and mainly use GenAI as an assistant, not only for understanding instructions, concepts and notions learned, or for information search and text rephrasing to help with their comprehension, but also for project development.

Table 9. Students' uses of GenAI

Reported uses	Orthosis	Prosthesis	Auxesis
Help with comprehension	1	12	
Help with planning activities	2		
Help with revision	2	3	
Find definitions		2	
Find examples	1	3	
Find ideas	3	3	
Search for information	4	5	
Search for bibliographic references (scientific articles)		2	
Rephrase texts/ideas	3	3	
Improve writing	1	1	
Create an outline	3	3	
Generate summaries of documents		2	
Generate a summary of a lesson		1	
Generate illustration/images		2	
Brainstorming	2	1	
Correct typos, spelling mistakes and grammatical errors	1	1	
Get feedback on work (quizzes, storyboard writing, etc)		3	
Project development (organizing ideas, generation quiz, content, ...)	6	5	

Most reported uses fall under the 'prosthesis' category or shared across both 'orthosis' and ' prosthesis '. Uses related to project development, such as organising ideas, generating quizzes, and producing content, were reported in both categories. Certain activities, including finding definitions, searching for information, generating summaries, illustrations or images appeared exclusively within the 'prosthesis' category. This is noteworthy given the reported inconveniences related to the need for vigilance and constant verification of answers, the difficulty in finding correct sources and errors in referencing, as well as students' recognition that some outputs may lack depth or precision and may include errors (Table 8). "Planning activities" emerge as the only use of GenAI tools as an orthosis, and no uses imply GenAI tools as an auxesis. Since the uses identified are the described ones, some uses remain unclassified; these include creating templates or presentation materials and translating articles.

The findings pointed out that students perceive GenAI tools as useful for helping them to develop the project, but also to learn the subject taught. However, while they acknowledge the inconveniences of using the tools for these purposes, they continue to employ them as a prosthesis, even for tasks requiring significant cognitive engagement. This raises the question of whether such patterns might be an early sign of deskilling.

5. DISCUSSION AND CONCLUSION

In this chapter, we have explored the use of GenAI in the context of project-based learning. The results display a large range of benefits, but also criticism identified by students while using GenAI. Delegating even some basic routine tasks (e.g., correcting spelling and grammatical errors) to GenAI, when done with minimal evaluation of the results, or as "Prosthesis", can use the risk of dependency (Jeunesse, 2025). Therefore, it can be assumed that such action can be strategically adopted to allow students to allocate more time and cognitive resources to more elaborate tasks. This study, however, pointed out that students were not delegating basic tasks to GenAI to engage more in higher-order, meta-cognitive activities. Instead, we have observed that students used GenAI for a limited set of activities, but not necessarily the basic ones. The most frequently identified activities were 'Helping with comprehension' and 'Project development' (organising ideas, generating quizzes and content, etc.). Both activities require critical thinking, which confirms their position as actions involving higher-order thinking skills. Furthermore, while students acknowledge the inconveniences of using the tools for these purposes, their uses largely correspond to a "Prosthesis" mode, replacing human ability to perform tasks, pointing out students' dependency on GenAI tools.

The findings remain more ambivalent as well for the delegation of basic tasks to GenAI, which would enable greater engagement in cooperative and collaborative activities. The predominance of individual and mixed modes of use (Table 5) indicates that GenAI is appropriated as personal rather than collective working tools. Group dynamics remain unclear since the quality of journal writing depends on the students' willingness. Further interviews will be necessary to examine hypothesis 2 in greater depth.

GenAI tools are instruments that offer opportunities for dialogue and act as critical "partners" capable of challenging students' work. Indeed, the aim of this work was multifaceted. Regarding its technical limits, the goal of its integration into the PBL setting was to raise students' awareness of it so that they can use GenAI tools as supports for their competency's development. However, the findings suggest that students' uses were less oriented toward the latter one and rather reflect a "Prosthesis" mode of use, which entails emerging risk of overdependence and highlights the importance of developing a pedagogical approach encouraging critical use of GenAI tools. Given the feeling of being in dialogue, in future research, it would also be interesting to explore the sense of presence in individual work with GenAI and the emotions that arise in interaction with it.

Building on this chapter, the risk of overdependence on GenAI emerges as a central issue, closely linked to *how* students appropriate the tool rather than how often they use it.

The predominance of a "prosthesis" mode of use indicates that GenAI is not merely supporting learning but, in some cases, substituting students' cognitive activity. Overdependence becomes a risk when the tool progressively assumes functions that are central to learning processes: structuring ideas, validating understanding, or generating content that students might otherwise struggle with productively. While these activities are classified as higher-order, delegating them systematically to GenAI can lead potentially to: (1) a reduction in epistemic struggle, which is essential for conceptual change and deep learning; (2) a weakening of metacognitive regulation, as students rely on the tool to judge relevance, coherence, or quality; (3) an illusion of competence, where fluent outputs mask shallow understanding.

The predominance of individual and mixed modes of use could further contribute to overdependence risks. When GenAI is appropriated as a personal working tool, opportunities for collective regulation, such as peer questioning, negotiation of meaning, and shared decision-making, are reduced. In collaborative settings, such regulation often acts as a safeguard against blind reliance on external resources. Its absence may partially explain why delegation does not translate into increased cooperative engagement, contrary to expectations.

Overall, these results highlight the need for further pedagogical research to frame the use of GenAI in higher education. While GenAI offers valuable support for comprehension and project development, students' spontaneous uses tend to favour a "prothesis" mode, with risks of overdependence and limited metacognitive engagement. Additional research is therefore required to identify the didactic conditions that encourage critical, reflective, and dialogical uses of GenAI. In particular, studies should examine how instructional design, scaffolding, and assessment can support the development of academic and professional competencies rather than task substitution. Longitudinal and design-based approaches would also help understand how students' relationships with GenAI evolve and how these practices transfer to professional contexts.

REFERENCES

Adinda, D. (2020). *Stratégies d'accompagnement des étudiants en formations hybrides : Effets sur l'autodirection dans l'apprentissage* [Doctoral dissertation]. Université de Strasbourg.

Adinda, D., & Denami, M. (2023). Blended Learning and Self-Direction : The Use of E-Forum. In A. S. Munna, V. Nadda, T. A. Allahyari, G. Cantafio, & S. Bilan (Eds.), *Advances in Educational Technologies and Instructional Design* (p. 110-165). IGI Global. DOI: 10.4018/978-1-6684-8282-7.ch006

Bandura, A. (2001). Social cognitive theory: An agentic perspective. *Annual Review of Psychology*, *52*(1), 1–26. DOI: 10.1146/annurev.psych.52.1.1 PMID: 11148297

Barron, B. J., Schwartz, D. L., Vye, N. J., Moore, A., Petrosino, A., Zech, L., & Bransford, J. D. (1998). Doing with understanding: Lessons from research on problem- and project-based learning. *Journal of the Learning Sciences*, *7*(3–4), 271–311.

Biggs, J. (1996). Enhancing teaching through constructive alignment. *Higher Education*, *32*(3), 347–364. DOI: 10.1007/BF00138871

Billett, S. (2001). *Learning in the workplace: Strategies for effective practice*. Allen & Unwin.

Boaler, J. (1998). Open and closed mathematics: Student experiences and understandings. *Journal for Research in Mathematics Education*, *29*(1), 41–62. DOI: 10.2307/749717

Brown, T., Mann, B., Ryder, N., Subbiah, M., Kaplan, J., Dhariwal, P., & Amodei, D. (2020). *Language Models are Few-Shot Learners* (Vol. 33). Advances in Neural Information Processing Systems, https://arxiv.org/abs/2005.14165

Calamel, C. (2012). Prendre en compte les situations non formelles d'apprentissage: *Agora débats/jeunesses, 62*(3), 33-43. https://doi.org/DOI: 10.3917/agora.062.0033

Carré, P. (2020). *Pourquoi et comment les adultes apprendre : De la formation à l'apprenance*. Dunod. DOI: 10.3917/dunod.carre.2020.01

Carretero, S., Vuorikari, R., & Punie, Y. (2017). *DigComp 2.1: The Digital Competence Framework for Citizens with eight proficiency levels and examples of use*. Publications Office of the European Union., DOI: 10.2760/38842

Crisp, G., & Cruz, I. (2009). Mentoring college students: A critical review of the literature between 1990 and 2007. *Research in Higher Education*, *50*(6), 525–545. DOI: 10.1007/s11162-009-9130-2

Cristol, D., & Muller, A. (2013). Les apprentissages informels dans la formation pour adultes: *Savoirs, n° 32*(2), 11-59. https://doi.org/DOI: 10.3917/savo.032.0011

Cukurova, M. (2025). The interplay of learning, analytics and artificial intelligence in education : A vision for hybrid intelligence. *British Journal of Educational Technology, 56*(2), 469–488. DOI: 10.1111/bjet.13514

Dewey, J. (1938). *Experience and education*. Macmillan.

Dionne, K., & Carlile, P. (2016). Le pouvoir transformationnel des hackathons. *Gestion, 41*(2), 62–63. DOI: 10.3917/riges.412.0062

Ehlers, U.-D., Lindner, M., Sommer, S., & Rauch, E. (2023). *AICOMP - Future Skills in a World Increasingly Shaped By AI*. Ubiquity Proceedings., DOI: 10.5334/uproc.91

Engeström, Y. (2001). Expansive learning at work: Toward an activity-theoretical reconceptualization. *Journal of Education and Work, 14*(1), 133–156. DOI: 10.1080/13639080020028747

Eraut, M. (2004). Informal learning in the workplace. *Studies in Continuing Education, 26*(2), 247–273. DOI: 10.1080/158037042000225245

Goodfellow, I., Pouget-Abadie, J., Mirza, M., Xu, B., Warde-Farley, D., Ozair, S., & Bengio, Y. (2014). *Generative adversarial nets* (Vol. 27). Advances in neural information processing systems, https://arxiv.org/abs/1406.2661

Greenhow, C., & Lewin, C. (2016). Social media and education: Reconceptualizing the boundaries of formal and informal learning. *Learning, Media and Technology, 41*(1), 6–30. DOI: 10.1080/17439884.2015.1064954

Guile, D., & Griffiths, T. (2001). Learning through work experience. *Journal of Education and Work, 14*(1), 113–131. DOI: 10.1080/13639080020028738

Guszcza, J. (2018). *Smarter together: Why artificial intelligence needs human-centered design*. Deloitte Insights.

Hart, A. (2013, Juin). *Apprentissage formel, informel, non-formel, des notions difficiles à utiliser… pourquoi?* https://oce.uqam.ca/apprentissage-formel-informel-non-formel-des-notions-difficiles-a-utiliser-pourquoi/

Holmes, W., Porayska-Pomsta, K., Holstein, K., Sutherland, E., Baker, T., Shum, S. B., Santos, O. C., Rodrigo, M. T., Cukurova, M., Bittencourt, I. I., & Koedinger, K. R. (2021). Ethics of AI in education: Towards a community-wide framework. *International Journal of Artificial Intelligence in Education, 32*(3), 504–526. DOI: 10.1007/s40593-021-00239-1

Ito, M.. (2013). *Connected learning: An agenda for research and design.* Digital Media and Learning Research Hub.

Jenkins, H., Purushotma, R., Clinton, K., Weigel, M., & Robison, A. J. (2006). *Confronting the challenges of participatory culture: Media education for the 21st century.* MacArthur Foundation.

Jeunesse, C. (2025). *Des usages des technologies pour apprendre aux Environnements Personnels d'Apprentissage augmentés par l'Intelligence Artificielle Générative (IAGEN)* [thèse d'HDR, Université Paris Nanterre]. https://hal.science/tel-05328100

Johnson, D. W., & Johnson, R. T. (1999). *Learning together and alone: Cooperative, competitive, and individualistic learning.* Allyn & Bacon.

Kaldi, S., Filippatou, D., & Govaris, C. (2011). Project-based learning in primary schools: Effects on pupils' learning and attitudes. *Education* 3–13, 39(1), 35-47.

Karaçalli, S., & Korur, F. (2014). The Effects of Project-Based Learning on Students' Academic Achievement, Attitude, and Retention of Knowledge : The Subject of "Electricity in Our Lives". *School Science and Mathematics, 114*(5), 224–235. Advance online publication. DOI: 10.1111/ssm.12071

Kasneci, E., Sessler, K., Küchemann, S., Bannert, M., Dementieva, D., Fischer, F., Gasser, U., Groh, G., Günnemann, S., Hüllermeier, E., Krusche, S., Kutyniok, G., Michaeli, T., Nerdel, C., Pfeffer, J., Poquet, O., Sailer, M., Schmidt, A., Seidel, T., & Kasneci, G. (2023). ChatGPT for good? On opportunities and challenges of large language models for education. *Learning and Individual Differences, 103*, 102274. DOI: 10.1016/j.lindif.2023.102274

Kilpatrick, W. H. (1918). The project method. *Teachers College Record, 19*(4), 319–335. DOI: 10.1177/016146811801900404

Kilpatrick, W. H. (1921). Dangers and Difficulties of the Project Method and how to Overcome Them—A Symposium1. *Teachers College Record: The Voice of Scholarship in Education, 22*(4), 1-6. https://doi.org/ (Original work published 1921)DOI: 10.1177/016146812102200407

Kolb, D. A. (1984). *Experiential learning: Experience as the source of learning and development.* Prentice-Hall.

Koltay, T. (2023). The age of artificial intelligence: Challenges for information literacy. *Journal of Academic Librarianship, 49*(1), 102666. DOI: 10.1016/j.acalib.2022.102666

Krajcik, J., & Shin, N. (2014). *Project-based learning. The Cambridge handbook of the learning sciences.* Cambridge University Press.

Krajcik, J. S., & Blumenfeld, P. C. (2006). The Cambridge Handbook of the Learning Sciences. R. Keith Sawyer (ed). Cambridge University Press DOI: 10.1017/CBO9780511816833

Larmer, J., Mergendoller, J., & Boss, S. (2015). *Setting the standard for project based learning : A proven approach to rigorous classroom instruction.* ASCD.

Laurillard, D. (2002). *Rethinking university teaching: A conversational framework for the effective use of learning technologies.* Routledge. DOI: 10.4324/9780203160329

Long, D., & Magerko, B. (2020). What is AI literacy? Competencies and design considerations. In *Proceedings of the 2020 ACM CHI Conference on Human Factors in Computing Systems* (pp. 1–16). ACM. https://doi.org/DOI: 10.1145/3313831.3376727

Luckin, R.. (2009). Learner-generated contexts: A framework to support the effective use of technology to support learning. *Learning, Media and Technology, 34*(4), 341–355.

Luckin, R., Holmes, W., Griffiths, M., & Forcier, L. B. (2019). *Intelligence unleashed: An argument for AI in education.* Pearson.

Lund, B. D., & Wang, T. (2023). ChatGPT and academic libraries. *Library Hi Tech News, 40*(3), 26–29. DOI: 10.1108/LHTN-01-2023-0009

Mal Walder, A. (2016). Les innovations technologiques sont-elles à l'origine des nouveaux rythmes et temporalités de l'université contemporaine ? *Distances et médiations des savoirs, (16).* DOI: 10.4000/dms.1605

Merrill, M. D. (2002). First principles of instruction. *Educational Technology Research and Development, 50*(3), 43–59. DOI: 10.1007/BF02505024

Morlaix, S. (2015). Les compétences sociales à l'école primaire: essai de mesure et effets sur la réussite. *Carrefours de l'éducation, 40*(2), 183-200. .DOI: 10.3917/cdle.040.0183

NextEducation. (n.d.). *AIComp – Artificial Intelligence Competences.* Retrieved from https://next-education.org/en/projects/ai-comp/

OECD. (2022). *"OECD Framework for the Classification of AI systems", OECD Digital Economy Papers, No. 323.* OECD Publishing., DOI: 10.1787/cb6d9eca-

Perkins, D. N. (1995). L'individu-plus. Une vision distribuée de la pensée et de l'apprentissage. *Revue française de pédagogie, 111*, 1995. Psychologie de l'éducation: Nouvelles approches américaines. https://doi.org/DOI: 10.3406/rfp.1995.1232

Piaget, J., & Inhelder, B. (1973). *The Psychology Of The Child*. Basic Books.

Rabardel, P. (1995). *Les hommes et les technologies: Approche cognitive des instruments contemporains*. Armand Colin.

Rose, J. (2018). La professionnalisation des formations supérieures: Facettes multiples et effets incertains. *Cahiers de la recherche sur l'éducation et les savoirs. Hors-série*, *6*, 59–70.

Santelmann, P. (2019). Quel usage des compétences transversales. Santelmann P. (dir.) Partir des compétences transversales pour lire autrement le travail. *Education Permanente HS*, *13*, 33–43.

Schön, D. A. (1983). *The reflective practitioner: How professionals think in action*. Basic Books.

Schugurensky, D. (2007). « Vingt mille lieues sous les mers » : Les quatre défis de l'apprentissage informel. *Revue Française de Pédagogie*, *160*, 13–27. DOI: 10.4000/rfp.583

Sefton-Green, J. (2004). *Report 7: Literature review in informal learning with technology outside school*. Futurelab.

Selwyn, N. (2009). The digital native—Myth and reality. *Aslib Proceedings*, *61*(4), 364–379. DOI: 10.1108/00012530910973776

Sharples, M.. (2014). *Innovating pedagogy 2014: Exploring new forms of teaching, learning and assessment, to guide educators and policy makers*. The Open University.

Stewart, R. A. (2007). Investigating the link between self-directed learning readiness and project-based learning outcomes: The case of international Masters students in an engineering management course. *European Journal of Engineering Education*, *32*(4), 453–465. DOI: 10.1080/03043790701337197

Susnjak, T. (2022). ChatGPT: The end of online exam integrity? *Journal of Applied Learning & Teaching*, *5*(2). Advance online publication. DOI: 10.37074/jalt.2022.5.2.9

Thomas, J. W. (2000). *A review of research on project-based learning*. The Autodesk Foundation.

Van Laer, S., & Elen, J. (2017). In search of attributes that support self-regulation in blended learning environments. *Education and Information Technologies*, *22*(4), 1395–1454. Advance online publication. DOI: 10.1007/s10639-016-9505-x

Veletsianos, G. (2016). *Social media in higher education: Critical perspectives.* Routledge.

Vygotsky, L. S. (1978). *Mind in society: The development of higher psychological processes*. Harvard University Press.

Weber, A. (1982). Savoirs sociaux et savoirs scolaires. Pour une problématique articulation. *Pratiques*, *36*(1), 24–36. DOI: 10.3406/prati.1982.1244

Wenger, E. (1998). *Communities of practice: Learning, meaning, and identity.* Cambridge University Press. DOI: 10.1017/CBO9780511803932

Zou, J., Schiebinger, L., & Washington, A. (2023). AI and the end of originality? *Nature Human Behaviour*, *7*, 1529–1532. DOI: 10.1038/s41562-023-01632-w

Chapter 9
Applications of AI in Educational Research

Ardra Rianisa
http://orcid.org/0009-0005-0304-1195
Universitas Esa Unggul, Indonesia

Binastya Anggara Sekti
http://orcid.org/0000-0001-5489-4888
Universitas Esa Unggul, Indonesia

ABSTRACT

This chapter explores the role of Artificial Intelligence (AI) in educational research, focusing on its applications, methodologies, and ethical considerations. AI's integration into educational research has streamlined processes such as data analysis, hypothesis testing, and literature reviews, while also enhancing personalized learning experiences. The chapter addresses AI's potential to improve student engagement and outcomes through adaptive learning systems, AI-powered tutoring, and predictive analytics. However, ethical concerns, including biases in AI algorithms, data privacy, and the transparency of AI-driven decisions, are discussed in depth. The chapter concludes with a look at the future of AI in educational research, emphasizing the need for responsible and ethical AI deployment to ensure that AI complements, rather than replaces, the human aspects of education, such as creativity and critical thinking.

1. INTRODUCTION

The presence of Artificial Intelligence (AI) in educational research has garnered significant attention in recent years. This continuously evolving technology prom-

DOI: 10.4018/979-8-2600-1458-5.ch009

ises immense potential to revolutionize how education is researched, developed, and delivered. AI enables researchers to analyze large datasets more efficiently, automate repetitive tasks, and provide more personalized learning experiences. AI also facilitates the creation of dynamic educational content and allows the use of predictive analytics to map student learning outcomes. In this context, AI plays a major role in improving the efficiency of educational research methodologies and offering new insights for the development of pedagogy and educational technology (Bećirović et al., 2025; Bottrighi et al., 2025).

However, despite its benefits, the application of AI also raises significant ethical challenges that must be addressed. One of the concerns is the risk of excessive dependence on technology, which can diminish human creativity and intuition in decision-making during research. Over-relying on AI in the research process could undermine the critical thinking and analytical capabilities that have traditionally been the foundation of knowledge and educational research. Additionally, there are concerns about data privacy and the potential for bias in the AI systems used for educational data analysis. Therefore, it is crucial to understand both the advantages and risks of AI so that its application can be done judiciously and responsibly (Campillo-Ferrer et al., 2025; Shata & Hartley, 2025).

AI not only has the potential to speed up data analysis but also offers opportunities to design learning experiences that are more tailored to individual student needs. For example, in teaching contexts, AI can provide more personalized instruction by adjusting the difficulty level and content based on student performance data. The use of this technology can enhance student engagement, reduce academic failure rates, and facilitate independent learning with real-time feedback. Thus, AI has great potential to improve the overall quality of education, but careful control is required to avoid misuse or overdependence on these tools (Fletscher et al., 2025; Gao et al., 2025).

Looking ahead, AI is predicted to continue developing and become an integral part of educational research methodologies. New technologies, such as machine learning and natural language processing (NLP), will further enhance AI's ability to process data and suggest data-driven solutions to improve educational outcomes. As such, AI's role in educational research will likely evolve from being a tool to becoming a strategic partner that offers innovative insights and enhances teaching and learning. However, for AI to be used effectively, researchers and educators must have good literacy regarding this technology and understand how to apply it ethically in educational settings (Shata & Hartley, 2025; Zhang, 2025).

Finally, it is important to consider the long-term impact of AI in education. While AI can improve efficiency and effectiveness in education, excessive reliance on this technology may diminish the ability to think critically and independently. Therefore, education that involves technology should also include the development of critical skills, creativity, and the ability to evaluate and interpret AI-generated results carefully. This will help ensure that students do not just rely on technology but also develop the necessary analytical skills needed to solve real-world problems (Daher, 2025; Manganello et al., 2025).

2. OBJECTIVES

The goal of this chapter is to provide a deeper understanding of the role of AI in educational research and how AI can be applied in various aspects of teaching, learning, and academic performance. In this chapter, we will identify the main contributions of AI to educational research methodologies, particularly in data analysis and information gathering that improve accuracy and efficiency. The first objective is to explore how AI can be used to collect, process, and analyze data on a large scale and how this technology can improve the accuracy and efficiency of educational research (Deval et al., 2025; Gao et al., 2025).

Next, the chapter aims to explore AI's applications in creating more personalized learning experiences. AI technologies allow for the development of curricula that are tailored to the needs of each student, offering them a more engaging and interactive learning experience. For example, AI can adjust the learning materials based on students' progress, offer additional practice on areas that need more attention, and provide real-time feedback that helps students improve their understanding. The second objective of this chapter is to dive deeper into how AI can enhance adaptive learning that is responsive to individual needs (Campillo-Ferrer et al., 2025; Fletscher et al., 2025).

Additionally, the chapter aims to investigate the ethical challenges and concerns that arise as AI becomes more integrated into educational research. While AI holds the potential to optimize many educational processes, issues such as bias in algorithms, data privacy, and the lack of transparency in the use of this technology are significant challenges that need to be addressed. Thus, this chapter will also discuss the importance of developing clear policies and guidelines regarding the use of AI in education to ensure that the technology is applied ethically and fairly (Bećirović et al., 2025; Bottrighi et al., 2025).

Another objective is to provide insights into the latest trends and innovations in the application of AI within educational research. AI technologies not only enhance how we collect and analyze data, but they also enable the development of new research tools that can accelerate the research process and provide more relevant results that can be applied in educational contexts. By understanding these trends, we can prepare for a future that is increasingly driven by AI and optimize the potential of this technology for global educational advancement (Daher, 2025; Shata & Hartley, 2025).

Ultimately, the primary goal of this chapter is to ensure that readers can understand the implications of AI adoption in education and how best to integrate this technology while maintaining a balance between technology and human roles. This chapter will guide educators, researchers, and policymakers in effectively leveraging AI to improve education quality while safeguarding academic integrity and creativity (Deval et al., 2025; Zeng et al., 2025).

3. UNDERSTANDING AI AND ITS CORE TECHNOLOGIES

Figure 1. AI Technology Workflow in Educational Research

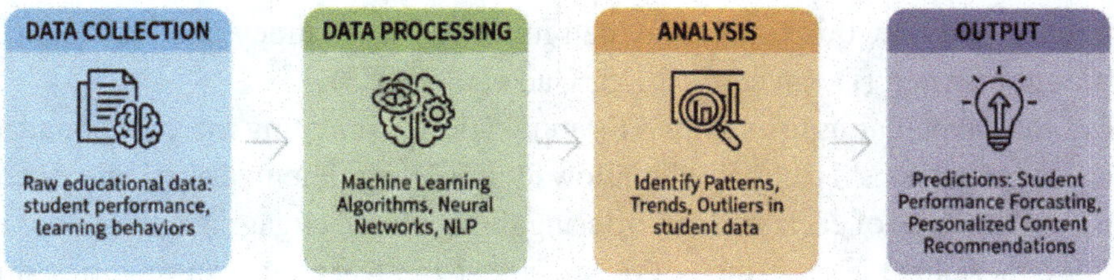

Artificial Intelligence (AI) has emerged as a transformative force across various sectors, including education. AI can be broadly defined as a field of computer science focused on creating systems capable of performing tasks that would normally require human intelligence. These tasks include decision-making, problem-solving, speech recognition, and learning. The core technologies driving AI's application in educational research are machine learning, natural language processing (NLP), and neural networks. These technologies allow AI systems to analyze vast amounts of educational data, identify patterns, and make predictions about student performance, thus enhancing the efficiency and scalability of educational research (Caiza et al., 2025; Gao et al., 2025).

Machine learning (ML), a subset of AI, enables computers to learn from data without being explicitly programmed. This technology is particularly useful in educational research, where large datasets are common. For example, ML algorithms can identify patterns in student behavior, predict academic success, and provide insights into effective teaching strategies. NLP, another key technology, allows AI systems to understand and process human language, making it ideal for analyzing open-ended responses, student essays, and other text-based data. NLP-powered systems can categorize text, extract key insights, and even generate content, thus facilitating the analysis and synthesis of educational research findings (Bećirović et al., 2025; Zhang, 2025).

Neural networks, inspired by the structure of the human brain, are used in deep learning models to process complex patterns in large datasets. These networks are especially powerful in applications such as image recognition, speech recognition, and personalized learning pathways. In educational research, neural networks can be employed to create models that predict student outcomes based on historical data, thus allowing researchers to develop more accurate educational interventions (Gao et al., 2025; Zeng et al., 2025). Through these technologies, AI can automate tedious tasks, freeing up time for researchers to focus on more creative aspects of their work.

AI's role in educational research extends beyond data analysis and prediction. With the help of AI, researchers can automate literature reviews, conduct hypothesis testing, and synthesize findings more quickly than ever before. For example, AI-powered systems can search through large academic databases to identify relevant studies, summarize key findings, and propose new research questions based on gaps in the literature. This ability to streamline the research process not only saves time but also helps ensure that educational research is more comprehensive and up-to-date (Jaramillo et al., 2025).

Finally, as AI technologies continue to evolve, their applications in educational research will become increasingly sophisticated. Emerging innovations, such as AI-powered collaborative learning systems, will enable real-time, data-driven decision-making, enhancing both research and classroom practices. These systems will likely transform how researchers and educators interact with data, further integrating AI into the fabric of educational inquiry. By understanding the core technologies behind AI, educational researchers can better leverage these tools to enhance their work and create more personalized, efficient, and scalable educational environments (Shata & Hartley, 2025; Zhu et al., 2025).

4. AI IN DATA ANALYSIS AND RESEARCH METHODOLOGY

Artificial Intelligence (AI) has revolutionized the way educational researchers approach data analysis, significantly increasing both efficiency and accuracy. Machine learning (ML) algorithms, which are at the heart of AI technologies, are particularly beneficial in processing large datasets that would otherwise be too complex or time-consuming for human researchers to analyze. In educational research, where vast amounts of data are generated from assessments, surveys, and learning management systems, AI tools can identify patterns and trends that might not be immediately apparent. These tools enable researchers to make data-driven decisions and predictions, offering new insights into student performance, teaching strategies, and overall learning outcomes (Gao et al., 2025; Zhang, 2025). For instance, AI can predict which students are at risk of underperforming, allowing educators to implement timely interventions before academic problems become severe.

In addition to predictive capabilities, AI has streamlined the process of literature reviews, hypothesis testing, and the synthesis of research findings. Traditionally, researchers spent countless hours manually reviewing large volumes of literature to identify gaps and trends in existing studies. AI tools, such as natural language processing (NLP) systems, have made this task more efficient by automatically scanning and categorizing research articles, extracting key concepts, and providing summaries. NLP tools can also analyze qualitative data, such as open-ended survey responses or student essays, to uncover themes and insights that are valuable for researchers seeking to understand student attitudes, behaviors, and learning experiences. This automation not only saves time but also ensures that researchers do not overlook important studies, thus contributing to more comprehensive and up-to-date reviews of the literature (Jaramillo et al., 2025).

Furthermore, AI-powered systems assist researchers in hypothesis testing by automating complex statistical analyses. Machine learning algorithms can analyze multiple variables and determine relationships between them without requiring the manual computation of equations. These systems can run simulations to test different research hypotheses and provide instant feedback on whether the data supports or refutes a given theory. This capability is particularly useful in large-scale educational studies, where researchers are often dealing with thousands of data points. AI's ability to automate these processes reduces the margin of error in statistical analysis, leading to more reliable results. It also allows researchers to test hypotheses faster and more efficiently, facilitating quicker advancements in educational theory and practice (Manganello et al., 2025).

Another important aspect of AI's impact on educational research is its role in improving research methodology itself. AI tools help researchers identify gaps in their own methodology by analyzing data for inconsistencies or areas where the research design may need improvement. For example, AI can assess whether the data collected is representative of the target population and suggest modifications to the research design if necessary. This ensures that the research findings are more generalizable and reliable. Additionally, AI technologies can assist in ensuring that research methodologies adhere to ethical guidelines by flagging potential biases in data collection or analysis. This feature is especially important in education, where bias in research can lead to misleading conclusions and perpetuate inequalities in the learning system (Bećirović et al., 2025; Deval et al., 2025).

Despite its significant advantages, the use of AI in educational research is not without its challenges. One of the primary concerns is the potential for bias in AI algorithms. Since AI systems are often trained on historical data, they may inadvertently replicate existing biases, such as those based on socioeconomic status, ethnicity, or gender. This can skew research findings and lead to unfair or inaccurate conclusions, particularly when AI is used to predict student performance or analyze educational outcomes. To address this issue, researchers must ensure that AI algorithms are trained on diverse datasets that accurately represent the populations being studied. Additionally, it is crucial to continuously monitor AI systems for signs of bias and adjust the models as necessary to ensure that the research remains ethical and equitable (Fletscher et al., 2025; Shata & Hartley, 2025).

In conclusion, AI's impact on data analysis and research methodology in education is profound, enabling researchers to analyze complex datasets, automate repetitive tasks, and enhance the accuracy and reliability of their findings. The ability of AI to identify patterns, predict outcomes, and provide real-time feedback is transforming educational research, making it more efficient and effective. However, it is important to be mindful of the ethical implications of AI in research, particularly regarding bias and fairness. As AI technologies continue to evolve, it is essential that educational researchers work alongside AI experts to develop solutions that address these challenges and ensure that AI's potential is harnessed responsibly to advance knowledge and improve educational practices (Manganello et al., 2025; Zhang, 2025).

5. AI IN PERSONALIZED LEARNING AND ADAPTIVE SYSTEMS

Figure 2. AI-Driven Personalized Learning System

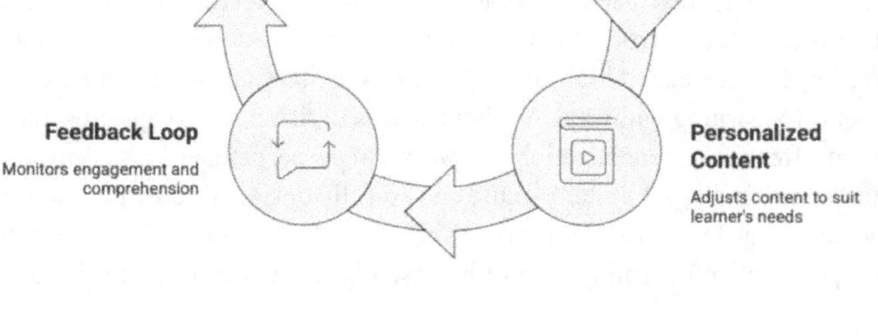

One of the most promising applications of Artificial Intelligence (AI) in education is its ability to deliver personalized learning experiences. Personalized learning, an approach that tailors education to individual students' needs, is greatly enhanced by AI technologies. Through machine learning algorithms, AI can analyze a student's learning patterns, progress, and preferences to adjust the content and pace of learning. This customization allows for a more effective educational experience, as students receive targeted resources and activities that address their unique strengths and challenges. AI-driven adaptive learning systems can dynamically modify the learning environment, offering different levels of difficulty or personalized feedback based on real-time data, which improves student engagement and outcomes (Caiza et al., 2025; Fletscher et al., 2025).

AI's role in personalized learning is not limited to simply adjusting content difficulty. It can also be employed to develop individualized learning pathways, providing students with a more customized curriculum that aligns with their specific needs and goals. These systems, when properly implemented, allow students to progress at their own pace, revisiting concepts that they may not have fully understood or advancing quickly through material they have mastered. This type of adaptive learning ensures that each student is working within their optimal zone of development, a concept that closely aligns with Vygotsky's Zone of Proximal Development (ZPD), which highlights the importance of providing tailored support that fosters student growth (Jaramillo et al., 2025; Zeng et al., 2025).

Moreover, AI technologies support the creation of intelligent tutoring systems (ITS), which function as virtual tutors that can provide one-on-one support to students, much like a human teacher would. These ITS use AI to analyze students' responses and provide immediate feedback, making the learning experience interactive and dynamic. The use of AI in this context not only allows for scalable individualized support but also enables real-time monitoring of student progress, allowing educators to intervene early if a student is struggling. In settings where personalized human attention might be limited due to class size or resource constraints, AI-powered tutoring systems bridge the gap, ensuring that all students can receive the support they need to succeed academically (Campillo-Ferrer et al., 2025; Zhang, 2025).

However, while AI has shown significant promise in personalizing learning, there are challenges that need to be addressed to fully realize its potential. One challenge is the need for robust data to train AI systems, as AI algorithms require access to large, diverse, and high-quality datasets to make accurate predictions and adjustments to learning pathways. Without access to rich data, AI systems may fail to provide effective personalization, or worse, may perpetuate biases present in the data. Additionally, AI systems must be carefully designed to respect students' privacy, ensuring that sensitive information is handled securely. As AI continues to shape personalized learning, it will be essential for educational institutions to adopt policies that protect student data while ensuring the benefits of personalized learning are accessible to all students, regardless of their background (Bećirović et al., 2025; Daher, 2025).

Looking toward the future, AI is poised to further enhance personalized learning by integrating with other emerging technologies, such as augmented reality (AR) and virtual reality (VR). These technologies, when combined with AI, can create immersive learning environments that adapt in real-time based on a student's actions, providing even more tailored experiences. For example, VR environments could simulate real-world situations where students can practice skills in a safe, controlled space. AI would monitor the student's interactions within these environments and provide personalized feedback, enhancing both engagement and learning outcomes. As these technologies continue to evolve, the integration of AI with VR and AR could redefine the future of personalized education, making learning more interactive, immersive, and effective (Fletscher et al., 2025; Meng, 2025).

In conclusion, AI is transforming personalized learning by offering adaptive systems that respond to the unique needs of each student. These systems enhance engagement, support diverse learning styles, and provide real-time feedback, ensuring that education is more tailored and efficient. While there are challenges related to data quality, privacy concerns, and algorithmic biases, the future of AI in personalized learning holds immense promise. As AI continues to advance, it will be crucial for educators, researchers, and policymakers to ensure that these systems are developed and implemented responsibly, making personalized learning accessible to all students and ensuring that technology enhances, rather than replaces, the human aspects of teaching and learning (Caiza et al., 2025; Fletscher et al., 2025).

6. NATURAL LANGUAGE PROCESSING IN EDUCATIONAL RESEARCH

Natural Language Processing (NLP) has emerged as a transformative tool in educational research, offering powerful capabilities to analyze and interpret textual data. NLP, a branch of AI that focuses on enabling machines to understand, interpret, and generate human language, is becoming increasingly integrated into educational settings. In educational research, NLP tools are used to analyze open-ended student responses, essays, discussion posts, and even large volumes of academic papers. These systems can automate the process of coding qualitative data, helping researchers extract meaningful patterns and themes from text-based data more quickly and accurately than traditional methods. NLP algorithms can identify key phrases, categorize content, and detect sentiment, thus making it easier to analyze student feedback and assess learning outcomes (Jaramillo et al., 2025; Zhu et al., 2025).

One of the key advantages of NLP in educational research is its ability to handle large datasets that would be unmanageable for human researchers. For example, when analyzing open-ended survey responses, NLP systems can process hundreds or even thousands of responses in a matter of seconds, categorizing and summarizing the content based on predetermined themes or keywords. This ability to handle large amounts of text data allows researchers to focus on higher-level analysis, such as drawing conclusions and making recommendations, rather than spending hours manually processing data. Moreover, NLP-powered systems can detect nuances in language, such as student misunderstandings or misconceptions, which can inform educators on how to adjust their teaching strategies to address specific learning needs (Bottrighi et al., 2025; Shata & Hartley, 2025).

In addition to simplifying data analysis, NLP tools are also useful in automating content creation. For instance, AI-driven systems can assist in generating educational materials such as quizzes, summaries, and instructional content by analyzing existing learning resources and student performance data. These systems use NLP to identify the most relevant content for a specific topic and generate new learning resources that are tailored to individual students' needs. As a result, educators can save valuable time in creating content while also ensuring that the materials are highly relevant and personalized for their students. NLP tools can also help create interactive learning modules where students can receive personalized feedback based on their responses, enhancing the learning experience through real-time interaction (Meng, 2025; Zhu et al., 2025).

However, as promising as NLP is, there are significant challenges and limitations that need to be addressed. One challenge is the potential for misinterpretation or loss of context in NLP algorithms. While these systems are designed to process human language, they may struggle with understanding context, sarcasm, or cultural nuances, which can lead to incorrect categorization or misunderstanding of the data. For instance, a student's positive feedback might be misinterpreted as negative if the system does not fully grasp the context or tone. This limitation can affect the accuracy of research findings and the quality of automated feedback provided to students. Therefore, researchers and developers must continuously improve NLP algorithms to ensure that they can more effectively understand and interpret the subtleties of human language, especially in educational contexts where language use can vary widely (Caiza et al., 2025; Gao et al., 2025).

Looking toward the future, NLP in educational research is expected to become even more sophisticated, offering deeper insights into student learning. As AI systems continue to improve, they will be able to generate more accurate analyses of student behavior, provide personalized recommendations for learning, and assist in creating adaptive learning environments that evolve with the student. For example, AI-powered NLP tools could be integrated into educational platforms to offer real-time analysis of student writing, suggesting improvements and helping students refine their critical thinking and writing skills. Additionally, NLP could be used to analyze trends across educational research papers, synthesizing findings from diverse studies and identifying areas that require further investigation. The growing capabilities of NLP in education will open up new opportunities for researchers to better understand student engagement, achievement, and learning behaviors, ultimately helping to improve educational practices (Bottrighi et al., 2025; Jaramillo et al., 2025).

In conclusion, Natural Language Processing is a powerful and rapidly developing tool in educational research, enabling researchers to analyze large amounts of textual data more efficiently, automate content creation, and provide personalized learning experiences. While there are challenges related to context and interpretation, ongoing advancements in AI and NLP technologies promise to overcome these obstacles, further enhancing their applicability in education. As NLP tools become more accurate and sophisticated, they will play a key role in transforming educational research methodologies, offering deeper insights into student learning and engagement, and helping to create more adaptive, effective learning environments. As the technology continues to evolve, it will be essential for researchers and educators to work together to integrate these tools in ways that are both ethical and effective, ensuring that AI-driven solutions are used to complement, not replace, human judgment (Bećirović et al., 2025; Zhang, 2025).

7. ETHICAL CONCERNS AND CHALLENGES IN AI-DRIVEN EDUCATIONAL RESEARCH

Table 1. Ethical Concerns and Solutions in AI-Driven Educational Research

Ethical Concern	Description	Potential Solution
Bias in Algorithms	AI systems may perpetuate biases in data, leading to unfair outcomes (e.g., biased performance predictions).	Regular auditing of AI systems for fairness; diverse training datasets.
Data Privacy	AI systems often require access to sensitive student data, raising privacy concerns.	Adhering to strict data privacy regulations like GDPR; anonymizing student data.
Transparency	AI systems can operate as “black boxes,” making it difficult to understand how decisions are made.	Developing explainable AI systems that provide clear insights into decision-making processes.

continued on following page

Table 1. Continued

Ethical Concern	Description	Potential Solution
Dehumanization of Education	Over-reliance on AI could reduce the role of human educators in the classroom, leading to a lack of empathy and creativity.	Ensuring AI complements, rather than replaces, human interaction in education.
Access Inequality	ot all students or institutions have equal access to AI-driven educational tools, exacerbating the digital divide.	Policies to ensure equitable access to AI technologies and resources in underserved areas.

As Artificial Intelligence (AI) continues to permeate educational research, it brings with it a host of ethical concerns and challenges that need to be addressed. One of the primary ethical issues revolves around the potential biases present in AI algorithms. AI systems, especially those used in educational research, often rely on historical data to make predictions and decisions. If the data used to train these algorithms contains biases whether related to socioeconomic status, gender, ethnicity, or disability there is a significant risk that these biases will be perpetuated in the research outcomes. In educational contexts, this could lead to unfair treatment or misrepresentation of certain student groups, resulting in biased academic predictions, unequal learning opportunities, and the reinforcement of existing educational inequalities (Shata & Hartley, 2025; Yan et al., 2025). Therefore, it is crucial that AI systems be developed with fairness in mind and that the data used to train these systems is regularly audited for bias.

Another critical ethical concern in AI-driven educational research is privacy and data security. AI systems typically rely on large datasets, often containing sensitive student information, such as academic records, personal identifiers, and behavioral data. This reliance on extensive data collection raises significant concerns regarding data privacy. Researchers must ensure that AI tools comply with existing data protection regulations, such as the General Data Protection Regulation (GDPR), which provides guidelines for safeguarding personal information. Moreover, the use of AI in educational settings may expose students to risks if their data is mishandled or accessed without consent. As such, it is essential that educational institutions implement strict protocols for data security, including encryption, anonymization, and secure data storage, to protect students' privacy and ensure the responsible use of AI technologies (Bećirović et al., 2025; Markus et al., 2025).

The issue of transparency in AI decision-making is another important ethical challenge in educational research. Many AI systems, particularly those based on machine learning and neural networks, operate as "black boxes," meaning that the decision-making processes behind their predictions and actions are not always clear to human users. In educational research, this lack of transparency can be problematic, especially when AI systems are used to make decisions about student performance, grading, or the design of personalized learning experiences. Without a clear understanding of how AI systems arrive at their conclusions, educators and researchers may struggle to trust the results, leading to skepticism and resistance to AI adoption. To address this issue, it is necessary to develop AI systems that provide explainable and interpretable outputs, ensuring that users can understand how and why certain decisions are made. This transparency will foster trust in AI systems and encourage their ethical integration into educational practices (Daher, 2025; Manganello et al., 2025).

AI also raises concerns about the potential dehumanization of education. While AI-driven tools, such as adaptive learning platforms and intelligent tutoring systems, can provide personalized support, there is a fear that overreliance on technology could reduce the role of human teachers in the classroom. Education is not just about transferring knowledge; it involves social interaction, empathy, and the development of critical thinking and emotional intelligence skills that AI is currently unable to replicate. If AI were to replace too many aspects of the educational process, it could result in a loss of the human connection that is essential for effective teaching and learning. Therefore, it is important to strike a balance between AI-driven tools and human input, ensuring that AI complements rather than replaces the role of educators (Fletscher et al., 2025; Zeng et al., 2025).

Lastly, as AI becomes increasingly integrated into educational research, the ethical implications of its potential for widespread adoption must be considered. While AI can bring about numerous benefits, including efficiency, scalability, and personalized learning, it is crucial that its integration into education is carried out with careful thought and consideration. One significant challenge is ensuring equitable access to AI technologies, especially in underserved regions or among marginalized student populations. If AI tools are not equally accessible, there is a risk of exacerbating the digital divide, where students with greater access to technology have a distinct advantage over those without. Therefore, policymakers must consider how to make AI tools and the benefits they bring accessible to all students, ensuring that no one is left behind in the AI-driven educational revolution (Caiza et al., 2025; Zhu et al., 2025).

In conclusion, the ethical challenges associated with AI in educational research are vast and complex. These include issues related to bias, privacy, transparency, dehumanization of education, and equitable access to technology. While AI offers tremendous potential to improve educational research and practices, it is essential that its integration be done responsibly, with careful attention to these ethical concerns. By addressing these issues, researchers, educators, and policymakers can ensure that AI is used in ways that benefit all students and preserve the core human aspects of education, including creativity, critical thinking, and social interaction (Morello & Chick, 2025; Shata & Hartley, 2025).

8. AI IN EDUCATIONAL CONTENT CREATION AND ENHANCEMENT

Artificial Intelligence (AI) is revolutionizing the way educational content is created and enhanced. Traditionally, the process of creating educational materials such as textbooks, quizzes, assignments, and multimedia resources required significant time and effort from educators. However, AI technologies, particularly those powered by natural language processing (NLP) and machine learning, are transforming content creation by automating various aspects of this process. AI systems can generate personalized content tailored to individual student needs, creating more engaging and relevant learning materials. For example, AI-driven platforms can automatically generate quizzes based on the topics covered in a lesson, adjust the level of difficulty according to each student's performance, and even provide immediate feedback on students' responses, enhancing their learning experience (Bećirović et al., 2025; Zhang, 2025).

One of the most impactful uses of AI in content creation is the development of dynamic and interactive educational simulations. AI-powered simulations can create virtual learning environments where students can interact with the content in real-time, allowing them to practice skills in a controlled setting. For instance, AI can simulate complex scientific experiments, historical events, or mathematical problems, providing students with the opportunity to learn through active participation rather than passive observation. These simulations can be personalized to meet the learning needs of each student, allowing them to progress at their own pace and receive real-time feedback. By incorporating AI into educational simulations, educators can provide students with immersive learning experiences that enhance their understanding of complex concepts (Caiza et al., 2025; Zeng et al., 2025).

Additionally, AI is playing a crucial role in enhancing the accessibility of educational content. For students with disabilities, AI-driven technologies can offer tailored solutions that make learning more inclusive. For example, AI-powered speech recognition and text-to-speech systems enable students with visual impairments to access written content, while language translation tools help students who speak different languages understand the material. Furthermore, AI can automatically generate captions for videos, making multimedia content accessible to students with hearing impairments. These technologies ensure that educational resources are more inclusive, allowing all students, regardless of their abilities or backgrounds, to benefit from the learning experience (Fletscher et al., 2025; Zhu et al., 2025).

Another significant contribution of AI in educational content creation is its ability to analyze student data to generate personalized learning paths. By analyzing how students engage with the content, AI can recommend resources that are most relevant to each student's learning needs. For example, if a student struggles with a specific concept in a subject, AI can suggest additional readings, videos, or exercises that address that area of difficulty. This type of personalization ensures that students receive the support they need to succeed academically and allows them to engage with the material in ways that are most beneficial to them. AI systems also enable educators to monitor student progress in real-time, allowing them to adjust their teaching strategies accordingly ((Jaramillo et al., 2025; Szűts et al., 2025).

Despite the numerous advantages of AI in content creation, there are challenges that need to be addressed. One major concern is the potential for AI-generated content to lack the depth and creativity that human educators bring to the classroom. While AI can efficiently generate learning materials, it may struggle to create content that fully captures the nuances of a subject or fosters critical thinking and creativity in students. Additionally, the use of AI in content creation raises concerns about the ownership and authorship of educational materials. If AI systems are responsible for generating educational content, it becomes unclear who owns the intellectual property rights to that content. These issues highlight the need for a balanced approach in integrating AI into content creation, where human educators and AI systems collaborate to produce high-quality, meaningful, and creative learning materials (Daher, 2025; Shata & Hartley, 2025).

In conclusion, AI is significantly transforming the process of educational content creation and enhancement. From generating personalized learning materials and interactive simulations to improving accessibility and providing real-time feedback, AI has the potential to make education more engaging, inclusive, and efficient. However, as AI continues to play a greater role in content creation, it is essential to address the challenges related to creativity, ownership, and the potential limitations of AI-generated content. By carefully considering these factors, educators can harness the power of AI to enhance educational experiences while maintaining the human touch that is critical to fostering creativity, critical thinking, and personal growth in students (Fletscher et al., 2025; Zhu et al., 2025).

9. OVERDEPENDENCE ON AI: RISKS AND IMPLICATIONS FOR ACADEMIC RESEARCH

As Artificial Intelligence (AI) becomes increasingly integrated into academic research, the potential for overdependence on these technologies poses significant risks. While AI offers the promise of efficiency, scalability, and accuracy, the over-reliance on AI tools in research may lead to unintended consequences, such as diminishing human creativity, critical thinking, and the capacity for independent thought. Academic research is deeply rooted in human intellectual processes problem formulation, theory development, and hypothesis testing functions that rely heavily on human intuition, experience, and creativity. Overreliance on AI could undermine these elements, resulting in research that lacks the depth, originality, and nuance that human researchers traditionally provide. Additionally, when researchers rely too heavily on AI for generating insights or even conducting entire analyses, they may inadvertently overlook important contextual factors that require human judgment (El Mourabit et al., 2025; Zeng et al., 2025).

AI tools, particularly those used for data analysis, are often seen as objective and impartial, but they are not free from limitations. These systems operate based on the data they are fed, and if the data used to train AI models is incomplete, biased, or flawed, the resulting conclusions may be similarly flawed. For example, AI systems used to predict student performance or analyze learning outcomes may reinforce existing educational inequalities if the data is skewed by socio-economic or demographic factors. Overdependence on AI for decision-making in academic research may lead to the replication of these biases, further entrenching inequalities and limiting the scope of research findings. It is therefore crucial that researchers remain critical of the outputs provided by AI systems, ensuring that they are used as tools to augment, rather than replace, human analysis and interpretation (Zhang, 2025; Zhu et al., 2025).

Moreover, AI-driven automation in research raises concerns about the erosion of traditional research skills. Many researchers, particularly in fields such as qualitative research, have spent years developing methods for data collection, coding, and analysis. AI tools, while capable of automating many of these tasks, may reduce the need for researchers to engage directly with the data, potentially leading to a loss of key research skills. This automation could result in the erosion of the human touch in research, which is essential for interpreting complex social, cultural, and emotional factors that may not be easily captured by algorithms. Researchers must strike a balance between leveraging AI to improve efficiency and ensuring that they retain their ability to engage deeply with their research subjects (Deval et al., 2025; Manganello et al., 2025).

Another risk of overdependence on AI in academic research is the potential for diminishing critical thinking. The convenience and speed with which AI systems can generate solutions or answers might lead to a decline in the rigor of thought that is essential to the scientific process. For example, researchers may be tempted to accept AI-generated findings without thoroughly questioning or interpreting them, thereby bypassing the critical evaluation that is fundamental to good research. Furthermore, if AI is used predominantly for data analysis or literature reviews, researchers might become reliant on the technology to identify patterns or gaps in the literature, potentially overlooking novel approaches or theories that may not align with AI's algorithms. To prevent this, it is important for researchers to use AI as a tool for enhancing, rather than replacing, human insight (Bottrighi et al., 2025; Shata & Hartley, 2025).

In the long term, the increasing dependence on AI for academic research could have broader societal implications. As AI technologies become more advanced, there is a real concern that they may replace not only researchers but also educators, potentially leading to job displacement in academic fields. The rise of AI-driven research assistants, automated content creation tools, and intelligent tutoring systems could reduce the demand for traditional academic roles, particularly in administrative and support capacities. However, this shift could also lead to new opportunities for educators and researchers who can adapt to the changing landscape and develop skills in working alongside AI. To ensure that the academic workforce remains competitive, there must be a focus on training researchers and educators to understand and utilize AI technologies in ways that enhance their work without undermining their roles (Jaramillo et al., 2025; Shata & Hartley, 2025).

In conclusion, while AI offers numerous benefits for academic research, overdependence on these technologies presents significant risks. These include the potential erosion of human creativity and critical thinking, the replication of biases in research, the loss of traditional research skills, and the implications of job displacement. To mitigate these risks, it is crucial for researchers to maintain a balanced approach to AI adoption, using AI as a tool to augment their work while ensuring that human judgment, insight, and ethical considerations remain central to the research process. The future of academic research will depend on the ability of researchers to harness AI's potential responsibly and thoughtfully, ensuring that it enhances the quality and integrity of research while preserving the essential human elements that drive scientific discovery (Caiza et al., 2025; Deval et al., 2025).

10. THE FUTURE OF AI IN EDUCATIONAL RESEARCH: TRENDS AND INNOVATIONS

The future of AI in educational research holds immense promise, with emerging technologies poised to further revolutionize the way research is conducted, analyzed, and applied. As AI continues to evolve, its integration with other advanced technologies, such as augmented reality (AR) and the Internet of Things (IoT), will create more immersive and dynamic educational environments. For example, AI-powered systems integrated with AR could provide real-time feedback on student performance in physical or virtual classrooms, enabling a deeper, more personalized learning experience. These innovations will not only improve educational outcomes but also expand the scope of research by facilitating new ways to observe and measure student engagement, behavior, and learning processes. As AI and related technologies become more sophisticated, educational research will likely shift towards more real-time, data-driven methodologies that can adapt to the ever-changing dynamics of teaching and learning (Jaramillo et al., 2025; Zhu et al., 2025).

One significant trend in the future of AI in educational research is the increased use of AI-powered collaborative learning systems. These systems will allow students to work together in real-time, supported by AI tools that can assess their individual and collective progress, offer personalized suggestions, and track the development of their skills. AI-driven collaborative platforms will enable students to engage in problem-solving and knowledge-building activities more effectively, even when they are geographically dispersed. This trend aligns with the growing demand for online and hybrid learning environments, where students and researchers need to collaborate and share knowledge despite physical distances. AI's role in enhancing collaborative learning will also enable more diverse and interdisciplinary research teams to work together seamlessly, breaking down the barriers that often hinder collaborative efforts in traditional educational settings (Fletscher et al., 2025; Shata & Hartley, 2025).

Another emerging trend is the development of AI-powered research assistants, which will become increasingly integral to the academic research process. These AI systems will assist researchers in tasks such as literature reviews, data collection, hypothesis generation, and even the drafting of research papers. AI research assistants, using natural language processing and machine learning algorithms, will be able to analyze vast amounts of academic literature, identify trends, and suggest relevant studies that researchers may have missed. These assistants will help researchers stay up to date with the rapidly expanding body of knowledge in their fields, allowing them to focus on higher-level analysis and idea development. The use of AI-driven research assistants will dramatically speed up the research process, making it more efficient and comprehensive, and enhancing the overall quality of academic work (Bećirović et al., 2025; Bottrighi et al., 2025).

AI's impact on educational research will also extend to predictive analytics, enabling researchers to forecast learning outcomes more accurately and in real-time. By analyzing historical data, AI can predict student performance, identify potential academic risks, and suggest interventions tailored to individual students. This ability to predict outcomes and intervene proactively is particularly important in addressing the needs of students who may be at risk of falling behind or dropping out. Predictive analytics powered by AI can help educators and researchers design more effective and targeted interventions, ensuring that students receive the support they need before their academic performance begins to decline. This shift towards more proactive and personalized learning strategies will be critical in achieving equitable educational outcomes for all students, especially in diverse and underserved educational settings (Caiza et al., 2025; Zhang, 2025).

Despite these promising innovations, several challenges remain in integrating AI into educational research. One of the most pressing concerns is ensuring that AI systems are developed in ways that are ethical, transparent, and accountable. As AI takes on more responsibilities in educational settings, it will be important for policymakers, researchers, and educators to ensure that these systems do not perpetuate biases or inequalities. The development of ethical frameworks for AI in education will be essential to address concerns about data privacy, algorithmic bias, and the potential for AI to replace human judgment in areas that require empathy, creativity, and moral reasoning. Ensuring that AI tools are designed and implemented responsibly will be key to maximizing their positive impact on educational research while minimizing any negative consequences (Caiza et al., 2025; Manganello et al., 2025).

Looking forward, the future of AI in educational research will likely be characterized by continued advancements in AI technologies, alongside growing attention to their ethical implications. As AI becomes increasingly integrated into both research and classroom environments, it will be essential to foster a balanced approach that combines the efficiency and precision of AI with the human touch that is crucial to quality education. Researchers and educators will need to develop a deep understanding of how AI can enhance educational practices, while also recognizing its limitations and potential risks. By adopting a responsible and forward-thinking approach to AI, educational research can continue to evolve in ways that are both innovative and ethical, ensuring that AI serves as a tool to enrich, rather than replace, human-driven education (Zhu et al., 2025).

CONCLUSION

In conclusion, Artificial Intelligence (AI) has proven to be a transformative force in educational research, offering unparalleled opportunities for enhancing data analysis, personalizing learning experiences, and automating various aspects of the research process. The integration of AI technologies has streamlined the way educational data is collected, processed, and analyzed, enabling researchers to uncover insights that were once difficult or even impossible to access. From predictive analytics to natural language processing, AI has facilitated a deeper understanding of student performance, learning behaviors, and educational outcomes. As AI continues to evolve, its potential to further enhance the efficiency, scalability, and accessibility of educational research grows, promising a future where research and teaching can be more dynamic and responsive to the needs of students.

However, with these advancements come significant ethical considerations that must be addressed to ensure that AI is used responsibly and fairly in educational contexts. The potential for bias in AI algorithms, the privacy concerns associated with the use of student data, and the risk of overdependence on AI systems are issues that must be carefully managed. As AI becomes more integrated into both research and classroom environments, it will be crucial for educators, researchers, and policymakers to work together to develop frameworks that ensure transparency, fairness, and accountability in the use of these technologies. This will involve creating ethical guidelines, ensuring equitable access to AI tools, and maintaining human oversight to safeguard the integrity of educational practices. The role of AI in personalized learning is another area where significant strides have been made. AI-powered adaptive learning platforms have allowed for more individualized and tailored educational experiences, providing students with the support they need to succeed at their own pace. This has been particularly beneficial for students with diverse learning styles and needs, helping to bridge gaps in education and improve learning outcomes across a range of contexts. As AI continues to enhance personalized learning, it will not only support students in their academic journeys but also empower educators to design more effective and targeted instructional strategies that cater to the unique strengths and challenges of each student.

Despite the immense promise of AI, it is essential to recognize the limitations of these technologies. AI, at its core, is still a tool that relies on human input for design, implementation, and ethical considerations. While AI can augment research processes and support educational practices, it cannot replace the critical thinking, empathy, and ethical reasoning that human educators and researchers bring to their work. The balance between AI-driven insights and human judgment will be crucial in ensuring that AI serves as a tool that enhances, rather than replaces, the human elements of education. Furthermore, as AI continues to develop, it will be essential for educators and researchers to remain adaptable, continually learning how to use these technologies to their full potential while retaining their ability to critically assess the implications of their use.

Looking ahead, the future of AI in educational research holds great promise, but it also requires careful planning and thoughtful implementation. The continued integration of AI will likely shape the next generation of educational research methodologies, allowing for more accurate predictions, more engaging learning experiences, and more efficient research practices. However, this future must be one where technology is not only advancing rapidly but is also being thoughtfully guided by ethical considerations and human values. The future of AI in education will ultimately depend on how we balance innovation with responsibility, ensuring that the technologies we develop today serve to create a more inclusive, equitable, and effective education system for tomorrow.

REFERENCES

Bećirović, S., Polz, E., & Tinkel, I. (2025). Exploring students' AI literacy and its effects on their AI output quality, self-efficacy, and academic performance. *Smart Learning Environments*, *12*(1), 29. Advance online publication. DOI: 10.1186/s40561-025-00384-3

Bottrighi, A., Grosso, F., Ghiglione, M., Maconi, A., Nera, S., Piovesan, L., Raina, E., Roveta, A., & Terenziani, P. (2025). A Symbolic AI Approach to Medical Training. *Journal of Medical Systems*, *49*(1), 2. Advance online publication. DOI: 10.1007/s10916-024-02139-y PMID: 39786677

Caiza, G., Villafuerte, C., & Guanuche, A. (2025). Interactive Application with Virtual Reality and Artificial Intelligence for Improving Pronunciation in English Learning. *Applied Sciences (Basel, Switzerland)*, *15*(17), 9270. Advance online publication. DOI: 10.3390/app15179270

Campillo-Ferrer, J. M., López-García, A., & Miralles-Sánchez, P. (2025). Student Perceptions of the Use of Gen-AI in a Higher Education Program in Spain. *Digital*, *5*(3), 29. Advance online publication. DOI: 10.3390/digital5030029

Daher, R. (2025). Integrating AI literacy into teacher education: A critical perspective paper. *Discover Artificial Intelligence*, *5*(1), 217. Advance online publication. DOI: 10.1007/s44163-025-00475-7

Deval, Ö., Öztürk Kösenciğ, K., & Acirli, Z. (2025). Integration of artificial intelligence tools into interior architecture education: A study on textual and visual representations. *Estoa*, *14*(28), 109–120. DOI: 10.18537/est.v014.n028.a08

El Mourabit, I., Andaloussi, S. J., Ouchetto, O., & Miyara, M. (2025). AI Chatbots in Higher Education: Opportunities and Challenges for Personalized and Mobile Learning. *International Journal of Interactive Mobile Technologies*, *19*(12), 19–37. DOI: 10.3991/ijim.v19i12.54163

Fletscher, L., Mercado, J., Gómez, A., & Mendoza-Cardenas, C. (2025). Innovating Personalized Learning in Virtual Education Through AI. *Multimodal Technologies and Interaction*, *9*(7), 69. Advance online publication. DOI: 10.3390/mti9070069

Gao, J., Zhang, J., & Li, Y. (2025). Do AI chatbot-integrated writing tasks influence writing self-efficacy and critical thinking ability? An exploratory study. *Computers and Education: Artificial Intelligence*, *9*, 100472. Advance online publication. DOI: 10.1016/j.caeai.2025.100472

Jaramillo, J. J., Chiappe, A., & Delgado, F. S. (2025). From Struggle to Mastery: AI-Powered Writing Skills in ESL Education. *Applied Sciences (Basel, Switzerland)*, *15*(14), 8079. Advance online publication. DOI: 10.3390/app15148079

Manganello, F., Nico, A., & Boccuzzi, G. (2025). Theoretical Foundations for Governing AI-Based Learning Outcome Assessment in High-Risk Educational Contexts. *Information (Basel)*, *16*(9), 814. Advance online publication. DOI: 10.3390/info16090814

Markus, A., Carolus, A., & Wienrich, C. (2025). Objective measurement of AI literacy: Development and validation of the AI competency objective scale (AI-COS). *Computers and Education: Artificial Intelligence*, *9*, 100485. Advance online publication. DOI: 10.1016/j.caeai.2025.100485

Meng, L. (2025). Evaluating the Impact of Mobile-Based Generative AI Tools on Visual Design Education. *International Journal of Interactive Mobile Technologies*, *19*(16), 189–203. DOI: 10.3991/ijim.v19i16.57603

Morello, L. T., & Chick, J. C. (2025). Human-AI Symbiotic Theory (HAIST): Development, Multi-Framework Assessment, and AI-Assisted Validation in Academic Research. *Informatics (MDPI)*, *12*(3), 85. Advance online publication. DOI: 10.3390/informatics12030085

Shata, A., & Hartley, K. (2025). Artificial intelligence and communication technologies in academia: Faculty perceptions and the adoption of generative AI. *International Journal of Educational Technology in Higher Education*, *22*(1), 14. Advance online publication. DOI: 10.1186/s41239-025-00511-7

Szűts, Z., Lengyelné Molnár, T., Racskó, R., Vaughan, G., Ceglédi, S., & Dominek, D. L. (2025). Examining the Flow Dynamics of Artificial Intelligence in Real-Time Classroom Applications. *Computers*, *14*(7), 275. Advance online publication. DOI: 10.3390/computers14070275

Yan, Y., Liu, H., Zhang, H., Chau, T., & Li, J. (2025). Designing a Generalist Education AI Framework for Multimodal Learning and Ethical Data Governance. *Applied Sciences (Basel, Switzerland)*, *15*(14), 7758. Advance online publication. DOI: 10.3390/app15147758

Zeng, S., Rahim, N., & Xu, S. (2025). Integrating Mobile AI in Art Education: A Study on Children's Engagement and Self-Efficacy. *International Journal of Interactive Mobile Technologies*, *19*(11), 112–142. DOI: 10.3991/ijim.v19i11.54847

Zhang, Y. (2025). Optimizing Personalized Learning Paths in Mobile Education Platforms Based on Data Mining. *International Journal of Interactive Mobile Technologies, 19*(12), 4–18. DOI: 10.3991/ijim.v19i12.56393

Zhu, W., Wei, L., & Qin, Y. (2025). Artificial Intelligence in Education (AIEd): Publication Patterns, Keywords, and Research Focuses. *Information (Basel), 16*(9), 725. Advance online publication. DOI: 10.3390/info16090725

Chapter 10
Accurate or Artificial? Comparing AI and Human Peer Review Feedback

Ahmed M. Alaa
http://orcid.org/0000-0003-4900-3635
Badr University in Cairo, Egypt

ABSTRACT

Peer review stands as the foundation of academic publishing, shaping the quality and credibility of scholarly work. However, concerns remain about its consistency and reliability. The emergence of large language models (LLMs) presents a transformative opportunity in this regard. This study examines the quality of peer review feedback generated by a general AI tool, ChatGPT, and a specialized one, SCiNiTO, compared to human reviewers. Four research articles, each previously reviewed by human experts with different conclusions, were uploaded to the selected LLMs for evaluation. The review reports of the four research articles were analyzed for the final decision reached and the score of certain quality dimensions based on a developed rubric. The analysis showed that both AI tools gave almost similar decisions, but they were mostly different from the decisions given by human reviewers. In addition, AI tools showed superior quality performance. Eventually, the study findings uncover AI's promise and possible implications toward enhancing academic evaluation and communication.

INTRODUCTION

Peer review is one of the pillars of academic research. It has an immense impact on both the quality and credibility of scholarly work. Scholars are required to publish sound research in recognized journals to achieve visibility, credit, and career growth.

DOI: 10.4018/979-8-2600-1458-5.ch010

The typical process of peer review (Figure 1) starts when the author submits his/her research article to a certain journal. The article thus goes through the first phase of review, which is called pre-screening. In this phase, the journal's editor performs some initial checks to make sure the article aligns with the journal's scope and standards. Then, if accepted, it moves to the next phase, where the editor assigns the article to peer reviewers who are experts in its field to review its originality, significance, and rigor. This is followed by a decision from the peer reviewers, usually one of 4 decisions: reject, accept with major revisions, accept with minor revisions, and accept. Once the research article is deemed ready for publication, it goes through some final checks including proofreading and technical checks. Thus, as can be seen from the process, peer review lies at the heart of the publication process and is a crucial high-stake element in scholarly work.

Figure 1. The peer review process (from Checco et al., 2021).

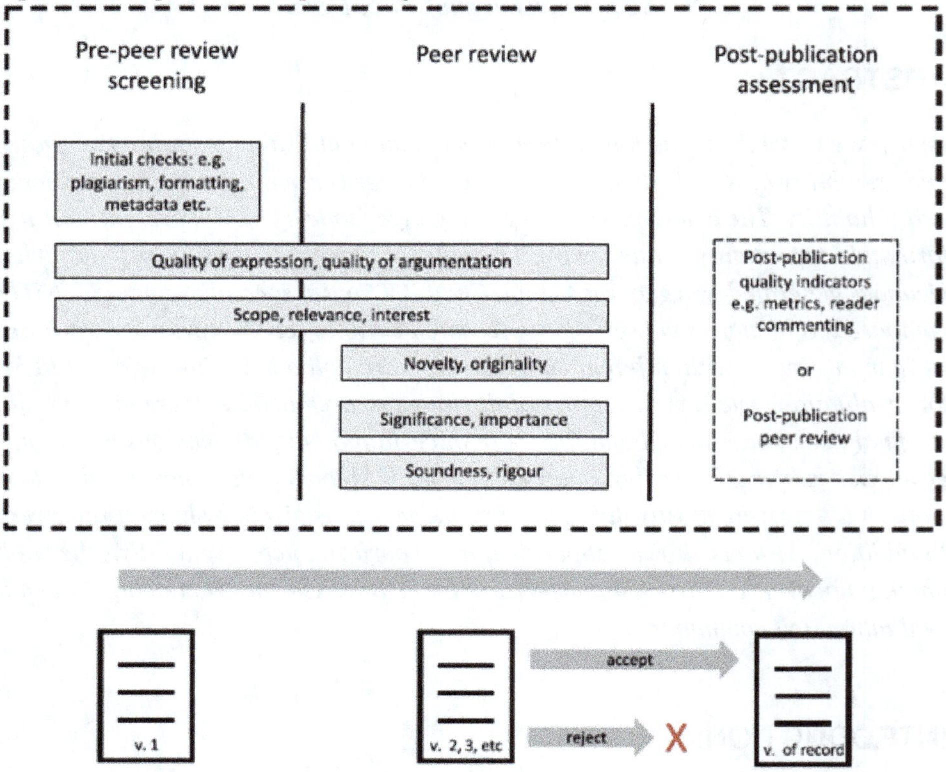

However, due to the prolific production of research into different journals, challenges have arisen regarding the feasibility and accuracy of traditional peer review (Checco et al., 2021; Biswas et al., 2023). It has been even argued that the volume of manuscript submissions far outpaces the workload of qualified reviewers willing to dedicate some time of their busy schedules to conduct detailed and precise evaluation of their peers' works, especially that these reviewers receive no material credit for their peer review work. Therefore, there has been a true struggle to keep the review process going efficiently (Papatriantafyllou, 2017; Biswas et al., 2023; Krausman, 2023).

One magical solution to this struggle could be artificial intelligence (AI). The rise of AI and large language models (LLMs) has been of great assistance to optimize different processes. This development has resulted in the extensive use of AI tools in many fields, to the point that it is now a worldwide phenomenon (Al Sawi & Alaa, 2024). Scholars have consequently shown an interest in exploring the possibilities of using AI tools, especially generative AI (GenAI), to solve peer review challenges (Alqahtani et al., 2023; Deng & Lin, 2023; Krausman, 2023; Lin, 2023; Oliveira et al., 2023; Varghese & Chapiro, 2024; Gatrell et al., 2024; Mehta et al., 2024).

Among the leading GenAI tools is ChatGPT. ChatGPT might be considered the biggest GenAI platform in the world, developed by OpenAI. It performs exceptionally well in a range of natural language processing (NLP) tasks, including its exceptional comprehension and production of natural language and its ability to produce human-like responses. Add to this its essential characteristics, such as the ability to comprehend and adjust to various languages and contexts while generating adjustable responses. In spite of these benefits, ChatGPT also has several limitations. Firstly, it can produce biased or inaccurate results since it depends on the information provided by its programmers and users. Secondly, its effectiveness depends on the quality of the prompts introduced. Lastly, ChatGPT may encounter difficulties when tasked with complex assignments. Despite its general abilities, it requires further training, and its output should be examined closely (Ang et al., 2023; Schou et al., 2023; Rice et al., 2024; Ali et al., 2025).

Another possible solution to the peer review challenges is AI tools specialized in academic services. One such platform is SCiNiTO. This website is developed by NotionWave, a company that offers AI solutions to redefine learning and research. SCiNiTO offers a research ecosystem, powered by OpenAlex database and AI. It offers full text access to millions of Open Access articles. It also offers many useful tools for researchers, such as AI Chat that serves as a modern research assistant, Journal Recommendation, PDF Analysis, and a dedicated AI Reviewer Agent (https://www.scinito.ai/). Still, it remains an AI tool that may have the same limitations as any other AI tool. Despite the obvious advantages of using AI in reviewing research articles, such as easing the load on human reviewers, increasing consistency, and reducing time and cost, concerns arise regarding whether this is ethical and whether AI is a reliable peer reviewer (Checco et al., 2021; Biswas et al., 2023; Krausman, 2023; Miao et al., 2023). Additionally, transparency, privacy, and authorship responsibility are concerns that need to be addressed as well (Deng & Lin, 2023; Dwivedi et al., 2023; Lin, 2023).

The current study attempts to address a gap in the literature by comparing AI-generated peer review with human expert peer review. A general AI tool, that is, ChatGPT, and a specialized one, that is, the reviewer agent of SCiNiTO, were used to assess four research manuscripts in linguistics and translation previously reviewed by human peer reviewers. The main aim of this comparison is to document the potential of AI as a peer reviewer regarding relevance, completeness, accuracy, constructiveness, and feedback clarity and depth, which are critical dimensions to evaluate (Lim et al., 2025). This may help show if AI can provide peer review comparable to human reviewers as well as contribute to the emerging discussion about the responsible use of AI in academia. What is more, the significance of this study goes beyond technical evaluation since it targets broader implications for scholarly evaluation and communication.

Recent studies investigated the feasibility of using AI in reviewing research articles. Checco et al. (2021) explored the ability of using AI to assist in peer review. They trained an AI model on more than 3000 conference papers and their review reports. They then tested this model with an unseen paper to see whether it would generate a review decision similar to that it received from its human reviewers. They found that the AI model was successful in predicting the peer review decision. While that study had solid empirical insight, it did not focus on a certain discipline and it relied mainly on surface level textual features. Biswas et al. (2023) compared the performance of ChatGPT in reviewing published research against reviews provided by human peer reviewers. The study found that ChatGPT's feedback aligned with human reviewer feedback. Particularly, ChatGPT exhibited competency in identifying methodological flaws, providing feedback on theoretical frameworks, and assessing the overall contribution of research. These preliminary findings suggested that AI tools possess fundamental capabilities for reviewing academic work. Hosseini and Horbach (2023) explored the benefits and risks of using ChatGPT and other LLMs in peer review. They employed five discussion themes taken from another study by Tennant and Ross-Hellauer (2020), that is, reviewers' role, editors' role, functions and quality of peer reviews, reproducibility, and the social and epistemic functions of peer reviews. The authors concluded that LLMs like ChatGPT have obvious advantages such as enhancing efficiency, language quality, and inclusivity. They warned, however, that they pose serious threats regarding confidentiality, bias, and epistemic accountability. The study fails, however, to offer an empirical sample or analysis, as it sufficed with a conceptual and theoretical discussion.

Another study compared ChatGPT review with human peer review but on a larger scale of more than 4000 published papers (Liang et al., 2023). The study found that AI-generated feedback was comparable to human feedback to a great extent. It also detected higher effectiveness of AI review in lower-quality submissions. In addition, researchers participating in that study reported high value in AI-generated review, considering it helpful and beneficial. Lim et al. (2025) investigated the performance of GenAI tools in peer review in the field of occupational health. They compared the effectiveness of Microsoft Copilot, ChatGPT (GPT-3.5), and Google Gemini 1.0 against five human reviewers. They also created a scoring system to evaluate the feedback based on relevance, completeness, accuracy, and the ability to identify errors. The study found that GenAI tools were significantly more effective than human reviewers in providing feedback. However, human reviewers performed significantly better at providing recommendations. The authors concluded that although human oversight remains needed to verify AI output, using GenAI would improve the speed and accuracy of the review process prior to publication.

The literature demonstrates that AI tools possess measurable capacity to contribute to peer review processes, demonstrating strengths in speed, consistency, and identification of technical issues. The empirical evidence does not yet support replacing human peer review with automated AI tools but rather suggests carefully designed hybrid models combining AI efficiency for initial screening and diagnostic feedback with human expertise for practical evaluation and constructive guidance. Moreover, to the best of the researcher's knowledge, none of the previous studies compared the performance of AI with human experts in reviewing articles in the fields of linguistics, translation, and education. More importantly, no study compared the AI review of a general AI tool with one specialized in research and academic services. This is the first study that measures the performance of specialized AI review tools, represented here by SCiNiTO's AI Reviewer Agent. Thus, the current study is considered a worthy contribution to the body of literature regarding investigating the use of AI in peer review.

METHODS

Research Design

This study adopts a comparative design examining the similarities and differences between AI-generated and human peer review feedback. This comparison lays the foundation for sound judgment on the effectiveness of AI when assuming the role of a peer reviewer. The study follows a mixed-methods approach to ensure reaching valid results. The review reports are given scores based on a set rubric, as informed by Lim (2025), which represents the quantitative side. The review content and quality are also analyzed, representing the qualitative side. Combining insights from both the quantitative and qualitative sides can help reach a comprehensive picture of the topic under investigation.

Sample and Tools

Four peer-reviewed research articles previously evaluated by human peer reviewers were selected for inclusion in this study. Article selection criteria included: (1) availability of complete human peer review reports with assigned decision or recommendations, (2) representation across different subdisciplines within the researcher's field of expertise, and (3) submission recency (within the past 5 years). The selected research articles were in the fields of linguistics, translation, and education. They had different review decisions, where Article 1 was accepted with major revision, Article 3 was accepted with minor revision, and Articles 2 and 4 were rejected. Articles were sourced from journals with diverse review systems to ensure variation in review criteria and standards. Any information that may denote the identity of the articles, the journals, or the peer reviewers was removed to achieve privacy and anonymity.

Although the sample may be considered limited in size, this was deliberate due to feasibility and to allow a deeper and more detailed analysis both qualitatively and quantitatively. This intensive examination of the data is unfeasible for large data. Note that the full review reports could not be shown within the article due to size restrictions.

Besides, two GenAI tools were selected to act as the AI peer reviewer. The first platform was ChatGPT, using GPT 5.0, which is an LLM that is used for general purposes. The second platform was SCiNiTO, which is an LLM that offers specialized AI research tools, including the tool of interest in this study, which is the AI Reviewer Agent. Both platforms are also accessible to the public and have strong track records. The selection of a general AI tool and a specialized one was intended to add depth to the comparison and investigate whether even different AI tools with different scopes can have majorly different outcomes. Hence, this study has a dual-comparison approach, where not only does it compare AI and human reviews, but it also compares general and specialized AI reviews.

Data Collection

Concerning ChatGPT, standard prompts were developed to elicit peer review feedback. The main prompt used was as follows: "*You are an expert linguist, researcher, and peer reviewer in a prestigious journal. Conduct a detailed and accurate peer review of the attached research article, and end your review with your recommendation concerning the publication of this article*." This was succeeded by a follow-up prompt to make sure the review has numerical evaluation as well to serve the quantitative dimension of the study: "*If you will give it a score out of 100, what will it be based on your review of it?*" Concerning SCiNiTO, no prompts were used since the AI Reviewer tool does not require any. The tool only requires uploading the PDF file of the article to be then analyzed and assessed to reach a final detailed downloadable review report. You can also check an option which adds a score to each section and to the whole article based on the review to add a numerical aspect to it, which was activated by the researcher. Concerning human peer review, the review reports of each of the selected articles were collected from the researcher's historical records, being earlier versions of research articles that were submitted for review at recognized journals.

Analysis Procedure

In order to assess the quality of the different review reports, a rubric was developed, building on the work of Lim (2025). The rubric consisted of 5 elements (i.e., relevance, completeness, accuracy, constructiveness, and feedback clarity and depth), each measured according to a range of 0–2 marks to reach a maximum score of 10. Table 1 explains the assessment rubric.

Table 1. The rubric used to assess the review reports.

Criterion	0 – Poor	1 – Fair	2 – Excellent
Relevance	Comments are unrelated or trivial	Mix of relevant and irrelevant points	All feedback is directly relevant to the article's quality
Completeness	Fails to address most sections and the strengths and limitations	Addresses some sections and covers only strengths or limitations	Addresses manuscript sections comprehensively and covers both strengths and limitations
Accuracy	Fails to identify issues, or points out things that are not errors, and contains inaccuracies or misinterpretations	Identifies some correct issues, but misses key ones and has few inaccuracies	Correctly identifies all major strengths/weaknesses and entirely accurate
Constructiveness	Makes vague or false claims with no evidence	Provides some justification, but weak or incomplete	Supports feedback with clear evidence from the text/data
Feedback clarity and depth	Superficial, general and unclear statements	Moderate detail, but lacks thoroughness	Detailed, precise, and insightful analysis

The data were then analyzed qualitatively, by examining the content of each review report and identifying patterns that are similar or different between AI and human review reports as well as between general and specialized AI review reports. The analysis of each criterion was then reviewed by an expert peer reviewer specialized in the fields of the selected articles to achieve inter-rater agreement and maximize reliability.

RESULTS AND DISCUSSION

This study compared AI-generated peer reviews from two distinct platforms (ChatGPT and SCiNiTO) and human peer reviewer feedback on 4 research articles, based on both the final decision and the rating the AI tools gave to each article. In addition, a comprehensive rubric evaluating 5 critical dimensions of review quality was employed to further compare and assess the review done by AI and human experts. The scores were later reviewed by an expert peer reviewer to confirm or modify them.

An interesting finding was the final recommendation for publishing decision for each article. Table 2 shows the final decision each AI review report recommended for each of the 4 articles, compared to the actual decision the articles received in real life. Each AI tool was asked not only to review the research articles, but also to provide a final decision of whether the article is accepted or rejected and to give that decision a score.

Table 2. Comparative final decisions across the four research articles reviewed.

Article	ChatGPT	SCiNiTO	Human Reviewers	Article Rank according to Decision Score
Article 1	Accept with moderate revision	Accept with major revision	Accept with major revision	Human: 2 ChatGPT: 1 SCiNiTO: 2
Article 2	Accept with moderate revision	Accept with major revision	Reject	Human: 3, 4 ChatGPT: 2 SCiNiTO: 3
Article 3	Accept with major revision	Accept with major revision	Accept with minor revision	Human: 1 ChatGPT: 4 SCiNiTO: 4
Article 4	Accept with major revision	Accept with major revision	Reject	Human: 3, 4 ChatGPT: 3 SCiNiTO: 1

As can be found in the table, there were both similarities and differences between the decisions of both AI tools and the real-life decisions done by human peer reviewers. Both ChatGPT and SCiNiTO were almost similar in the decisions they gave to the 4 articles, with the exception of Articles 1 and 2 that had a better decision with ChatGPT than the one suggested by SCiNiTO ("Accept with moderate revision" vs "Accept with major revision", respectively). This near similarity was partly reflected in the numerical rating offered by both tools, where both of them agreed that Article 3 would have the lowest rating of the 4 articles. However, they had different opinions concerning the other 3 articles, where ChatGPT considered Article 1 to be the strongest, while SCiNiTO gave that rank to Article 4.

When compared to the human reviewers, there was almost no agreement, except for that between SCiNiTO and human reviewers regarding Article 1's decision and rank. The other 3 articles showed marked differences, where Articles 2 and 4, for instance, were rejected by human reviewers, while both AI tools accepted them, with ChatGPT considering Article 2 the second best of the 4 articles and SCiNiTO considering Article 4 the best of the 4. This contrast between AI review decisions and real-life review decisions may raise questions about which decision is more accurate and representative of the articles, as well as starting discussions about issues previous studies pointed out when studying AI and human review reports. These possible issues could be bias, inconsistency, inaccuracy, and any other possible variables (e.g., Checco et al., 2021; Biswas et al., 2023; Hosseini & Horbach, 2023; Kousha & Thelwall, 2023).

On the other hand, when assessing the quality of the reviews according to the rubric created, the scores revealed that both AI tools achieved perfect scores (10/10) across all evaluated dimensions, while human reviewers achieved a lower score (6/10), with particular gaps in completeness, accuracy, constructiveness, and analytical depth. The comparative scoring results are presented in Table 3.

Table 3. Comparative performance scores across review quality dimensions.

Dimension	**ChatGPT**	**SCiNiTO**	**Human Reviewers**
Relevance	2	2	2
Completeness	2	2	1
Accuracy	2	2	1
Constructiveness	2	2	1
Clarity and Depth	2	2	1
Total Score	**10**	**10**	**6**

Both AI tools demonstrated "Excellent" scores (2/2), indicating remarkable consistency in their review generation capabilities. Human reviewers, by contrast, had a "Fair" score (1/2) on four of five dimensions, suggesting some areas of improvement compared to both AI tools. The following sections discuss the results of each quality dimension.

Relevance

All three reviewers (ChatGPT, SCiNiTO, and human) achieved maximum scores on relevance. This indicates that the review feedback addressed manuscript quality directly without any off points. This finding shows that AI tools can successfully identify and focus on specific quality issues without hallucinating or generating irrelevant feedback. This aligns with Liang et al.'s (2023) large-scale study which found that GPT-4 feedback generally aligned with the feedback given by human reviewers.

Completeness

A clear disagreement emerged on the completeness dimension. Both AI tools achieved perfect scores by systematically addressing every major manuscript component: title, abstract, theoretical framework, methodology, data analysis, discussion, conclusion, and so on. SCiNiTO's structured approach explicitly covered each manuscript section through its IMRD (Introduction, Methods, Results, Discussion) framework, while ChatGPT achieved similar comprehensiveness through a more narrative assessment. Human reviewers, in contrast, demonstrated uneven performance. Some human reviewers provided detailed commentary across multiple manuscript dimensions (e.g., Article 3), while others were briefer and more concentrated narrowly on specific aspects without systematically addressing all components (e.g., Article 4). This finding contradicts the assumption that human reviewers, with their discipline-specific knowledge and expertise, naturally conduct more comprehensive reviews. However, it might be argued that rejection reports are usually not very detailed like the ones that recommend major revisions or even the ones that follow a preset review form that has required review points to address.

This result well aligns with prior findings. Lim et al.'s (2025) occupational health study found that GenAI tools were significantly more effective than human reviewers in providing comprehensive feedback addressing relevance, completeness, and accuracy across structured dimensions. Similarly, Liang et al. (2023) found that while there was some similarity between AI-human feedback and human-human feedback, AI tools provided more uniform and consistent review of the different elements of the research articles.

Accuracy

Both ChatGPT and SCiNiTO demonstrated exceptional accuracy in identifying valid quality concerns. ChatGPT correctly identified specific technical issues including reliability issues, statistical requirements, and methodological gaps. SCiNiTO showed comparable precision, spotting exact methodological issues and specific areas of improvement, with zero detected misinterpretations across the four articles. Human reviewers, on the other hand, scored lower on accuracy, though not necessarily in all 4 articles analyzed. The accuracy gap appeared in two identified patterns: first, human reviewers sometimes failed to identify key issues that both AI tools spotted (e.g., some comments that both AI tools had concerning the Literature Review of Article 3 which were not mentioned in the human reviewers' report); second, human reviewer feedback occasionally tackled surface-level issues, like linguistic or stylistic issues, without engaging the methodological concerns underlying them.

This finding is particularly notable because it challenges the conventional assumption that human expertise guarantees accuracy in specialized assessment. The AI tools' superior accuracy suggests that systematic, algorithmic approaches to error-checking may surpass human reviewers' ability even in specialized contexts like peer review. Importantly, this result differs from Biswas et al.'s (2023) feasibility study, which found that ChatGPT exhibited "commendable capability in identifying methodological flaws" but noted potential "ambiguities" with complex research articles that might lead to "nuanced discrepancies between AI and human reviews" (p. 415). In the present study, such discrepancies were not observed; instead, AI accuracy exceeded human accuracy.

Constructiveness

An obvious distinction arose in the constructiveness dimension. Both AI tools accompanied every identified issue with evidence-based guidance grounded in manuscript content. ChatGPT provided specific recommendations (e.g., "add inter-rater reliability test," "reorder discussion by frequency") with clear justification. SCiNiTO demonstrated even higher constructiveness through well-supported recommendations that included examples or explicit rationale for each correction. In contrast, human reviewers frequently provided advice lacking clear justification or supporting evidence. Comments such as "redraft some sections" or "the information is insufficient" appeared without specifying the substantive basis for such recommendations or concrete guidance on implementation. This pattern suggests that human reviewers may have possessed implicit understanding of quality standards that they failed to articulate explicitly.

This finding contradicts Lim et al.'s (2025) study finding, where human reviewers performed significantly better than AI tools at providing recommendations. The present study's finding of superior AI constructiveness could suggest checking the meaning of "recommendations". If recommendations mean high-level suggestions (which human reviewers excelled at), humans may outperform AI. However, if they mean specific, evidence-based guidance, AI tools showed superior performance, as found in the present study.

Feedback Clarity and Depth

Both AI tools again achieved top scores, outperforming human reviewers. ChatGPT's reviews were well-organized, clearly reasoned, and insightful while maintaining professional academic tone, coherent structure, and correct language. SCiNiTO's reports were less organized, but intensively deeper, where each section was scrutinized to lead to the final decision, recommendations, and action plan. Human reviewers' feedback, while readable and professional, demonstrated less analytical depth in general. Commentary frequently appeared fragmented or procedurally oriented rather than interpretive; reviewers might note issues without fully saying the conceptual or empirical basis for them. This shortcoming might be, like in constructiveness, due to potential constraints such as time limitation, exhaustion from reviewing multiple manuscripts, or simply differences among reviewers (Bauchner & Rivara, 2024).

Finally, it is worth noting that the exceptional scores achieved by both AI tools warrant special attention, especially given existing literature emphasizing AI limitations (Biswas et al., 2023; Hosseini & Horbach, 2023; Liang et al., 2023). Although the rubric used for the current study is comprehensive and based on previous research, it may have been particularly well-suited to evaluating AI-generated reviews that are mostly systematic, complete, and evidence-based. The rubric's emphasis on dimensions like completeness and constructiveness may have unintentionally given AI an advantage over human variable review approaches. Other rubrics focusing on different dimensions like innovation, originality, and theoretical insight might produce different results.

CONCLUSION

Summary of Key Findings and Implications

This comparative study examined the quality of peer reviews generated by two AI tools (ChatGPT and SCiNiTO) and human reviewers on 4 research articles, employing a comprehensive rubric assessing relevance, completeness, accuracy, constructiveness, and feedback clarity and depth. The quantitative findings were remarkable: both AI tools achieved "Excellent" scores (10/10) across all evaluated dimensions, while human reviewers achieved a noticeably lower score (6/10), showing a "Fair" score in completeness, accuracy, constructiveness, and feedback clarity and depth. Only on the relevance dimension did all three reviewer types achieve excellence.

Moreover, the analysis explored whether there was agreement in the final decision of all three reviewers for the 4 articles. It was found that ChatGPT and SCiNiTO reached mostly similar decisions with slight difference, while the decisions of both AI tools were almost totally different from those of human reviewers. Additionally, when asked to provide a score for each article based on their review, dissimilarity arose between ChatGPT and SCiNiTO. However, this dissimilarity was not as much as that found with the human reviews as well.

These findings revealed that AI tools excelled at systematic, methodological assessment, while human reviewers provided contextual judgment but with variable depth and completeness. Both AI tools demonstrated almost identical performance, suggesting the existence of somehow an algorithmic consistency, whereas human reviewers displayed more variability and subjectivity. The findings challenge assumptions in existing literature that AI and human peer review performance are close to each other (Checco et al., 2021; Liang et al., 2023; Lim et al., 2025); instead, this study documents more AI advantages on multiple measurable dimensions, despite important limitations to consider regarding sample size, evaluation framework, and the nature of the dimensions assessed.

On another note, the study findings support several strong implications. First, systematic methodology is substantial for a high-quality peer review. AI tools' completeness and constructiveness advantages appear to stem from systematic, comprehensive approaches that cover all relevant quality dimensions. Human reviewer training and the peer review process can hence improve by following a more systematic approach. Second, a hybrid human-AI model can be an ideal choice when doing peer review. Rather than putting boundaries between AI and human review, a collaborative approach can have the best of both worlds, with AI's organization and detailed efficiency and human's expertise and judgment. The Lim et al. (2025) finding, for example, that AI excels at feedback while humans excel at recommendations adds further support to this point encouraging collaboration rather than replacement. Third, responsible use requires attention to fairness and bias. The potential for AI tools to improve fairness in peer review access must be weighed against risks of automating or amplifying any biases. Therefore, critical monitoring of peer review results should take place. Fourth, the question of how and whether to disclose AI use in peer review is still not answered. There should be clear policies informed by empirical evidence and ethical principles. Hosseini and Horbach's (2023) recommendations for mandatory disclosure and reviewer responsibility provide a starting point but require implementation across diverse publishing contexts. Finally, while the input of AI tools may excel at analytical details, human reviewers remain essential for supervising and mentoring that input to avoid any possible inaccuracy or misalignment to academic culture. Realizing AI's potential to strengthen scholarly communication while mitigating risks requires thoughtful implementation within transparent frameworks that prioritize fairness, accountability, and preservation of peer review's essential functions and unshakable role in academia.

Limitations

Several important limitations affect the generalizability of the study findings. The study examines a small sample size of 4 research articles. While this limited sample may limit generalizability, the combination of both qualitative and quantitative in-depth analyses acts as a counter to this limitation. Another possible argument is the likelihood of having rubric design bias. The current study rubric may be more suited to systematic systems and therefore may favor AI over human review by design. Nevertheless, this rubric was built upon empirical studies and evidence (Lim, 2025) which safeguards its results from such claims. What is more, unlike the study of Liang et al. (2023) which employs strong external validation regarding authors' views on AI reviews, the current study suffices with the comparison and analysis results' interpretation and insights. Although author's views are important and are a worthy addition to the study's strength, that was not within the scope of the current comparative study. Lastly, the perfect scores achieved by both AI tools may raise skepticism. Theoretically, a perfect performance is very difficult to attain in complex tasks like research work, and only one rater might not be enough to achieve enough reliability. Blind evaluation by multiple independent raters employing standardized scoring procedures would strengthen confidence in scoring.

Recommendations for Future Research

The findings of this study open the door for many research directions. Studies comparing the peer review of AI performance versus human reviewers across different disciplines would help reach a wider view of the topic. Another possible area for research is tracking possible bias in peer review toward some groups like non-English-native scholars, early career researchers, small-scale institutions, or low-income countries. Moreover, based on this study's implications, future research can investigate the application of a hybrid AI-human peer review approach to measure its efficiency and effectiveness. In addition, the input of other AI tools can be examined to compare the quality of their performance to human reviewers and fellow AI tools. Lastly, a longitudinal study inspecting the evolution of AI tools' performance over time can present valuable conclusions.

ACKNOWLEDGMENT

The author made use of AI tools to polish the language of the writing of some parts of this study. Any AI input was then reviewed to avoid any possible inaccuracy and to maintain the originality of the study.

REFERENCES

Al Sawi, I., & Alaa, A. (2024). Navigating the impact: A study of editors' and proofreaders' perceptions of AI tools in editing and proofreading. *Discover Artificial Intelligence*, *4*(1), 23. DOI: 10.1007/s44163-024-00116-5

Ali, M. M., Alaa, A. M., Alharbi, W., & AlQurashi, I. (2025). Investigating the impact of ChatGPT on reading proficiency in EFL context. *International Journal of Technology in Education*, *8*(4), 1222–1244. DOI: 10.46328/ijte.1203

Alqahtani, T., Badreldin, H. A., Alrashed, M., Alshaya, A. I., Alghamdi, S. S., Bin Saleh, K., Alowais, S. A., Alshaya, O. A., Rahman, I., Al Yami, M. S., & Albekairy, A. M. (2023). The emergent role of artificial intelligence, natural learning processing, and large language models in higher education and research. *Research in social & administrative pharmacy. Research in Social & Administrative Pharmacy*, *19*(8), 1236–1242. DOI: 10.1016/j.sapharm.2023.05.016 PMID: 37321925

Ang, T. L., Choolani, M., See, K. C., & Poh, K. K. (2023). The rise of artificial intelligence: Addressing the impact of large language models such as ChatGPT on scientific publications. *Singapore Medical Journal*, *64*(4), 193–195. DOI: 10.4103/singaporemedj.SMJ-2023-055 PMID: 37006087

Bauchner, H., & Rivara, F. P. (2024). Use of artificial intelligence and the future of peer review. *Health Affairs Scholar*, *2*(5), qxae058. Advance online publication. DOI: 10.1093/haschl/qxae058 PMID: 38757006

Biswas, S., Dobaria, D., & Cohen, H. L. (2023). ChatGPT and the future of journal reviews: A feasibility study. *Cureus*, *15*(9), 415–420. Advance online publication. DOI: 10.59249/SKDH9286 PMID: 37780993

Checco, A., Bracciale, L., Loreti, P., Pinfield, S., & Bianchi, G. (2021). AI-assisted peer review. *Humanities & Social Sciences Communications*, *8*(1), 1–10. DOI: 10.1057/s41599-020-00703-8 PMID: 38617731

Deng, J., & Lin, Y. (2023). The emergent role of artificial intelligence, natural learning processing, and large language models in higher education and research. *Frontiers in Computing and Intelligent Systems*, *2*, 81–83. DOI: 10.54097/fcis.v2i2.4465

Dwivedi, Y. K., Kshetri, N., Hughes, L., Slade, E. L., Jeyaraj, A., Kar, A. K., Baabdullah, A. M., Koohang, A., Raghavan, V., Ahuja, M., Albanna, H., Albashrawi, M. A., Al-Busaidi, A. S., Balakrishnan, J., Barlette, Y., Basu, S., Bose, I., Brooks, L., Buhalis, D., ... Wright, R. (2023). Opinion Paper: "So what if ChatGPT wrote it?" Multidisciplinary perspectives on opportunities, challenges and implications of generative conversational AI for research, practice and policy. *International Journal of Information Management, 71*, 102642. Article 102642. DOI: 10.1016/j.ijinfomgt.2023.102642

Gatrell, C., Muzio, D., Post, C., & Wickert, C. (2024). Here, there and everywhere: On the responsible use of artificial intelligence (AI) in management research and the peer-review process. *Journal of Management Studies*, *61*(4), 1023–1042. DOI: 10.1111/joms.13045

Hosseini, M., & Horbach, S. P. J. M. (2023). Fighting reviewer fatigue or amplifying bias? Considerations and recommendations for use of ChatGPT and other large language models in scholarly peer review. *Research Integrity and Peer Review*, *8*(1), 8. DOI: 10.1186/s41073-023-00133-5 PMID: 37434258

Kousha, K., & Thelwall, M. (2023). Artificial intelligence to support publishing and peer review: A summary and review. *Learned Publishing*, *36*(4), 456–472. DOI: 10.1002/leap.1570

Krausman, P. R. (2023). Managing artificial intelligence. *The Journal of Wildlife Management*, *87*(8), e22492. DOI: 10.1002/jwmg.22492

Liang, W., Zhang, Y., Cao, H., Wang, B., Ding, D. Y., Yang, X., Vodrahalli, K., He, S., Smith, D. S., Yin, Y., McFarland, D. A., & Zou, J. (2023). Can large language models provide useful feedback on research papers? A large-scale empirical analysis. *arXiv preprint arXiv:2310.01783*. https://doi.org//arxiv.2310.01783DOI: 10.48550

Lim, G. H., Tan, M., Hoe, V. C. W., & Koh, D. (2025). Generative AI in peer review process for occupational health. *Occupational Medicine*, *75*(5), 351–357. DOI: 10.1093/occmed/kqaf051 PMID: 40601499

Lin, Z. (2023). Why and how to embrace AI such as ChatGPT in your academic life. *Royal Society Open Science*, *10*(8), 230658. DOI: 10.1098/rsos.230658 PMID: 37621662

Mehta, V., Mathur, A., Arun, A., & Fiorillo, L. (2024). The application of ChatGPT in the peer-reviewing process. *Oral Oncology Reports*, *5*, 100227. DOI: 10.1016/j.oor.2024.100227

Miao, J., Thongprayoon, C., Suppadungsuk, S., Garcia Valencia, O. A., Qureshi, F., & Cheungpasitporn, W. (2023). Ethical dilemmas in using AI for academic writing and an example framework for peer review in nephrology academia: A narrative review. *Clinics and Practice*, *14*(1), 8. DOI: 10.3390/clinpract14010008 PMID: 38248432

Oliveira, E., Rios, S. A., & Jiang, Z. (2023). AI-powered peer review process. *Australasian Journal of Educational Technology*, *39*(3), 1–15. DOI: 10.14742/apubs.2023.482

Papatriantafyllou, M. (2017). Peer review – The future is here. *FEBS Letters*, *591*(17), 2571–2574. DOI: 10.1002/1873-3468.12792 PMID: 28805250

Rice, S., Crouse, S. R., Winter, S. R., & Rice, C. (2024). The advantages and limitations of using ChatGPT to enhance technological research. *Technology in Society*, *76*, 102426. DOI: 10.1016/j.techsoc.2023.102426

Schou, S., Cobanaj, I., Kaushik, N., Schlagwein, D., Van Der Heide, R., & Baskerville, R. L. (2023). "So what if ChatGPT wrote it?" Multidisciplinary perspectives on opportunities, challenges, and implications of generative conversational AI for research, practice, and policy. *Journal of the Association for Information Systems*, *24*(5), 939–979. DOI: 10.17705/1jais.00819

SCiNiTO. (n.d.). https://www.scinito.ai/

Tennant, J. P., & Ross-Hellauer, T. (2020). The limitations to our understanding of peer review. *Research Integrity and Peer Review*, *5*(6), 6. Advance online publication. DOI: 10.1186/s41073-020-00092-1 PMID: 32368354

Varghese, J., & Chapiro, J. (2024). ChatGPT: The transformative influence of generative AI on science and healthcare. *Journal of Hepatology*, *80*(6), 977–980. DOI: 10.1016/j.jhep.2023.07.028 PMID: 37544516

Compilation of References

Aarseth, E. J. (1997). *Cybertext: Perspectives on ergodic literature*. JHU Press. DOI: 10.56021/9780801855788

Abd Malek, S. N., & Ahmad, A. L. (2023). International Students' Academic Adjustment in Private Universities in Malaysia. *Jurnal Komunikasi: Malaysian Journal of Communication*, *39*(4), 224–246. DOI: 10.17576/JKMJC-2023-3904-12

Adinda, D. (2020). *Stratégies d'accompagnement des étudiants en formations hybrides : Effets sur l'autodirection dans l'apprentissage* [Doctoral dissertation]. Université de Strasbourg.

Adinda, D., & Denami, M. (2023). Blended Learning and Self-Direction : The Use of E-Forum. In A. S. Munna, V. Nadda, T. A. Allahyari, G. Cantafio, & S. Bilan (Eds.), *Advances in Educational Technologies and Instructional Design* (p. 110-165). IGI Global. DOI: 10.4018/978-1-6684-8282-7.ch006

Ahmad, S. A., Soo, K. Y., Mohamed Yunos, R., & Mohd Amin, J. (2019). Exploring Lecturers' Readiness for 21st Century Education in Malaysian Higher Learning Institutions. *European Journal of Teacher Education*, *1*(1), 15–29. DOI: 10.33422/ejte.2019.10.27

Akbarighatar, P. (2025). Operationalizing responsible AI principles through responsible AI capabilities. *AI and Ethics*, *5*(2), 1787–1801. DOI: 10.1007/s43681-024-00524-4

Al Sawi, I., & Alaa, A. (2024). Navigating the impact: A study of editors' and proofreaders' perceptions of AI tools in editing and proofreading. *Discover Artificial Intelligence*, *4*(1), 23. DOI: 10.1007/s44163-024-00116-5

Al Yakin, A., Al Matari, A.S., Muthmainnah M., Herawan, E., Auliya, Z.G., Wiradinata, R., & Obaid, A.J. (2026). Intelligent Blended Agents (IBAs) to Promote Computational Behaviour and Design Thinking in the Cyborg Education 7.0 Manifesto for Future of AI-Augmented Sociology Education. In Dutta, S., Bhattacharya, A., Bose, S., Polkowski, Z. (eds) Proceedings of International Conference on Computational Intelligence and Information Retrieval. ICCIIR 2025. Lecture Notes in Networks and Systems, vol 1617. Springer, Cham. DOI: 10.1007/978-3-032-04539-3_34

Al Yakin, A., Cardoso, L., Al Matari, A. S., Muthmainnah, M., Alnoor, A., & Obaid, A. J. (2024, September). Optimizing Artificial Intelligence (AI) Cici-Chatbot Teaching Mode on 4 Skills for Future Trends in Sociology Education Landscape at University. In *International Conference on Artificial Intelligence and Networking* (pp. 193-210). Singapore: Springer Nature Singapore.

Alberts, K. (2025). Unravelling the web: exploring the dynamics of online disinformation and its impact on democracy in Africa. *Canadian Journal of African Studies/Revue canadienne des études africaines, 59*(2), 333-359.

Albukhari, I. N. (2025). The role of artificial intelligence (AI) in architectural design: A systematic review of emerging technologies and applications. *Journal of Umm Al-Qura University for Engineering and Architecture*, 1-20.

Alexander, J. M. (2016). *Capabilities and social justice: The political philosophy of Amartya Sen and Martha Nussbaum*. Routledge. https://www.taylorfrancis.com/books/mono/10.4324/9781315260914/capabilities-social-justice-john-alexander

Ali, M. M., Alaa, A. M., Alharbi, W., & AlQurashi, I. (2025). Investigating the impact of ChatGPT on reading proficiency in EFL context. *International Journal of Technology in Education*, *8*(4), 1222–1244. DOI: 10.46328/ijte.1203

Alqahtani, T., Badreldin, H. A., Alrashed, M., Alshaya, A. I., Alghamdi, S. S., Bin Saleh, K., Alowais, S. A., Alshaya, O. A., Rahman, I., Al Yami, M. S., & Albekairy, A. M. (2023). The emergent role of artificial intelligence, natural learning processing, and large language models in higher education and research. *Research in social & administrative pharmacy. Research in Social & Administrative Pharmacy*, *19*(8), 1236–1242. DOI: 10.1016/j.sapharm.2023.05.016 PMID: 37321925

Ammar, W., Groeneveld, D., Bhagavatula, C., Beltagy, I., Crawford, M., Downey, D., & Etzioni, O. (2018). Construction of the literature graph in Semantic Scholar. *Proceedings of the 2018 Conference of the North American Chapter of the Association for Computational Linguistics: Human Language Technologies: Industry Papers, 3*, 84–91. DOI: 10.18653/v1/N18-3011

Ang, T. L., Choolani, M., See, K. C., & Poh, K. K. (2023). The rise of artificial intelligence: Addressing the impact of large language models such as ChatGPT on scientific publications. *Singapore Medical Journal*, *64*(4), 193–195. DOI: 10.4103/singaporemedj.SMJ-2023-055 PMID: 37006087

Arendt, H. (1961). *Between past and future: Eight exercises in political thought.* Viking Press.

Arslankara, V. B., Demir, A., Oztaş, O., & Usta, E. (2022). Digital Well-Being Scale Validity and Reliability Study. *Journal of Teacher Education and Lifelong Learning*, *4*(2), 263–274. DOI: 10.51535/tell.1206193

Austin, L. A. (2025). *Polarization in the Era of News Media Metamorphosis: A Critical Exploration of Implications for Democracy and Human Rights* (Doctoral dissertation, University of Calgary (Canada)).

Autor, D. H. (2015). Why are there still so many jobs? The history and future of workplace automation. *The Journal of Economic Perspectives*, *29*(3), 3–30. DOI: 10.1257/jep.29.3.3

Autor, D. H., Levy, F., & Murnane, R. J. (2003). The skill content of recent technological change: An empirical exploration. *The Quarterly Journal of Economics*, *118*(4), 1279–1333. DOI: 10.1162/003355303322552801

Aydin, M. A., Yıldız, M., Kiyici, M., Yildiz, M., Kirksekiz, A., & Kızıloğlu, Ş. (2024). The effect of digital obesity and phubbing level on life satisfaction: Latent profile analysis. *BMC Psychology*, *12*, 754. DOI: 10.1186/s40359-024-02256-w

Ayyaz, S. (2025). AI translation tools in language learning: Bridging gaps and enhancing skills. In *AI Applications for English Language Learning* (pp. 43–72). IGI Global Scientific Publishing. DOI: 10.4018/979-8-3693-9077-1.ch003

Baars, B. (2005). In Laureys, S. (Ed.), Progress in Brain Research: Vol. 45-52. *Global workspace theory of consciousness: toward a cognitive neuroscience of human experience.*

Bahar, F. H. M., Roslan, N. S., Ping, N. P. T., & Yusoff, M. S. B. (2024). Digital Well-Being among Learners in Higher Education: A Scoping Review Protocol. *Education in Medicine Journal*, *16*(4), 181–186. DOI: 10.21315/eimj2024.16.4.14

Bandura, A. (1986). *Social Foundations of Thought and Action: A Social Cognitive Theory*. Prentice Hall. https://api.semanticscholar.org/CorpusID:142519016

Bandura, A. (2001). Social cognitive theory: An agentic perspective. *Annual Review of Psychology*, *52*(1), 1–26. DOI: 10.1146/annurev.psych.52.1.1 PMID: 11148297

Barnett, V., & Lewis, T. (1994). *Outliers in Statistical Data* (3rd ed.). John Wiley & Sons, Kluwer Academic Publishers.

Barrafrem, K., Vastfjall, D., & Tinghog, G. (2024). Financial homo ignorans: Measuring vulnerability to behavioral biases in household finance. *Journal of Behavioral and Experimental Finance*, *42*, 100936. DOI: 10.1016/j.jbef.2024.100936

Barron, B. J., Schwartz, D. L., Vye, N. J., Moore, A., Petrosino, A., Zech, L., & Bransford, J. D. (1998). Doing with understanding: Lessons from research on problem- and project-based learning. *Journal of the Learning Sciences*, *7*(3–4), 271–311.

Barron, L. (2023). AI and Literature. In *AI and popular culture* (pp. 47–87). Emerald Publishing Limited. DOI: 10.1108/978-1-80382-327-020231003

Barthes, R. (1992). *The death of the author, 1968*. na.

Bauchner, H., & Rivara, F. P. (2024). Use of artificial intelligence and the future of peer review. *Health Affairs Scholar*, *2*(5), qxae058. Advance online publication. DOI: 10.1093/haschl/qxae058 PMID: 38757006

Bećirović, S., Polz, E., & Tinkel, I. (2025). Exploring students' AI literacy and its effects on their AI output quality, self-efficacy, and academic performance. *Smart Learning Environments*, *12*(1), 29. Advance online publication. DOI: 10.1186/s40561-025-00384-3

Beel, J., Gipp, B., Langer, S., & Breitinger, C. (2016). Research-paper recommender systems: A literature survey. *International Journal on Digital Libraries*, *17*(4), 305–338. DOI: 10.1007/s00799-015-0156-0

Benton, P. (2023). AI Literacy: A Primary Good. In Pillay, A., Jembere, E., & Gerber, A. J. (Eds.), *Artificial Intelligence Research* (Vol. 1976, pp. 31–43). Springer Nature Switzerland., DOI: 10.1007/978-3-031-49002-6_3

Biedermann, D., Kister, S., Breitwieser, J., Weidlich, J., & Drachsler, H. (2024). Use of digital self-control tools in higher education – a survey study. *Education and Information Technologies*, *29*(8), 9645–9666. DOI: 10.1007/s10639-023-12198-2

Biggs, J. (1996). Enhancing teaching through constructive alignment. *Higher Education*, *32*(3), 347–364. DOI: 10.1007/BF00138871

Bilandzic, H., & Gall Myrick, J. (2024). Information Seeking and Avoidance in the COVID-19 Pandemic as a Function of Political Ideology and National Context: A Survey Comparing the US and Germany. *Health Communication*, *39*(11), 2276–2289. DOI: 10.1080/10410236.2023.2263220

Billett, S. (2001). *Learning in the workplace: Strategies for effective practice*. Allen & Unwin.

Birhane, A., Kalluri, P., Card, D., Agnew, W., Dotan, R., & Bao, M. (2022). The values encoded in machine learning research. In *Proceedings of the 2022 ACM Conference on Fairness, Accountability, and Transparency* (pp. 173–184). DOI: 10.1145/3531146.3533083

Biswas, S., Dobaria, D., & Cohen, H. L. (2023). ChatGPT and the future of journal reviews: A feasibility study. *Cureus*, *15*(9), 415–420. Advance online publication. DOI: 10.59249/SKDH9286 PMID: 37780993

Blei, D. M., & Lafferty, J. D. (2009). Topic models. In Srivastava, A., & Sahami, M. (Eds.), *Text mining: Classification, clustering, and applications* (pp. 101–124). Chapman & Hall/CRC.

Boaler, J. (1998). Open and closed mathematics: Student experiences and understandings. *Journal for Research in Mathematics Education*, *29*(1), 41–62. DOI: 10.2307/749717

Bolaños, F., Salatino, A., Osborne, F., & Motta, E. (2024). Artificial intelligence for literature reviews: Opportunities and challenges. *Artificial Intelligence Review*, *57*(10), 259. DOI: 10.1007/s10462-024-10902-3

Bolter, J. D. (2016). Posthumanism. In Jensen, K. B., Rothenbuhler, E. W., Pooley, J. D., & Craig, R. T. (Eds.), *The International Encyclopedia of Communication Theory and Philosophy*., DOI: 10.1002/9781118766804.wbiect220

Bond, M., Bedenlier, S., Marín, V. I., & Handel, M. (2021). Emergency remote teaching in higher education: Mapping the first global online semester. *International Journal of Educational Technology in Higher Education*, *18*(1), 50. DOI: 10.1186/s41239-021-00282-x

Borgman, C. L. (2015). *Big data, little data, no data: Scholarship in the networked world*. MIT Press. DOI: 10.7551/mitpress/9963.001.0001

Bornmann, L., & Mutz, R. (2015). Growth rates of modern science: A bibliometric analysis based on the number of publications and cited references. *Journal of the Association for Information Science and Technology*, *66*(11), 2215–2222. DOI: 10.1002/asi.23329

Bottrighi, A., Grosso, F., Ghiglione, M., Maconi, A., Nera, S., Piovesan, L., Raina, E., Roveta, A., & Terenziani, P. (2025). A Symbolic AI Approach to Medical Training. *Journal of Medical Systems*, *49*(1), 2. Advance online publication. DOI: 10.1007/s10916-024-02139-y PMID: 39786677

Bozkurt, A., Junhong, X., Lambert, S., Pazurek, A., Crompton, H., Koseoglu, S., & Romero-Hall, E. (2023). Speculative futures on ChatGPT and generative artificial intelligence (AI): A collective reflection from the educational landscape. *Asian Journal of Distance Education, 18*(1), 53–130.

Brown, P. (2013). Education, opportunity and the prospects for social mobility. *British Journal of Sociology of Education, 34*(5–6), 678–700. DOI: 10.1080/01425692.2013.816036

Brown, T. B., Mann, B., Ryder, N., Subbiah, M., Kaplan, J., Dhariwal, P., & Amodei, D. (2020). Language models are few-shot learners. *Advances in Neural Information Processing Systems, 33*, 1877–1901.

Brown, T., Mann, B., Ryder, N., Subbiah, M., Kaplan, J., Dhariwal, P., & Amodei, D. (2020). *Language Models are Few-Shot Learners* (Vol. 33). Advances in Neural Information Processing Systems, https://arxiv.org/abs/2005.14165

Brynjolfsson, E., & McAfee, A. (2014). *The second machine age: Work, progress, and prosperity in a time of brilliant technologies*. W. W. Norton.

Buchi, M. (2024). Digital well-being theory and research. *New Media & Society, 26*(1), 172–189. DOI: 10.1177/14614448211056851

Bulathwela, S., Pérez-Ortiz, M., Holloway, C., Cukurova, M., & Shawe-Taylor, J. (2024). Artificial intelligence alone will not democratise education: On educational inequality, techno-solutionism and inclusive tools. *Sustainability (Basel), 16*(2), 781. DOI: 10.3390/su16020781

Caiza, G., Villafuerte, C., & Guanuche, A. (2025). Interactive Application with Virtual Reality and Artificial Intelligence for Improving Pronunciation in English Learning. *Applied Sciences (Basel, Switzerland), 15*(17), 9270. Advance online publication. DOI: 10.3390/app15179270

Calamel, C. (2012). Prendre en compte les situations non formelles d'apprentissage: *Agora débats/jeunesses, 62*(3), 33-43. https://doi.org/DOI: 10.3917/agora.062.0033

Campbell, J. L., & Pedersen, O. K. (2011). Knowledge regimes and comparative political economy. *Ideas and Politics in Social Science Research, 167*, 172–190.

Campillo-Ferrer, J. M., López-García, A., & Miralles-Sánchez, P. (2025). Student Perceptions of the Use of Gen-AI in a Higher Education Program in Spain. *Digital, 5*(3), 29. Advance online publication. DOI: 10.3390/digital5030029

Carré, P. (2020). *Pourquoi et comment les adultes apprendre : De la formation à l'apprenance*. Dunod. DOI: 10.3917/dunod.carre.2020.01

Carretero, S., Vuorikari, R., & Punie, Y. (2017). *DigComp 2.1: The Digital Competence Framework for Citizens with eight proficiency levels and examples of use*. Publications Office of the European Union., DOI: 10.2760/38842

Carvalho, M. (2024, March 4). *Grads earn more now but skills mismatch still high, survey finds*. The Star. https://www.thestar.com.my/news/nation/2024/03/04/grads-earn-more-now-but-skills-mismatch-still-high-survey-finds

Cavlovic, T., Koford, B. C., & Rentschler, L. (2024). Information avoidance: An experimental test of anticipated regret. *Journal of Risk and Uncertainty*, *69*(3), 323–348. DOI: 10.1007/s11166-024-09447-1

Chatterjee, D. (2025). An empire of artificial intelligence: Exploring an intersection of politics, society, and creativity. *International Journal of Politics Culture and Society*, *38*(1), 81–110. DOI: 10.1007/s10767-024-09484-3

Checco, A., Bracciale, L., Loreti, P., Pinfield, S., & Bianchi, G. (2021). AI-assisted peer review. *Humanities & Social Sciences Communications*, *8*(1), 1–10. DOI: 10.1057/s41599-020-00703-8 PMID: 38617731

Chen, C. (2017). Science mapping: A systematic review of the literature. *Journal of Data and Information Science*, *2*(2), 1–40. DOI: 10.1515/jdis-2017-0006

Chigbu, B. I., & Makapela, S. L. (2025). AI in education, sustainability, and the future of work: An integrative review of industry 5.0, education 5.0, and work 5.0. *Journal of Open Innovation*, *11*(4), 100645. DOI: 10.1016/j.joitmc.2025.100645

Chiu, T. K., & Rospigliosi, P. A. (2025). Encouraging human-AI collaboration in interactive learning environments. *Interactive Learning Environments*, *33*(2), 921–924. DOI: 10.1080/10494820.2025.2471199

Chong, P. S. J., & Guan, T. E. (2022). Life Satisfaction, Academic Achievement and Work Readiness Among Undergraduate Students. *International Journal of Education. Psychology and Counseling*, 7(48), 527–535. DOI: 10.35631/ijepc.748040

Clark, B. R. (1986). *The higher education system: Academic organization in cross-national perspective*. University of California Press.

Cohen, J. (1988). *Statistical power analysis for the behavioral sciences* (2nd ed.). Lawrence Erlbaum.

Collins, H. (2025). Why artificial intelligence needs sociology of knowledge: Parts I and II. *AI & Society*, *40*(3), 1249–1263. DOI: 10.1007/s00146-024-01954-8

Collins, R. (1979). *The credential society: An historical sociology of education and stratification*. Academic Press.

Contractor, Z., & Reyes, G. (2025). Generative AI in higher education: Evidence from an Elite College. *arXiv*. /arXiv.2508.00717DOI: 10.48550

Crawford, K. (2021). *The atlas of AI: Power, politics, and the planetary costs of artificial intelligence*. Yale University Press.

Crisp, G., & Cruz, I. (2009). Mentoring college students: A critical review of the literature between 1990 and 2007. *Research in Higher Education*, *50*(6), 525–545. DOI: 10.1007/s11162-009-9130-2

Cristol, D., & Muller, A. (2013). Les apprentissages informels dans la formation pour adultes: *Savoirs, n° 32*(2), 11-59. https://doi.org/DOI: 10.3917/savo.032.0011

Crompton, H., & Burke, D. (2023). Artificial intelligence in higher education: The state of the field. *International Journal of Educational Technology in Higher Education*, *20*(1), 22. DOI: 10.1186/s41239-023-00392-8

Crupi, A., Marinelli, L., & Cacciatore, E. (2025). Generative AI and Society 5.0: Enabling a Collaborative, Inclusive Future. In *The Generative AI Impact: Reframing Innovation in Society 5.0* (pp. 3-20). Emerald Publishing Limited.

Csernoch, M., Kiss, J. T., Takacs, V., & Mate, D. (2024). Exploring higher education competencies through spreadsheet self-assessment & time. *Proceedings of the EuSpRIG 2024 Conference "Spreadsheet Productivity & Risks."* https://doi.org/DOI: 10.48550/arXiv.2409.12974

Cukurova, M. (2025). The interplay of learning, analytics and artificial intelligence in education : A vision for hybrid intelligence. *British Journal of Educational Technology*, *56*(2), 469–488. DOI: 10.1111/bjet.13514

Cynthia, R., & Chong, P. Y. (2023). Factors Influencing International Students' Choice to Study at Malaysian Private Higher Education Institutions. [MJSSH]. *Malaysian Journal of Social Sciences and Humanities*, *8*(5), e002281. DOI: 10.47405/mjssh.v8i5.2281

Daher, R. (2025). Integrating AI literacy into teacher education: A critical perspective paper. *Discover Artificial Intelligence*, *5*(1), 217. Advance online publication. DOI: 10.1007/s44163-025-00475-7

Dale, R. (2021). GPT-3: What's it good for? *Natural Language Engineering*, *27*(1), 113–118. DOI: 10.1017/S1351324920000601

Daniels, G. (Director). (2020-2024). *Upload* [Motion Picture].

Deane, P. D. (2020). Building and Justifying Interpretations of Texts: A Key Practice in the English Language Arts ETS RR-20-20

Demir, O., Cinar, M., & Keskin, S. (2023). Participation style and social anxiety as predictors of active participation in asynchronous discussion forums and academic achievement. *Education and Information Technologies*, •••, 1–22. Advance online publication. DOI: 10.1007/s10639-022-11517-3

Deng, J., & Lin, Y. (2023). The emergent role of artificial intelligence, natural learning processing, and large language models in higher education and research. *Frontiers in Computing and Intelligent Systems*, *2*, 81–83. DOI: 10.54097/fcis.v2i2.4465

Deng, L., Zhou, Y., & Broadbent, J. (2024). Distraction, multitasking and self-regulation inside university classroom. *Education and Information Technologies*, *29*(18), 23957–23979. DOI: 10.1007/s10639-024-12786-w

Deval, Ö., Öztürk Kösenciğ, K., & Acirli, Z. (2025). Integration of artificial intelligence tools into interior architecture education: A study on textual and visual representations. *Estoa*, *14*(28), 109–120. DOI: 10.18537/est.v014.n028.a08

Devarakonda, M., & Kilicoglu, H. (2022). *AI-assisted systematic reviewing: A state-of-the-art review*. Morgan & Claypool.

Devisakti, A., Muftahu, M., & Xiaoling, H. (2024). Digital divide among B40 students in Malaysian higher education institutions. *Education and Information Technologies*, *29*(2), 1857–1883. DOI: 10.1007/s10639-023-11847-w

Dewey, J. (1938). *Experience and education*. Macmillan.

Dewey, J. (1938). *Logic: The theory of inquiry*. Holt.

Dijkstra, T. K., & Henseler, J. (2015). Consistent partial least squares path modeling. *Management Information Systems Quarterly*, *39*, 297–316. DOI: 10.25300/MISQ/2015/39.2.02

Dili, G., & Ansong, E. D. (2025). Human–AI Collaboration: A Paradigm Shift in Decision-Making. In *The Power of Agentic AI: Redefining Human Life and Decision-Making: In Industry 6.0* (pp. 59–80). Springer Nature Switzerland. DOI: 10.1007/978-3-031-89424-4_5

Ding, D., & Yusof, M. B. (2025). Investigating the role of AI-powered conversation bots in enhancing L2 speaking skills and reducing speaking anxiety: A mixed methods study. *Humanities & Social Sciences Communications*, *12*(1), 1–16. DOI: 10.1057/s41599-025-05550-z

Dionne, K., & Carlile, P. (2016). Le pouvoir transformationnel des hackathons. *Gestion*, *41*(2), 62–63. DOI: 10.3917/riges.412.0062

Docherty, T. (2016). *Postmodernism: A reader.* Routledge. DOI: 10.4324/9781315504612

Dogru, M., Celik, M., Koca, C., & Tongal, A. (2022). Development of Life and Career Skills Scale for University Students. *Asian Journal of Contemporary Education, 6*(1), 30–43. DOI: 10.55493/5052.v6i1.4425

Dritsas, E., & Trigka, M. (2025). Machine Learning and Data Science in Social Sciences: Methods, Applications, and Future Directions. *IEEE Access : Practical Innovations, Open Solutions, 13*, 105334–105352. DOI: 10.1109/ACCESS.2025.3578906

Dwivedi, Y. K., Kshetri, N., Hughes, L., Slade, E. L., Jeyaraj, A., Kar, A. K., Baabdullah, A. M., Koohang, A., Raghavan, V., Ahuja, M., Albanna, H., Albashrawi, M. A., Al-Busaidi, A. S., Balakrishnan, J., Barlette, Y., Basu, S., Bose, I., Brooks, L., Buhalis, D., ... Wright, R. (2023). Opinion Paper: "So what if ChatGPT wrote it?" Multidisciplinary perspectives on opportunities, challenges and implications of generative conversational AI for research, practice and policy. *International Journal of Information Management, 71*, 102642. Article 102642. DOI: 10.1016/j.ijinfomgt.2023.102642

Eaton, S. E. (2025). Global trends in education: Artificial intelligence, postplagiarism, and future-focused learning for 2025 and beyond–2024–2025 Werklund Distinguished Research Lecture. *International Journal for Educational Integrity, 21*(1), 12. DOI: 10.1007/s40979-025-00187-6

Ehlers, U.-D., Lindner, M., Sommer, S., & Rauch, E. (2023). *AICOMP - Future Skills in a World Increasingly Shaped By AI.* Ubiquity Proceedings., DOI: 10.5334/uproc.91

El Mourabit, I., Andaloussi, S. J., Ouchetto, O., & Miyara, M. (2025). AI Chatbots in Higher Education: Opportunities and Challenges for Personalized and Mobile Learning. *International Journal of Interactive Mobile Technologies, 19*(12), 19–37. DOI: 10.3991/ijim.v19i12.54163

Engeström, Y. (2001). Expansive learning at work: Toward an activity-theoretical reconceptualization. *Journal of Education and Work, 14*(1), 133–156. DOI: 10.1080/13639080020028747

Eraut, M. (2004). Informal learning in the workplace. *Studies in Continuing Education, 26*(2), 247–273. DOI: 10.1080/158037042000225245

Etikan, I., & Bala, K. (2017). Sampling and Sampling Methods. *Biometrics & Biostatistics International Journal, 5*, 00149. Advance online publication. DOI: 10.15406/bbij.2017.05.00149

Faza, A., & Lestari, I. A. (2025). Self-Regulated Learning in the Digital Age: A Systematic Review of Strategies, Technologies, Benefits, and Challenges. *International Review of Research in Open and Distance Learning*, *26*(2), 23–58. DOI: 10.19173/irrodl.v26i2.8119

Fletscher, L., Mercado, J., Gómez, A., & Mendoza-Cardenas, C. (2025). Innovating Personalized Learning in Virtual Education Through AI. *Multimodal Technologies and Interaction*, *9*(7), 69. Advance online publication. DOI: 10.3390/mti9070069

Floridi, L. (2025). Distant Writing: Literary Production in the Age of Artificial Intelligence. *Minds and Machines*, *35*(3), 1–26. DOI: 10.1007/s11023-025-09732-1

Floridi, L., Cowls, J., Beltrametti, M., Chatila, R., Chazerand, P., Dignum, V., Luetge, C., Madelin, R., Pagallo, U., Rossi, F., Schafer, B., Valcke, P., & Vayena, E. (2018). AI4People – An ethical framework for a good AI society. *Minds and Machines*, *28*(4), 689–707. DOI: 10.1007/s11023-018-9482-5 PMID: 30930541

Følstad, A., Araujo, T., Law, E. L.-C., Brandtzaeg, P. B., Papadopoulos, S., Reis, L., Baez, M., Laban, G., McAllister, P., Ischen, C., Wald, R., Catania, F., Meyer von Wolff, R., Hobert, S., & Luger, E. (2022). Future directions for chatbot research: An interdisciplinary research agenda. *Computing*, *104*(12), 2915–2942. DOI: 10.1007/s00607-021-01016-7

Fornell, C., & Larcker, D. F. (1981). Evaluating structural equation models with unobservable variables and measurement error. *JMR, Journal of Marketing Research*, *18*(1), 39–50. DOI: 10.2307/3151312

Foucault, M. (2003). *What is an author? Reading Architectural History*. Routledge.

Francis, P., & Wolton, D. (2025). *A future of faith: the path of change in politics and society*. Macmillan+ ORM.

Frické, M. (2019). The knowledge pyramid: The DIKW hierarchy. *Knowledge Organization*, *46*(1), 33–46. DOI: 10.5771/0943-7444-2019-1-33

Gao, J., Zhang, J., & Li, Y. (2025). Do AI chatbot-integrated writing tasks influence writing self-efficacy and critical thinking ability? An exploratory study. *Computers and Education: Artificial Intelligence*, *9*, 100472. Advance online publication. DOI: 10.1016/j.caeai.2025.100472

Gardner, C. (2003). Meta-interpretation and hypertext fiction: A critical response. *Computers and the Humanities*, *37*(1), 33–56. DOI: 10.1023/A:1021803606361

Gatrell, C., Muzio, D., Post, C., & Wickert, C. (2024). Here, there and everywhere: On the responsible use of artificial intelligence (AI) in management research and the peer-review process. *Journal of Management Studies, 61*(4), 1023–1042. DOI: 10.1111/joms.13045

Gehl Sampath, P. (2021). Governing Artificial Intelligence in an Age of Inequality. *Global Policy, 12*(S6), 21–31. DOI: 10.1111/1758-5899.12940

Ghiurău, D., & Popescu, D. E. (2024). Distinguishing reality from AI: Approaches for detecting synthetic content. *Computers, 14*(1), 1. DOI: 10.3390/computers14010001

Giroux, H. A. (2020). *On critical pedagogy*. Bloomsbury Publishing. DOI: 10.5040/9781350145016

Goodfellow, I., Pouget-Abadie, J., Mirza, M., Xu, B., Warde-Farley, D., Ozair, S., & Bengio, Y. (2014). *Generative adversarial nets* (Vol. 27). Advances in neural information processing systems, https://arxiv.org/abs/1406.2661

Greenhow, C., & Lewin, C. (2016). Social media and education: Reconceptualizing the boundaries of formal and informal learning. *Learning, Media and Technology, 41*(1), 6–30. DOI: 10.1080/17439884.2015.1064954

Guglielmo, M., Ahrweiler, P., Barberà, O., Brockschmidt, D. S., Critch, N., de Moraes Azenha, A. L., Del Río, A. F., Ennis, C. A., García Guijarro, P., Gomís Jaen, E., Luke, D., Luque Capellas, B., Malý, M., Mansouri, M. I., Medrado, A., O'Loughlin, B., Ritchie, D., Sánchez Montell, M., Sentí Navarro, C., & Ward, B. (2025). Us and artificial intelligence: Questioning agency and the need for critical and humanist perspectives. *Open Research Europe, 5*, 318. DOI: 10.12688/openreseurope.21477.1

Guile, D., & Griffiths, T. (2001). Learning through work experience. *Journal of Education and Work, 14*(1), 113–131. DOI: 10.1080/13639080020028738

Guszcza, J. (2018). *Smarter together: Why artificial intelligence needs human-centered design*. Deloitte Insights.

Gutiérrez-Leefmans, M., Picazo-Vela, S., & Kareem, O. (2025). Adoption of artificial intelligence in higher education: A diffusion of innovation approach. *The TQM Journal*. Advance online publication. DOI: 10.1108/TQM-12-2024-0523

Haddaway, N. R., Bethel, A., Dicks, L. V., Koricheva, J., Macura, B., Petrokofsky, G., & Pullin, A. S. (2020). Eight problems with literature reviews and how to fix them. *Nature Ecology & Evolution, 4*(12), 1582–1589. DOI: 10.1038/s41559-020-01295-x PMID: 33046871

Haddaway, N. R., Lotfi, T., & Mbuagbaw, L. (2022). *Faster literature reviews: Using AI to keep up with the evidence*. Campbell Collaboration.

Hair, J. F., Black, W. C., Babin, B. J., & Anderson, R. E. (2019). *Multivariate data analysis* (8th ed.). Cengage Learning.

Hair, J. F., Hult, G. T. M., Ringle, C. M., & Sarstedt, M. (2022). *A Primer on Partial Least Squares Structural Equation Modeling (PLS-SEM)* (3rd ed.). Sage., DOI: 10.1007/978-3-030-80519-7

Halim, F. S. A., Luaran, J. E., & Jill, L. S. S. (2024). Unravelling Challenges of Higher Education Institutions in Implementing Effective Micro-Credentials: A Multi-Stakeholder Qualitative Study. *Asian Journal of University Education, 20*(1), 114–126. DOI: 10.24191/ajue.v20i1.25698

Haney, W. S. (2006). *Cyberculture, Cyborgs and Science Fiction: Consciousness and the Posthuman*. Conscious Literature and the Arts. DOI: 10.1163/9789401202701

Haraway, D. (2010). A Cyborg Manifesto (1985). *Cultural theory: An anthology, 454*.

Haraway, D. (1985). *Cyborg Manifesto: Science, Technology, and Socialist-Feminism in the Late Twentieth Century*. Socialist Review.

Harley, N. (2020, April 29). *Upload Review (Spoiler Free)*. Retrieved September 21, 2025, from Den of Geek: https://www.denofgeek.com/tv/upload-review/

Haroud, S., & Saqri, N. (2025). Generative ai in higher education: Teachers' and students' perspectives on support, replacement, and digital literacy. *Education Sciences, 15*(4), 396. DOI: 10.3390/educsci15040396

Hart, A. (2013, Juin). *Apprentissage formel, informel, non-formel, des notions difficiles à utiliser… pourquoi?* https://oce.uqam.ca/apprentissage-formel-informel-non-formel-des-notions-difficiles-a-utiliser-pourquoi/

Hashmi, N., & Bal, A. S. (2024). Generative AI in higher education and beyond. *Business Horizons, 67*(5), 607–614. DOI: 10.1016/j.bushor.2024.05.005

Hayles, N. K. (1993). The materiality of informatics. *Configurations, 1*(1), 147–170. DOI: 10.1353/con.1993.0003

Hayles, N. K. (1999). *How We Become Posthuman: Virtual Bodies in Cybernetics, Literature and Informatics*. The University of Chicago Press. DOI: 10.7208/chicago/9780226321394.001.0001

Hayles, N. K. (2002). *Writing Machines*. MIT Press. DOI: 10.7551/mitpress/7328.001.0001

Hayles, N. K. (2008). *Electronic literature: New horizons for the literary*. University of Notre Dame Press.

Head, M. L., Holman, L., Lanfear, R., Kahn, A. T., & Jennions, M. D. (2021). The extent and consequences of p-hacking in science. *PLoS Biology*, *19*(3), e3001162. DOI: 10.1371/journal.pbio.3001162 PMID: 25768323

Henseler, J., Ringle, C. M., & Sarstedt, M. (2015). A new criterion for assessing discriminant validity in variance-based structural equation modeling. *Journal of the Academy of Marketing Science*, *43*(1), 115–135. DOI: 10.1007/s11747-014-0403-8

Hillygus, D. S., & Holbein, J. B. (2023). Refocusing civic education: Developing the skills young people need to engage in democracy. *The Annals of the American Academy of Political and Social Science*, *705*(1), 73–94. DOI: 10.1177/00027162231177798

Hixson, N. K., Ravitz, J., & Whisman, A. (2012). *Extended Professional Development in Project-Based Learning: Impacts on 21st century teaching and student achievement*. In West Virginia Department of Education. https://files.eric.ed.gov/fulltext/ED565466.pdf

Hofstra, B., Kulkarni, V. V., Munoz-Najar Galvez, S., He, B., Jurafsky, D., & McFarland, D. A. (2020). The diversity–innovation paradox in science. *Proceedings of the National Academy of Sciences of the United States of America*, *117*(17), 9284–9291. DOI: 10.1073/pnas.1915378117 PMID: 32291335

Holmes, W., Porayska-Pomsta, K., Holstein, K., Sutherland, E., Baker, T., Shum, S. B., Santos, O. C., Rodrigo, M. T., Cukurova, M., Bittencourt, I. I., & Koedinger, K. R. (2021). Ethics of AI in education: Towards a community-wide framework. *International Journal of Artificial Intelligence in Education*, *32*(3), 504–526. DOI: 10.1007/s40593-021-00239-1

Hosseini, M., & Horbach, S. P. J. M. (2023). Fighting reviewer fatigue or amplifying bias? Considerations and recommendations for use of ChatGPT and other large language models in scholarly peer review. *Research Integrity and Peer Review*, *8*(1), 8. DOI: 10.1186/s41073-023-00133-5 PMID: 37434258

Hultell, D., & Gustavsson, J. P. (2008). A psychometric evaluation of the satisfaction with life scale in a Swedish nationwide sample of university students. *Personality and Individual Differences*, *44*(5), 1070–1079. DOI: 10.1016/j.paid.2007.10.030

Hwang, Y., Lee, S., & Jeon, J. (2025). Integrating AI chatbots into the metaverse: Pre-service English teachers' design works and perceptions. *Education and Information Technologies*, *30*(4), 4099–4130. DOI: 10.1007/s10639-024-12924-4

Ifenthaler, D., Cooper, M., Daniela, L., & Sahin, M. (2023). Social anxiety in digital learning environments: An international perspective and call to action. *International Journal of Educational Technology in Higher Education*, *20*(1), 50. DOI: 10.1186/s41239-023-00419-0

Ilcic, A., Fuentes, M., & Lawler, D. (2025). Artificial intelligence, complexity, and systemic resilience in global governance. *Frontiers in Artificial Intelligence*, *8*, 1562095. DOI: 10.3389/frai.2025.1562095 PMID: 40529642

Ito, M.. (2013). *Connected learning: An agenda for research and design*. Digital Media and Learning Research Hub.

Iyer, V. (2025). *Digital Humanities Research Methods*. Educohack Press.

Jacob, J. U. U., & Vajjhala, N. R. (Eds.). (2025). *AI and the Future of Democracy: Building Resilient and Inclusive Societies*. CRC Press. DOI: 10.1201/9781003594185

Jacobson, T. L. (2016). Amartya Sen's capabilities approach and communication for development and social change. *Journal of Communication*, *66*(5), 789–810. DOI: 10.1111/jcom.12252

Jain, V. (2024). Quality Education Through E-Learning for Sustainable Development. *Transforming Vocational Education and Training Using AI*, 211.

Janfada, M., Heidari, E., & Lin, A. (2025). Transcending multiliteracies pedagogies in, for, through AI-oriented learning spaces: A dialogic perspective. *Pedagogies*, •••, 1–23. DOI: 10.1080/1554480X.2025.2563621

Jaramillo, J. J., Chiappe, A., & Delgado, F. S. (2025). From Struggle to Mastery: AI-Powered Writing Skills in ESL Education. *Applied Sciences (Basel, Switzerland)*, *15*(14), 8079. Advance online publication. DOI: 10.3390/app15148079

Jenkins, H., Purushotma, R., Clinton, K., Weigel, M., & Robison, A. J. (2006). *Confronting the challenges of participatory culture: Media education for the 21st century*. MacArthur Foundation.

Jeunesse, C. (2025). *Des usages des technologies pour apprendre aux Environnements Personnels d'Apprentissage augmentés par l'Intelligence Artificielle Générative (IAGEN)* [thèse d'HDR, Université Paris Nanterre]. https://hal.science/tel-05328100

Jha, A., & Singh, S. R. (2025). Integrating Artificial Intelligence in Media Education: Revolutionizing Learning, Creativity, and Critical Thinking. In Teachers' Roles and Perspectives on AI Integration in Schools (pp. 297-328). IGI Global Scientific Publishing.

Jia, C., & Li, P. (2024). Generation Z's Health Information Avoidance Behavior: Insights From Focus Group Discussions. *Journal of Medical Internet Research, 26*, e54107. DOI: 10.2196/54107

Jiang, Y., Zhao, J., Yuan, Y., Zhang, T., Huang, Y., Zhang, Y., . . . Li, X. (2025). Never compromise to vulnerabilities: A comprehensive survey on ai governance. *arXiv preprint arXiv:2508.08789.*

Johnson, D. W., & Johnson, R. T. (1999). *Learning together and alone: Cooperative, competitive, and individualistic learning*. Allyn & Bacon.

Kadum, B. M. C. M., & Karpudewan, M. (2025). Influence of self-efficacy and metacognition on malaysian pre-university students' chemistry academic motivation: The moderating role of gender and locality. *Chemistry Education Research and Practice, 26*(3), 682–700. DOI: 10.1039/D4RP00334A

Kalaycı, R., & Eşgi, N. (2024). Development of the 21St Century Information Literacy Skills Scale, Validity and Reliability Study. *European Journal of Education Studies, 11*(3), 55–75. DOI: 10.46827/ejes.v11i3.5221

Kaldi, S., Filippatou, D., & Govaris, C. (2011). Project-based learning in primary schools: Effects on pupils' learning and attitudes. *Education* 3–13, 39(1), 35-47.

Kant, I. (2000). *Kritik der Urteilskraft*. Meiner. (Original work published 1790)

Karaçalli, S., & Korur, F. (2014). The Effects of Project-Based Learning on Students' Academic Achievement, Attitude, and Retention of Knowledge : The Subject of "Electricity in Our Lives". *School Science and Mathematics, 114*(5), 224–235. Advance online publication. DOI: 10.1111/ssm.12071

Karadži, E., & Redžepi, F. (2025). Uvod u kritičku analizu biopolitičkog genocidnog rata u pojasu Gaze: Teorijski izazovi i društvene implikacije/Introduction to a Critical Analysis of the Biopolitical Genocidal War in the Gaza Strip: Theoretical Challenges and Social Implications. *Pregled: časopis za društvena pitanja/Periodical for social issues, 66*(2), 83-111.

Kasneci, E., Sessler, K., Küchemann, S., Bannert, M., Dementieva, D., Fischer, F., Gasser, U., Groh, G., Günnemann, S., Hüllermeier, E., Krusche, S., Kutyniok, G., Michaeli, T., Nerdel, C., Pfeffer, J., Poquet, O., Sailer, M., Schmidt, A., Seidel, T., & Kasneci, G. (2023). ChatGPT for good? On opportunities and challenges of large language models for education. *Learning and Individual Differences, 103*, 102274. DOI: 10.1016/j.lindif.2023.102274

Kavitha, K., Joshith, V. P., Rajeev, N. P., & S, A. (2024). Artificial Intelligence in Higher Education: A Bibliometric Approach. *European Journal of Educational Research, volume–13–2024*(volume–13–issue–3–july–2024), 1121–1137. DOI: 10.12973/eu-jer.13.3.1121

Khan, M. S., Umer, H., & Faruqe, F. (2024). Artificial intelligence for low income countries. *Humanities & Social Sciences Communications*, *11*(1), 1–13. DOI: 10.1057/s41599-024-03947-w

Kilpatrick, W. H. (1921). Dangers and Difficulties of the Project Method and how to Overcome Them—A Symposium1. *Teachers College Record: The Voice of Scholarship in Education, 22*(4), 1-6. https://doi.org/ (Original work published 1921)DOI: 10.1177/016146812102200407

Kilpatrick, W. H. (1918). The project method. *Teachers College Record*, *19*(4), 319–335. DOI: 10.1177/016146811801900404

Kim, S. J., Sun, Y., Bucy, E. P., & Shah, D. V. (2025). Digital Dilemmas: Crises in the Fourth Age of Political Communication. In *Public Communication in Freefall: Revisiting the work of Jay Blumler* (pp. 59–88). Springer Nature Switzerland. DOI: 10.1007/978-3-031-83364-9_4

Kline, R. B. (2011). Principles and practice of structural equation modeling. In *Guilford Publication*. Guilford Press.

Kock, N. (2015). Common Method Bias in PLS-SEM: A Full Collinearity Assessment Approach. [IJeC]. *International Journal of e-Collaboration*, *11*, 1–10. DOI: 10.4018/ijec.2015100101

Kohnke, L., Moorhouse, B. L., & Zou, D. (2023). Exploring generative artificial intelligence preparedness among university language instructors: A case study. *Computers and Education: Artificial Intelligence*, *5*, 100156. DOI: 10.1016/j.caeai.2023.100156

Kolb, D. A. (1984). *Experiential learning: Experience as the source of learning and development*. Prentice-Hall.

Koltay, T. (2023). The age of artificial intelligence: Challenges for information literacy. *Journal of Academic Librarianship*, *49*(1), 102666. DOI: 10.1016/j.acalib.2022.102666

Kousha, K., & Thelwall, M. (2023). Artificial intelligence to support publishing and peer review: A summary and review. *Learned Publishing*, *36*(4), 456–472. DOI: 10.1002/leap.1570

Krajcik, J. S., & Blumenfeld, P. C. (2006). The Cambridge Handbook of the Learning Sciences. R. Keith Sawyer (ed). Cambridge University Press DOI: 10.1017/CBO9780511816833

Krajcik, J., & Shin, N. (2014). *Project-based learning. The Cambridge handbook of the learning sciences*. Cambridge University Press.

Krausman, P. R. (2023). Managing artificial intelligence. *The Journal of Wildlife Management*, *87*(8), e22492. DOI: 10.1002/jwmg.22492

Kshetri, N. (2024). Linguistic Challenges in Generative Artificial Intelligence: Implications for Low-Resource Languages in the Developing World. *Journal of Global Information Technology Management*, *27*(2), 95–99. DOI: 10.1080/1097198X.2024.2341496

Kundu, A., & Bej, T. (2025). Empowering Students' Autonomy in EFL Learning: AI Innovations in Schools of the Global South. *The Electronic Journal on Information Systems in Developing Countries*, *91*(6), e70041. DOI: 10.1002/isd2.70041

Larmer, J., Mergendoller, J., & Boss, S. (2015). *Setting the standard for project based learning : A proven approach to rigorous classroom instruction*. ASCD.

Laurillard, D. (2002). *Rethinking university teaching: A conversational framework for the effective use of learning technologies*. Routledge. DOI: 10.4324/9780203160329

Leander, K. M., & Burriss, S. K. (2020). Critical literacy for a posthuman world: When people read, and become, with machines. *British Journal of Educational Technology*, *51*(4), 1262–1276. DOI: 10.1111/bjet.12924

Leba, S. M. R., Nggaruaka, T., & Butarbutar, R. (2025). Smart Teaching in Rural Indonesia: Harnessing AI-Assisted Deep Learning for Teacher Professional Development. *EthAIca: Journal of Ethics. AI and Critical Analysis*, (4), 419.

Leonhardt, C., Danielsen, D., & Andersen, S. (2025). Associations between screen use, learning and concentration among children and young people in western countries: a scoping review. *Children and Youth Services Review, 177*, 108508 Contents. https://doi.org/DOI: 10.1016/j.childyouth.2025.108508

Liebowitz, M. R. (1987). Social phobia. *Modern Problems of Pharmacopsychiatry*, *22*, 141–173. DOI: 10.1159/000414022

Li, K., Jiang, S., Yan, X., & Li, J. (2024). Mechanism study of social media overload on health self-efficacy and anxiety. *Heliyon*, *10*, e23326. DOI: 10.1016/j.heliyon.2023.e23326

Lim, G. H., Tan, M., Hoe, V. C. W., & Koh, D. (2025). Generative AI in peer review process for occupational health. *Occupational Medicine, 75*(5), 351–357. DOI: 10.1093/occmed/kqaf051 PMID: 40601499

Lind, T., Ahmed, A., Skagerlund, K., Strömbäck, C., & Västfjäll, D., & Ting hög G. (2020). Competence, confidence, and gender: The role of objective and subjective financial knowledge in household finance. *Journal of Farm Economics, 41*, 626–638. DOI: 10. 1007/ s10834- 020- 09678-9

Lin, Z. (2023). Why and how to embrace AI such as ChatGPT in your academic life. *Royal Society Open Science, 10*(8), 230658. DOI: 10.1098/rsos.230658 PMID: 37621662

Long, D., & Magerko, B. (2020). What is AI literacy? Competencies and design considerations. In *Proceedings of the 2020 ACM CHI Conference on Human Factors in Computing Systems* (pp. 1–16). ACM. https://doi.org/DOI: 10.1145/3313831.3376727

Lorenzo, R., Sagula, J. E., Zayas-Figueras, E. E., Quishpe-Solano, R., & Pérez-Rodríguez, R. (2024, October). Development of Educational 4.0 Environments Through the Dynamic Integration of Natural (Human) and Artificial Intelligences. In *Workshop in R&D+ i & International Workshop on STEM of EPS* (pp. 387-398). Cham: Springer Nature Switzerland.

Luckin, R.. (2009). Learner-generated contexts: A framework to support the effective use of technology to support learning. *Learning, Media and Technology, 34*(4), 341–355.

Luckin, R., Holmes, W., Griffiths, M., & Forcier, L. B. (2019). *Intelligence unleashed: An argument for AI in education.* Pearson.

Lund, B. D., & Wang, T. (2023). ChatGPT and academic libraries. *Library Hi Tech News, 40*(3), 26–29. DOI: 10.1108/LHTN-01-2023-0009

Machi, L. A., & McEvoy, B. T. (2021). *The literature review: Six steps to success* (4th ed.). Corwin Press.

Mail, M. (2024, April 30). *HR Ministry: Graduate employment mismatch rate shows sharp decline from 18.2pc in 2023 to 40.5pc in previous year.* https://www.malaymail.com/news/malaysia/2024/04/30/hr-ministry-graduate-employment-mismatch-rate-shows-sharp-decline-from-182pc-in-2023-to-405pc-in-previous-year/131778

Mal Walder, A. (2016). Les innovations technologiques sont-elles à l'origine des nouveaux rythmes et temporalités de l'université contemporaine ? *Distances et médiations des savoirs, (16).* DOI: 10.4000/dms.1605

Mamlok, D. (2025). Landscapes of sociotechnical imaginaries in education: A theoretical examination of integrating artificial intelligence in education. *Foundations of Science*, *30*(2), 529–540. DOI: 10.1007/s10699-024-09948-x

Manganello, F., Nico, A., & Boccuzzi, G. (2025). Theoretical Foundations for Governing AI-Based Learning Outcome Assessment in High-Risk Educational Contexts. *Information (Basel)*, *16*(9), 814. Advance online publication. DOI: 10.3390/info16090814

Marginson, S. (2016). *The dream is over: The crisis of Clark Kerr's California idea of higher education*. University of California Press. http://library.oapen.org/handle/20.500.12657/32075

Margolis, E. (2019). The Day A Computer Wrote A Novel. Retrieved on December 3, 2025

Markus, A., Carolus, A., & Wienrich, C. (2025). Objective measurement of AI literacy: Development and validation of the AI competency objective scale (AI-COS). *Computers and Education: Artificial Intelligence*, *9*, 100485. Advance online publication. DOI: 10.1016/j.caeai.2025.100485

Marshall, I. J., & Wallace, B. C. (2019). Toward systematic review automation. *Systematic Reviews*, *8*(1), 163. DOI: 10.1186/s13643-019-1074-9 PMID: 31296265

Marsh, E., Vallejos, E. P., & Spence, A. (2022). The digital workplace and its dark side: An integrative review. *Computers in Human Behavior*, *128*, 107118. DOI: 10.1016/j.chb.2021.107118

Maskun, R., Mat Khairi, S. M., Sulaiman, M. N. A., Mohd Aris, N., Omar, M. M., & Mohamed, M. N. (2025). Digital Wellbeing Among Generation Y in Malaysia: Implications, Challenges, and the Path Forward. *Asia-Pacific Journal of Business, Humanities, and Education*, *10*(1), 44–57.

Matar, S. (2025). The Development of Educational Technology and Artificial Intelligence and Their Impact on the Future of Education: Opportunities and Risks. *Journal of Posthumanism*, *5*(7), 1271–1292. DOI: 10.63332/joph.v5i7.2915

Mavridi, S. (2025). Hype, fear, and everything in between: A critical typology of responses to AI and their implications for language teacher education. *Technology in Language Teaching & Learning*, *7*(2), 103219–103219. DOI: 10.29140/tltl.v7n2.103219

Mawdsley, M. (2023). *On materiality: an analysis of the medium's role in electronic literature* (Master's thesis, University of Malta).

Mayiwar, L., Asutay, E., Tinghög, G., Västfjäll, D., & Barrafrem, K. (2025). Determinants of digital well-being. *AI & Society*, *40*, 3063–3073. DOI: 10.1007/s00146-024-02071-2

Meadows, A. J. (2015). *The history of scientific publishing*. Edward Elgar.

Mehta, V., Mathur, A., Arun, A., & Fiorillo, L. (2024). The application of ChatGPT in the peer-reviewing process. *Oral Oncology Reports*, *5*, 100227. DOI: 10.1016/j.oor.2024.100227

Meng, L. (2025). Evaluating the Impact of Mobile-Based Generative AI Tools on Visual Design Education. *International Journal of Interactive Mobile Technologies*, *19*(16), 189–203. DOI: 10.3991/ijim.v19i16.57603

Merrill, M. D. (2002). First principles of instruction. *Educational Technology Research and Development*, *50*(3), 43–59. DOI: 10.1007/BF02505024

Meyer, J. W., Ramirez, F. O., Frank, D. J., & Schofer, E. (2006). Higher education as an institution. Center on Democracy, Development, and the Rule of Law Working Papers No. 57. https://fsi9-prod.s3.us-west-1.amazonaws.com/s3fs-public/Meyer_No_57.pdf

Meyer, J. W., & Rowan, B. (1977). Institutionalized organizations: Formal structure as myth and ceremony. *American Journal of Sociology*, *83*(2), 340–363. DOI: 10.1086/226550

Miao, J., Thongprayoon, C., Suppadungsuk, S., Garcia Valencia, O. A., Qureshi, F., & Cheungpasitporn, W. (2023). Ethical dilemmas in using AI for academic writing and an example framework for peer review in nephrology academia: A narrative review. *Clinics and Practice*, *14*(1), 8. DOI: 10.3390/clinpract14010008 PMID: 38248432

Miller, R. L. (2015). Rogers' innovation diffusion theory (1962, 1995). In *Information seeking behaviour and technology adoption: Theories and trends* (pp. 261–274). IGI Global Scientific Publishing. https://www.igi-global.com/chapter/rogers-innovation-diffusion-theory-1962-1995/127136

Mittelstadt, B. (2019). Principles alone cannot guarantee ethical AI. *Nature Machine Intelligence*, *1*(11), 501–507. DOI: 10.1038/s42256-019-0114-4

Mohamad Fadzil, N. F., Samad, P. N. S. N., Mohd Nawawi, A. F., Mohamed Pandi, N. Z., & Puteh, F. (2022). Towards a High Standards of Excellence in Malaysia's Higher Education Institutions: Obstacles and Enablers. *The Journal of American Science*, *19*(2), 162–192.

Mohamed, N. F., Ting, J., Tan, A. M., Norhafizah, M. S., Farhana, I., Chan, M. F., Fadlin, M., Rahmatullah, B., Govindasamy, P., & Abdulla, K. (2024). Prevalence and predictors of social anxiety disorders among Malaysian secondary school students during the COVID-19 pandemic: Exploring the influence of internet gaming disorder and impulsivity. *Clinical Child Psychology and Psychiatry, 13591045231206968.* Advance online publication. DOI: 10.1177/13591045231206967

Mohr, J. W., & Bogdanov, P. (2013). Topic models: What they are and why they matter. *Poetics*, *41*(6), 545–569. DOI: 10.1016/j.poetic.2013.10.001

Moo, K. H., & Da Wan, C. (2023). Graduate Employability in Malaysia: Unpacking the Concept, Policy and Practices. *IIUM Journal of Educational Studies*, *11*(2), 3–25. DOI: 10.31436/ijes.v11i2.471

Morello, L. T., & Chick, J. C. (2025). Human-AI Symbiotic Theory (HAIST): Development, Multi-Framework Assessment, and AI-Assisted Validation in Academic Research. *Informatics (MDPI)*, *12*(3), 85. Advance online publication. DOI: 10.3390/informatics12030085

Morlaix, S. (2015). Les compétences sociales à l'école primaire: essai de mesure et effets sur la réussite. *Carrefours de l'éducation, 40*(2), 183-200. .DOI: 10.3917/cdle.040.0183

Mou, Q., Zhuang, J., Wu, Q., Zhong, Y., Dai, Q., Cao, X., Gao, Y., Lu, Q., & Zhao, M. (2024). Social media addiction and academic engagement as serial mediators between social anxiety and academic performance among college students. *BMC Psychology*, *12*(1), 190. DOI: 10.1186/s40359-024-01635-7

Muthmainnah, M., ... (2026). Navigating the Impact of Augmentation Computing Intelligence, AI Literacy, and Human Integration in English Language Education 7.0 by Using Computer-Assisted Language Learning and Augmented (CALLedA) Model. In: Dutta, S., Bhattacharya, A., Bose, S., Polkowski, Z. (eds) Proceedings of International Conference on Computational Intelligence and Information Retrieval. ICCIIR 2025. Lecture Notes in Networks and Systems, vol 1617. Springer, Cham. DOI: 10.1007/978-3-032-04539-3_35

Muthmainnah, M., Cardoso, L., Marzuki, A. G., & Al Yakin, A. (2025). A new innovative metaverse ecosystem: VR-based human interaction enhances EFL learners' transferable skills. *Discover Sustainability, 6*(1), 156.

Mutunhu, B., Nyathi, T., & Dube, S. (2021). An Analysis on the Adoption of High-Performance Computing (HPC): A Case of Zimbabwe State Universities. *2021 IST-Africa Conference (IST-Africa)*, 1–8. https://ieeexplore.ieee.org/abstract/document/9576909/

Nature. (2023). Editorial: Tools such as ChatGPT threaten transparent science. *Nature, 613*(7945), 612. DOI: 10.1038/d41586-023-00191-1

Nayyar, P. (2023, February). *Posthumanism.* Retrieved August 28, 2025, from Oxford Bibliographies: https://www.oxfordbibliographies.com/display/document/obo-9780190221911/obo-9780190221911-0122.xml

Neagu, S. N., & Vieriu, A. M. (2025). Digital and Psychological Well-Being Among Technical University Students: Exploring the Impact of Digital Engagement in Higher Education. *Education Sciences, 15*(9), 1192. DOI: 10.3390/educsci15091192

NextEducation. (n.d.). *AIComp – Artificial Intelligence Competences.* Retrieved from https://next-education.org/en/projects/ai-comp/

Neyazi, , T. AKhai, Ee, TKuru, , O. (2025). Campaign Deepfakes and Affective Polarization: The Role of Artificial Intelligence in Campaigns in Shaping Voter Attitudes. *Social Science Computer Review*, •••, 08944393251362247.

Ng, S.-L., & Ho, C.-C. (2025). Generative AI in education: Mapping the research landscape through bibliometric analysis. *Information (Basel), 16*(8), 657. DOI: 10.3390/info16080657

Ningxue, F. (2025, May). Ethical Challenges of AI Integration in Open University Online Education: A Multidimensional Analysis. In *2025 5th International Conference on Artificial Intelligence and Education (ICAIE)* (pp. 45-49). IEEE. DOI: 10.1109/ICAIE64856.2025.11158646

Nunnally, J. C. (1978). *Psychometric theory* (2nd ed.). McGraw-Hill.

O'Brien, A. G., Foust, J. L., & Taber, J. M. (2024). Physical health mindsets and information avoidance. *Journal of Behavioral Medicine*, *47*(6), 1052–1066. DOI: 10.1007/s10865-024-00514-1

O'Mara-Eves, A., Thomas, J., McNaught, J., Miwa, M., & Ananiadou, S. (2015). Using text mining for study identification in systematic reviews. *Systematic Reviews*, *4*(1), 5. DOI: 10.1186/2046-4053-4-5 PMID: 25588314

OECD. (2022). *"OECD Framework for the Classification of AI systems", OECD Digital Economy Papers, No. 323.* OECD Publishing., DOI: 10.1787/cb6d9eca-

Okolo, C. T. (2023). Addressing global inequity in AI development. In *Handbook of Critical Studies of Artificial Intelligence* (pp. 378–389). Edward Elgar Publishing., https://www.elgaronline.com/edcollchap/book/9781803928562/book-part-9781803928562-40.xml DOI: 10.4337/9781803928562.00040

Olanipekun, S. O.Samson Olufemi Olanipekun. (2025). Computational propaganda and misinformation: AI technologies as tools of media manipulation. *World Journal of Advanced Research and Reviews*, *25*(1), 911–923. DOI: 10.30574/wjarr.2025.25.1.0131

Oliveira, E., Rios, S. A., & Jiang, Z. (2023). AI-powered peer review process. *Australasian Journal of Educational Technology*, *39*(3), 1–15. DOI: 10.14742/apubs.2023.482

Omar, S., Hussein, N. H., Hanapi, N. F., Abdullah, Y. S., Mohd Noor, A. L., & Saidi, S. B. (2023). Self-Efficacy and Self-Regulated Learning Among Undergraduate in Learning Arabic As a Foreign Language Via Online. *Issues in Language Studies*, *12*(2), 227–245. DOI: 10.33736/ils.5566.2023

Ong, S. H., & Ramasamy, R. (2024). Exploring Students' Satisfaction and Loyalty in Private Universities, Malaysia. *Semarak International Journal of Applied Psychology*, *1*(1), 40–50. DOI: 10.37934/sijap/1.1.4050b

Ooi, T. L. (2025). *Strengthening Malaysia's Private Higher Education Sector through a Structural Revamp*. https://penanginstitute.org/wp-content/uploads/2025/05/Strengthening-Malaysias-Private-Higher-Education-Sector-through-a-Structural-Revamp.pdf

Osborne, E. L., Ainsworth, B., Hooper, N., & Atkinson, M. J. (2023). Experiences of Using Digital Mindfulness-Based Interventions: Rapid Scoping Review and Thematic Synthesis. *Journal of Medical Internet Research*, *25*, e44220. DOI: 10.2196/44220

Osman, I., Ibrahim, A., Mohd, I. H., Jameelah, M., Hashim, M., & Ahmad, N. N. (2025). Graduate soft skills and employability in Malaysia: The view of employers from different manufacturing companies. *Social and Management Research Journal*, *22*(1), 1–16. DOI: 10.24191/smrj.v22i1

Osrečki, F. (2025). *Eine Soziologie des Nichtwissens*. Suhrkamp.

Oyelude, A. A. (2024). Artificial intelligence (AI) tools for academic research. *Library Hi Tech News*, *41*(8), 18–20. DOI: 10.1108/LHTN-08-2024-0131

Padalko, H., Chumachenko, D., Kaur, N., Hussain, I. Z., Kaur, J., Lotto, M., Butt, Z. A., & Morita, P. P. (2025). Investigation of machine learning approaches to classify war-related content during Russian full-scale invasion of Ukraine. *Social Network Analysis and Mining*, *15*(1), 1–17. DOI: 10.1007/s13278-025-01501-3

Panwar, K., Sihag, V., Choudhary, G., & Dragoni, N. (2023, August). A threat and risk analysis of internet communication technology use. In *International Conference on ICT for Sustainable Development* (pp. 407-414). Singapore: Springer Nature Singapore. DOI: 10.1007/978-981-99-5652-4_36

Papatriantafyllou, M. (2017). Peer review – The future is here. *FEBS Letters, 591*(17), 2571–2574. DOI: 10.1002/1873-3468.12792 PMID: 28805250

Park, J., Paxtle-Granjeno, J., Ok, M. W., Shin, M., & Wilson, E. (2025). Preventing digital distraction in secondary classrooms: A quasi-experimental study. *Computers & Education, 227*, 105223. https://doi.org/https://doi.org/10.1016/j.compedu.2024.105223

Pascarella, E. T., Salisbury, M. H., & Blaich, C. (2011). Exposure to Effective Instruction and College Student Persistence: A Multi-Institutional Replication and Extension. *Journal of College Student Development, 52*(1), 4–19. DOI: 10.1353/csd.2011.0005

Pavlović, J. (2025). *Partnering with AI in Coaching and Human Skills Development: A Constructivist Guidebook for Innovation*. Taylor & Francis. DOI: 10.4324/9781003583141

Pennington, J., Socher, R., & Manning, C. D. (2014) Glove: global vectors for word representation. In: *Proceedings of the 2014 conference on empirical methods in natural language processing (EMNLP)*, pp. 1532–1543 (2014) DOI: 10.3115/v1/D14-1162

Perkins, D. N. (1995). L'individu-plus. Une vision distribuée de la pensée et de l'apprentissage. *Revue française de pédagogie, 111*, 1995. Psychologie de l'éducation: Nouvelles approches américaines. https://doi.org/DOI: 10.3406/rfp.1995.1232

Peters ME, Neumann M, Iyyer M, Gardner M, Clark C, Lee K, Zettlemoyer L (2018) Deep contextualized word representations. ArXiv abs/1802.05365

Piaget, J., & Inhelder, B. (1973). *The Psychology Of The Child*. Basic Books.

Pierson, P. (2000). Increasing returns, path dependence, and the study of politics. *The American Political Science Review, 94*(2), 251–267. DOI: 10.2307/2586011

Podsakoff, P. M., MacKenzie, S. B., Lee, J. Y., & Podsakoff, N. P. (2003). Common method biases in behavioral research: A critical review of the literature and recommended remedies. *The Journal of Applied Psychology, 88*(5), 879–903. DOI: 10.1037/0021-9010.88.5.879

Ponton, M. K., & Rhea, N. E. (2006). Autonomous Learning from a Social Cognitive Perspective. *New Horizons in Adult Education and Human Resource Development*, *20*(2), 38–49. DOI: 10.1002/nha3.10250

Project, A. I. (2016). "The Day a Computer Writes a Novel" *The day a computer writes a novel* [AI-generated novella]. Hoshi Shinichi Prize Committee.

Prouteau, F. (2024). For a Regenerated Humanism in the Anthropocene. In *Anthropology of the Anthropocene: Ideas for a Courageous Education* (pp. 29–72). Springer Nature Switzerland. DOI: 10.1007/978-3-031-75419-7_2

Puiu, S., Udri tioiu, M. T., Petri or, I., Yılmaz, S. E., Pfefferová, M. S., Raykova, Z., Yildizhan, H., & Marekova, E. (2024). Students' Well-Being and Academic Engagement: A Multivariate Analysis of the Influencing Factors. *Healthcare (Basel, Switzerland)*, *12*(15), 1492. DOI: 10.3390/healthcare12151492

Purmayanti, D. (2022). The Challenges of Implementing Digital Literacy in Teaching and Learning Activities for EFL Learners in Indonesia. *BATARA DIDI: English Language Journal*, *1*(2), 101–110. DOI: 10.56209/badi.v1i2.38

Rabardel, P. (1995). *Les hommes et les technologies: Approche cognitive des instruments contemporains*. Armand Colin.

Rahman, S., Munam, A. M., Hossain, A., Hossain, A. S. M. D., & Bhuiya, R. A. (2023). Socio-economic factors affecting the academic performance of private university students in Bangladesh: A cross-sectional bivariate and multivariate analysis. *SN Social Sciences*, *3*(2), 26. DOI: 10.1007/s43545-023-00614-w

Raji, I. D., Smart, A., White, R. N., Mitchell, M., Gebru, T., Hutchinson, B., & Barnes, P. (2020). Closing the AI accountability gap. *Proceedings of the 2020 ACM Conference on Fairness, Accountability, and Transparency*, 33–44. DOI: 10.1145/3351095.3372873

Rapanta, C. (2025). Postdigital Citizenship Education and Argumentation: Can AI Support Students' Critical Literacy? In *Discourses of Globalisation and Citizenship Education* (pp. 69–86). Springer Nature Switzerland. DOI: 10.1007/978-3-031-86145-1_5

Rasa, T. (2025). Postdigital Dissensus: On the Complexity of Debating Technology in Higher Education Futures. *Postdigital Science and Education*, 1-20.

Razak, A. A., Raime, S., Misron, A., & Zailani, N. F. I. (2025). Conceptualising Educational Experience towards STREAMS Skills Attainment among MBA Students. *International Journal of Academic Research in Business & Social Sciences*, *15*(6), 1090–1102. DOI: 10.6007/ijarbss/v15-i6/25578

Rice, S., Crouse, S. R., Winter, S. R., & Rice, C. (2024). The advantages and limitations of using ChatGPT to enhance technological research. *Technology in Society*, *76*, 102426. DOI: 10.1016/j.techsoc.2023.102426

Riquelme, S. (2025). Citizenship Education, Crisis of the Democratic Belief and World without Adults: Challenges and Educational Perspectives. In *Latin American University Students and Global Citizenship: Perspectives and Engagement* (pp. 19–33). Springer Nature Switzerland. DOI: 10.1007/978-3-032-03057-3_2

Romanishyn, A., Malytska, O., & Goncharuk, V. (2025). The Problem of AI-Driven Disinformation. Policy recommendations in respect to fighting disinformation. *Frontiers in Artificial Intelligence*, *8*, 1569115. DOI: 10.3389/frai.2025.1569115 PMID: 40821951

Rose, J. (2018). La professionnalisation des formations supérieures: Facettes multiples et effets incertains. *Cahiers de la recherche sur l'éducation et les savoirs. Hors-série*, *6*, 59–70.

Rudin, C. (2019). Stop explaining black box machine learning models. *Nature Machine Intelligence*, *1*(5), 206–215. DOI: 10.1038/s42256-019-0048-x PMID: 35603010

Sackett, D. L., Rosenberg, W. M., Gray, J. M., Haynes, R. B., & Richardson, W. S. (1996). *Evidence based medicine: what it is and what it isn't*. British Medical Journal Publishing Group.

Sahar, R., & Munawaroh, M. (2025). Artificial intelligence in higher education with bibliometric and content analysis for future research agenda. *Discover Sustainability*, *6*(1), 401. DOI: 10.1007/s43621-025-01086-z

Sahin, A., Yoon, M., & Kim, M. (2019). The Development and Validation of a 21st Century Skills Instrument: Measuring Secondary School Students' Skills. *Journal of Research in Science. Mathematics and Technology Education*, *2*(2), 85–103. DOI: 10.31756/jrsmte.223

Samadhiya, A., Kumar, A., Mulat-Weldemeskel, E., Luthra, S., Garza-Reyes, J. A., & Yadav, S. (2025). Next-gen quality learning: How can AI technologies shape education 4.0 and 5.0 towards the SDGs from multiple stakeholders' perspective? *The TQM Journal*. Advance online publication. DOI: 10.1108/TQM-11-2024-0441

Santelmann, P. (2019). Quel usage des compétences transversales. Santelmann P. (dir.) Partir des compétences transversales pour lire autrement le travail. *Education Permanente HS*, *13*, 33–43.

Santiago-Torner, C., Corral-Marfil, J. A., Jiménez-Pérez, Y., & Tarrats-Pons, E. (2025). Impact of ethical leadership on autonomy and self-efficacy in virtual work environments: The disintegrating effect of an egoistic climate. *Behavioral Sciences (Basel, Switzerland)*, *15*(1), 95. DOI: 10.3390/bs15010095 PMID: 39851899

Sarafis, D., Karamitsios, K., & Kravari, K. (2025, February). AI and Civic Engagement: A Brief Exploration of Applications and Opportunities. In *2025 International Conference on Advancement in Data Science, E-learning and Information System (ICADEIS)* (pp. 1-6). IEEE. DOI: 10.1109/ICADEIS65852.2025.10933183

Schmidt, T. A., & Raines, J. M. (2019). Analyzing Class Attendance and Student Achievement in Prescribed College Mathematics Courses. *Global Journal of Educational Studies*, *5*(2), 12–23. DOI: 10.5296/gjes.v5i2.15352

Schön, D. A. (1983). *The reflective practitioner: How professionals think in action.* Basic Books.

Schou, S., Cobanaj, I., Kaushik, N., Schlagwein, D., Van Der Heide, R., & Baskerville, R. L. (2023). "So what if ChatGPT wrote it?" Multidisciplinary perspectives on opportunities, challenges, and implications of generative conversational AI for research, practice, and policy. *Journal of the Association for Information Systems*, *24*(5), 939–979. DOI: 10.17705/1jais.00819

Schugurensky, D. (2007). « Vingt mille lieues sous les mers » : Les quatre défis de l'apprentissage informel. *Revue Française de Pédagogie*, *160*, 13–27. DOI: 10.4000/rfp.583

SCiNiTO. (n.d.). https://www.scinito.ai/

Sefton-Green, J. (2004). *Report 7: Literature review in informal learning with technology outside school.* Futurelab.

Selwyn, N. (2009). The digital native—Myth and reality. *Aslib Proceedings*, *61*(4), 364–379. DOI: 10.1108/00012530910973776

Senin, M. S., Ali, S., Hau, T. C., Jamaluddin, N. S., & Rahman, S. A. (2023). Relationship between Self–Efficacy and Student Psychology in Blended Learning Courses. *Journal for ReAttach Therapy and Developmental Diversities*, *6*(3s), 70–80.

Shahzad, M. F., Shuo, X., Weng, M. L., Yang, X., & Khan, Q. R. (2024). Artificial intelligence and social media on academic performance and mental well-being: Student perceptions of positive impact in the age of smart learning. *Heliyon*, *10*, e29523. DOI: 10.1016/j.heliyon.2024.e29523

Sharples, M.. (2014). *Innovating pedagogy 2014: Exploring new forms of teaching, learning and assessment, to guide educators and policy makers*. The Open University.

Shata, A., & Hartley, K. (2025). Artificial intelligence and communication technologies in academia: Faculty perceptions and the adoption of generative AI. *International Journal of Educational Technology in Higher Education*, *22*(1), 14. Advance online publication. DOI: 10.1186/s41239-025-00511-7

Shmueli, G., Sarstedt, M., Hair, J. F., Cheah, J.-H., Ting, H., Vaithilingam, S., & Ringle, C. M. (2019). Predictive model assessment in PLS-SEM: Guidelines for using PLSpredict. *European Journal of Marketing*, *53*(11), 2322–2347. DOI: 10.1108/EJM-02-2019-0189

Shneiderman, B. (2020). *Human-centered artificial intelligence*. Oxford University Press.

Sidiq, M., Janakiraman, B., Kashoo, F., Jastania, R., Alhusayni, A. I., Alzahrani, A., Chahal, A., Thiyagarajan, A., Khan, I., Kumar, C., Vasanthi, R. K., Alanazi, F., Ahmad, M., Sehgal, C. A., Khan, S., & Alghadier, M. (2025). Screen time exposure and academic performance, anxiety, and behavioral problems among school children. *PeerJ*, *13*(5). Advance online publication. DOI: 10.7717/peerj.19409

Singh, H., Murali, P., & Singh, A. (2022). Semantic Scholar: An AI-powered academic search engine. *Communications of the ACM*, *65*(4), 76–83. DOI: 10.1145/3488564

Singh, S., & Strzelecki, A. (2025). Academics as adopters of generative AI: An application of diffusion of innovations theory. *Education and Information Technologies*. Advance online publication. DOI: 10.1007/s10639-025-13835-8

Singun, A. J. (2025). Unveiling the barriers to digital transformation in higher education institutions: A systematic literature review. *Discover Education*, *4*(1), 37. DOI: 10.1007/s44217-025-00430-9

Smyth, R. S., Parker, K., & Sharif, M. O. (2020). General Data Protection Regulation-are we up to date? *British Dental Journal*, ●●●, 1–5. DOI: 10.1038/s41415-020-1844-8

Snyder, H. (2019). Literature review as a research methodology. *Journal of Business Research*, *104*, 333–339. DOI: 10.1016/j.jbusres.2019.07.039

Stauffer, B. (2022). *What are 21st century skills? ICEV.* https://www.icevonline.com/blog/what-are-21st-century-skills

Stevens, C. (2025). Teachers and teaching: Pedagogy, digital skills and professional development. *Open Learning*, *40*(1), 1–3. DOI: 10.1080/02680513.2024.2436665

Stevenson, N. (2010). Critical pedagogy, democracy, and capitalism: Education without enemies or borders. *Review of Education, Pedagogy & Cultural Studies, 32*(1), 66–92. DOI: 10.1080/10714410903482674

Stewart, R. A. (2007). Investigating the link between self-directed learning readiness and project-based learning outcomes: The case of international Masters students in an engineering management course. *European Journal of Engineering Education, 32*(4), 453–465. DOI: 10.1080/03043790701337197

Stokel-Walker, C. (2022). AI bot ChatGPT writes smart essays—Should professors worry? *Nature*. https://www.nature.com/articles/d41586-022-04397-7

Stromback, C., Skagerlund, K., Vastfjall, D., & Tinghog, G. (2020). Subjective self-control but not objective measures of executive functions predicts financial behavior and well-being. *Journal of Behavioral and Experimental Finance, 27*, 100339. https://doi.org/https://doi.org/10.1016/j.jbef.2020.100339

Subaveerapandiyan, A., Paladhi, M. M., & Maruthaveeran, V. (2023). Evaluating AI literacy proficiency among LIS researchers in ASEAN. *Library Hi Tech News, 41*(4), 6–8.

Susnjak, T. (2022). ChatGPT: The end of online exam integrity? *Journal of Applied Learning & Teaching, 5*(2). Advance online publication. DOI: 10.37074/jalt.2022.5.2.9

Susskind, R., & Susskind, D. (2015). *The future of the professions: How technology will transform the work of human experts*. Oxford University Press. DOI: 10.1093/oso/9780198713395.001.0001

Szczuka, Z., Kulis, E., Boberska, M., Banik, A., Siwa, M., Zaleskiewicz, H., Knoll, N., Revenson, T. A., & Luszczynska, A. (2023). Dyadic reciprocal associations between self-efficacy and planning predict sedentary behaviour. *British Journal of Health Psychology, 28*(2), 451–466. DOI: 10.1111/bjhp.12633

Szűts, Z., Lengyelné Molnár, T., Racskó, R., Vaughan, G., Ceglédi, S., & Dominek, D. L. (2025). Examining the Flow Dynamics of Artificial Intelligence in Real-Time Classroom Applications. *Computers, 14*(7), 275. Advance online publication. DOI: 10.3390/computers14070275

Tang, K. S., & Putra, G. B. S. (2025). Generative AI as a Dialogic Partner: Enhancing Multiple Perspectives, Reasoning, and Argumentation in Science Education with Customized Chatbots. *Journal of Science Education and Technology*, •••, 1–13.

Tee, P. K., Wong, L. C., Dada, M., Song, B. L., & Ng, C. P. (2024). Demand for digital skills, skill gaps and graduate employability: Evidence from employers in Malaysia. *F1000 Research, 13*(389). Advance online publication. DOI: 10.12688/f1000research.148514.1

Tehseen, S., Ramayah, T., & Sajilan, S. (2017). Testing and Controlling for Common Method Variance: A Review of Available Methods. *Journal of Management Sciences*, *4*, 142–168. DOI: 10.20547/jms.2014.1704202

Tejero, A., Pisoni, G., Lashkari, Z. H., & Aguilar, S. R. (2025). Combating Misinformation and Polarization in the Corporate Sphere: Integrating Social, Technological and AI Strategies. *International Journal of Interactive Multimedia and Artificial Intelligence*, *9*(4), 117–125. DOI: 10.9781/ijimai.2024.03.003

Tennant, J. P., & Ross-Hellauer, T. (2020). The limitations to our understanding of peer review. *Research Integrity and Peer Review*, *5*(6), 6. Advance online publication. DOI: 10.1186/s41073-020-00092-1 PMID: 32368354

Thomas, J. W. (2000). *A review of research on project-based learning*. The Autodesk Foundation.

Tihonova, E. V., Borisova, T. P., & Bunov, E. G. (2022, January). Cyberspace as a New Social Reality in the Era of Globalization. In *Proceedings of the International Scientific Conference "Smart Nations: Global Trends In The Digital Economy" Volume 2* (pp. 274-280). Cham: Springer International Publishing. DOI: 10.1007/978-3-030-94870-2_35

Tompkins, J. (1988). A Short Course in Post-Structuralism. *College English*, *50*(7), 733–747. DOI: 10.58680/ce198811361

Trow, M. (1973). *Problems in the transition from elite to mass higher education.* Carnegie Commission on Higher Education.

Truman, S. E. (2017). *Speculative Methodologies and Emergent Literacies: Walking and Writing as Research-Creation*. University of Toronto.

Tshitoyan, V., Dagdelen, J., Weston, L., Dunn, A., Rong, Z., Kononova, O., Persson, K. A., Ceder, G., & Jain, A. (2019). Unsupervised word embeddings capture latent knowledge. *Nature*, *571*(7763), 95–98. DOI: 10.1038/s41586-019-1335-8 PMID: 31270483

United Nations. (2021). *ITU: 2.9 billion people still offline*. United Nations; United Nations. https://www.un.org/en/delegate/itu-29-billion-people-still-offline

Upadhyaya, P., & Vrinda. (2021). Impact of technostress on academic productivity of university students. *Education and Information Technologies*, *26*(2), 1647–1664. DOI: 10.1007/s10639-020-10319-9

van de Schoot, R., de Bruin, J., Schram, R., Zahedi, P., de Boer, J., Weijdema, F., & Oberski, D. L. (2021). An open-source ML framework for systematic reviews. *Nature Machine Intelligence*, *3*(2), 125–133. DOI: 10.1038/s42256-020-00287-7

Van Esch, P., & Cui, Y. (2025, January 8). *Logging off Life, Living On: How AI is redefining death, memory and immortality.* Retrieved September 18, 2025, from Conversation: https://theconversation.com//loggong-off-life-but-living-on-how-ai-is-redefining-death-memory-and-immortality 246306?utm_medium=article_clipboard_share&utm_source=theconversation.com

Van Laer, S., & Elen, J. (2017). In search of attributes that support self-regulation in blended learning environments. *Education and Information Technologies*, *22*(4), 1395–1454. Advance online publication. DOI: 10.1007/s10639-016-9505-x

Van Le, H. (2024). Silence in the classroom: Unraveling the cultural dynamics affecting participation and critical thinking in Malaysian and Vietnamese engineering education. *Cogent Education*, *11*(1), 2404780. DOI: 10.1080/2331186X.2024.2404780

Varghese, J., & Chapiro, J. (2024). ChatGPT: The transformative influence of generative AI on science and healthcare. *Journal of Hepatology*, *80*(6), 977–980. DOI: 10.1016/j.jhep.2023.07.028 PMID: 37544516

Vaswani, A., Shazeer, N., Parmar, N., Uszkoreit, J., Jones, L., Gomez, A. N., & Polosukhin, I. (2017). Attention is all you need. *Advances in Neural Information Processing Systems*, *30*, 5998–6008.

Velander, J., Otero, N., & Milrad, M. (2024). What is critical (about) AI literacy? Exploring conceptualizations present in AI literacy discourse. In *Framing futures in postdigital education: Critical concepts for data-driven practices* (pp. 139–160). Springer Nature Switzerland. DOI: 10.1007/978-3-031-58622-4_8

Veletsianos, G. (2016). *Social media in higher education: Critical perspectives*. Routledge.

Vygotsky, L. S. (1978). *Mind in society: The development of higher psychological processes*. Harvard University Press.

Wang, S., Wang, F., Zhu, Z., Wang, J., Tran, T., & Du, Z. (2024). Artificial intelligence in education: A systematic literature review. *Expert Systems with Applications*, *252*, 124167. DOI: 10.1016/j.eswa.2024.124167

Wang, X., Wan Jaafar, W. M., & Sulong, R. M. (2025). Building better learners: Exploring positive emotions and life satisfaction as keys to academic engagement. *Frontiers in Education, 10*, 1535996. DOI: 10.3389/feduc.2025.1535996

Wang, X., & Xie, F. (2025). Global artificial intelligence governance research in the digital and intelligent era: Advances, trends and countermeasures. *Journal of Knowledge Management*.

Weber, A. (1982). Savoirs sociaux et savoirs scolaires. Pour une problématique articulation. *Pratiques*, *36*(1), 24–36. DOI: 10.3406/prati.1982.1244

Wenger, E. (1998). *Communities of practice: Learning, meaning, and identity*. Cambridge University Press. DOI: 10.1017/CBO9780511803932

Wong, W., Aristidou, A., & Scheuermann, K. (2025). The future of learning or the future of dividing? Exploring the impact of general artificial intelligence on higher education. *Data & Policy*, *7*, e44. DOI: 10.1017/dap.2025.10011

World Bank. (2025). *World Bank Open Data—Individuals using the Internet (% of population)*. World Bank Open Data. https://data.worldbank.org

Xethakis, L. J., Rupp, M., & Plummer, B. R. B. (2024). Why students feel anxious in group work: An investigation into students' perspectives on the sources of their anxious experiences in group work. *Frontiers in Education*, *9*, 1461747. DOI: 10.3389/feduc.2024.1461747

Xu, L., Hinds, A., Rakisheva, A., El Souefi, N., & Witt, A. (2025). Beyond borders: Virtual Global Engagement in teacher education. *Teaching and Teacher Education*, *165*, 105133. DOI: 10.1016/j.tate.2025.105133

Yadav, D. (2024). The role of Artificial Intelligence in literary analysis: A computational approach to understand literary styles. *International Journal of Emerging Knowledge Studies*, *3*(9), 558–565. DOI: 10.70333/ijeks-03-09-006

Yan, Y., Liu, H., Zhang, H., Chau, T., & Li, J. (2025). Designing a Generalist Education AI Framework for Multimodal Learning and Ethical Data Governance. *Applied Sciences (Basel, Switzerland)*, *15*(14), 7758. Advance online publication. DOI: 10.3390/app15147758

Yim, I. H. Y. (2024). A critical review of teaching and learning artificial intelligence (AI) literacy: Developing an intelligence-based AI literacy framework for primary school education. *Computers and Education: Artificial Intelligence*, *7*, 100319. DOI: 10.1016/j.caeai.2024.100319

Yuan, W., Neubig, G., & Liu, P. (2022). Can generative models generate novel hypotheses? *Transactions of the Association for Computational Linguistics*, *10*, 1340–1354. DOI: 10.1162/tacl_a_00507

Zdravkov, S., & Ilieva-Trichkova, P. (2025). Participation in Online Courses from the Perspective of Bourdieu's Cultural Capital Theory: A European Comparative Study. *European Education*, *57*(3), 209–227. DOI: 10.1080/10564934.2025.2531529

Zeng, S., Rahim, N., & Xu, S. (2025). Integrating Mobile AI in Art Education: A Study on Children's Engagement and Self-Efficacy. *International Journal of Interactive Mobile Technologies*, *19*(11), 112–142. DOI: 10.3991/ijim.v19i11.54847

Zhang, C., Shao, Y., Yuan, Y., & Shen, W. (2025). Artificial Intelligence Reshapes Creativity: A Multidimensional Evaluation. *PsyCh Journal*, *14*(6), 831–840. DOI: 10.1002/pchj.70042 PMID: 40764253

Zhang, Y. (2025). Optimizing Personalized Learning Paths in Mobile Education Platforms Based on Data Mining. *International Journal of Interactive Mobile Technologies*, *19*(12), 4–18. DOI: 10.3991/ijim.v19i12.56393

Zheng, L., & Lee, K. C. (2023). Examining the Effects of "Small Private Online Course and Flipped-Classroom"-Based Blended Teaching Strategy on First-Year English-Major Students' Achievements. *Sustainability*, *15*(21). Advance online publication. DOI: 10.3390/su152115349

Zhou, K., & Kantor, J. (2020). Automatic citation recommendation. *Journal of the Association for Information Science and Technology*, *71*(11), 1375–1391. DOI: 10.1002/asi.24377

Zhou, X., Li, Y., Chai, C. S., & Chiu, T. K. (2025). Defining, enhancing, and assessing artificial intelligence literacy and competency in K-12 education from a systematic review. *Interactive Learning Environments*, *33*(10), 1–23. DOI: 10.1080/10494820.2025.2487538

Zhu, W., Wei, L., & Qin, Y. (2025). Artificial Intelligence in Education (AIEd): Publication Patterns, Keywords, and Research Focuses. *Information (Basel)*, *16*(9), 725. Advance online publication. DOI: 10.3390/info16090725

Zou, J., Schiebinger, L., & Washington, A. (2023). AI and the end of originality? *Nature Human Behaviour*, *7*, 1529–1532. DOI: 10.1038/s41562-023-01632-w

About the Contributors

Muhammad Mooneeb Ali is leading AI and Linguistics at Saudi Aramco, Saudi Arabia. is a scholar of AI and English, Applied Linguistics, Educational technology, Technology in Education, critical pedagogy, and digital ethics. He has more than 60 research publications. He is also an author of 40 academic books and authored monograph on technology-based Teaching and learning. His latest work is AI applications in English Language which is Scopus Indexed. His research focuses on the intersection of emerging technologies and academic responsibility, particularly in the Global South. With a background in applied linguistics, educational technology, and sociocultural critique, Dr. Ali has published extensively on academic transformation in the AI age. He advocates for balanced, inclusive, and critically-informed frameworks that place human agency at the center of technological adoption in academia.

Muhammad Mujtaba Asad is serving as a Head of Educational Technology and TVET Research at Sukkur IBA University, Pakistan. Dr. Asad has extensive research experience in the domain of Educational Technologies in Higher Education, Innovative Techno-pedagogical Approaches, Techno-Ethics and AI integration in Education 4.0 Classrooms. He has published more than 100 research publications in reputed indexed journals. Also, four edited books are under his credit related to Educational Technologies.

***

Norsafriman B. Abd Rahman holds an MBA (IMI Switzerland, 2008), a B.Sc. in Marketing (RIT USA, 1998), and a Diploma in Banking Studies (UiTM, 1994). He has taught diploma and bachelor-level courses at UNITAR since 1999. His earlier career included roles in hospitality, manufacturing, and retail. His research spans social sciences, encompassing cultural tourism (2006–2011); business management, education management and technology management (2018 onward). Since the early 2000s, he has also provided consultancy in events and F&B. He can be contacted at email: safriman@unitar.my

Dina Adinda holds a PhD in Education and is an associate professor at the University of Paris Nanterre. Her research interests include students' self-direction, technology for teaching and learning, and higher education.

Huma Ahmed is an accomplished academic with over nine years of teaching experience in higher education. She has successfully supervised more than ten theses at the BS, MA, and M.Phil levels and has published over ten research articles in national and international journals. Her scholarly interests encompass literary theory, literary pedagogy, postcolonial theory and literature, feminist theory and literature, and literary aesthetics. Dr. Ahmed's work reflects a deep engagement with critical theory and a commitment to advancing literary scholarship and education.

Ahmad Al Yakin is a distinguished academic, researcher, and educator affiliated with Universitas Al Asyariah Mandar (UNASMAN) in West Sulawesi, Indonesia. Known for his interdisciplinary scholarship bridging education, digital technology, and human development, Dr. Ahmad Al Yakin has established himself as one of the leading figures in the study of educational innovation, instructional design, and technology-enhanced learning in the Indonesian higher education landscape. He earned his doctoral degree in Educational Technology and Curriculum Development, focusing on digital pedagogy and transformative learning models in higher education. His academic journey reflects a consistent commitment to improving educational access and quality through technology integration, cross-cultural collaboration, and applied research in Education 5.0 and 7.0 frameworks. As a lecturer and researcher at Universitas Al Asyariah Mandar, Dr. Al Yakin has contributed extensively to curriculum development and educational technology initiatives that align with the national vision for digital transformation in higher education. Dr. Ahmad Al Yakin's research interests span virtual learning environments, generative AI in education, academic well-being, feedback literacy, digital resilience, and the ethics of AI-based learning ecosystems. His body of work explores how educators and students can leverage artificial intelligence and immersive technologies to foster creativity, empathy, and inclusivity in teaching and learning processes. His current research examines how AI and virtual reality tools can enhance learners' cognitive engagement and mental well-being, particularly in post-pandemic learning contexts. In addition to his academic role, Dr. Al Yakin has been actively involved in international editorial boards and collaborative research projects, contributing to global discussions on educational reform and digital pedagogy. He has served as an editor, reviewer, and chapter contributor for several international academic publishers, including IGI Global, Taylor & Francis, and Springer Nature. His collaborations often focus on comparative education, human–AI interaction, and the social dimensions of technology in the learning process. As an educator, Dr. Al Yakin is deeply committed to student-centered learning and community engagement. He regularly mentors early-career academics and postgraduate students, encouraging them to adopt innovative methodologies and interdisciplinary approaches in their research. His pedagogical philosophy emphasizes the integration of local wisdom (kearifan lokal) with global educational paradigms, reflecting his belief that sustainable education must be both culturally grounded and globally adaptive. Dr. Ahmad Al Yakin is also a frequent speaker at national and international conferences, addressing themes such as digital literacy, AI in education, and well-being in virtual learning spaces. His publications and presentations have earned recognition for their originality and relevance to emerging global challenges in higher education. Beyond academia, Dr. Al Yakin is a strong advocate for ethical AI deployment and the humanization of digital learning, arguing that technological advancement must serve as a tool for empathy, empowerment, and equity. His intellectual leadership continues to inspire a new generation of scholars in Indonesia and beyond to envision education as a transformative, humane, and digitally fluent enterprise.

Ahmed Alaa holds a Ph.D. in Linguistics from the Faculty of Arts, Cairo University. He also has a TESOL Certificate from Arizona State University. He works as an Assistant Professor at the School of Linguistics and Translation, Badr University in Cairo (BUC). He is a published author with Q1 Scopus-indexed, WoS-indexed international journals. He is also a reviewer for many international journals affiliated with world-class publishers such as Elsevier, Springer- Nature, Taylor & Francis, and PLoS. He is interested in linguistics, discourse analysis, sociolinguistics, writing, translation, EAP, and ELT. You can follow Dr. Ahmed Alaa at https://www.linkedin.com/in/dr-ahmedalaa/.

Shazia Ayyaz is an Assistant Professor of English at Al Zahra College for Women, Muscat, holding a PhD in Linguistics with specialization in English Language Teaching (ELT). Her research focuses on Critical Discourse Analysis, AI-supported language learning, and research-informed pedagogy in higher education. She has presented at international conferences and contributed to scholarship on AI integration in ELT and academic integrity in AI-enhanced contexts.

Maria Denami is Associate Professor in the field of Education. Interested in Higher Education Pedagogy, her main research topic is students' professionalisation and development of their professional skills. In this sense, her research objective is to understand how experiential learning combined with reflexivity support leads to the awareness/development of students' professional competences. She is a member of LISEC-UR 2310. Maria Denami has worked for three years in the Student Success Unit and has designed and managed various projects to support integration and success. During the winter semester 2021-2022, she was a visiting professor at the University of Dresden to participate in the training of future teachers in pedagogical engineering and training.

Willam D.C. Enrique is currently the Vice President for Academic Affairs and Dean of the School of Graduate Studies at the City of Malabon University, Malabon City, Philippines. He earned his Doctor of Philosophy in Educational Management at De La Salle Araneta University (DLSAU) in 2014 with Highest Distinction. Due to his educational qualification and leadership skills, he was appointed as Education Program Chair from 2012-2014, and from 2014-2016, he became the College of Education Dean, where he was given a chance to lead the college accreditation level II under the Philippine Association of Colleges and Universities - Commission on Accreditation (PACUCOA). In 2015, he was given a chance to lead DLSAU Graduate School as Vice Dean from 2015 to 2016. His exposure and experiences in different managerial positions gave him the opportunity to lead the College of Education of Baliuag University from 2016 to 2019 before he joined the management of his present school. Aside from being the college dean, he also handled the directorship of the physical education department and the special program for international students of the university. He's also involved in the Lasallian Supervised Schools Office (LASSO) as a Supervisor under the PEAC – LEAP Program. His research interest includes educational management, fitness and wellness, innovation and development in learning practices, operations, and leadership of schools.

Ken Paul M. Espinosa graduated Benemeritus Magna Cum Laude from Our Lady of Fatima University. He is a licensed professional teacher with a major in biological science and a registered nurse, holding two master's degrees—one in nursing administration and another in educational management. He also earned a Doctor of Philosophy in Educational Management from De La Salle Araneta University, where he was also awarded Outstanding Alumnus in Research. Also, he holds a post-doctoral graduate Diploma in Research and Development Management under the Faculty of Management and Development Studies at the University of the Philippines Open University. Dr. Espinosa has received numerous awards and citations from various organizations and institutions both locally and internationally. As a writer, researcher, and speaker, he has published multiple books and scientific research papers. Throughout his career in academia, he has served in several administrative roles, including positions in student affairs, the registrar's office, directorships, and even as president of an international organization. At present, he is the Director of the Center for Research and Development at Baliuag University and a graduate studies professor, teaching master's and doctoral programs to both local and international students. He has also been recognized for his outstanding contributions to research as Baliuag University's top scientist, earning a place in the AD Scientific Index.

Sheikh Rashid Bin Islam is a Doctoral Student at the Graduate School of International Cooperation Studies (GSICS), Kobe University, Japan. He previously served as a consultant at the UNESCO International Institute for Educational Planning (IIEP) in France. He has also contributed to a wide range of research and consultancy projects supported by organizations such as UNICEF, the Asian Development Bank (ADB), the Japan Society for the Promotion of Science (JSPS), the Global Partnership for Education (GPE), UNDP and the Government of Bangladesh, the Japan Foundation, the Japan External Trade Organization (JETRO), and the University of Dhaka. His professional and research work spans multiple countries, including Japan, Bangladesh, Mongolia, the Pacific Islands, Lao PDR, and Myanmar. His research interests include education economics, education financing, education sector planning, and comparative education.

Aervina Misron is a Senior Lecturer at the Faculty of Business and Management, Quest International University. She received a Bachelor of Science (2016), a Master of Business Administration (2018), and a Doctor of Philosophy (2022) from Universiti Teknologi Malaysia. She brings industry experience in both the information technology and hospitality and tourism sectors. In academia, she is actively involved in research projects, curriculum development, and postgraduate supervision. She also serves as a reviewer for reputable international journals, and an examiner for theses and dissertations. She can be contacted at email: aervina.misron@qiu.edu.my

Mahmuda Naznin is a research and policy analyst specializing in development economics, economics of education, public policy, and digitalization of key development sectors, including education. She has received her degrees on Master of Social Science and Master of Development Economics, both from University of Dhaka, Bangladesh. She has contributed to a wide range of research and policy projects supported by organizations such as the World Bank, JICA, JETRO, GPE, the LEGO Foundation, FHI 360, and the Government of Bangladesh. She has also published in peer-reviewed Q1 journals and books. Her work spans diverse areas including education sector analysis, labor market intelligence, financial inclusion,

AI in education, digitalization of education, climate literacy and public policy analysis, with applications across Bangladesh and comparative contexts involving South, Southeast and East Asian regions.

Sharfika Raime is a Senior Lecturer at City University Malaysia, bringing together strong academic credentials and industry experience in the oil and gas sector. Her research spans human resource, education, tourism, and technology management. Since 2023, she has been actively involved in consultancy work and collaborative projects, including matching grants with local and international universities. She recently received a writing workshop grant funded by The British Academy in collaboration with Heriot-Watt University, Scotland. She aims to grow as a prolific researcher, building partnerships with leading scholars worldwide and expanding her work into interdisciplinary fields. She aspires to serve as a Research Scientist at renowned institutions such as The British Academy, the Institute of Ethnic Studies (KITA), or the Institute of Development Studies (UK).

Ardra Rianisa is an Information Technology professional with a strong interest in digital technology and information systems. Ardra actively engages in writing academic papers and popular articles that discuss current trends, innovations, and developments in the field of information technology. With a solid understanding of technology and its practical applications, Ardra is committed to continuously expanding knowledge and contributing insights to the digital and academic community.

Binastya Anggara Sekti has been a lecturer at the Faculty of Computer Science, Esa Unggul University, Jakarta, since 2016. He is actively involved in the Artificial Intelligence and Information Security Study Group. He holds a Bachelor's degree in Informatics Engineering from the Bandung Institute of Technology and a Master's degree in Information Systems Management from Trisakti University, Jakarta. Prior to entering academia, he accumulated over 25 years of professional experience as an IT practitioner in various companies across Jakarta. His work focused on developing data centers for internet service providers and delivering IT solutions for the manufacturing and oil & gas sectors. His research interests include artificial intelligence, cybersecurity, and the development of IT infrastructure.

MuthmainnahYakin is a respected scholar and educator at Universitas Al Asyariah Mandar (UNASMAN), West Sulawesi, Indonesia. Renowned for her dedication to advancing inclusive education and pedagogical innovation, she has become a leading figure in the intersection of language education, educational psychology, and digital learning transformation. Her academic and professional pursuits reflect a strong commitment to empowering learners through evidence-based teaching practices, digital literacy, and the integration of cultural values into modern educational contexts. Dr. Muthmainnah earned her doctoral degree in Education and Language Pedagogy, where her research explored how feedback literacy, student motivation, and reflective learning processes shape academic success in higher education environments. Her academic journey is characterised by a continuous pursuit of excellence and innovation, positioning her among the emerging voices in Indonesian higher education who bridge traditional educational values with the rapidly evolving landscape of Education 5.0 and Education 7.0 paradigms. As a faculty member at Universitas Al Asyariah Mandar, Dr. Muthmainnah has contributed significantly to curriculum reform, teacher professional development, and the enhancement of language education programmes. Her work often integrates psychological dimensions of learning, focusing on well-being, emotional regulation, and feedback engagement among students in multilingual and multicultural classrooms. She advocates for the creation of emotionally intelligent and technologically adaptive learning environments that prioritise both cognitive and affective development. Her research interests encompass language learning strategies, feedback literacy, gender and education, virtual pedagogy, and the integration of artificial intelligence (AI) in language instruction. She has authored and co-authored numerous papers in national and international journals, particularly addressing the psychological dimensions of learner engagement and the pedagogical implications of digital transformation. Her recent studies examine the role of AI-enhanced feedback systems in improving student writing and self-efficacy an area that situates her research within the global discourse on digital education ethics and innovation. Dr. Muthmainnah is also an active collaborator in international research networks and a contributor to several edited volumes and conference proceedings with reputable publishers such as IGI Global and Springer Nature. She serves as a peer reviewer and editorial board member for academic journals in the areas of educational psychology, language education, and instructional design. Her involvement in these networks reflects her vision of positioning Indonesian scholarship within broader international academic conversations. Beyond her research and teaching, Dr. Muthmainnah is passionately committed to empowering female academics and students in higher education. She actively promotes gender equity, leadership development, and mentorship initiatives that inspire young women to pursue careers in academia and research. As a teacher, she is admired for her interactive, student-centred pedagogical style, which blends technological innovation with cultural empathy. She believes that education should not only transmit knowledge but also cultivate resilience, creativity, and humanity. Her approach aligns with her broader mission to harmonise local wisdom (kearifan lokal) with global educational standards. Dr. Muthmainnah's scholarly contributions and leadership have positioned her as a dynamic advocate for sustainable and human-centred education in Indonesia. Through her teaching, research, and mentorship, she continues to shape the next generation of educators and researchers equipped to thrive in the era of intelligent and ethical digital learning.

Index

A

B

C

D

E

G

H

K

L

www.ingramcontent.com/pod-product-compliance
Lightning Source LLC
LaVergne TN
LVHW060002031026
849161LV00025B/1314